Economics of Business Policy

Economics of Business Policy

Dibyendra Nath Sengupta

Anindya Sen

OXFORD
UNIVERSITY PRESS

OXFORD

UNIVERSITY PRESS

YMCA Library Building, Jai Singh Road, New Delhi 110 001

Oxford University Press is a department of the University of Oxford. It furthers the
University's objective of excellence in research, scholarship, and education
by publishing worldwide in

Oxford   New York

Auckland   Bangkok   Buenos Aires   Cape Town   Chennai
Dar es Salaam   Delhi   Hong Kong   Istanbul   Karachi   Kolkata
Kuala Lumpur   Madrid   Melbourne   Mexico City   Mumbai   Nairobi
Sao Paulo   Shanghai   Taipei   Tokyo   Toronto

Published in India
By Oxford University Press, New Delhi

First published 2004

ISBN   0 19 565507 9

Typeset in RK Computer Services Delhi 110 051
Printed at Roopak Printers , Delhi 110 032
Published by Manzar Khan, Oxford University Press
YMCA Library Building, Jai Singh Road, New Delhi 110 001

Acknowledgements

The idea of this book first came up when Rakesh Basant and Dibyendra Nath Sengupta were teaching a course in *Industrial Organization and Policy* at the Indian Institute of Management, Ahmedabad. Rakesh Basant contributed significantly to the initial conceptualization and planning of the book, but could not continue with it owing to other demands on his time. The project was revived at the Indira Gandhi Institute of Development Research, Mumbai, where DNS and Anindya Sen started work on the book. The final stages of the writing of the book took place at the Indian Institute of Management, Calcutta. The authors have benefited a great deal from interactions with and feedback from colleagues and students at all three institutes. However, the responsibility for any shortcomings and errors rests squarely with the authors.

The authors thank the editors at OUP for their help and for putting up patiently with the delays in submitting the manuscript. Anindya Sen wishes to thank OUP for permission to draw on material from his book *Microeconomics: Theory and Applications* for use in the present volume.

Finally, DNS takes this opportunity to remember fondly his late parents who encouraged him to write this book but could not see its completion.

Contents

Introduction

What is Business Policy?

Business Policy, also called *Strategic Management*, is concerned with setting long-term goals for a firm in line with the expectations of its stakeholders, developing an action plan for meeting these goals, and allocating resources for meeting the plan. There are a number of theories about how the firm should go about this. The basic steps are as follows. The firm should first take a view of where it wants to be in, say, 5–10 years. It should then make an assessment of how the business and competitive environments are likely to unfold and identify the products and markets that it should be in. The selection of products and markets should be based on how promising they are in terms of profitability and growth and how well equipped the firm is to compete for them. The firm should then take stock of its existing resources, capabilities, and governance structures, decide what changes and additions to these are necessary, and make these changes and additions by making the required investments. Finally, the firm should keep reviewing the progress made and revising its plan as required.

Thanks to the work done by business schools, consulting firms, and management theorists, Business Policy has now evolved into a research-based, intellectually stimulating discipline in its own right.

What is Industrial Organization?

In this book, we are concerned with a field of Economics, which is called *Industrial Organization* in America and *Industrial Economics* in Europe. It studies how some organizing mechanism like the market or the firm brings the productive activities in an industry in harmony with the demand for its goods or services, and how imperfections in these mechanisms affect the efficiency with which this demand is met. The scope of Industrial Organization is best explained by using the so-called *Structure–Conduct–Performance* (SCP) paradigm, which is illustrated in Fig. 1. An industry's *performance*, or how efficiently it meets the demand for its goods and services, depends on the *conduct* or behaviour of the firms that constitute the industry. The conduct of firms, in turn, depends on the *structure*, or factors that determine the competitiveness, of the industry. The structure of an industry depends on some *basic conditions* governing demand and supply, like the material inputs required, economies of scale and scope, market size, price elasticity of demand, heterogeneity of consumers' needs and preferences, etc. The cause-and-effect relationship is, however, not unidirectional. Firms can also affect the basic conditions and structure through their conduct. They can, for example, alter production methods or consumer preferences through their R&D and advertising activities. They can also change the industry structure by integrating vertically, diversifying horizontally, or differentiating their products. The last component of the SCP paradigm is *public policy*. If the government considers the performance of an industry unsatisfactory, it may try to correct it by influencing the structure of the industry or the conduct of firms through public investments, taxes and subsidies, regulations and controls, and other means.

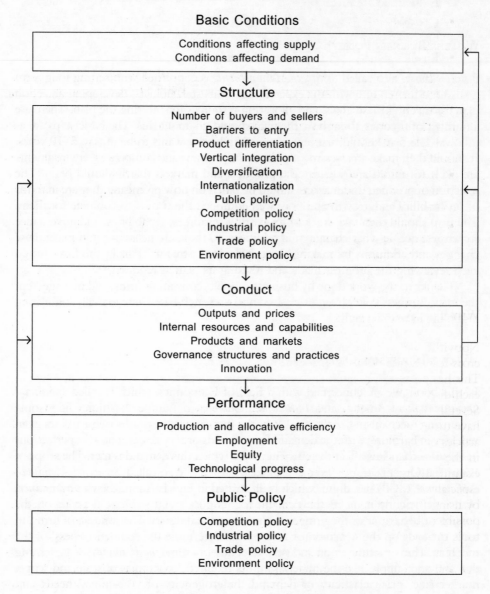

Fig. 1 The Structure-Conduct-Performance Paradigm

COMMONALITY AND DIFFERENCES

Thus, both Business Policy and Industrial Organization are concerned with the behaviour of firms. While Business Policy tries to spell out how firms should behave, Industrial Organization tries to find out how firms actually behave and why. There is, therefore, a common ground between the two. However, the perspectives and approaches are quite different, as outlined below.

- Business Policy is concerned with the private welfare of stakeholders, while Industrial Organization is concerned with social welfare.
- Consequently, Business Policy addresses business managers, while Industrial Organization addresses policy makers.
- Business Policy is multi-disciplinary and uses ideas from Economics, Political Science, Behavioral Sciences, and other fields of management. However, Industrial Organization is firmly rooted in Economics.
- As a result, Business Policy tries to analyse behaviour from a number of perspectives. Industrial Organization, on the other hand, assumes that firms maximize profits, subject to the availability of relevant information and the need to reconcile the aspirations of different stakeholders.
- Business Policy is process-oriented: it tells firms how they should go about doing what they do. Industrial Organization, by contrast, is logic-oriented: it analyses why firms do what they do.
- Business Policy derives its generalizations from in-depth studies of individual firms. Industrial Organization, on the other hand, derives its generalizations from models developed to explain data collected from large samples of firms.

WHY THIS BOOK?

Notwithstanding these differences, there has been in recent years, a fair amount of cross-fertilization of the concepts and analytical tools developed by the two disciplines. This has proved to be mutually beneficial and taken place in three ways. Scholars in each discipline have adapted concepts and tools of the other to their own discipline. Several economists have written books and articles on Business Policy, some of which have turned out to be very influential. A few economists have also written books and articles on Industrial Organization with a Business Policy perspective. This book falls in the third category and is probably the first effort in this direction in India. It examines how a firm can maximize short- and long-term gains to its stakeholders, especially shareholders, and addresses issues that are of interest to them. This is done by using the concepts and analytical tools of Industrial Organization. To the extent possible, Indian examples are used to illustrate the applicability of these concepts and tools to Business Policy situations.

It is hoped that the book will be useful in at least three ways:

- It will help students and practitioners of Business Policy think through the basic trade-offs involved in some important decisions and the ways in which these trade-offs may be optimized.

- It will help students and practitioners of Industrial Organization appreciate how business managers look at problems.

- It may also provide the basis for a course in Industrial Organization for students of management. Such courses are offered in business schools in America and Europe, though they are not very common in India yet.

TOPICS COVERED

The topics covered in this book encompass areas that should be of interest to business managers. The analytical framework of the SCP paradigm has been used to sequence the topics.

Chapters 1 to 3 explain some of the basic concepts and analytical tools used by economists. Chapter 1 explains the concepts of cost, rationality, and marginal analysis, while Chapter 2 expounds the concepts of value, demand, supply, and elasticity. Chapter 3 introduces the reader to game theory, which helps decision-makers decide in situations in which the pay-off depends on not only their own decisions but also the decision of their rivals.

Chapters 4 to 7 explain why imperfections in the structure of an industry arise and how firms exploit them by restricting output, charging a price that exceeds the cost of production, and extracting a monopoly rent. Chapter 4 shows how, given an imperfect structure, the firm can set its output and price to maximize its profit. Chapters 5 and 7 show how it can use the basic conditions affecting supply and demand, respectively, to create and exploit imperfections in the structure. Chapter 6 explains how it can increase its monopoly rent by using such devices as auctions, charging different prices to different groups of customers and making weak products ride on strong products.

In Chapters 8 to 12, we turn our attention from price and output setting behaviour to three other aspects of conduct, namely the way the firm builds and exploits its internal resources and capabilities, selects its products and markets, and establishes its governance structures and practices. Chapter 8 explains how the firm creates a competitive advantage for itself by creating or acquiring some unique assets and how it extracts a quasi-rent by restricting the supply of these assets. This allows us to analyse, in Chapters 9 and 10, why it often pays the firm to operate in more than one market. We argue that multi-market operations help the firm use its assets more efficiently and, in the process, gain market power and strategic advantages over its competitors. Within this framework, we examine a few topical issues like vertical integration vs. outsourcing, related vs. unrelated diversification, exports based on comparative advantage vs. exports based on competitive advantage, and international trade vs. international production. In Chapters 11 and 12, we deal with the question of governance structures and practices. We show how the firm minimizes transaction costs and promotes teamwork by establishing an authority-based internal architecture, consisting of an organization structure, a compensation system, and a performance evaluation system. We explain why in some situations it becomes more efficient to externalize transactions by setting up an external architecture, how these arrangements are self-enforced, and the circumstances in which they fail. We also examine how, and to what extent, various mechanisms for corporate governance align the interests of different stakeholders.

In Chapter 13, we adopt the Schumpeterian [Schumpeter, J.A. (1942), *Capitalism, Socialism and Democracy,* London: Oxford University Press] view of conduct, characterized by innovation and entrepreneurship, to explain why some firms prosper over time, while others fail. We link up a few important theories of innovation and growth to conclude that the requirements for long-term success are innovation, growth, a changing product portfolio, entrepreneurship, and luck.

Chapters 14 and 15 deal with the final component of the SCP paradigm, namely public policy. It is impossible to think of any aspect of Public Policy that does not affect industries and firms. However, four types of policies tend to impact the firm more directly than the others. They are: competition policy, which tries to promote an optimum level of competition; industrial policy, which tries to direct investment to socially desirable industries; trade policy, which tries to influence the balance and composition of international trade; and environment policy, which tries to curb negative externalities generated by firms. We discuss the rationale relating to some of these policies, as well as their situation in India. In view of its topical importance, we also discuss privatization in some depth.

1   Cost

The concept of cost is at the heart of the subject of Economics, which teaches how to correctly calculate the net gains from pursuing any course of action. The proper calculation of the costs of taking a decision and engaging in an action is the first and crucial step in this process. This chapter discusses various cost concepts that are used by economists. The concept of costs then leads us to consider the critical concept of value in the next chapter.

1.1   OPPORTUNITY COST

We start with the basic concept of *opportunity cost*. To motivate the concept of opportunity cost, it should be remembered that Economics studies how choices are made from among alternatives under conditions of scarcity. A number of points about this characterization should be emphasized.

- Economics as a discipline exists because resources are scarce. Scarcity exists when the necessary resources for producing the things that people desire are insufficient to satisfy all wants.

The economic concept of scarcity has to be kept distinct from the physical fact that resources are limited. Suppose that there are only three chairs in a room. Is there a scarcity of chairs? The answer depends on how many people want seats in the room and not on the number of chairs as such. If fifteen people are rehearsing for a play in the room but only the director of the play requires a seat, while all the other fourteen actors and actresses have to be on their feet, there is still no 'scarcity' of chairs. On the other hand, even resources like clean air and water, which at one time seemed to be available in inexhaustible amounts, often seem to be scarce in many of today's cities.

Moreover, even if physical resources are not limited, the concept of scarcity would exist because human beings have inherent limitations on their ability to consume and enjoy. Such limitations might exist for various reasons:

(i) Limited income: most people earn limited amounts of money every month to spend on various things. One then has to choose how much to spend and on which item. For example, from the point of view of one individual, there is no shortage of cars in the showrooms. But each individual's ability to buy cars is limited by her/his income. In a country like the USA, it is not rare to find families with two or three cars in their garage. In a developing country like India, most middle-income families are happy to own just one car.

(ii) Limited time: even if we never sleep, we have, at the most, only 24 hours at our disposal each day. We have to allocate these 24 hours between work hours and leisure hours. Our lifespans are finite and we must decide what to do during our finite lifetimes.

(iii) Limited human faculties: we have limited faculties of hearing, seeing, etc. It is almost impossible for most of us to listen to (consume) more than one piece of music at a time.

- If there were no scarcities, there would be no need to make choices. We can have anything we want and we can consume all that we want to.[1]

- Choice must be made from among alternatives. If there are no alternatives available, then the freedom to choose has very little meaning. When only bread is available from shops, even a rich individual cannot choose to buy cakes.

Choosing a particular alternative means comparing the benefits and costs of that alternative. Let $B(Z)$ be the benefits from choosing alternative Z, and $C(Z)$ the costs of choosing Z.

Then, Z should be chosen if $B(Z) > C(Z)$, not otherwise.

Put this way, the problem of choice seems to be almost trivial. However, there are subtle considerations involved in the calculations of B and C.

The first thing to do is to define B and C more precisely. These definitions may be expressed as:

$B(Z)$: maximum rupee amount you would be willing to pay to do or choose Z.

$C(Z)$: rupee value of the resources you must give up in order to do or choose Z.

As the definition of C shows, the cost must be calculated with reference to the other alternatives that were forgone, to get a proper idea of the net benefit from the alternative in question. We, therefore, come to the critical notion of opportunity cost.

Definition: The opportunity cost of an action refers to the rupee value of the *next best* alternative forgone.

Usually, in choosing an alternative Z, a number of alternatives will be forgone, say, W, X, Y, etc. The net benefit from Z should then be compared with the net benefit from the next best alternative; the latter is the opportunity cost of Z.

Example 1.1. A car manufacturer is considering whether to use manual seat adjusters or power seat adjusters in its 'large' cars. Power seat adjusters already exist for 'large luxury' cars and can be used in the large cars without any modification. To develop manual seat adjusters, Rs 10,000,000 would have to be invested. The cost per unit for manual seat adjusters would be lower by Rs 800 than that for power seat adjusters.

[1]Andrew Marvell, in his poem 'To his Coy Mistress' points out that he could have done justice to his love for his mistress only if he had an infinite amount of time. However, under the constant pressure of the knowledge that his days on earth are numbered ('But at my back I always hear/Time's winged chariot hurrying near'), he urges his mistress to abandon her coyness immediately and give way to her love for him.

The company expects to sell 100,000 units over the next five years, after which it would have to reconsider the nature of seat adjusters.

The opportunity cost of the capital for developing manual seat adjusters is calculated and at 18 per cent over 5 years, it amounts to Rs 22,877,780 (18 per cent is the best return from an alternative use of the funds). This obviously is much less than the saving in costs of Rs 80,000,000 from using manual seat adjusters. However, there are additional costs of engineering and testing the manual seat adjuster. It will cost Rs 5,000,000 to engineer such a seat adjuster, Rs 750,000 in prototype material and Rs 12,000,000 in testing expenses. At 18 per cent over five years, the total cost of capital (of Rs 27,750,000) is seen to be Rs 63,485,280. The decision to develop the manual seat adjuster is taken because this is still less than Rs 80,000,000. However, taking account of all the costs—explicit and hidden—takes the manual seat adjuster closer to the power seat adjuster so far as costs are concerned, and even a small change in the relevant parameters can change the decision.

1.1.1 Pitfalls in the Calculation of Opportunity Costs: Hidden Costs

As the above example shows, one has to be very careful in calculating the opportunity cost of any course of action. There are two pitfalls in the way of such a calculation: some relevant costs may be ignored in the calculation or some costs that should not be included may be included.

Some of the costs are implicit and some do not have any direct monetary valuation. One might easily overlook them in the computation of opportunity cost. Accounting costs are derived from financial reports that mainly categorize explicit rupee payments. As a result, accounting costs can miss out on some implicit or hidden costs. Examples of implicit costs that are not taken into account in accounting costs include (a) the salary that could have been earned elsewhere by the owner of the firm working for the firm but earning no salary and (b) the cost of funds invested in the firm that could have been used elsewhere.

One exception to the accountant's focus on explicit costs is the treatment of depreciation, the implicit cost of using up and wearing out of capital equipment and buildings. As a machine wears out, no explicit payment is made, but the implicit cost does reflect the use of a scarce resource and is included as part of the relevant opportunity cost.

Example 1.2. Suppose that a person invests Rs 1000 in some shares and gets a return of 20 per cent (Rs 200) annually. One day, he decides to start a small business of his own and sells off his shares and invests the money received in the business. At the end of the year, he finds that he has made a profit of Rs 100. This is a 10 per cent return on his investment. However, the economic view of the business will be that Rs 100 is being lost annually. Why? Because the opportunity cost of the funds is Rs 200, and this must be subtracted from the profit to provide a correct picture of the viability of the business.

1.1.2 Pitfalls in the Calculation of Opportunity Costs: Sunk Costs

Some costs should not be included in the opportunity cost but often are. People include sunk costs in their calculations of the opportunity cost, even though they should not do so. A *sunk cost* is one that cannot be recovered. From a firm's point of view, sunk costs arise when an investment in an asset cannot be recovered by subsequent resale. Therefore, an investment is a sunk cost when its opportunity cost is zero. Once incurred, sunk costs are not part of the firm's alternatives because they cannot be put to alternative use.

Example 1.3. A dam is built at a very high cost. At the time of construction, the cost of energy produced by the dam was Rs 3 per unit, of which Rs 2 corresponded to the amortized cost of the initial investment and Re 1 to recurrent cost. Suppose that after the dam is built, an alternative source of energy is found that allows production of energy at Rs 2 per unit. It might seem that the dam should be abandoned and the new source tapped. However, Rs 2 per unit of the energy cost from the dam represents sunk cost. This cost is now unrecoverable and should not enter into the decision to choose between the two sources of energy since 'one should not cry over spilt milk'. Therefore, we should persist with the dam.[2]

Example 1.4. The most important piece of equipment required to provide air service is the aircraft, which carries a big price tag (a wide-bodied aircraft can cost US$100 million). Is this investment a sunk cost? If an airlines wants to leave the market, it can sell or lease the aircraft to another firm. It can also use the aircraft in some other market. Hence, much of the investment in the aircraft is not sunk. Similarly, if the airlines plans to leave a particular city, the rental of the terminal space will stop and the ground equipment can be moved to another location. However, the airlines has to incur some other costs which are sunk. These include the cost of hiring and training staff, advertising to inform the customers that it is operating in a certain route, setting up baggage-handling facilities, etc.

1.1.3 Switching Costs

A switching cost is a one-time cost incurred when an agent switches from one product to another. This cost may be incurred by a buyer when she switches from one supplier's product to another. Porter (1980) mentions the following as examples of switching costs:

- employee retraining costs,
- cost of new ancillary equipment,
- cost and time in testing or qualifying a new source,
- need for technical help as a result of reliance on seller engineering aid, product redesign,
- or even the psychic costs of severing a relationship.

It is obvious that a switching cost reduces the opportunity cost of an action and thereby can have a lock-in effect. In other words, if a switching cost is present, then an economic agent finds it more difficult to shift from one product to another, or from one decision to another.

---

[2]This example is from Cabral (2000).

BOX 1.1. SWITCHING COSTS IN THE INFORMATION ECONOMY

Shapiro and Varian (1999) observe that switching costs are the norm, not the exception, in the information economy. They make a comparison between cars and computers to illustrate this. If a person has been driving a Maruti car, there is no compelling reason for him to buy another Maruti if he decides to replace his car. The driving skills acquired on the Maruti car and the technical knowledge gained can very easily be transferred to a Santro or an Indica car. On the other hand, somebody who has been using a Macintosh computer has also invested significantly in complementary assets like Mac software, Mac printer, etc. The switch to a PC or Unix machine involves a substantial switching cost for this user, since all the complementary assets, too, will have to be replaced. Such switching costs will make it more difficult for the user to change to another technology. In other words, the user will face a lock-in effect.

Source: Shapiro, C. and Hal Varian, (1999), *Information Rules*, Harvard Business School Press, Boston, Ma.

1.2 THE PRODUCTION POSSIBILITIES CURVE

It is not only individuals who must make choices from among alternatives. The economy, too, at any point of time has a fixed amount of resources, and must decide what to produce and in what quantities, with these resources. The opportunity cost of producing more of a commodity X is the bundle of other commodities that could have been produced with the resources used to produce this extra amount of X.

Suppose that an economy can produce only two types of goods: 'N-bombs' (military spending) and 'rice' (civilian spending). With the society's resources, various combinations of N-bombs and rice can be produced. Some possible combinations are:

N-bombs (hundreds)	Rice (millions of tonnes)
100	0
90	40
70	70
40	90
0	100

These combinations can be represented by means of a *production possibilities curve (PPC)* as shown in Fig. 1.1. A number of things about the production possibilities curve in the figure are to be noted.

First, any point such as A inside the area bounded by the curve is inefficient, in the sense that with the society's resources, more of at least one commodity can be produced at a point such as B on the curve which lies to the north-east of A. A point like B is efficient because we cannot find a point anywhere inside or on the curve where more of at least one commodity can be produced compared to the bundle given by B.

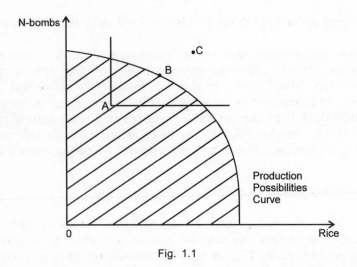

Fig. 1.1

Secondly, a point like *C* lying *outside* the *PPC* is unattainable: it represents a bundle that cannot be produced with the current resources of the society. All points on or inside the *PPC* (the shaded area) form the feasible set, i.e. the set of bundles that can be produced with the current resources.

Thirdly, the *PPC* is concave to the origin, i.e. bowed away from the origin. This has an important implication in terms of the trade-offs that the society faces. First, consider a situation where only N-bombs are being produced. Now, the society decides to produce some rice, too, and makes fewer N-bombs, releasing some resources for rice growing. It makes sense to release those resources that are particularly suited for rice-production, for example, agricultural labourers rather than nuclear scientists. Hence, a small sacrifice in terms of N-bombs (1000 bombs) can yield substantial gains in terms of rice production (40 million tonnes of rice). However, as less and less resources are devoted to making bombs, and transferred into rice production, the addition to rice production per unit of sacrifice of bombs declines (if nuclear scientists are forced to produce rice, they turn out, not surprisingly, to be rather inept at it). The sacrifice of 2000 bombs (from 9000 to 7000) does not generate 80 million tonnes of rice, but only an additional 30 million tonnes (an increase from 40 to 70 million tonnes). This is reflected in the concave shape of the *PPC*.

The *PPC* illustrates the concepts of scarcity, choice, and opportunity cost. Scarcity is implied by the unattainable combinations beyond the boundary; choice by the need to choose among the alternative points on the boundary; and opportunity cost by the negative slope of the boundary, which shows that obtaining more of one commodity necessitates having less of the other. In the example developed here, the slope gets steeper as the economy moves along the *PPC* from left to right, which means that it becomes more and more difficult to produce additional amounts of rice by decreasing the production of bombs. More and more bombs have to be forgone to get the same amount of rice as before. The increasing (absolute) slope, therefore, indicates increasing opportunity cost.

If the economy is using all its resources efficiently, it is on a point on the *PPC*. Then the only way it can produce more of everything is by increasing its resources or by using better technology. Either of these two will shift the *PPC* outwards to the right.

A similar consideration is faced by any firm which produces more than one product. At any point of time, a firm has given resources of land, labour, capital, and entrepreneurship. It also faces a production-possibility boundary that defines the maximum it can produce of any output, given the amounts of the other outputs it has decided to produce. If it wants to produce more of one product it has to produce less of another, if it is operating efficiently on the boundary. It can also shift its boundary by investing in more capital or hiring more workers or applying superior techniques.

1.3 TRANSACTION COSTS

There are many ways of organizing economic activities. The most visible alternatives are the market and the firm. One can think of an entire automobile being produced by a firm. On the other hand, different items like the steering wheel, gear-box, tyres, etc. can be produced separately by a number of firms and then purchased and assembled by a firm. Even within the firm, different organizational forms may be employed, e.g. centralized versus decentralized structures. Economic efficiency implicitly presupposes that the most efficient way of organizing activities is being employed.

Specialization means that economic agents engage in different activities. There is hence a need to coordinate these activities to reach the desired goals. Different types of organizations solve in different ways the problems of coordination and communication in an overall framework of specialization. Coordination necessitates the reaching of agreements to work towards a common goal and, therefore the formulation of contracts, whether implicit or explicit. When I go to the neighbourhood grocery store to buy a tube of toothpaste, I simply pay the money over the counter, get a sales receipt and the toothpaste. When a steel producer buys coal from a coal mine, the contract can run into many pages and be valid for several years.

Transaction costs is the term used to describe the impediments to reaching and enforcing agreements. They are associated with activities such as bargaining, contracting, and monitoring performance, activities that are not directly productive, but which are engaged in solely as a need to coordinate activities among transactors.

To concretize the notion of transaction costs further, we can distinguish between *ex ante* and *ex post* transaction costs. The former are the costs of drafting, negotiating, and safeguarding an agreement. The *ex post* costs include (i) the maladaptation costs when transactions drift out of alignment in relation to the original agreement, (ii) the haggling costs incurred if bilateral efforts are made to correct *ex post* misalignments, (iii) the set-up and running costs associated with the governance structures to which disputes are referred, and (iv) the bonding costs of securing agreements.

Example 1.5. Suppose that a firm contracts with the owner of an oil tanker for the delivery of a certain amount of oil at a certain place on a certain date. The *ex ante* costs refer to the costs of drawing up and entering into the contract. Now suppose that war breaks out in the Middle East and the usual routes for oil tankers are shut down. As a result, the oil is not delivered. The maladaptation costs refer to this particular transaction facing a difficulty not foreseen in the original agreement. The firm and the owner of the oil tanker might try to solve the issue bilaterally. The firm would cite the contract while the owner would cite the changed circumstances. If the dispute is not resolved, then it might have to be referred to the courts (which will be the governance structures available for such disputes). Finally, the court can mediate an agreement with some bonding costs as commitments on either side.

There are two major sources of transaction costs. First, human beings have bounded rationality. Bounded rationality refers to human behaviour that is *intendedly rational but only limitedly so*. That is, human beings try to behave rationally (optimize). However, they are faced with both neuro-physiological limits as well as language limits. There are limits on the power of individuals to receive, sort, retrieve, and process information without error. Language limits refer to the inability of individuals to articulate their knowledge or feelings by the use of words, numbers, or graphics in a way that permits them to be understood by others. Bounded rationality is important when the limits of rationality have been reached, i.e. under conditions of uncertainty and/or complexity.

The presence of bounded rationality means that comprehensive contracting is not a realistic organizational alternative: because of the existence of bounded rationality, the parties to a transaction cannot make provision for every possible contingency. That is, the transaction costs of negotiating and enforcing contracts make it prohibitively costly to write long-term contracts that specify all obligations under all contingencies.

The second source of transaction costs is opportunism, which refers to *self-seeking with guile*. Since contracts cannot be comprehensive, agents will try to behave opportunistically when unanticipated events arise (i.e. events for which no provision has been made in a contract). They can try to take advantage of existing loopholes in the contract or even try to modify the terms of the contract, either through actions that directly benefit them or by imposing costs on trading partners to elicit concessions (examples of the latter being strikes, false claims of dissatisfaction with the existing terms, etc.).

The costs of opportunism sometimes are direct, for example when a prolonged strike or lockout leads to production and income losses. The indirect costs of opportunism can be equally serious: investors may be unwilling to set up firms in a region where unions are known not to stick to wage bargaining agreements but to go on strike at every possible opportunity.

The problem of opportunism assumes a serious form under conditions of asset specificity. Asset specificity refers to investments that are specific to transactions in the sense that their values in alternative transactions are significantly lower. An example is a rail line built to carry coal from the pithead to a steel plant. If the coal mine were to close down, the rail line might be useless, i.e. there might not be any alternative goods to carry. Asset specific investments often permit significant cost savings to be realized (the cost of transporting coal by trucks will be much higher).

But such investments are risky, in that specialized assets cannot be redeployed without sacrifice of value if contracts should be interrupted or prematurely terminated. This creates the scope for opportunism: once two parties have entered into an agreement and one party (say party *A*) has made specific investments relying on the initial contract, the other party (say party *B*) realizes that, to some extent, *A* is at its mercy. *A* is 'locked into' this relationship because of the specific nature of its investment. Hence, *B* will

---

Box 1.2. Transaction Costs and Equity Markets

Bencivenga, Smith, and Starr (1996) argue that in financial markets, transaction costs are critical for affecting not just the level of investment, but the kinds of investments that occur. They draw on two fundamental insights to support their view. The first is that most productive capital investments often require the commitment of large amounts of funds for substantial periods: the pay-out period faced by the investors is relatively long. The second is that investors are unlikely to commit funds to such investments in the absence of well-functioning capital markets that can provide them with liquidity. That is, investors face two important timing decisions with respect to their capital investments— the time for pay-out or maturity and the holding period. In poorly developed capital markets, it is difficult to sell off stocks and the time for pay-out and the holding period are identical. Once equity markets allow the ownership of capital to be transferred economically, individuals can choose a maturity of investment that maximizes yield, and at the same time choose a holding period to satisfy the desired timing of their transactions.

Economic transfer of ownership of capital requires the lowering of transaction costs. Among the important transaction costs in the context of equity markets are the following:

- Brokerage fees: commissions paid by investors to brokers who execute the orders on their behalf.

- Counterparty risk: when a trade has been struck and one of the two parties to the transaction declares bankruptcy, the other party suffers.

- Settlement costs: these include the costs of paperwork, such as stamp duty. Additionally there is the risk to the buyer of getting stolen or forged certificates.

Another transaction cost is the 'impact cost'. This refers to the fact that trading in larger blocks leads to a change in the prices. An investor trying to sell shares can end up receiving less than he should have and somebody trying to buy shares can end up paying more.

In India, a number of steps have been taken to lower the transaction costs in equity markets. Among them are attempts to create a nationwide market in securities (so that the transaction costs do not differ significantly between the metro cities and other areas), setting up of the National Securities Clearing Corporation to eliminate counterparty risk, and creation of depositories and a movement towards dematerialized trading to lower settlement costs.

---

have an incentive to force A to give up more than the originally agreed upon share of gains, threatening otherwise to terminate the relationship. But realizing this possibility *ex ante*, A might be reluctant to enter into a contract with B. Thus, from society's point of view, some opportunities of welfare-enhancing trade could be forsaken. In our example, the mine owner who invests in the rail line may find herself at the mercy of the steel plant using the coal. The steel plant may threaten to get coal by using trucks. On the other hand, the steel plant might worry that after the railway is built, the mine will try to raise the freight rates, banking on the fact that alternative transportation modes are too expensive. This possibility of opportunistic behaviour is called the *hold-up problem*.

If contracts were complete, hold-up problems would not arise. The full range of possibilities and safeguards against these would be specified in the contract. Even though complete contracting is not possible, the parties can draw up long-term contracts, and try to build into the contract safeguards against such opportunism, for example, through price indexing clauses, cost-plus pricing clauses, liquidated damages, and arbitration provisions. However, when asset specificity is substantial, contractual governance may become very costly. Internal organization of the exchange may then be the more efficient governance structure, providing the rationale for the existence of firms.

1.4 RATIONALITY

One of the basic assumptions that economists make is that economic agents engage in cost–benefit calculations before undertaking any action. But do people really make such cost–benefit analyses? One answer is that they do so implicitly, sometimes without being aware of it. The other is that they will enrich both themselves and the society if they are more conscious of the costs and benefits from their actions.

We are assuming that people behave (or ought to behave) *rationally*, i.e. take decisions on the basis of cost–benefit analyses. But there might be other ways of making decisions, e.g. by simply tossing a coin, or by asking one's friends for advice (in this case, perhaps the person is assuming that the friends are in a better position to do the cost–benefit calculation because they will take a more 'objective' view, i.e. a view that is more aligned to rational analysis). Economics takes rationality as a basic principle guiding people's behaviour, to lend generality to its analysis of economic actions and motives.

BOX 1.3. CONCEPTS OF RATIONALITY

There might be some disagreement over what rationality really means. Does it refer to the 'self-interest standard of rationality', which says that rational persons assign significant weights only to those costs and benefits that affect directly themselves? This standard would preclude all charitable motives, motives to make other people happy, and so on. (Of course, one might say that charitable motives also flow from self-interest, from the pleasure that charity or its attendant publicity confers, compared with the actual costs of charity). Or is it the 'present-aim standard of rationality', which requires the person to act efficiently in the pursuit of whatever goals he/she happens to be pursuing at the moment? This standard can accommodate charitable motives, but is too broad, explaining everything tautologically. For example, if a person with a heart condition likes cholesterol-rich food, this is still rational by present-aim standards, so long as the person does not pay more for the food than is necessary.

Economists have sometimes formalized rationality to mean that agents solve optimization problems, i.e. they maximize or minimize certain objective functions subject to certain constraints. In other words, they try to do the best under the limitations faced by them. Thus, for example, they maximize their 'utility' subject to the fact that they cannot spend more than the income they receive. The posing of the individual's problem as one of optimization allows economists to be more precise in their formulations. The proper specification of the objective function and the constraints is the key to such analysis.

1.5 MARGINAL ANALYSIS

If people behave rationally, then they try to optimaliy allocate the limited resources at their disposal. *Marginal analysis,* a basic tool used by economists to analyse the optimal allocation of resources, focuses on the comparison of incremental benefits and costs from alternative courses of action. The example below illustrates the way in which marginal analysis can be used if there is a fixed amount of a certain resource that must be 'optimally' allocated between competing ends.

Example 1.6. Suppose that a firm has Rs 10 lakh to invest. The chief executive officer (CEO) can invest this money in only two projects, A and B. She has a fair idea of the profits she will get from each project given the funds she invests in each of the two projects. This information is provided in the table below. For simplicity, we assume that investments must be made in blocks of Rs 1 lakh. Π_A and Π_B refer to the total profits from the two projects, respectively. The CEO's aim is to obtain the maximum profits from the two projects together from the Rs 10 lakh at her disposal.

In this example, note that for any amount of funds invested, the total profit from Project A is always greater than Project B. It would, however, be a mistake to conclude that the CEO should only invest in Project A. She should compare the profits from an extra lakh of rupee's investment in each project. Starting from 0 rupees of investment, the first lakh rupees of investment yields Rs 9000 from Project A and Rs 4000 from Project B. Hence, the first lakh of rupees should be invested in Project A and the last column notes this. Similarly, the second lakh of rupees yields Rs 8000 from Project A and Rs 4000 from Project B, so this too should be spent on Project A.

Continuing in this manner, we find that the marginal (additional) gains from both projects are the same after the investment of Rs 5 lakh in Project A. But from Rs 6 lakh onwards, each extra lakh of rupees invested in Project B yields more profits. So, the CEO should invest Rs 6 lakh in Project A and Rs 4 lakh in Project B (or, alternatively, Rs 5 lakh in each). This nets her Rs 39,000 profits from Project A and Rs 16,000 profits from Project B, a total of Rs 55,000 in profits. This is the best she can do, and this solution is obtained by equating the marginal 'products' (profits) from the two projects. If she had invested only in Project A, she could expect to get Rs 45,000 at the most.

Rupees invested (lakh)	Π_A (Rs '000)	Π_B (Rs '000)	$\Delta\Pi_A$ (Rs '000)	$\Delta\Pi_B$ (Rs '000)	Project for investment
1	9	4			A
			8	4	A
2	17	8			
			7	4	A
3	24	12			
			6	4	A
4	30	16			
			5	4	A

			$\Delta\Pi_A$	$\Delta\Pi_B$	
5	35	20			
			4	4	A/B
6	39	24			
			3	4	B
7	42	28			
			2	4	B
8	44	32			
			1	4	B
9	45	36			
			0	4	B
10	45	40			

Note: $\Delta\Pi_A$ refers to the additional profits obtained by investing another Rs 1 lakh in Project A. Similarly for $\Delta\Pi_B$.

1.6 PRODUCTION COSTS

As already pointed out, the notion of cost that economists use is that of opportunity cost. The calculation of opportunity costs forces us to take into account both implicit and explicit costs. Examples of implicit costs include

- the owner of the firm working for the firm but getting no salary, and
- the cost of funds invested in the firm that could have been used elsewhere.

Production costs, as the term signifies, are the costs incurred in the process of production, while transaction costs relate to the exchange process. Economists have tried to categorize the different types of *production costs* from the economic point of view. A brief review of this categorization is provided below.

1.6.1 Costs in the Short Run

In the short run, at least one input is fixed in quantity. For example, if a courier firm rents a building for one year, then the services from the rented building (e.g. the floor space available) are independent of the production level of the firm (the amount of mail handled) for this year.

Economists often simplify matters by assuming that output Q is produced with the help of two inputs—capital services (K) and labour services (L). The production function F shows the maximum amount of Q that can be produced from a certain amount of K and L: $Q = F(K, L)$. It is conventional to assume that capital K is fixed in the short run, i.e. $K = K_0$. Then the minimum amount of L needed to produce some Q is obtained by solving $Q = F(K_0, L)$.

Example 1.7. Suppose $Q = K^{0.5}L^{0.5}$, and $K = 100$ in the short run. Then, from the definition of the production function, the minimum amount of L needed to produce any Q is $L = (Q/10)^2$.

Total cost in the short run, C, has two components:

- Total fixed cost (TFC), associated with the fixed K. $TFC = r K_0$, where r is the rental cost of capital. This part of the cost does not change when output level is changed. In our example, this is the rental on the building that must be paid every month. Moreover, fixed cost is incurred even when there is zero production.

- Total variable cost (TVC) = wL, 'w' being the wage rate. This part of the cost is dependent on the level of output, since the minimum L required to produce any Q changes when Q changes. To indicate this dependence, we can write $TVC = TVC(Q)$. Continuing with Example 1.7, $TVC(Q) = (wQ^2)/100$.

Therefore, $C(Q) = TFC + TVC(Q)$, i.e. total cost is the sum of total fixed cost and total variable cost.

Examples of variable cost include commissions to salespersons or the wages paid to contractual labour. General and administrative expenses are examples of fixed costs.[3] The line dividing fixed and variable costs is often fuzzy. Some types of advertisements that are used to establish a market presence are fixed costs because they are unrelated to the level of production of the firm. But for increasing the demand for a product, more advertising is generally needed to sustain higher sales. In this case, advertising expenditure will be a variable cost because it will be related to output.

It is important to realize that a cost is fixed when it is invariant to a firm's output. The cost can still be affected by other dimensions of a firm's operations or the decisions managers may take. The cost of providing a cable connection to a person depends on the distance of his TV from the nearest connecting point, not only on the number of channels he decides to subscribe to.

Whether a cost is fixed or not also depends on the time period involved. For example, consider the owner of a tea-shop on the street who rents a small kiosk to run his operations. He enters into a rental agreement for six months. The rent of the kiosk is a fixed cost for these six months. But after six months, the owner can decide to expand his operations and rent a bigger kiosk. Then the rental becomes a variable cost.

A final point should be noted. A fixed cost may or may not be sunk. Advertising expenditure invariant to the level of output is both fixed and sunk. On the other hand, if a firm purchases a building to house its administrative staff, the cost of purchase is a fixed cost, but it is not sunk, since the firm may be able to sell off the building if necessary and recover the initial cost.

Corresponding to each of these total cost concepts, we can define an average cost concept, i.e. the cost per unit of quantity produced, with similar definitions:

- Average total cost (AC) = C/Q.
- Average fixed cost (AFC) = TFC/Q. Unlike total fixed cost, average fixed cost depends on the level of output.
- Average variable cost (AVC) = TVC/Q. Using Example 1.7, $AVC = (wQ)/100$.

---

[3]In Indian companies, wages and salaries are often taken to be components of fixed costs because of the difficulty of laying off workers.

Note that $AC = C/Q = (TFC + TVC)/Q = (TFC/Q + TVC/Q) = AFC + AVC$. Like total cost, average total cost is the sum of the average fixed cost and the average variable cost.

The next important definition is that of (short run) marginal cost, which will play a crucial role in subsequent analysis. The marginal cost (MC) at any level of output is the extra cost incurred to produce an additional unit of output:

- Marginal cost (MC) = dC/dQ.

Moreover, $MC = d(TFC + TVC)/dQ = dTVC/dQ$, since total fixed cost by definition does not change when output changes. In Example 1.7, $MC = (2wQ)/100$.

If finite changes in Q are being considered, then marginal cost may be defined as $[C(Q+\Delta Q) - C(Q)]/\Delta Q$, where ΔQ is the change in output.

All the costs, it should be noted, depend parametrically on the input prices and the fixed level of K. In other words, we are defining our cost concepts on the basis of the assumption of unchanging input prices and a fixed K. If the input prices change or K is altered, then this leads to shifts in the cost curve.

1.6.2 Shapes of Short Run Cost Curves

Let us begin with the simplest concept, that of the total fixed cost curve. The total fixed cost is independent of the level of output; hence it can be represented by a horizontal straight line. On the other hand, $AFC = TFC/Q$. Since TFC is fixed, AFC always falls as more and more output is produced and asymptotically approaches the Q axis (since it never becomes 0). This process whereby AFC falls with output is sometimes referred to as 'spreading overhead costs'.

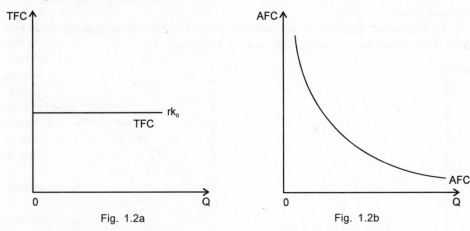

Fig. 1.2a   Fig. 1.2b

It will now be shown that an assumption about the shape of the TVC curve enables us to identify the shapes of all other cost curves. The TVC curve is often assumed to be inverse-S shaped. Since the marginal cost curve represents the slope of the TVC curve, it can be easily checked that if the TVC curve is inverse-S shaped, the MC curve must have a U shape.

How can we justify a U-shaped MC curve? One can appeal to the law of diminishing returns to justify the upward rising part of the MC curve. The *law of diminishing returns* states that if at least one input is a fixed input, then the marginal product of any other input (i.e. the extra product from an additional unit of the input) will, eventually, decrease as more of that input is applied. That is, in our model, since K is fixed in the short run, after a point, $\Delta Q/\Delta L$ will decrease as more of L is used. In other words, $\Delta L/\Delta Q$ will rise; production of extra amounts of Q will require more and more of L. This will lead to a rising MC curve.

Example 1.8

L	ΔL	Q	ΔQ	ΔQ/ΔL
1		10		
	1		2	2
2		12		
	1		3	3
3		15		
	1		3	3
4		18		
	1		2	2
5		20		

In Example 1.8, when L is increased from 4 to 5, only 2 additional units of Q are obtained and $\Delta Q/\Delta L$ falls to 2 from 3. Note that this implies a rise in $\Delta L/\Delta Q$. Similarly, in Example 1.7, $dL/dQ = Q/50$. For $Q = 1$, $dL/dQ = 1/50$; for $Q = 2$, $dL/dQ = 1/25$; and so on.

Remembering that $TVC = wL$, and $MC = \Delta TVC/\Delta Q$, we see that $MC = w(\Delta L/\Delta Q)$. This shows that eventually MC will be rising with Q.

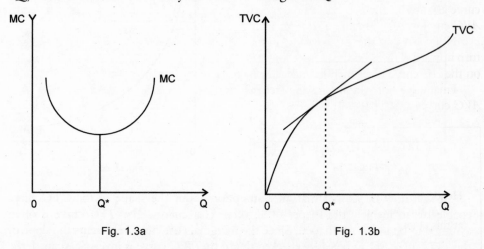

Fig. 1.3a   Fig. 1.3b

From the shape of the *TVC* curve, three things follow:

1. The *C* (total cost) curve will be the vertical summation of the *TFC* and *TVC* curves. Given that the *TFC* curve is a horizontal straight line, the *C* curve will have

exactly the same shape as the *TVC* curve, though it will lie above the *TVC* curve. Therefore, it will also have the inverse-S shape. The vertical distance between the two at any *Q* will equal *TFC*.

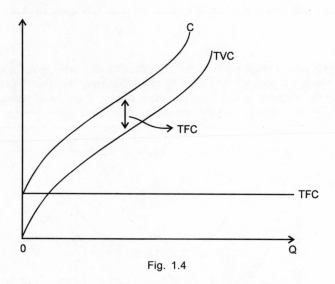

Fig. 1.4

2. The *AVC* for any *Q* is the slope of the ray from the origin to the *TVC* curve at that *Q*. Hence, given the shape of the *TVC* curve, it follows that the *AVC* curve must be U-shaped.

3. The *AC* curve, which represents the slope of the ray from the origin to the *C* curve at any *Q*, will also be U-shaped. It can also be represented by the vertical summation of the *AFC* and the *AVC* curves. Note that *AFC* = *AC* – *AVC*, i.e. the distance between the *AC* and *AFC* curves represents the *AFC* curve. Since the *AFC* curve asymptotically approaches the *Q*-axis, the vertical distance between the *AC* and *AVC* curves grows smaller as output is increased.

Note also that the *AC* curve continues to fall even after the *AVC* curve starts to turn upward. This is because the falling *AFC* curve continues to exert a downward pull on the *AC* curve until there is sufficient increase in *AVC* to neutralize it.

Finally, we note the interesting fact that the *MC* curve cuts both the *AC* and the *AVC* curves at their lowest points.

Box 1.4. *MC* CURVE CUTS *AC* CURVE AT ITS LOWEST POINT

$$MC = dC/dQ = d(AC.Q)/dQ = AC + Q(dAC/dQ).$$

Hence, $$dAC/dQ = (MC - AC)/Q.$$

At the lowest point of the *AC* curve, $dAC/dQ = 0$, which implies that *MC* = *AC* at this point.

The reader is advised to carry out the same exercise noting that $MC = dTVC/dQ$.

- Also, when *MC* > *AC*, $dAC/dQ > 0$, i.e. the *AC* curve must be rising.
- When *MC* < *AC*, $dAC/dQ < 0$, i.e. the *AC* curve must be falling.

In other words, when *MC* is less than *AC* (or *AVC*), the *AC* (*AVC*) curve is falling as *Q* increases. When *MC* is higher than *AC* (or *AVC*), the *AC* (*AVC*) curve is rising. Hence, *MC* is equal to both *AC* and *AVC* at the minimum points of these curves.

Box 1.5. Marginal and average

Suppose that your average grade in the first semester of studies is *B*. In the second semester, you get a grade of *A* in the first exam that you take. This *A* grade can be considered the marginal grade. After this exam is over, your average grade over the courses for the last semester and the new course, will definitely be above *B*.

The relationship between all the average and marginal cost curves is shown in Fig. 1.5.

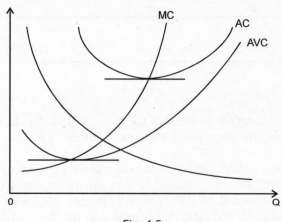

Fig. 1.5

1.6.3 Costs in the Long Run

In the long run, all inputs are variable. The firm's problem is to select that input combination that minimizes the cost of producing the targeted level of output.

There are no fixed costs in the long run; all costs are variable. Hence *LC* (long run total cost) = *LVC* (long run variable cost). This in turn implies that the long run average total cost (*LAC*) and long run average variable cost (*LAVC*) coincide, i.e. *LAC* = *LAVC*, where *LAC* = *LC/Q* and *LAVC* = *LVC/Q*.

The long run marginal cost (*LMC*) is defined as dLC/dQ. Noting that $LC = Q.LAC$, we can show that $dLAC/dQ = (LMC - LAC)/Q$. Thus the *LMC* curve lies below the *LAC* curve when the latter is downward sloping, intersects it at its lowest point, and lies above it when *LAC* is upward rising, as shown in Fig. 1.6.

1.6.4 Shape of the LAC Curve

In the long run, we cannot use the law of diminishing returns to determine the shapes of the cost curves, since all inputs are freely variable. Instead, in the long run, the

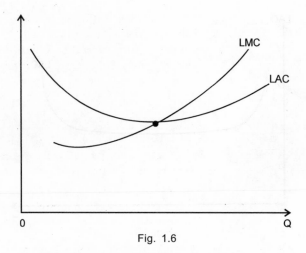

Fig. 1.6

concept of returns to scale is appropriate: the type of returns to scale that applies will determine the shape of the *LAC* curve.

1. Constant returns to scale *(CRS)*: In this case, when *L* and *K* are changed in the same proportion, output also changes in the same proportion. In other words, a change in output from *Q* to *tQ*, *t* > 0, can be achieved by changing *L* and *K* to *tL* and *tK*, respectively.[4] Hence *LAC(tQ)* = *LAC(Q)*, for any *t* > 0. The *LAC* curve, plotted against *Q*, is a horizontal straight line. It follows that the L*MC* curve coincides with the *LAC* curve.

2. Increasing returns to scale *(IRS)*: In this case, when *L* and *K* are increased in the same proportion, output increases by a larger proportion. In other words, a change in output from *Q* to *tQ*, *t* > 1, can be achieved by changing *L* and *K* to *t'L* and *t'K* respectively, where *t'* < *t*. Then *LAC(tQ)* < *LAC(Q)*, for any *t* > 1. If *L* and *K* are doubled, total cost doubles (assuming unchanged input prices), but output more than doubles. As a result, *LAC* falls. Hence when *IRS* prevails, the *LAC* declines as output is increased; the *LAC* curve is downward sloping.

3. Decreasing returns to scale *(DRS)*: When *L* and *K* are increased in the same proportion, output increases by a smaller proportion. It is easy to show that the *LAC* curve will be upward rising in this case.

Economists usually work with a U-shaped *LAC* curve. Implicitly, they are assuming that when the firm produces more and more in the long run, it first faces a condition of *IRS*, then *CRS* (when the curve reaches its minimum), and finally *DRS*. The minimum point of the U-shaped *LAC* curve is called the minimum efficient scale *(MES)*.

Empirical studies sometimes suggest that the *LAC* is a flat-bottomed curve, i.e., there is a range of outputs for which the condition of *CRS* prevails. See Fig. 1.7.

[4]The discerning reader will note that we still have to show that when output is increased by a factor of *t*, cost-minimization requires that all inputs have to be increased by a factor of *t*.

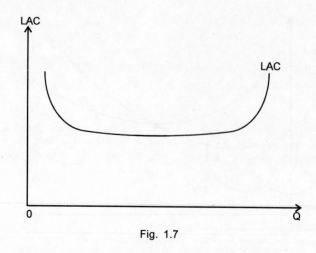

Fig. 1.7

1.6.5 The Relationship between Short Run and Long Run Cost Curves

In the long run, the firm is free to vary all inputs. Therefore, it has more flexibility and in general achieves a lower cost of production than in the short run.

The relationship between the long run and short run cost curves can be analysed as follows. Consider three possible levels of K. Each of these will determine a particular short run total cost curve. In the short run, given the level of K, the firm is stuck to one of these curves. However, in the long run, the firm is free to choose the level of K that minimizes a particular level of output. In Fig. 1.8, the level of K that minimizes the total cost from 0 to Q_1 is K_1, from Q_1 to Q_2 is K_2, and from Q_2 onwards, it is K_3. The long run total cost curve is then obtained by joining the corresponding segments of the short run total cost curves. It is the envelope of the short run cost curves, denoted by the thick curve.

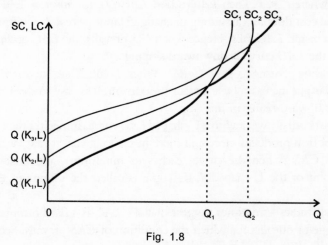

Fig. 1.8

Similarly, the *LAC* curve is the envelope of the *SAC* curves (Fig. 1.9a). If there is a continuum of short run curves, then the long run cost curve becomes smooth curve

(Fig. 1.9b). Note that in this case, each *SAC* curve touches the envelope *LAC* curve only once. Moreover, the point of tangency, in the upward and downward sloping segments of the *LAC* curve, is not the minimum point of the *SAC* curve. It is the minimum point of a *SAC* curve only when there is *CRS* in the long run, i.e. at the minimum point(s) of the *LAC* curve.

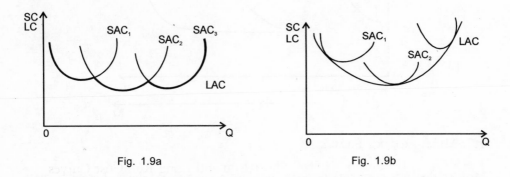

Fig. 1.9a   Fig. 1.9b

The long run marginal cost curve, *LMC* is built up from the corresponding *SMC*s. Take a particular output and consider the corresponding point on the *LAC* curve. It is a point of tangency with some *SAC* curve. At that point, the *LMC* is nothing but the corresponding short run marginal cost (e.g., point *A* in Fig. 1.10). Hence, the *LMC* curve is obtained from the points on the *SMC* curves at different levels of *Q*, the *SMC* curves corresponding to the *SAC* curves that minimize short run average costs at those *Q*.

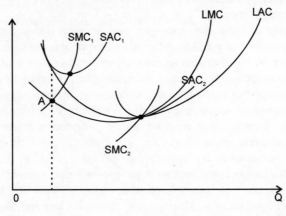

Fig. 1.10

If there is *CRS* for every level of production, then the *LAC* curve is a horizontal straight line and coincides with the *LMC* curve (Fig. 1.11). All the *SAC* curves are tangential to the *LAC* curve at their minimum points.

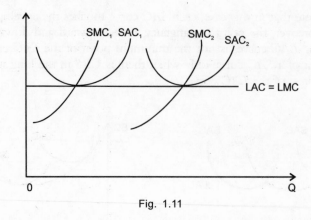

Fig. 1.11

1.7 MULTI-PRODUCT FIRMS

Most of the large corporations today produce a range of products. For such multi-product firms, the cost concepts we have developed earlier need to be modified and new concepts developed.

For example, if a firm produces two or more products, it makes no sense to talk about the average cost or the marginal cost, because output for the firm is a vector. Suppose that a firm produces two goods and has a total cost function $C(q_1, q_2)$, where q_1 and q_2 are the quantities of the two products. One can then define the incremental cost of increasing product 2 from 0 to q_2, holding product 1 constant: $IC_2 = C(q_1, q_2) - C(q_1, 0)$. The average incremental cost of increasing product 2 from 0 to q_2, holding product 1 constant, is then $AIC_2 = [C(q_1, q_2) - C(q_1, 0)]/q_2$.

With the help of these two concepts, we can then define the product-specific economies of scale (PS_i) of q_i holding the other output, q_j, constant: $PS_i = AIC_i/MC_i$, where MC_i is just $\partial C/\partial q_i$. Returns to the scale of product i are said to be increasing, decreasing, or constant as PS_i is greater than, less than, or equal to unity, respectively.

Another concept that is required in the case of multi-product firms is economies of scope. Economies of scope refer to the possibility of achieving lower costs by producing goods jointly rather than separately (sometimes referred to as 'synergy effects'). Such economies exist when $C(q_1, q_2) < C(q_1, 0) + C(0, q_2)$. Economies of scope (SC), are measured as $SC = [C(q_1, 0) + C(0, q_2) - C(q_1, q_2)]/ C(q_1, q_2)$.

Many possible factors contribute to economies of scope, one of the most important being common inputs. One example of such common input is the use of sheep to produce both wool and mutton. Mutton spoils unless refrigerated. Before refrigeration, it was sometimes more efficient to produce mutton and wool separately. The shearing centre could be so far from the population centre that the mutton would spoil by the time it arrived. The alternative of keeping the sheep near the population centre would not be cost-effective.

2 Value

2.1 INTRODUCTION

One might say that the fundamental purpose of all economic activity is to create value. Three questions then arise:

- What is value?
- How and when is value created?
- Who appropriates value?

The concept of value emerges in the context of the fundamental economic problem of choice among alternatives under conditions of scarcity. The creation of value depends on making the correct choices, i.e. properly evaluating the alternatives available. It is, therefore, intimately linked up with the notion of opportunity costs.

Before we go into the concept of value in detail, here is a simple example to illustrate how value is created and apportioned between different economic agents. Consider the case of an oil company, which imports crude petroleum, refines the crude into petrol, transports the petrol to petrol pumps, and sells it at a price P per litre. Motorists who buy petrol at that price obviously value the benefits they get from it at P per litre or more. It follows that the average of the maximum prices that these motorists would be willing to pay for a litre of petrol is more than P. Let us assume that this average figure is V, so that $V>P$. Let us also assume that the price that the company pays for its imported crude works out to M per litre of petrol. If the crude remains as crude, it has a value of M. If it is transformed into petrol and marketed to motorists, its value, as perceived by the motorists, is V. Thus, the value created (VC) by the process of transformation and marketing is $V - M$. In other words, the value created by a firm is the difference between the perceived value of its output and the market value of its material inputs. More formally,

$$VC = V - \mathrm{M} \tag{2.1}$$

Of the total value created, the difference between what motorists are willing to pay and what they actually pay accrues to the motorists as a consumers' surplus (CS). Formally,

$$CS = V - P \tag{2.2}$$

The rest of the value created, i.e. $P - M$ accrues to the oil company and is called value added (VA). Put differently, the value added by a firm is the difference between the market value of its output and the market value of its material inputs and can be written as

$$VA = P - M \qquad (2.3)$$

VA is lower than *VC* in that it does not include the consumers' surplus. Business Policy literature holds that *VC* reflects the true value of the transformation and marketing activities undertaken by a firm, or what economists call production. But V represents a subjective valuation by consumers and cannot be estimated accurately, while *P* represents an objective valuation by the market. Therefore, economists use *VA*, rather than *VC*, to measure production.

2.2 (Added) Value from the Point of View of the Firm: The Concept of Economic Profit

We start with the concept of economic profit which will be critical in defining value. Accounting profit is equal to total revenue minus explicit costs, while economic profit is equal to total revenue minus all opportunity costs. The opportunity costs consist of both explicit costs and all implicit costs.

If a firm is to continue operations in an industry, economic rationale demands that it make profit which is at least sufficient to cover the returns from alternative uses of its resources. This is its *normal profit*. Normal profit is said to be earned when economic profit is zero. If economic profit is greater than zero, then the firm is making supernormal profits, and resources are attracted into the industry. If it is less than zero, the firm can earn more elsewhere, and it would want to exit from the industry. Therefore, in economics, if we say that a firm is earning zero or negative profits, this does not mean that its accounting profit is zero or negative. The point is that even a positive accounting profit may hide the true cost of resources being used by the firm.

From the point of view of a single firm, we measure value by economic profit earned by that firm. Thus,

Value = Economic profit = Total revenue – Opportunity cost of the resources used by the firm.

The firm creates value by applying to material inputs, *labour* or physical and mental effort of human beings and *capital* or tangible and intangible assets that increase the productivity of human beings. It pays a wage (*W*) for the labour it uses and an interest (*I*) on the capital it employs. If all firms were equally efficient and could enter the product and factor markets freely, then competition among them for markets and factors would lower product prices and raise factor prices, until the entire value created is paid out to consumers, labour, and capital as consumers' surplus, wages, and interest charges, respectively. In reality, all firms are not equally efficient, nor is entry free. Therefore, as we shall see in subsequent chapters, some firms are able to appropriate a part of the value they create as an economic profit (Π), either by acquiring market power or by becoming more efficient than firms that just break even. In the former case, they charge a price that exceeds the cost of production and make a profit by reducing the consumers' surplus. In the latter case, they produce the same output with less material, labour, or capital than firms that break even, and make a profit at the expense of loss-making firms. To sum up,

$$VC = CS + W + I + \Pi, \qquad (2.4)$$

where the value of Π may be positive, negative, or zero. Combining (eqn 2.1), (eqn 2.2) and (eqn 2.4) and rearranging terms, we get

$$\Pi = P - M - W - I. \tag{2.5}$$

Chart 2.1 shows how value is to be calculated.

Chart 2.1

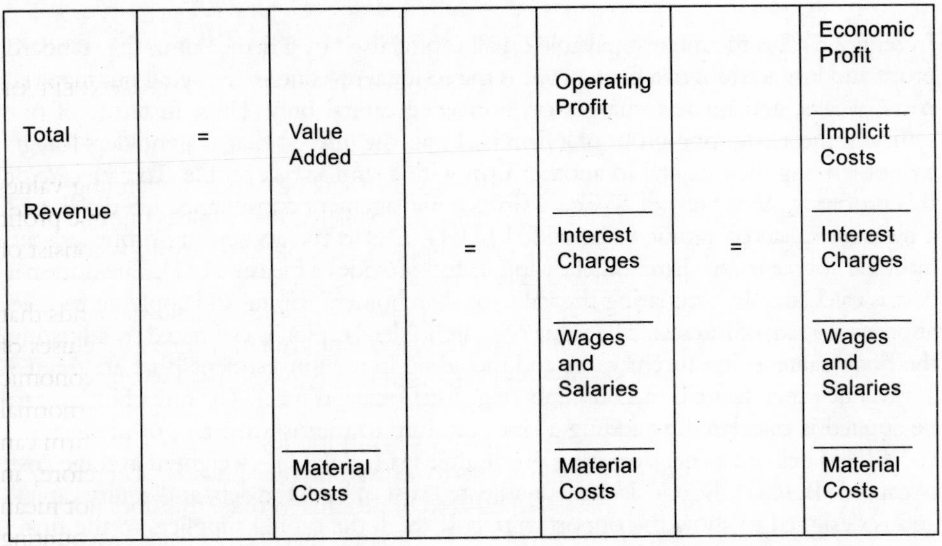

Total	=	Value Added		Operating Profit		Economic Profit
						Implicit Costs
Revenue			=	Interest Charges	=	Interest Charges
				Wages and Salaries		Wages and Salaries
		Material Costs		Material Costs		Material Costs

In Example 2.1, economic profits are calculated by subtracting explicit variable and fixed costs from the revenue of the firm to get accounting profit. From the accounting profit figure, two implicit costs are deducted to get economic profit —the return on firm's capital and owner's imputed wage.

Example 2.1. Profit and Loss Account for ABC Company for the year ending 31 March 1998

	Expenditure (Rs)		*Income (Rs)*
Variable Costs		*Revenue from sales*	1,000,000
Wages	200,000		
Materials	300,000		
Other	100,000		
Fixed Costs			
Rent	50,000		
Managerial salaries	60,000		
Interest on loans	90,000		
Depreciation allowance	50,000		
Total Expenditure	850,000		

Profit	150,000
Return on the firm's capital	−100,000
Owner's imputed wage	− 40,000
Economic Profit	10,000

Economic Value Added

In (eqn 2.5), I is the interest payable on all capital used by a firm. But in the standard profit and loss account of a firm, profit is the residual revenue after paying out material costs, wages, and interest charges on borrowed capital only. Thus, in terms of our symbols, the accounting profit of a firm is Π plus the interest that shareholders forego by not lending their capital to another firm with a similar risk profile. To take care of this problem, Stern Stewart & Co., a firm of management consultants, has developed a measure called economic value added (*EVA*). *EVA* is the accounting profit less the notional cost of using shareholders' capital, and provides a measure of Π. The notional cost is calculated by estimating the value of shareholders' capital and applying to it an appropriate rate of interest. The value of shareholders' capital is estimated by adjusting the book value to its current value and including in it all investments that are treated as revenue expenditure by accountants (e.g. R&D expenditure). The rate of interest to be applied is calculated by adding a risk premium to the risk-free rate of interest.

EVA is defined as net operating profit after tax (*NOPAT*) – weighted average cost of capital (*WACC*). *WACC* is the risk-adjusted cost of both the debt and equity capital and is designed to show the opportunity cost to all the capital suppliers to the firm.

Suppose there are three types of capital, K_1, K_2, K_3, used by a firm and their associated implicit returns are r_1, r_2, and r_3. Then the total cost of capital will be $r_1 K_1 + r_2 K_2 + r_3 K_3$. This can be written as rK, where $r = (r_1 K_1 + r_2 K_2 + r_3 K_3)/K$, and $K = (K_1 + K_2 + K_3)$. Then r is weighted average return on all the capital employed by the firm that could have been earned elsewhere (in the best possible alternate usages). The total cost of capital, rK, is then called the weighted average cost of capital because of the way we define r.

Interest charges are commonly deducted to arrive at the figure for operating profit. If we, however, treat interest charges as part of capital costs, then the operating profit figure has to be calculated without deducting interest costs.

It should be noted that *EVA* takes account of one implicit cost—the cost of capital such as equity capital or retained earnings. If there are other types of implicit costs, then the *EVA* will not be equal to the economic profit of the firm.

Stern Stewart & Co. recommends 160 adjustments to standard accounting data to arrive at a realistic estimate of the *EVA*. This is not only cumbersome, but often infeasible. Many of these adjustments are required to convert the accounts from 'accrual' to 'cash' basis and can be avoided if cash flow data are used to estimate economic profit. We can do this by calculating the internal rate of return (*IRR*). The *IRR* is the rate of discount that equates the present value of cash outflows with the present value of cash inflows and represents the gross rate of return realized by the firm on its capital. If it is netted for the risk-adjusted cost of capital, we get a measure of the economic profit earned by the firm. Boston Consulting Group, an American firm of management consultants, is a strong proponent of this approach.

Box 2.1. *EVA* of some Indian Companies

The *EVA* of some Indian companies for the year 1997–8 is given below. All figures are in Rs crore.

Company	Operating Capital Employed(CE)	NOPAT	WACC	EVA
HLL	916	474.9	129.5	345.4
ITC	2260	519.2	349.9	169.3
Castrol	293	151.5	44.7	106.8
Reliance	13,476	1748.4	2106.4	–358.0

Source : The Economic Times, 21 September 1998.

In 2000, the performances of these companies were as follows:

Company	Op.Capital Employed (CE)	NOPAT	WACC	EVA
HLL	3069	1098.28	529.16	569.12
ITC	3836	859.67	725.69	133.98
Castrol	364	204.40	59.25	145.15
Reliance	23,288	2995.79	4020.78	–1024.99

Source: Business Today, 6 March 2001.

Business Policy litreature tends to regard the economic profit of a firm as a measure of its efficiency. This is not strictly correct. As we shall see later, a firm may have a positive Π not because it is efficient, but because it is protected by externally ordered entry barriers like licensing restrictions, structural imperfections in the market, etc., and can charge a price that exceeds the cost of production.

2.3 Demand–supply Analysis and Value

We will now use the familiar analysis of supply and demand to illustrate the concepts of value creation and value appropriation in a market. The forces of demand and supply are balanced in an equilibrium, which therefore determines the price and quantity transacted in a market. This in turn determines how much value is created and how it is shared between buyers and sellers.

The first concept we need is that of a market. We will use a broad definition: A *market* consists of the buyers and sellers of a good or service. We are, therefore, abstracting from any concept of specific time and location of a market. Our definition can accommodate both fairs which meet on certain days of the year for specified time periods in certain locations as well as a Stock Exchange for which buyers and sellers are dispersed all over the country. In a market, the interaction of buyers and sellers determines the prices that are established and the quantities that are transacted. The two sides of a market are represented through the forces of demand and supply. We now turn to a consideration of these forces.

The market *demand schedule* shows the amounts of the commodity that buyers are prepared to buy at different prices. The market *demand function* expresses this relationship between quantities demanded and prices in a compact functional form. When the relationship between price and quantity demanded is plotted as a graph, we get a *demand curve*.

A demand curve, therefore, represents in the form of a graph the quantity demanded at each price. Alternatively, it might be thought of as representing the *maximum price* that buyers are willing to pay for each quantity.

Example 2.2. Consider the demand for toothpastes. Let the demand function be $Q^d = 12 - P$, where P is the price per unit and Q^d is the quantity demanded in some units (say number of tubes). Q^d refers implicitly to some period of time. Your demand for toothpastes must be expressed as either one tube per month (say) or 12 tubes per year. The demand schedule then is, for some representative prices:

Price	Quantity
1	11
2	10
3	9
.	.
12	0

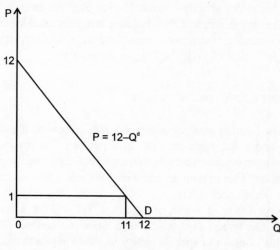

Fig. 2.1

For reasons of convenience, to draw the demand curve, economists first express price as a function of quantity, thereby deriving the *inverse demand curve*: $P = 12 - Q^d$. One can then measure P on the y-axis and Q^d on the x-axis and represent points on the inverse demand curve labelled *DD*.

In our example, the demand curve is linear, which means that its slope—given by the first derivative dQ^d/dP—is the same (here it is -1) everywhere on the demand curve, i.e. it is independent of P or Q^d. For non-linear curves, the slope of the demand curve will change from point to point on the demand curve. In general, we do not expect the demand curve to be linear, i.e. a straight line. However, for illustrative purposes, we will deal with linear demand curves to keep things simple.

The downward sloping demand curve that has been drawn above obeys the *law of demand*: quantity demanded decreases as price increases. The slope is negative (but may not be constant) at all points of the demand curve.

It is obvious from even casual observation or introspection that demand depends on many things. In general, the quantity demanded is expected to depend on

- own price
- incomes
- tastes and preferences
- prices of 'related' commodities
- expectations, etc.

When we draw the demand curve, we are focusing only on the relationship between price and quantity demanded. We can do this by assuming that 'everything else' is being kept fixed at certain levels. A change in any of these other factors thus leads to a shift in the entire curve. In Example 2.2, the number 12 captures the total influence on demand of all the other things that are being kept fixed. If any of the 'other things' change, then the entire demand curve shifts. It is very important, therefore, to distinguish between movements along an unchanging demand curve and shifts in the curve itself. When a movement along the curve is being analysed, it is customary to refer to a change in quantity demanded. A change in demand, on the other hand, refers to a shift in the demand curve.

Suppose that the equation of the inverse demand curve is $P = 10 - Q^d$, instead of $P = 12 - Q^d$. The new curve $D'\,D'$ will lie below and to the left of the old curve.

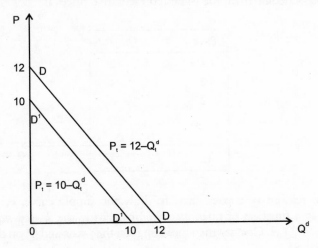

Fig. 2.2

How do we expect the 'other things' to influence demand?

- If I (income) increases, we expect more to be demanded at every price – the demand curve will shift to the right.
- If T (tastes and preferences) change such that buyers like a commodity more, again the same thing will happen.
- If the price of a substitute rises, we expect the demand to rise, too (as price of coffee rises, the demand curve for tea shifts upward and to the right). If the price of a complement rises, we expect the demand to fall (as price of sugar rises, the demand curve for tea shifts downward and to the left).
- An expectation that prices will rise in the future shifts the demand curve to the right.

The important thing to remember is that: a change in commodity's own price by itself can only represent a movement along the demand curve and not a shift in the curve; however, a change in any of the 'other things' will lead to a shift of the demand curve.

The market *supply schedule* shows the amounts of the commodity that sellers are prepared to sell at different prices. The market *supply function* expresses this relationship between quantities supplied and prices in compact functional form. When the relationship between price and quantity supplied is plotted as a graph, we get a *supply curve*.

A supply curve, therefore, represents in the form of a graph the quantity supplied at each price. Alternatively, it might be thought of as representing the *minimum price* that sellers want for supplying each quantity.

Example 2.3: Let the supply function be $Q^s = 2P$, where P is the price per unit and Q^s is the quantity supplied in some units (say kilograms). Q^s refers implicitly to some period of time. As before, the supply of toothpastes must be expressed as either one tube per month (say) or 12 tubes per year and the period chosen should be the same as the period chosen for the demand curve.

The supply schedule then, for some representative prices is:

Price	Quantity
1	2
2	4
3	6
.	.
.	.
12	24

Again, for reasons of convenience, to draw the supply curve, economists first express price as a function of quantity, thereby deriving the *inverse supply curve*. In Example 2.3, $P = Q^s/2$. One can then measure P on the y-axis and Q^s on the x-axis. The curve is labelled SS.

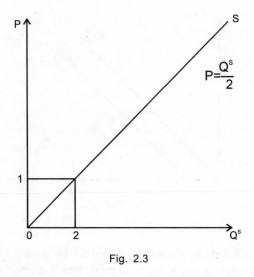

Fig. 2.3

The upward sloping supply curve that has been drawn above exemplifies the law of supply: quantity supplied increases as price increases.

Like demand, supply also depends on many things. In general, the quantity supplied is expected to depend on

• own price
• technological knowledge
• input prices,
• expectations, etc.

We have, therefore, to make the assumption of 'everything else constant' to obtain the supply function. It is then necessary to distinguish between *movements* along an unchanging supply curve and *shifts* in the curve itself. When own price changes and a movement along the curve occurs, we refer to a change in *quantity supplied*. A *change in supply*, on the other hand, refers to a shift in the supply curve, caused by a change in one or more of the 'other things'.

Suppose that the equation of the inverse supply curve is $P = Q^s/2 - 2$ instead of $P = Q^s/2$. The new curve will lie below and to the right of the old curve.

How do we expect the 'other things' to influence supply?

• A change in technology that allows the commodity to be produced more cheaply should shift the supply curve downwards and to the right.
• If input prices increase, exactly the opposite should happen.

What will be the actual price in the market and the actual quantity transacted? A *market equilibrium* occurs *when the prevailing price equates quantity demanded to quantity supplied*. The equilibrium refers to the (price, quantity) pair at which this takes place. At such a price, buyers find that they are able to buy exactly the amount that they are demanding at the prevailing price and suppliers are able to sell exactly the amount they are willing to supply at the prevailing price. In other words, there is no incentive for anyone in the market to change his or her behaviour.

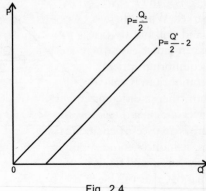

Fig. 2.4

The market equilibrium is, therefore, solved for by setting $Q^d = Q^s$, and solving for the resultant P. In diagrammatic terms, equilibrium is reached at the intersection of the (inverse) demand and supply curves DD and SS, since at the point of intersection, the quantities demanded and supplied are equal.

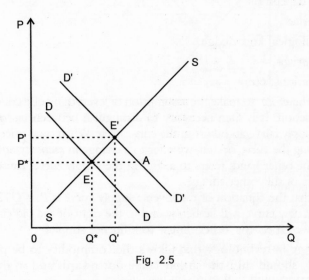

Fig. 2.5

Example 2.4. Let us bring the equations of the demand and supply curves from Examples 2.2 and 2.3 together. Setting $Q^d = Q^s$, we get $2P = 12 - P$, which can be solved for $P^* = 4$. At this price, $Q^d = Q^s = 8$.

What happens if the market price is other than P^*? For any $P > P^*$, in Fig. 2.6 we can see that $Q^d < Q^s$, so that there is *excess supply* in the market. An excess supply means that suppliers cannot sell off everything they want to at the current market price, and some of them will try to reduce prices to sell off their unsold stocks. The market price will tend to fall towards P^*. For any $P < P^*$, on the other hand, $Q^d > Q^s$, so that there is *excess demand* in the market. When there is excess demand, some buyers are unable to satisfy their demand, and will bid up prices to induce sellers to supply them the desired amount of goods. In either case, there are forces in the market pushing the actual price towards the equilibrium price.

A particular market equilibrium is valid only for a fixed set of demand and supply curves. If these curves shift, then a different equilibrium will obtain, as the diagram shows. In Fig 2.5, the inverse demand curve shifts from DD to $D'D'$. At the initial equilibrium price P^*, there is an excess demand EA which tends to push up the price. But as the price increases, it induces more supply from the sellers (represented by a movement along the supply curve) and tends to reduce demand. The new equilibrium is reached at the price–quantity pair of (P', Q').

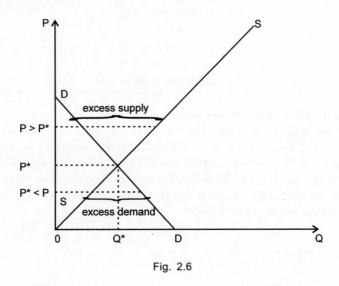

Fig. 2.6

Example 2.5. Suppose that the equation of the supply curve becomes $Q^s = 2P + 3$ while the equation of the demand curve remains the same as in Example 2.4. The equilibrium price now solves $2P + 3 = 12 - P$ and therefore $P^* = 3$. The quantity transacted now increases to 9.

In markets where demand and supply curves are rapidly shifting, the market may not be able to settle down to any equilibrium and actual prices and quantities will continue to be disequilibrium prices and quantities.

2.4 (ADDED) VALUE FROM THE POINT OF VIEW OF THE MARKET

From the point of view of the market as a whole, the concept of value relates to the gains obtained by economic agents from dealing with each other. The gain to the consumers is captured by the concept of *consumer surplus*. It is the difference between the maximum prices that the consumers are willing to pay for any amount rather than go without that amount, minus the price that they actually pay.[1] Under certain conditions, the consumer surplus is approximately the area below the demand curve and above the price line. In Fig. 2.7 below, it is shown by *DEP**.

It should be noted that this maximum price is net of (i) the user cost of the product (i.e. the costs of installing, learning how to use, operating, maintaining, and eventually disposing of the product) and (ii) any purchasing and transactions costs involved in the buying of the product, e.g. costs of search, transportation, etc.

Maximum price (gross perceived benefit)
Minus
User cost + Purchasing and transportation costs
Equals
Net perceived benefit
Minus
Price
Equals
Consumer Surplus

A similar concept called *producer surplus* can be used to represent the gains to firms from participating in the market. The producer surplus is the price that the seller obtains minus the minimum price at which the seller would have been willing to supply the good. The producer surplus can be measured by the area below the price line and above the supply curve. Therefore the aggregate producer surplus is represented in Fig. 2.7 by the area *P*ES*, i.e. the rectangle *P*OQ*E* (which is total revenue) minus the area under the supply curve *OSEQ**.

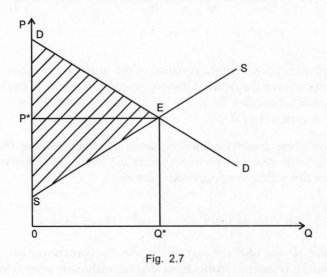

Fig. 2.7

[1]Besanko, Dranove, and Shanley (1996) term the maximum amount a consumer is willing to pay for a product as her 'perceived benefit' from the product.

The sum of consumer and producer surplus in equilibrium, representing the *total gains from trade to the participants in the market*, or the *total value created*, is the area *DES*. We can show that this is the maximum gain possible, i.e. for any other output and price, total value created or the joint gains to trade will be lower. We call this result the achievement of *static efficiency*.

To show that total value is maximized when price settles at P^* in the free market equilibrium, in Fig. 2.8a, we consider a situation where the market price P' is above P^* and in Fig. 2.8b, a situation where the market price P' is below the equilibrium price P^*. We assume that the 'short side of the market' rules, i.e. if quantity demanded (supplied) > quantity supplied (demanded), then quantity supplied (demanded) will be transacted. In both cases, consumer surplus plus producer surplus (the shaded areas) is less than *DES*. The difference, which is the area *ABE*, is known as the 'deadweight loss'. It is a deadweight loss in the sense that it represents potential gain from trade that is realized by neither the buyers nor the sellers in the market.

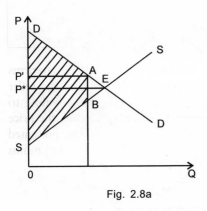

Fig. 2.8a

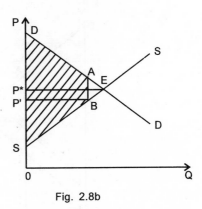

Fig. 2.8b

The concepts of consumer surplus and producer surplus also tell us how the total value is shared between buyers and sellers. When there is no deadweight loss, buyers get DEP^* and sellers get P^*ES. Note in this connection that if the supply curve is horizontal, then $P^*ES = 0$ and all the value accrues to the buyers.

We will see in Chapter 4 that a supply curve exists only under a certain type of market structure called perfect competition. Thus, we have just now shown that perfect competition maximizes value created in the market place. However, there are *imperfectly competitive* market structures where the total value generated will be less than the maximum realizable under perfect competition, but the sellers may be able extract more value than in the perfectly competitive situations. Therefore, there may be a conflict between the seller's goal of value appropriation and the wider (societal) goal of value creation.

2.5 GOVERNMENT INTERVENTION IN THE MARKET

If there is any intervention with the market forces, then even a perfectly competitive market structure will not maximize total value generated. In particular, governments sometimes try to interfere in the market to change the balance of value appropriation and tilt it in favour of the consumers. Examples are *rent control laws* and *minimum wage legislation*. Governments also impose *taxation* on the purchase and sale of certain commodities. We next show why such intervention prevents the maximum generation of value and also lead to certain unintended consequences.

2.5.1 Rent Control Laws

Governments sometimes try to set a *ceiling* on rents in the belief that rents in free market equilibrium would be too high for most people to afford renting flats/apartments. Thus in the market for housing, the maximum rent allowed is r^1 which is less than the equilibrium level r^* (see Fig. 2.9). At this r^1, there is excess demand, so that the actual transactions can take place only upto h^1. As a result, the consumer surplus plus producer surplus is only $DAh'O$ and there is a deadweight loss of ABC.

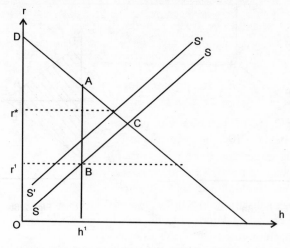

Fig. 2.9

At r^1, there will be excess demand for housing. One set of people will gain from this arrangement—the people who are able to get housing at the low rents. But some people will not be able to get housing and their unsatisfied demand shows up in various ways. First, landlords charge high deposits and 'pugrees'. Secondly, illegal transactions take place in the form of charging high rents without issuing corresponding receipts. Landlords also might use their discretion to screen applicants, e.g. some landlords might rent out flats only to tenants professing certain religious beliefs.

The smaller value from housing might discourage landlords from providing adequate maintenance services. It is not uncommon to see houses in dilapidated conditions when the Rent Control Act is enforced vigorously. More importantly, over time, funds are switched to other types of investment and less funds are deployed in the housing industry, thus shifting the supply curve to the left, (from SS to $S'S'$) and aggravating the initial condition of excess demand.

2.5.2 Minimum Wage Legislation

In contrast to rent control laws that set upper bounds on prices, minimum wage legislation is undertaken to ensure that wages paid to workers do not fall below a certain minimum. Hence, in the labour market, a *floor* is set on wages, i.e. wages are not allowed to fall below a certain level.

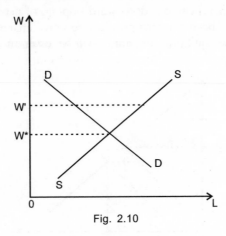

Fig. 2.10

Consider Fig. 2.10. In the absence of government intervention, the equilibrium wage rate would be W^*. But the government decrees that the wage rate cannot fall below W'. At this wage rate, there is excess supply of labour. Since some workers would have been willing to work for lower wages, a 'contract' system of wages tends to develop. Workers are employed for smaller periods or in smaller numbers, so that the minimum wage legislation does not apply, or they are not paid other benefits like medical benefits, Provident Fund, gratuity, etc. In the longer run, employers might switch to more machine-intensive processes to economize on labour costs.

Note that if $r^1 > r^*$ or $W' < W^*$, then the price ceiling or floor is not *binding*: the equilibrium price will not violate the constraint imposed by the government, and therefore the government's action is not expected to change the free market outcome substantially.

The foregoing analysis should not be taken to mean that interventions in the forms of price ceilings or price floors are always undesirable. There is some gain from each of these actions and there are some losses, and these must be balanced by society against each other. But when markets are not allowed to operate freely, forces build up that tend to bypass regulations, with unintended and undesirable outcomes. It is often argued that these outcomes could have been avoided if only the Acts and laws had been strictly enforced, and therefore, rather than giving up intervention, the government should focus on stringent implementation of such laws. This argument misses the point that in fact such stringent implementation is usually impossible and even if there is such implementation, there will still be losers and the forces for bypassing the laws will persist.

2.6 THE ELASTICITY CONCEPT

We know that when the demand and supply curves shift, then the equilibrium also shifts. That is, a new price is established on the market and a new quantity transacted. Now consider a situation where the demand curve does not shift but the supply curve shifts. The new equilibrium price and quantity are obtained on the same demand curve. Because the demand curve is downward sloping, of necessity, the equilibrium prices and quantities will be moving in opposite directions. That is, in a new equilibrium with a higher price, the equilibrium quantity will be lower and vice versa.

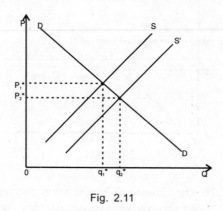

Fig. 2.11

Since p^* and q^* are moving in opposite directions, it becomes difficult to predict what happens to the product p^*q^* (total revenue).

2.6.1 Price-elasticity of Demand

A measure that helps us to make this prediction is the price-elasticity of demand. Consider a new equilibrium that involves a lower price but a higher quantity. If the percentage change in price were greater than the percentage change in quantity, the increase in volume would be unable to make up for the fall in per unit realization. Hence pq should fall. A natural 'elasticity' measure then is:

$$\varepsilon = \text{(percentage change in } Q) \div \text{by (percentage change in } P)$$
$$= -[(\Delta q/q)/(\Delta p/p)]$$
$$= -(p/q) \times (\Delta q/\Delta p).$$

where Δ refers to the change in the relevant variable. The negative sign is added to make the elasticity into a positive number—otherwise it will always be a negative number because of the downward sloping nature of the demand curve.

Since price-elasticity is being measured at a point on the market demand curve, we are assuming that all the other factors that affect market demand remain fixed. For example, the distribution of incomes among consumers, their tastes and preferences, prices of related commodities, etc., are all assumed to be constant.

- If the percentage change in q > the percentage change in p, then $\varepsilon > 1$, and we have *elastic* demand.

- If the percentage change in q = the percentage change in p, then $\varepsilon = 1$ and we say that the demand is *unit elastic*.
- If the percentage change in q < the percentage change in p, so that $\varepsilon < 1$, the demand is said to be *inelastic*.

For a fall in price,

$$TR = pq \begin{cases} \text{increases} & \text{if } \varepsilon > 1, \\ \text{stays constant} & \text{if } \varepsilon = 1, \\ \text{decreases} & \text{if } \varepsilon < 1. \end{cases}$$

For a rise in price, exactly the opposite will hold.

Example 2.6. Elasticity can be measured in different ways, as the following example shows. Suppose that we have the following two observations on price and quantity:

Situation 1	Situation 2
p_1 = Rs 10	p_2 = Rs 9.00
q_1 = 100	q_2 = 105

$\varepsilon = - [\Delta q/\Delta p] \times [p/q]$, where $\Delta q = q_2 - q_1 = 5$ and $\Delta p = p_2 - p_1 = -1$. However, there is now an ambiguity relating to which set of values to use for p/q. There are two possibilities.

We can use the price-quantity values from either of the two situations:

(a) $\varepsilon = - [\Delta q/\Delta p] \times [p_1/q_1] = -(-5) \times (10/100) = 5/10 = 0.5$

(b) $\varepsilon = - [\Delta q/\Delta p] \times [p_2/q_2] = -(-5) \times (9/105) = 9/21 = 3/7 = 0.42$

For 'small changes' in price, there will not be too much of a difference between the two values thus obtained. But for larger changes, the differences become substantial, as our example shows. Such elasticities are called *point-elasticity measures*.

To get rid of the ambiguity, we can use the *arc-elasticity measure*. We take an *average* of the values in the two situations:

$$\varepsilon = - [\Delta q/\Delta p][(p_2 + p_1)/2]/[(q_2 + q_1)/2]$$
$$= - [\Delta q/\Delta p][(p_2 + p_1)/(q_2 + q_1)]$$
$$= 5(19/205) = 0.46.$$

Three special types of the demand curve deserve mention at this stage:

- If the (inverse) demand curve is a horizontal straight line parallel to the quantity axis, then the slope of the demand curve is infinity (the slope of the inverse demand curve being 0) and the price-elasticity measure goes to infinity. We say that demand is perfectly elastic.
- If the (inverse) demand curve is a vertical straight line, then $\varepsilon = 0$ and demand is said to be perfectly inelastic.
- Suppose that the equation of the demand curve is of the form $q = Ap^{-b}$, where b is a constant. Then $\varepsilon = - [dq/dp] \times [p/q] = - (-Abp^{-b-1})/(Ap^{-b-1})$ $= b$. In other words, price-elasticity is the same at all points of the demand curve.

Among other things, the price-elasticity will depend on:

1. Availability of close substitutes: If close substitutes are available, then an increase in the price will lead to a large fall in demand, since consumers can easily and quickly shift to other commodities. On the other hand, if the commodity is a close substitute for other commodities, a fall in its price will lead to consumers of similar commodities switching to it in large numbers. A commodity like salt that has no close substitute is expected to be price-inelastic. But demand for a particular type of toothpaste is expected to be elastic, since consumers can quickly switch to other types of toothpaste. An aim of advertising often becomes to establish the uniqueness of a particular commodity as opposed to other, similar commodities. For example, advertisements might try to convince customers that a particular brand of toothpaste has medicinal properties not possessed by other brands. Once this is established, the producer can increase the price of her brand, secure in the knowledge that the quantity response will be smaller and will not outweigh the price effect on revenue.

2. Time period involved: The longer the period considered, the easier is it for buyers to make adjustments and hence the greater the elasticity of demand. A classic example of this was the effect of the OPEC oil price increase in 1973. The initial effect of this increase was a severe adverse effect on the balance of payments position of many countries, since oil import bills soared. However, over time, countries started exploiting their own oil reserves; technology for making smaller and more fuel-efficient cars was developed; alternative sources of energy like solar power began to be tapped. As a result of all these, countries like the US managed to considerably reduce their dependence on oil from the OPEC countries.

2.6.2 Other Elasticity Measures

We have already seen that the demand for a commodity depends, among other things, on

- own price
- incomes
- other 'related' prices.

Just as we derived the measure for the own-price elasticity of demand, we can derive elasticity measures related to the other factors affecting demand.

One may identify the close substitutes of a product by measuring the cross-price elasticity of demand between two products. Let the two products be Q and Y. Then the cross-price elasticity of demand for Q with respect to the price of Y is $\varepsilon_{QY} = [\Delta q/\Delta p_Y]\,[p_Y/q]$, where q is the quantity of the commodity Q and p_Y is the price of Y. When ε_{QY} is positive, it indicates that the consumers increase their purchase of Q when the price of good Y rises. For example, if the price of tea increases, the demand for tea would fall and that of a substitute commodity like coffee is expected to rise. Therefore, tea and coffee are substitutes.

If the supply curve does not shift but the demand curve does, then we can use the concept of price-elasticity of supply to predict the level of change in total revenue. Note that since the supply curve has a positive slope, there is no need to attach a negative sign to the elasticity to make it positive. Thus the price-elasticity of supply may be written as $e = (p/q) \times (\Delta q/\Delta p)$, where q now refers to the quantity supplied.

Finally, if both demand and supply curves shift, then the relevant elasticity will be a weighted average of both demand and supply elasticities.

3   Uncertainty, Information, and Game Theory

Economic agents have to operate in situations of uncertainty. Moreover, not everyone has access to all relevant information. In this chapter, we discuss the problems caused by uncertainty and lack of information. In later sections, we turn to game theory to analyse strategic situations.

3.1   Uncertainty

Uncertainty permeates almost all human activity. Consumers may be uncertain about how much income they will be able to earn. When trying to purchase something, they may be uncertain about the prices charged by different sellers or the qualities of the products they are buying. On the other hand, firms may be uncertain about production (there may be the possibility of random breakdowns in machines), market prices, strategies of rivals, etc.

Uncertainty may take several forms. Suppose that, before going to the market, a buyer is uncertain about the price that will be charged by a seller. Several situations are possible:

(a) The buyer may have some objective frequency distribution for prices, based upon her own experience and that of others. For example, she may know that a price of Rs 3 is charged 10 per cent of the time, a price of Rs 4 is charged 30 per cent of the time, and a price of Rs 4.50 is charged 60 per cent of the time.

(b) The buyer may only know that certain prices are more probable than others.

(c) The buyer may have some subjective beliefs about the probability distribution of prices, and proceed as if these are correct.

(d) The buyer may not be able to make any probability estimates, though she will still have some idea of the range of prices that are available.

(e) The buyer may have never purchased the commodity before and have no idea even about the range of prices available.

In trying to model uncertainty, we usually assume either (a) or (c), i.e. we assume that the buyer attaches some probabilities to the possible prices. This enables us to build a model of choice under uncertainty. The following elements of the problem are then specified for an individual decision-maker under uncertainty:

(a) A set of states of nature $(1, 2,...s,...S)$. A state of nature is a complete description of a possible environment, e.g. the possible states of nature may be 'fog with poor visibility', 'some mist', 'clear visibility'. The states of nature may not refer to weather conditions at all. For example, we may be interested in the economy and define a particular state of nature as 'stagflation'(high inflation rate coupled with low rate of growth).

(b) A probability p_i associated with the state of nature i. In other words, the probability that the state of nature i will occur is p_i, $0 \le p_i \le 1$. In the simplest case, 'Nature' chooses which state of nature will actually materialize.

(c) A set of acts $(1, 2, ... a, ... A)$ available to the individual. For example, the acts may be 'switch on the headlight of the car' or 'not switch on the headlight'.

(d) A consequence function $c(a, s)$ showing the outcome when action a is taken and state of nature s occurs. For example, the weather that might materialize together with the act of the individual will determine her pay-offs. If the state of nature is 'clear visibiliy', and the act is 'not switch on headlights', the pay-off to the individual will be greater than if the state of nature is 'fog', and the act is 'not switch on headlights'.

3.1.1 Choice under Uncertainty

In an uncertain environment, whenever an act is decided upon, the consequence is not certain; various consequences may follow with different probabilities. Therefore, every act is like a gamble or a *lottery*. A lottery may be defined more formally as follows:

Suppose an act a is chosen. This has consequences/pay-offs $c(a, 1)$, $c(a, 2)$, ... , with associated probabilities $p_1, p_2, ...$ When we couple these consequences with their associated probabilities, we have a *lottery* or a *gamble*:

$$L(a) = [\{p_1, c(a, 1)\}, \{p_2, c(a, 2)\}...].$$

Therefore, in an uncertain situation, the individual in essence has to *choose between lotteries*. Example 3.1 gives an illustration of a lottery involving a toss of a coin:

Example 3.1. There are two possibilities when tossing a coin: Either (1) do not toss the coin, in which case you get nothing or (2) toss a fair coin. If the coin comes up heads, you win Re 1, if it comes up tails, you lose Re. 0.50.

If the first action is taken (not tossing the coin), there is only one consequence with certainty, a payment of 0. If the coin is tossed, there are two possibilities, head or tail, with associated probabilities 0.5 and consequences/pay-offs Re 1 and – Re 0.50.

One important property of a lottery is its expected value (EV), which is the weighted average of all its possible outcomes, with the weights being the respective probabilities. In exemple 3.1, the expected value if the coin is tossed is

$$EV = (0.5).(1) - (0.5)(0.5) = 0.5 - 0.25 = 0.25.$$

One way of choosing between lotteries would be to select the lottery that has the highest expected value. In Example 3.1, it would seem that the decision should be to toss the coin, because this gives an expected value of 0.25, whereas not tossing the coin gives 0.

However, the expected value criterion suffers from the weakness that it does not distinguish between consequences and utilities from consequences. The formal economic theory of choice in situations of uncertainty is due to John von Neumann and Oskar Morgenstern. The central assumption of this theory is that people choose the alternative that provides the highest *expected utility*, and not the highest expected value.

To explain the theory simply, let us assume that the outcome of a lottery is determined uniquely by the amount of total wealth W to which it corresponds. If certain conditions are fulfilled, then the agent will have a utility function $u(W)$, called the von Neumann–Morgenstern (*vNM*) utility function. If the agent takes an action, various outcomes are possible, each characterized by a different W_i, hence a different $u(W_i)$ and having associated probabilities p_i. The expected utility (EU) is then

$$EU = p_1 u(W_1) + p_2 u(W_2) + \ldots\ldots\ldots p_S u(W_S) = \Sigma p_i u(W_i).$$

According to the expected utility theory, the individual will take that action which maximizes her EU.

Note that if $u(W_i) = W_i$, then the expected utility becomes identical with the expected value.

Example 3.2. The *vNM* utility function of an individual is $v = \sqrt{W}$ or $W^{0.5}$, and her initial wealth is 36. Will she accept a gamble in which she wins 13 with a probability 2/3 and loses 11 with probability 1/3?

The expected utility of the gamble is given by $EU = (2/3)\sqrt{(36 + 13)} + (1/3)\sqrt{(36 - 11)} = (2/3)7 + (1/3)5 = 19/3 > \sqrt{36} = 6$ (which is what the individual will get if she does not gamble). Hence the gamble should be accepted.

3.1.2 Attitudes towards Risk

Suppose that the consumer's preferences under uncertainty can be represented by a *vNM* utility function $u(.)$. Different people have different attitudes towards risk. How can we categorize these risks?

Definition: The consumer is said to be *risk-averse* if she strictly prefers a certain consequence to a risky prospect whose mathematical expectation of consequences equals the certain consequence.

That is, the consumer is risk-averse if $u(r) > Eu(c)$, where $r = Ec$, i.e. $u(Ec) > Eu(c)$. Written out more fully, this means that $u(\Sigma p_s c_s)] > \Sigma p_s u(c_s)$, where $c_s = c(a, s)$ for some act a and p_s are the probabilities, $\Sigma p_s = 1$.

The consumer is *risk-loving* if $u(Ec) < Eu(c)$, and is *risk-neutral* if $u(Ec) = Eu(c)$.

If u is a twice continuously differentiable function, then it can be shown that $u''(c) < 0 => Eu(c) < u(Ec)$, i.e. concavity of u denotes risk-averse behaviour. If u is linear, then the individual is risk-neutral, and if it is convex, then she is risk-loving. To simplify matters, from now on we assume that the consequence function is denominated in terms of just one variable—wealth, w. Moreover, the individual always prefers more wealth to less, i.e. $u'(w) > 0$.

The utility function of a risk-averse individual is shown below. Suppose that there are two possible outcomes w_1 and w_2 with associated probabilities p and $1 - p$. Then expected utility $pu(w_1) + (1 - p)u(w_2)$, $0 \le p \le 1$, will be represented by a point D on the chord AB in Fig. 3.1. The chord joining two points on the curve always lies below the curve. Hence $u(pw_1 + (1 - p)w_2)$, which is a point on the utility function, will always lie above the point D.

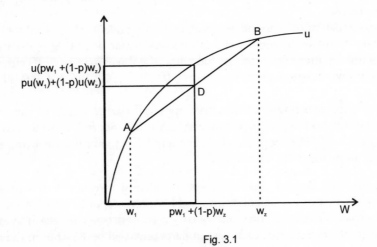

Fig. 3.1

Example 3.3. Suppose that an individual's $u(w) = w^2$. Then $u''(w) = 2 > 0$, and the person is a risk-lover. Will the person accept a gamble where there is a 50 per cent chance of winning 20 and a 50 per cent chance of losing 20, if the person's initial wealth is 100?

If the person does not accept the gamble, then utility is $100^2 = 10,000$. If the gamble is accepted, the expected utility is $0.5(120^2) + 0.5(80^2) = 0.5(14400 + 6400) = 10,400$. Hence the gamble will be accepted.

It can be shown that if $u = w$, the person is risk-neutral and will be indifferent between accepting or rejecting the gamble.

3.1.3 Value of Information and Option Value

Faced with uncertainty, the individual may act *passively*, i.e. take a decision given the constraints posed by the uncertain environment or try to be *active*, i.e. spend resources to acquire additional, more precise, information.

Under uncertainty, the consequences of an action are not known immediately for certain. Over time, as events unfold, more information becomes available and, therefore, uncertainty is resolved by the passage of time. Resolving uncertainty can improve pay-offs, and therefore additional information will have value, as the following examples show.

Example 3.4. Kajol has a *vNM* utility function given by $u = 1 - 1/W$, where W is the present value of her lifetime income. If Kajol becomes a teacher, she will make $W = 5$ with probability 1. If she becomes an actress, she will make $W = 400$ if she becomes a star, but only $W = 2$ if she fails to become a star. The probability of her becoming a star is 0.01.

If Kajol has no other information, which career should she pursue? In this situation, her expected utility if she becomes a teacher is $1 - 1/5 = 0.8$ while if she becomes an actress, it is $Eu = 0.01(1 - 1/400) + 0.99(1 - 1/2) = 0.465$. Therefore, she should become a teacher.

Suppose that Sippy is an infallible judge of acting talent. He can tell for sure after an interview with Kajol whether she can become a star or not. Suppose that Sippy charges b for the interview. After the interview, Kajol will have pay-offs either of 400 or 5. Then Kajol's expected utility is $Eu' = 0.01\{1 - 1/(400 - b)\} + 0.99\{1 - 1/(5 - b)\}$.

What is the maximum amount that Sippy can charge Kajol for the interview? Without information, Kajol's maximum pay-off is 0.8. Set $Eu' = 0.8$ and solve for b. We find that $b = 0.0494$ approximately. For any b less than this, it is better for Kajol to consult Sippy for more information.

Example 3.5. Suppose that a firm is considering investment in a project. The project would involve an immediate irreversible (sunk) cost of Rs 800. The net revenue from the project will depend on which of two states of nature emerges in a year's time. In one state, the net revenue each year in perpetuity will be Rs 150, in the other Rs 50. Both the states are equally likely. The appropriate discount rate is 10 per cent.

What will the net present value (*NPV*) criterion suggest in this case? The expected net revenue each year will be Rs 100 and the present value of this will be Rs 1000. Hence the *NPV* is (= – 800 + 1000) Rs 200, so that the firm should go ahead with the investment.

But suppose the firm waits one year and goes ahead with the project only if the revenue stream of Rs 150 materializes, cancelling the project otherwise. The present value of the project then will be $0.5(-800 + 1500) = $ Rs 350. Hence the present value of waiting one year is greater than the present value of investing now. The value of that wait-and-see option is Rs 150. This is an example of how a firm can benefit by actions that reduce uncertainty.

3.2 INFORMATION

3.2.1 The Principal–Agent Framework

One aspect of uncertainty is that people do not have perfect information about all the factors that can possibly affect them. An important subcase of this is the presence of asymmetric information. A 'principal' appoints an 'agent' to carry out a task. However, the agent may be in possession of better information than the principal. The Board of Directors of a company appoints a Chief Executive Officer (CEO) to run the company. The shareholders want the CEO to maximize the value of shares by maximizing profits. This involves the CEO working long and arduous hours—quite costly from the CEO's point of view. Unless appropriate incentives are given to the CEO, she will not put in the needed amount of effort.

Suppose that the company makes losses. Are the losses due to the fact that the CEO has not put in enough effort in the company? The CEO will know how much effort she has put in, but the Board of Directors will, in general, be unable to observe effort. Since the quantum of 'effort' is difficult to measure and therefore unverifiable, the Board may base the incentive scheme of the CEO not on the (unobservable) effort but on the observable outcome, i.e. profit. Profit depends on the CEO's effort, but it may also depend on general business conditions.

The agreement between the principal and the agent is characterized by a contract. A *contract* is a mutual agreement between people to act in some specified way. In some contracts, there is an agreement to pay a sum of money on the occurrence of some event that may or may not be controlled by one of the parties. For example, a bookie may agree to pay you a certain sum of money if a particular horse wins at the races or if a particular team wins a tournament. In this case, neither party to the agreement controls the occurrence of the stipulated event. In some contracts, a payment is contingent on a certain performance. A CEO may be offered a bonus plan: if the profit of the firm exceeds some level, a part of the profits would be paid to the CEO. In this case, the CEO can control the stipulated event to some extent.

When a transaction takes place at a single point of time, the contract does not have to deal with uncertain events. Spot contracts usually remain implicit or unwritten. When I buy vegetables from the market, a part of the contract is that I should not be cheated on the weight of the vegetables bought. But the vegetable seller and I do not sit down to write out a contract on a piece of paper. The terms of the contract tend to be unambiguous and, therefore, the problem of verification or enforcement of the contract is not severe.

Contracts become important when the agreement and the events to which they refer are separated by time or space. Fire insurance is bought before any fire accident actually occurs, but the insurance company cannot reimburse the loss until after the fire actually occurs. A bank lends to a firm to expand its operations, but cannot know beforehand with certainty whether these expansions will be profitable or involve a loss leading to bankruptcy.

A contract is entered into voluntarily by persons who think that they will make mutual gains from the contract. Contracts, therefore, provide an instrument for gains from trade to be realized. However, people will not enter into a contract unless it is *enforceable*. Courts are thought to provide a mechanism for the enforcement of contracts. However, sometimes contract clauses are contingent on certain things happening and courts may find it difficult to assess whether these things have happened. For example, if a patient suffers additional illnesses while in the hospital, a court will find it difficult to assess whether this was due to the hospital's negligence or because the patient's immunity was low as a result of the original illness. Moreover, courts often take a long time to decide upon cases and court cases can be very expensive.

Non-enforceability in the courts do not make contracts valueless. It becomes necessary to design contracts such that each party chooses to stick to the terms of the contract. Such contracts are said to be *self-enforcing*.

In the simplest principal–agent framework, the principal offers the agent a contract. The agent then accepts or rejects it. Typically, the contract consists of a pair—a payment schedule and a specification of the performance schedule on which the payments depend. For example, the contract may consist of wage rates together with rates of output.

Attention has been focused on two types of constraints that are imposed on agents in self-enforcing contracts. The first is the *individual rationality* or *participation constraint*. The principal has to make sure that the agent agrees to the contract. If the contract falls through, then the agent gets a utility level (say) of u'. Then if the contract is to be accepted by the agent, the agent must get at least u' level of utility from the contract. This condition is known as the individual rationality constraint.

The second type of constraint is called the *incentive compatibility constraint*. The principal must take into account the fact that whatever be the terms of the contract, the agent will maximize his own utility, which will generally be different from the principal's. For example, suppose that a shop (the principal) stocks shirts. It knows that richer buyers in general are willing to pay a higher price than poorer buyers. It must then offer a contract which couples the quality purchased with price for that quality. This contract must be offered to any buyer who comes into the shop. The shop must then take into account the fact that faced with the contract, a buyer will maximize his/her utility. In particular, even a richer buyer may choose a (low quality, low price) shirt aimed more at the poorer buyers, if this gives her greater utility than a (high quality, high price) shirt.

Example[1] 3.6. Suppose that a principal employs an agent to work on a certain project. If successful, the project will yield Rs 600,000, and if it is a failure, Rs 0. The agent can either 'work' or 'shirk'. If she shirks, the probability of success is 60 per cent, while if she works, the probability is pushed up to 80 per cent. Even while shirking, the agent must be paid a minimum of Rs 100,000. If she works, she faces a disutility from the extra effort, and must be compensated with an additional Rs 50,000. The principal is risk-neutral.

If the principal can observe whether the agent is working or shirking, he can offer the following contract to induce the agent to work. The agent will be paid a base salary of Rs 100,000 if she shirks and another Rs 50,000 if she works. The agent will accept this offer and work. This also benefits the principal, because if the agent works, he expects to get $(0.8)(600,000) - 150,000 = $ Rs 330,000, while if the agent shirks, he expects to get less: $(0.6)(600,000) - 100,000 = $ Rs 260,000. Note that under this arrangement, the agent does not bear any risk.

But suppose that the principal cannot observe whether the agent has worked or shirked. Then the contract cannot be based on the effort level, but must be based on performance. Let us consider contracts where a base salary of s is paid, with a bonus b that depends on the success of the project.

Under this contract, if the agent works, she expects to get $s + 0.8b$; while if she shirks, she expects to get $s + 0.6b$. She will therefore work only if the extra expected payment $(s + 0.8b - s - 0.6b) = 0.2b$ is greater than or equal to the compensation needed for disutility from extra effort, i.e. Rs 50,000. But $0.2b > 50,000$ implies $b > 250,000$. Hence the *incentive compatibility constraint* is that the bonus should be at least Rs 250,000.

[1]This example is taken from Dixit and Skeath (1999).

BORDERS.

BORDERS
BOOKS AND MUSIC
400 POST STREET
SAN FRANCISCO CA 94102
(415) 399-1633

STORE: 0057   REG: 01/75   TRAN#: 4875
SALE   07/08/2005   EMP: 00067

CLAP HANDS HERE COMES ROSIE
6235791   CD T   12.74
25% COUPON   16.99
COUPON 159003420000000000
ECONOMICS OF BUSINESS POLICY
7755178   SC T   45.00

Subtotal   57.74
CALIFORNIA 8.5%   4.91
2 Items   Total   62.65
VISA   62.65

ACCT # /S XXXXXXXXXXXXXX2518
AUTH: 072770

CUSTOMER COPY

07/08/2005 11:06PM

The *participation constraint* requires that the total compensation when the agent works must be greater than or equal to 150,000, i.e. s + 0.8b > 150,000.

Suppose we also require s and b to be non-negative. Then the minimum base salary that must be paid is 0. This, together with the incentive compatibility constraint, means that the expected payment to the agent is s + 0.8b = 0.8b > 200,000 (since b > 250,000). The minimum expected payment (which will maximize the principal's pay-off) to the agent is then Rs 200,000. This is Rs 50,000 more than the amount need to make the agent work if effort is observable. The agent can extract this extra amount from the principal because she has an informational advantage—she knows whether she is working or shirking, but the principal cannot observe her action.

3.2.2 Moral Hazard and Adverse Selection

We can distinguish between two types of problems in asymmetric information. A *moral hazard* problem arises when a party to a contract can, after the contract is agreed upon, take an action that might affect the outcome. However, the action is not verifiable. An example is of a person taking out a car theft insurance, and then becoming more careless in locking the car doors. In the absence of insurance, the person would have been sufficiently careful. But with the insurance available, the car-owner no longer has to bear the full cost of the car theft and hence becomes less careful, thereby increasing the probability of theft. Since the premium originally set by the insurance company ignored the moral hazard problem, it might be too low in the context of the increased probability of theft. Another example is that of an employee on a probationary contract who worked very hard but, once given a regular, long-term contract, starts to take things easy. The presence of moral hazard creates the need for monitoring and devising proper incentive schemes. Firms, for example, hire supervisors to oversee workers.

Adverse selection occurs when one party to the contract has information relevant to the contract that is not known to the other party before the contract is signed and not verifiable afterwards. A firm when hiring a worker is never absolutely sure whether the worker will turn out to be hard-working or lazy, though the worker himself has this information in advance. A person taking out a medical insurance may have a past history of illnesses which the insuring firm finds difficult to discover.

The lemons model is an example of the problems created by adverse selection. Consider a market where 100 people want to sell their used Maruti cars and there are many potential buyers of used cars. Used cars may either be 'plums', i.e. good quality cars, or 'lemons', i.e. bad quality cars. Everyone knows that 50 of the cars are plums and 50 are lemons. The owner of a lemon is willing to sell it for Rs 50,000, while the owner of a plum wants to get at least Rs 100,000. Buyers are willing to pay a maximum of Rs 60,000 for lemons and Rs 110,000 for plums.

If the quality of a car is easily verifiable, then there is no problem in the market for used cars. Lemons will sell for some amount between Rs 50,000 and Rs 60,000, while plums will sell for a price between Rs 100,000 and Rs 110, 000. But now suppose that only the owners know whether their cars are plums or lemons. A buyer can discover the quality of a car only after purchasing the car and driving it around for some time.

BOX 3.1. INFORMATION ABOUT QUALITY MAY BE DIFFICULT TO OBTAIN

Information about the quality of many products or services may be difficult or costly to obtain. for various reasons:
- the product is too complex for the consumer to inspect its quality directly (e.g. laptop computers)
- the consumer lacks the knowledge or expertise necessary to evaluate the quality (e.g. buying a used car, car repairs, medical opinion of a doctor).
- evaluation can only be done *ex post*, i.e. after the consumer purchases and tries the product (e.g. a bottle of wine, fruits).

In this case, buyers will have to guess how much a car is worth. Let us make the simplifying assumption that a buyer is willing to pay the expected value of a car. This turns out to be $0.5 \times 60,000 + 0.5 \times 110,000 = $ Rs 85,000. But at this price, the owners of plums will not sell their cars. The only cars on the market will be the lemons. However, if the buyers are certain that only lemons will be sold, they will not be prepared to pay more than Rs 60,000. The price in the market will be between Rs 50,000 and Rs 60,000 and no plum will come on the market.

To bypass this problem, owners of plums may try to *signal* the quality of their cars. One way of doing this is to issue a warranty. The owner of a plum will undertake to pay the bill of any subsequent repairs. She can do this, because she knows that this will not really be needed. An owner of a lemon cannot afford to undertake such a warranty. Therefore, the warranty signals the quality of the car and a market for plums can exist.

This *costly-to-fake* principle is very important in using signals to establish product quality. Compare two firms, one of which has invested very heavily in a lavishly decorated showroom, while the other operates from a small, congested godown. The second firm's product quality will be more suspect. It can dupe the customers by selling 'lemons' and then overnight close shop if necessary. On the other hand, the first type of firm has incurred large sunk costs and will try very hard to remain in business. That is why it is less probable that the first firm's quality will be inferior.

Another important principle is the *full-disclosure principle*. This says that if some agents stand to benefit by revealing some favourable information, others will be forced to disclose also, even though their types are less favourable. Suppose that there are three firms, whose product qualities can be assigned ranks 2, 4, 6, 8 (on an increasing scale). The firm with the rank 8 obviously has an incentive to disclose this information. But what about the firms with rank 6? If it does not disclose and is given the average rank by customers, its rank turns out to be 4, less than the actual rank. So it is better for it to disclose its rank. But if it does disclose its rank, by a similar logic, the firm with rank 4 should disclose, otherwise it would be perceived to be of rank 3. And, by default, the lowest ranking firm's identity will also be disclosed.

BOX 3.2. ASYMMETRIC INFORMATION IN THE LABOUR MARKET

One of the puzzles about labour markets is why they do not seem to work on the lines suggested by supply–demand analysis. Current wage rates seem to be high; there are lots of people who would be happy to work at these wage rates and who yet cannot find work. But this excess supply does not lead to the wage rates being bid down to the market-clearing levels.

There are some reasons why firms might keep wages high. Suppose there are two types of workers—'good' workers and 'bad' workers. Workers know their own types before hiring, but firms do not. Good workers have reservation wages (the minimum wages at which they are prepared to work) higher than those of bad workers. If the firm lowers the wage it offers, this will lead to the poorer quality workers also applying for jobs with the firm. Hence keeping the wage rate high may be one way of tackling the adverse selection problem.

Once in employment, workers will tend to work harder if they are satisfied with the wages they are getting and they feel that the cost of losing the current job is high. If wages are low, then workers are more likely to be indifferent between staying and leaving and will have less incentive to work hard. Higher wages, therefore, also solves the moral hazard problem.

3.3 GAME THEORY: NORMAL FORM GAMES

Game theory was developed to analyse situations in which strategic decisions have to be made. In this chapter, we look at some basic elements of game theory which can help us to think coherently in strategic situations.

Games can be represented either in the normal form or in extensive form. Let us first deal with a game in a normal form. A *normal form game* consists of *n* players, their strategies, and their pay-offs. The pay-off to each player will, in general, depend on the set of strategies chosen by *all* the players. Such a strategy might refer to the price level chosen by the firm or the quantity produced, or advertising expenditure, etc. Players choose their strategies *simultaneously* and the game is played only once. Players are 'rational' in the sense that their choices of strategies are dictated only by the pay-offs consequent upon such choices. The game is represented in the form of a pay-off matrix.

3.3.1 The Prisoners' Dilemma Game: Dominant Strategy Equilibrium

Although in strategic situations, what one player does is contingent on the other players' decisions, we begin with the famous Prisoners' Dilemma game where the best strategy for each player is independent of what the other player does.

Amar and Akbar have been caught while trying to burgle a flat. The officer in-charge (OC) of the police station in which they are jailed knows that they had earlier been involved in a train dacoity, but has no proof of this. The OC has the two prisoners put in separate cells. He visits them in turn and says to each: 'If you confess to the dacoity, but the other doesn't, then you will get no jail sentence, while the other prisoner will be jailed for 8 years. If neither confesses, then we can only jail you for burglary, and each will get a sentence of 1 year. If both confess, then each will be jailed for 4 years'.

The pay-off matrix, as the prisoners see it, will appear as follows:

		Amar	
		Confess	Not Confess
Akbar	Confess	(4, 4)	(0, 8)
	Not Confess	(8, 0)	(1, 1)

(The first number in each cell refers to the row player's pay off)

The aim of each prisoner is to minimize the number of years spent in jail. Obviously, if both keep quiet, they each spend only 1 year in jail. However, it can be checked that *regardless of what the other prisoner does, the best strategy for each prisoner is to confess*. We say that confessing is a *dominant strategy* for both prisoners, because regardless of what the other player does, this strategy gives any player strictly superior pay-offs. For example, if Amar confesses, then the optimal strategy for Akbar is to confess and get a 4 year sentence, rather than remaining silent and getting 8 years. If Amar does not confess, Akbar gets 0 years by confessing as compared with 1 year by not confessing. Therefore, for each player, the best strategy is to confess, and in the *dominant strategy equilibrium*, each ends up spending 4 years in jail.

The Prisoners' Dilemma game is an example of a *non-cooperative game* in which players cannot communicate with each other and enter into mutually beneficial binding agreements.

We will encounter Prisoners' Dilemma type of situations again and again.

Note that once the players are caught in a Prisoners' Dilemma situation, they find it very difficult to escape from such a situation.

Consider the following price-setting game which we will encounter again in Chapter 5. Two firms are forced into a situation where each charges a low price and the price war inflicts damages on both.

		Firm 2	
		Charge Rs 6 Cooperate)	Charge Rs 6 (Cheat)
Firm 1	Charge Rs 6	(2, 2)	(0, 3)
	Charge Rs 5	(3, 0)	(1.5, 1.5)

Suppose that firm 1 takes the initiative and raises its price, hoping that firm 2 will follow suit. But till firm 2 increases the price to Rs 6, it will continue to enjoy a pay-off of Rs 3 (rather than Rs 2 from raising the price), while firm 1 is earning 0. Thus firm 2 has every incentive to delay increasing the price. Fear of further delays can convince firm 1 that it should revert back to the lower price.

3.3.1.1 Ways out of the Prisoners' Dilemma: (1) The Criminal's Revenge

One can get out of a Prisoners' Dilemma situation by changing the pay-offs. If Amar and Akbar could have entered into a binding agreement with a hit man (say Anthony) outside the jail to eliminate the prisoner who confessed to the dacoity, then the pay-offs would be changed. Suppose that if only one prisoner confesses and escapes the jail term, the hit man will punish him, and this punishment is equivalent to 3 years in prison. The pay-off matrix now is:

		Amar	
		Confess	Not Confess
Akbar	Confess	(4, 4)	(3, 8)
	Not Confess	(8, 3)	(1, 1)

The best strategy for each prisoner now depends on what the other player does. If Amar confesses, Akbar should confess and vice versa. If Amar does not confess, however, Akbar should also not confess, and vice versa. This mutual dependence of strategies means that we have to employ a new concept of equilibrium.

In practice, how do the players transform the Prisoners' Dilemma game into a Criminal's Revenge game? Many rules of behaviour that lead to desired cooperative outcomes are enforced by the creation of *social norms* and not through formal legislation. Deviation from the social norm is punished by social disapproval which imposes some costs. If these costs are not too high, we can still get a Prisoners' Dilemma outcome in which people do not cooperate with each other. But if the costs are high enough, we can escape the Prisoners' Dilemma outcome.

Let x be the social cost of cheating. The social norms game is represented by the following pay-off matrix:

		2	
		Cooperate	Cheat
1	Cooperate	(10, 10)	$(0, 15 - x)$
	Cheat	$(15 - x, 0)$	(5, 5)

It can be easily seen that if $x < 5$, we have a Prisoners' Dilemma outcome, in which both players cheat. If $x > 5$, on the other hand, two equilibria are possible and no dominant strategies exist for the players.

3.3.1.2 Ways out of the Prisoners' Dilemma: (2) Repeated Games

When players interact repeatedly, there arises the possibility of punishing a cheater. 'Punishment' in this context does not necessarily refer to physical punishment. More generally, the possibility of punishment arises from the fact of repeated interactions between players. Thus consider the following hypothetical game (the pay-offs are in millions of dollars per day):

Iraq's Output (millions of barrels per day)

		2 (Cooperate)	4 (Cherat)
Iran's Output (million of barreks per day)	2	(46, 42)	(26, 44)
	4	(52, 22)	(32, 24)

Suppose Iran cheats for a day successfully, while Iraq stays honest. Iran gains $6 million. When Iraq finds out Iran has cheated, the mutual trust breaks down. The two settle down to a regime of high outputs. Relative to cooperation, Iran now loses $14 million a day. Even if it takes Iraq a while to detect the cheating, Iran loses in the long run. For example, if it takes Iraq a month to detect the cheating, Iran's gain is $180 million. Once cheating is detected, it takes only 13 days ($13 \times 14 = 182$) to wipe out Iran's gain from cheating. Punishment, in its broader sense, means a refusal to cooperate. The result of punishment is that the cheater forgoes the higher pay-offs that accrue from cooperation.

However, a repeated game does not by itself generate cooperation. Suppose that the Prisoners' Dilemma game is repeated a *finite number of times* and each player knows exactly when the game will end. Selten has demonstrated that the only *subgame-perfect* equilibrium in this game is where each player cheats in every round of the game. Why? Consider the last or the n-th round. Everyone knows that the game will end after this round is played, so this is like a one-round Prisoners' Dilemma game, and both players will cheat. Next consider the last-but-one round, i.e. $(n-1)$th round. Since players will cheat in the last round regardless of what went on before, they will consider this round again independently of other rounds, and cheat. And so on.

One can briefly represent the gains and losses from cheating in a repeated game as:

$$B = G - pdTL,$$

where B is the net benefit from cheating, G is the immediate gain from cheating, p is the probability of detection, L is the loss from cheating if detected, T is a multiplier to signify the long-term value of this loss, and d is a discount term.

Hence, to induce cooperation, we require either that the game be played an infinite number of rounds or that players be uncertain about the exact date of termination of the game. The punishment threat is also stronger, the larger is p, T, or d (future losses should not be discounted too much).

3.3.2 Iterated Elimination of Dominated Strategies

In many games, players may not have dominant strategies. However, elimination of dominated strategies can still be useful and in some cases, may even provide us with a solution to the game. Thus consider the following example:

		Player 2 Left	Player 2 Right
	Up	(1, 1)	(0, 1)
Player 1	Middle	(0, 2)	(1, 0)
	Down	(0, −1)	(0, 0)

First, consider player 1's strategies. Neither Up nor Middle dominate each other, but both weakly dominate Down. For example, Up carries the pay-offs of 1 and 0 and Down carries 0 and 0, so that if player 2 plays Left, it is better for player 1 to play Up rather than Down. Hence one can assume that player 1 will never play Down as a rational player. But if player 2 realizes this, then the only two strategies of player 1 that phayer 2 has to take into account are Up and Middle.

| | | Player 2 | |
		Left	Right
	Up	(1, 1)	(0, 1)
Player 1			
	Middle	(0, 2)	(1, 0)

In this case, Left weakly dominates Right for player 2, and player 1 can safely assume that Right will never be played by player 2. The game reduces to the following form:

| | | Player 2 |
		Left
	Up	(1, 1)
Player 1		
	Middle	(0, 2)

Finally, player 1 will select Up, assuming that player 2 only plays Left, so that (Up, Left) is the solution reached by an *iterated elimination of dominated strategies*.

An example of a game in which the iterated elimination of dominated strategies can yield an outcome is a duopoly price-setting game. There are two firms 1 and 2 who can choose to price high, medium, or low. If a firm prices high, the other firm can steal the entire market by pricing medium or low, but of course, the low price will yield less profit. The pay-off matrix is as follows:

| | | Player 2 | | |
		High	Medium	Low
	High	(6, 6)	(0, 10)	(0, 8)
Player 1	Medium	(10, 0)	(5, 5)	(0, 8)
	Low	(8, 0)	(8, 0)	(4, 4)

In this game, the medium price makes sense only against a high price. However, the high price is weakly dominated by both the medium price and the low price strategies. Hence it can be eliminated. If it is eliminated for both players, the game becomes:

| | | Player 2 | |
		Medium	Low
	Medium	(5, 5)	(0, 8)
Player 1			
	Low	(8, 0)	(4, 4)

Note that now a low price is the dominant strategy for both players, so that in equilibrium, both players end up selecting a low price.

3.3.3 Nash Equilibria: Problems of Coordination and Differentiation

The concept of Nash equilibrium seems to be the weakest concept of equilibrium appropriate to games like that of Criminal's Revenge. A set of strategies, one for each player, constitutes a Nash equilibrium if the strategy for each player is the best, *given that all other players are playing the corresponding strategies in the set*. Thus, in a Nash equilibrium, strategies are optimal only against each other, unlike a dominant strategy equilibrium where each player's strategy is optimal regardless of the strategy of the other players. It may be helpful to understand Nash equilibrium in a negative sense: a set of strategies cannot be an equilibrium if there is at least one player who can do better by choosing a different strategy. Therefore, a set of strategies forms an equilibrium if no player can do better by deviating from the prescribed strategy.

In the social norms game, if $x > 5$, two Nash equilibria are possible, one in which both cheat and the other in which both cooperate.

Battle of the Sexes Game: The Problem of Coordination

A husband and a wife are planning to spend the evening together. They can either go shopping or stay home and watch television. The husband would rather stay at home while the wife would rather go shopping. But spending the evening together is still preferable for each to doing things separately. The payoffs are given below (the first number in each cell refers to the wife's payoff).

		Husband	
		Go Shopping	Watch TV
	Go Shopping	(2, 1)	(0, 0)
Wife			
	Watch TV	(0, 0)	(1, 2)

There are two Nash equilibria in this game: (go shopping, go shopping) and (watch TV, watch TV). If the wife wants to go shopping, for example, the husband's best strategy is to choose to go shopping and get a pay-off of 1, rather than watch TV alone and get a pay-off of 0. If the husband wants to go shopping, it is also the best strategy for the wife.

In the Battle of the Sexes game, we face a problem of coordination. The players are better off if they do the same thing rather than if they do different things. For example, it is necessary for a CEO to ensure that the general manager (marketing) is on the same wavelength as the general manager (production). If the former acts on the assumption of slack sales while the latter acts on the assumption of high sales, then inventories keep piling up.

Two Nash equilibria are possible in the Battle of Sexes game, and the question is which equilibrium will actually materialize. In practice, there are various ways of resolving the non-uniqueness problem in the Battle of the Sexes game:

1. Commitment: Prior commitment is one way of determining the unique equilibrium. If the wife cuts off the cable connection, then shopping is the

only viable option left. If the husband 'loses' the car key, the wife may not feel like going out if this involves travelling by crowded buses.

2. Hierarchy: Hierarchy breaks the essential symmetry of the game by putting somebody in charge. The wife decides where the couple will go, or perhaps the husband does. Hierarchy is needed here not because one of the players has a superior decision-making power, but simply because somebody must decide.

3. Availability of alternatives. Suppose that while the husband or wife are arguing with each other, it suddenly strikes them that there is a third option, namely making a social call. The pay-off matrix now is:

		Husband		
		Watch TV	Social call	Shopping
Wife	Watch TV	(1, 5)	(0, 0)	(0, 0)
	Social call	(0, 0)	(3, 3)	(0, 0)
	Shopping	(0, 0)	(0, 0)	(5, 1)

The third option is one which does not involve any strong dislikes. It can be a convenient way out of the dilemma. One problem is that if either player suggests it, the other player can read some hidden motives behind the suggestion. It is usually better for a third party to make the suggestion—this will be accepted more readily by both players.

4. Strong preferences: If one player has a very strong preference for one rather than the other choice, and the second player is relatively indifferent between the two, we expect to find the player with the strong preference getting what he/she wanst.

		Husband	
		Go Shopping	Watch TV
Wife	Go Shopping	(2,1)	(0,0)
	Watch TV	(0,0)	(1,6)

The Game of Chicken: The Problem of Differentiation

Two teenage boys drive their cars at each other, watched by admiring girlfriends. The one who loses nerve and swerves is 'chicken' and loses face. If both stay on course, then there is an accident with unpleasant outcomes for both. If both swerve, then both are 'chicken' and not much damage to reputation occurs.

		B	
		Stay	Swerve
A	Stay	(−10, −10)	(5, −1)
	Swerve	(−1, 5)	(0, 0)

There are two Nash equilibria, in each of which one player swerves and the other stays. Examples of such situations are markets that are too small to accommodate more than one large player profitably. If one firm exits, then the other can make a profit. Suppose that Boeing and Airbus are both considering developing a megacarrier. If they both develop such carriers, there will be excess capacity in the market and both will make losses.

		Boeing	
		Develop	Not Develop
Airbus	Develop	(−2, −2)	(3, −1)
	Not Develop	(−1, 3)	(0, 0)

The two possible Nash equilibria are ones in which either Boeing and Airbus develops and the other does not develop. Again, how does one solve the non-uniqueness problem in these games?

1. Commitment: If one of the players can commit to 'stay', then the other player's best strategy will be to 'swerve'. It has been suggested that one of the players can take out the steering wheel and throw it out of the window to demonstrate his commitment to stay on course. But this is a dangerous gesture because this can be reciprocated by the other player.

2. Third party intervention: Suppose that Airbus is given a subsidy of 7 if it develops the megacarrier. If a similar subsidy is not offered to Boeing, then the pay-off matrix becomes

		Boeing	
		Develop	Not develop
Airbus	Develop	(5, −2)	(10, −1)
	Not develop	(−1, 3)	(0, 0)

Now, the dominant strategy for Airbus is to develop the megacarrier. Realizing this, Boeing will not develop, because the pay-off from developing is negative.

One way of dealing with the problem of multiple Nash equilibria is to strengthen the concept of equilibrium itself. Game theorists have therefore tried to strengthen the concept of Nash equilibrium to rule out some strategies on the ground that these are in some sense or other 'unreasonable' . One way of doing this is to explicitly introduce the sequences of moves by the players and we take this up in section 3.4.

3.3.4 Mixed Strategies

In the Battle of the Sexes game, the players had two choices—either to watch television (TV) or to go shopping. That is, we are assuming that the players either choose to watch TV with certainty or to go shopping with certainty. But suppose that the wife tries out a new strategy: she decides to toss a fair coin and watch TV if it comes up heads. Then she has a new strategy which is a mixture of the original strategies: go shopping with probability 0.5 and watch TV with probability 0.5 .This is called a *mixed strategy*.

The original strategies of 'watch TV' and 'go shopping' are called pure strategies. Note that pure strategies are special types of mixed strategies—'watch TV' is equivalent to a strategy of playing 'watch TV' with probability 1 and 'go shopping' with probability 0.

There are several reasons why we might be interested in mixed strategies. One (relatively) technical reason is that without mixed strategies, Nash equilibria may not exist. That is, there may not be a single equilibrium in pure strategies. However, at least one Nash equilibrium in mixed strategies will always exist.

A second reason is that mixed strategies may dominate pure strategies. Consider the following game:

		Player 2 L	Player 2 R
Player 1	U	(1, 0)	(4, 2)
	M	(2, 4)	(2, 0)
	D	(4, 2)	(1, 4)

Player 1 can consider a mixed strategy in which U and D are played with equal probabilities of 0.5 each. This mixed strategy will give the expected pay-off of 2.5 against either L or R. Therefore this mixed strategy (weakly) dominates the pure strategy of M which yields the pay-off of 2 against any pure strategy played by 2. The reason is that U does well against R but badly against L while the opposite is true for D. By putting equal weights on U and D, player 1 can 'insure' herself.

A third (intuitive) reason is that a mixed strategy keeps the opponent guessing. Dixit and Nalebuff give the example of a tennis match. The receiver's forehand return is stronger than the backhand return and the percentage of returns also depends on being able to anticipate correctly where the ball is coming. By mixing up the shots, the server can keep the receiver guessing and the percentage of returns down.

3.4 GAME THEORY: EXTENSIVE FORM GAMES

Until now, we have restricted our attention to games in which all players make their moves simultaneously. However, in many situations, choices are made *sequentially* and this sequencing of choices can confer advantages or disadvantages on players.

Let us again consider the 'Battle of the Sexes'. We have seen that this game in the normal form has two Nash equilibria. Now we assume that one of the players, (say) the wife, makes her choice before the husband does. Once the wife has made her choice, the husband makes his. The sequence of moves can be represented by means of a *game tree*:

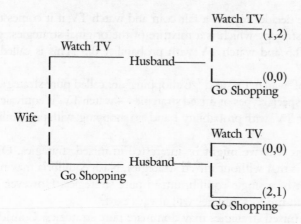

A 'node'in the game tree is a point at which a player chooses a strategy. A 'branch' stands for a particular choice by a player. Once a player makes a choice, the players are in a 'subgame' consisting of the strategies and payoffs available to them from that point on. Thus if the wife chooses to watch TV, there is a subgame in which the husband can choose to watch TV or go shopping, and the associated payoffs are determined by the husband's choice conditional on the wife's choice. There are three subgames in this example: (a) the entire game, (b) the subgame when the wife chooses to watch TV, and (c) the subgame when the wife chooses to go shopping.

We now strengthen the requirement of equilibrium: a combination of strategies must be a Nash equilibrium not only for the entire game, but also in each of the subgames. Such a combination of strategies forms a *subgame-perfect equilibrium* and can be obtained by *backward induction*.

In the original normal form game, one Nash equilibrium consisted of both players watching TV. Is this also a *reasonable* equilibrium? Suppose that the husband threatens to 'always watch TV'. If the wife takes this threat seriously, she should choose to watch TV and get a pay-off of 1. If she chooses to go shopping and he watches TV, her pay-off will be 0.

But is this a credible threat? If the wife does go shopping, it is in the husband's best interest not to watch TV and get 0, but go shopping and get 1. The wife will realize this and go shopping, and the husband will follow suit. Therefore, the only equilibrium consists of both players choosing to go shopping. The wife has a *first-mover advantage*. Because she gets to move first, she can anticipate the subsequent decisions of her husband and make the move that is most advantageous to herself.

In the simple game considered here, it is easy to work out the equilibrium by *backward induction*. Start with the last stage of the game and find out the husband's optimal choices in each subgame. The optimal choice is watching TV if the wife watches TV and going shopping if the wife goes shopping. The associated payoffs are (1, 2) and (2, 1). The wife then compares her payoffs from these two choices and decides to go shopping because then her pay-off is 2 rather than 1.

4   Market Structures

Value, as defined in Chapter 1, is created through production and subsequent voluntary exchange of commodities in the market place. In this chapter, we show that the processes of value creation and value appropriation depend critically on the market structure in which they take place. The amount of value created from the same production process is different in different market structures and so is the ability of the market players—firms and consumers—to appropriate value.

Economists distinguish between market structures on the basis of the *extent of strategic interaction* between sellers in the market/industry. At one extreme, one can think of perfectly competitive markets where there are 'many sellers' and no seller takes account of the possible reactions from rivals. At the other extreme is a monopoly where there is only one seller and therefore this seller does not have to worry about other sellers. In between are oligopolistic markets, where there are 'few' sellers who have to explicitly take account of how rivals are going to react.

Perfect Competition	Oligopoly	Monopoly
Many sellers	Few sellers	One seller

We start by considering market structures as if they are exogenously given to the firms in the market. However, the actions of the sellers in the market can also affect the market structure. For example, a firm may be able to enjoy a monopoly position in a market in spite of the presence of potential rivals by erecting certain *barriers to entry*. These possibilities are explored in the next chapter.

4.1   PERFECT COMPETITION

Perfect competition is an idealized market structure that acts as a benchmark for comparing what happens in other market structures. In a perfectly competitive market, sellers cannot appropriate any 'extra' value in the long run. They can only earn normal profits. It is, therefore, important to understand how departures from perfectly competitive conditions can enable a firm to appropriate value in the market place.

A perfectly competitive industry is characterized by the following features:

1. All firms sell a *homogeneous product*, i.e. the outputs of all firms are identical from the viewpoint of buyers.

2. There is unrestricted mobility of resources in the long run. In particular, firms can enter and exit from the market freely.

3. The number of buyers and sellers in the market is 'large'. This means that each agent in the market believes that her actions will have negligible effect on the market price. Therefore, all agents in the market act as if the market price is fixed independently of their own actions, i.e. everyone in the market is a 'price-taker'.

4. Finally, we assume that all agents possess perfect information.

   (i) All firms have the same production function and the same cost function.

   (ii) All firms are aware of the prices of inputs and opportunities available in other industries.

   (iii) All buyers are instantaneously aware of all the prices charged by all the sellers.

The implication of all these assumptions taken together is that a uniform price is established throughout the market and all firms/sellers behave as if they are unable to affect this price by their own individual actions. For example, a buyer would not be willing to pay a higher price for one seller's product than another's, since products from all sellers are viewed as identical.

We assume as a behavioural rule that the objective of the firm in a perfectly competitive market (or any other market structure, for that matter) is to maximize economic profit.

It is hard to think of an industry that fits the definition of perfect competition. However, perfect competition is useful as a benchmark market structure, as will be demonstrated later. The conceptual difference between the short run and the long run will be helpful in clarifying how value is created and appropriated in perfectly competitive industry. In the short run, at least one input is fixed in quantity. It is conventional to assume that capital K is fixed in the short run i.e $K = K_o$. In the long run, all inputs are variable. In particular, a firm is free to enter or exit from the industry. We will find that in the short run a firm, under perfect competition, can earn super-normal or sub-normal profits. But in the long run, forces exist that tend to drive the profits to normal levels. Hence, in the long run, value is entirely appropriated by buyers. Firms, therefore, would have an incentive to create obstacles to the operation of the forces that drive profits down to normal levels. We already know under what conditions perfectly competitive conditions prevail. Firms would, therefore, have incentive to take actions that move them away from all or some of these conditions.

4.1.1 Short-run Profit Maximization

The consequence of the assumptions made about perfect competition is that any firm in a perfectly competitive market takes the output price to be fixed: $p = p^*$. The firm tries to maximize economic profit, where

$$\Pi = p^*q - C(q) = TR - C(q),$$

where q is the output of any firm (we will reserve Q to denote industry output) and TR denotes the total revenue. *Profit is maximized by setting price = marginal cost*, subject to the constraint that the MC curve is upward sloping at the profit-maximizing output.

In Fig. 4.1, p^* is a horizontal straight line because from the firm's viewpoint, market price is given independently of its own output. Both q' and q^* are characterized by the equality of the market price with marginal cost. However, only at q^* is the MC curve upward sloping. Accordingly, it is the output at which profit is maximized.

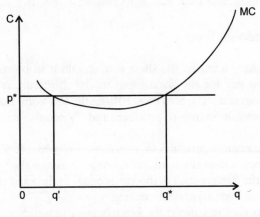

Fig. 4.1

What is the intuition behind the price = marginal cost condition? You should be able to see that the technique of marginal analysis is being used to solve the firm's problem, i.e. choosing the level of productions that maximizes economic profit. Starting from any level of production, let the firm consider the effect on profit of producing an additional Δq units. This will add $p^*\Delta q$ to revenue and ΔC to total costs. If $p^*\Delta q > \Delta C$, the extra units add more to revenue than to cost, and should be produced. If $p^*\Delta q < \Delta C$, the extra units add more to costs than to revenue, and the firm would be better off by producing a lesser amount: this way, it can increase profit by cutting down on costs. The profit-maximizing point is reached when $p^*\Delta q = \Delta C$, which means that $p^* = \Delta C/\Delta q = MC$ (it should be remembered that this discussion is subject to the fulfilment of the second order condition; check that if the MC curve is downward-sloping, then the firm would be minimizing profit when $p^* = MC$).

Example 4.1.

Q	p^*	$TR=p^*q$	C	$\Pi = TR - C$	$MR = \Delta TR$	$MC = \Delta C$
0	10	0	12	−12	—	—
1	10	10	14	−4	10	2
2	10	20	15	5	10	1
3	10	30	17	13	10	2
4	10	40	20	20	10	3
5	10	50	25	25	10	5
6	(10)	(60)	(35)	(25)	(10)	(10)
7	10	70	50	20	10	15
8	10	80	81	−1	10	31

These numbers are only illustrative. Note that profit is maximized at output levels 5 and 6. Price is equated to *MC* only at output level 6, however. The second order condition is also satisfied since *MC* is increasing at $q = 6$.

4.1.2 The Shutdown Point

If the firm is making a loss in the short run, should it stop production? (As the firm must continue to pay for the fixed input in the short run, it cannot exit from the industry in the short run.) The firm must balance the loss from shutting down production with the loss from continuing to produce, and choose the action that minimizes the loss.

If the firm continues production, it makes a loss equal to $TR - (TFC + TVC)$. If it shuts down, then it does not earn any revenue. It avoids the variable costs, but must continue to pay the fixed costs, i.e. the loss is equal to the fixed cost. The firm will then decide to continue even when it is making a loss if $- [TR - (TFC + TVC)] < TFC$ (the minus sign is used to convert the loss to a positive number so that we can compare it with the size of the fixed cost).

This condition, after some manipulation, reduces to $TR > TVC$, i.e. $p^* > AVC$. The reason for this should be easy to see. The firm incurs fixed cost in any case. If by continuing to produce, *it can cover all its variable costs and have something left over to cover its fixed cost*, it should do so. If it is unable to do this, then it is incurring some variable costs over and above its fixed cost and should shut down operations. The two situations are shown in Fig. 4.2.

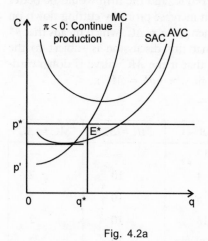

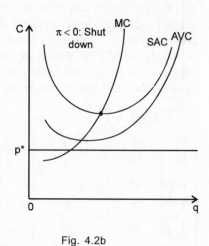

Fig. 4.2a   Fig. 4.2b

The market price p^* is given to the firm. Then the condition for continuing to produce becomes $p^* > \min AVC$, i.e. the line representing market price should be above the minimum point of the *AVC* curve. If $p^* = AVC$, the firm is indifferent between shutting down and continuing to produce.

4.1.3 The Short-Run Supply Curve

To summarize, in the short run the firm's decisions should be conditioned on the relationship between the market price and various costs:

If p^* < min AVC, then discontinue production.

If p^* ≥ min AVC, then choose q^* such that $p^* = MC$ and $dMC/dq > 0$.

These two conditions enable us to derive the firm's short-run supply curve, which shows the amount the firm will supply at any given market price. For p^* < min AVC, $q = 0$, which means that the supply curve is the y-axis for such p. For p^* ≥ min AVC, the firm is going to choose an output such that $p^* = MC$ (the second order condition is automatically satisfied because for outputs lying beyond the minimum point of AVC, the MC curve must be rising). Hence for p^* ≥ min AVC, the supply curve at each price is the corresponding point on the MC curve. In other words, the MC curve above the minimum point of the AVC curve is the short run supply curve of the firm. For p^* < min AVC, supply is zero. In Fig. 4.2a, the supply curve coincides with the vertical axis for $p < p'$, and is the thickly marked portion of the MC curve for $p > p'$.

The industry supply curve is then obtained from the supply curves of the firms. At each price, the MC curves are added horizontally. In fact, we have assumed that the firms have the same technologies, and hence the same MC curves. The industry supply curve will then be nMC, where n is the number of firms in the industry in the short run. The derivation of the industry supply curve if only two firms are in the market is shown in Fig. 4.3.

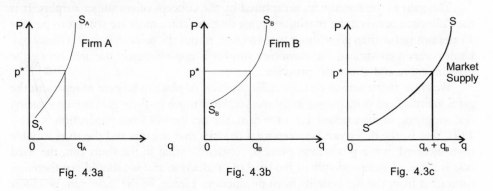

Fig. 4.3a   Fig. 4.3b   Fig. 4.3c

We can now bring the industry demand and supply curves together to determine the short run equilibrium market price p^* and the quantity Q^* (see Fig. 4.4b). Given p^*, we can also immediately find out the level of output produced by each firm from Fig. 4.4a. Given our assumption of identical firms, $q^* = Q^*/n$. In the short run, the firm can make either an economic profit or loss. Even if it is making a loss, it can continue to produce if the market price is above the AVC.

In addition to satisfying the two conditions to determine the profit-maximizing output of the firm, the short-run competitive equilibrium is also characterized by the condition that market demand must equal market supply.

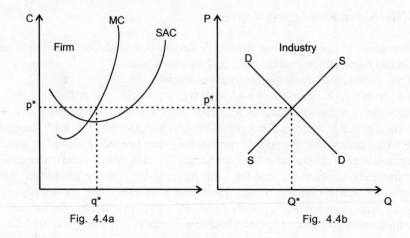

Fig. 4.4a   Fig. 4.4b

4.1.4 Property of the Market Equilibrium

Suppose that the industry is perfectly competitive and we are able to derive a market supply curve. The price-quantity pair at the intersection of the market demand and supply curves constitutes an equilibrium. Chapter 2 has already discussed how total value is maximized at such an equilibrium. We now give a more precise derivation of this result.

The gain to the consumers is captured by the concept of consumer surplus. It is the difference between the maximum price that the consumers are willing to pay for an amount rather than go without that amount, minus the price that they actually pay. Under certain conditions the consumer surplus is approximately the area below the demand curve and above the price line.

We know that a similar concept called *producer surplus* can be used to represent the gains to firms from participating in the market. How much do firms gain from producing and supplying in the market? For each firm, the net benefit from production is $TR - TVC$, that is, the difference between total revenue that it earns and the total variable costs incurred in the production process. Remember that in the short run, the fixed cost is incurred independently of the level of production and we should not therefore subtract it from the net benefits from production. Hence, in the short run, producer surplus is equal to $TR - TVC = \Pi + TFC$. The *aggregate* producer surplus is then just the aggregate of the difference between total revenue and total variable cost for all the firms.

The total variable cost for a particular level of output is found by adding the marginal cost for each successive unit of output upto that point: $TVC(Q) = MC(1) + MC(2) + \ldots + MC(Q)$. When output can be changed continuously, $TVC(Q)$ is the area below the MC curve for the firm. The industry supply curve is obtained by horizontally summing all the firms' MC curves. Therefore, the aggregate producer surplus is represented by the rectangle p^*OQ^*E (which is total revenue) minus the area under the supply curve $OSEQ^*$ in Fig. 4.5. It is then the area p^*ES.

The rest of our results have already been anticipated in Chapter 2. The sum of consumer and producer surplus will be maximized when price is p^* and quantity

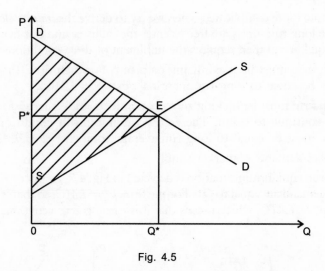

Fig. 4.5

transacted is Q^*. At any other level of price and quantity, the sum of consumer and producer surplus will be less.

4.1.5 The Long-Run Supply Curve

In the long run, firms are free to enter or leave the market. Let us first derive the long run supply curve of the firm. In the long run, all costs are variable. Hence, $LTC = LVC$. The firm maximizes profit by equating price with the long run marginal cost: $p^* = LMC$. The second order condition is that the LMC curve is upward sloping at the point of equilibrium.

In contrast to the short run situation, the firm shuts down production and *exits from the industry* if it makes less than normal profit. Therefore, its long run supply curve is given by the portion of LMC that lies above the $LATC$ curve.

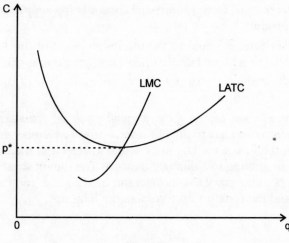

Fig. 4.6

Matters are more complicated when we try to derive the *industry* long run supply curve. In the long run, firms are free to enter the industry and exit from the industry. Long-run equilibrium then requires the fulfilment of three conditions:

1. Each firm must be maximizing its profit. For each firm, this requires that price be equal to long run marginal cost ($p = LMC$).

2. Each firm must be making zero economic profit. Otherwise, entry and exit will continue to occur. The zero economic profit condition implies that price must be equal to long run average total cost ($p = LATC$).

3. Market demand = market supply.

A long-run equilibrium situation is depicted in Fig. 4.7. At price p^*, both industry supply and demand are equal to Q^*. For the firm, $p^* = LMC$, so that it is maximizing profit. But $p^* = LATC$, which means that it is earning zero economic profit.

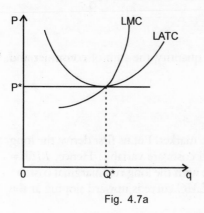

| Fig. 4.7a | Fig. 4.7b |

Thus, there are some remarkable features of competitive long run equilibrium:

- Price is equal to marginal cost, which means that all possibilities for mutually beneficial trades have been exhausted. Everybody who is willing to pay a price at least equal to the additional cost of being supplied a unit is able to buy the product.

- The market price is equal to the minimum point of the *LAC* curve (zero supernormal profits are being earned), implying that unit cost is minimum.

- Finally, all producers earn only the opportunity cost of the resources they are using in the firms.

In long run equilibrium, because of the zero profit condition, consumers receive all of the surplus because producers earn zero profits. However, we must remember that zero economic profit means that the firm is earning just enough to keep it in the industry; it would not be better off by shifting to a different industry. The sum of consumer surplus and producer surplus becomes equal to consumer surplus. Producer surplus is zero, because profits are zero and there are no fixed costs in the long run.

BOX 4.1. ELECTRONIC COMMERCE AND PERFECT COMPETITION

Economists are hard put to it to provide examples of perfect markets outside textbooks. In the real world, some of the more liquid financial markets come closest to the ideal of perfection. But even they have serious flaws: often access is restricted, and better-informed insiders are at an advantage. Most other traditional markets are even further from perfection. Prices often do not seem to respond to supply and demand. For example, in some markets, sellers publish a menu of prices, which customers can take or leave. Such prices are often not those that would bring supply and demand into equilibrium, and can be slow to change.

In certain markets, transactions costs are too high and limit the potential gain from transactions. Competitive auctions are usually more efficient than traditional markets, but their usefulness is limited by the need to assemble all potential bidders at once. Some high-value transactions can be priced by a 'reverse auction'—i.e. held on behalf of a buyer rather than seller. The buyer issues a 'request for quote', in which she spells out what she wants. But this imposes large transaction costs on the sellers, who have to prepare detailed quotes, most of which will fail.

High hopes have been held out for the Internet which has created new market places, promising far greater efficiency, based on the Net's ability to gather in the same virtual place, at hardly any cost, lots of information and processing power and vast numbers of potential buyers and sellers. Hundreds of online exchanges and other 'eHubs' in 'business to business' (B2B) markets bring together firms and their suppliers to auction, negotiate, or simply compare prices. Does this mean that e-commerce will take place in perfectly competitive markets?

Steven Kaplan and Mohanbir Sawhney[1] identify two main ways in which B2B eHubs can enhance economic efficiency. The first is 'aggregation': bringing together a huge number of buyers and sellers with a fixed menu of prices, and cutting transaction costs through one-stop shopping. The second is 'matching': a dynamic process in which buyers and sellers interact until they find the best match between what a buyer wants and a seller can supply.

But will traditional markets be replaced by e-commerce? In most markets, price is only one of many dimensions in which suppliers compete. Paul Milgrom of Stanford University suggests that Internet exchanges that allow competition only on price will not attract many of the suppliers or customers now in those markets offline. As Milgrom points out, arguments that online exchanges will produce big increases in efficiency implicitly assume that the Internet will make markets perfectly competitive—with homogeneous products, and competition on price alone. But markets for most goods and services in fact have 'imperfect competition'—similar but slightly differentiated products competing on many things besides price. There is no reason this should change simply because of the advent of e-commerce.

Source: *The Economist*, 12–18 February 2000
[1]'B2B E-Commerce Hubs: Towards a Taxonomy of Business Models', *Harvard Business Review*, May-June 2000.

4.2 MONOPOLY

A perfectly competitive industry can be viewed as one with the most intense competition among the sellers in the market. No firm in a perfectly competitive market believes that it can affect the market price by its action. The assumptions of product homogeneity and perfect information effectively rule out the scope for any strategic interactions in the market place. At the other extreme, we can think of a situation where there is only one firm facing no immediate competition. Such an industry is called a monopoly. The monopolist also does not have to strategically interact with other firms in the market. In between are oligopolistic market structures where a 'few' firms compete with each other.

A monopoly is the sole producer of a commodity that has no close substitutes. The firm and the industry are identical. The demand curve faced by the firm is the downward-sloping industry demand curve. We are, therefore, giving up the assumption of a large number of sellers that is so crucial to perfect competition. In contrast to a perfectly competitive firm that behaves as a price-taker so that the demand curve facing it is horizontal, a monopoly acts as a price-maker. It knows that it can set its own price. If the monopoly is to remain a monopoly, we must also give up the assumption of free entry into the industry.

Of course, the existence of the downward-sloping demand curve sets a constraint on the monopolist's actions. The monopolist can either set the price and then sell the quantity indicated by the demand curve. Or it can choose which quantity to sell and then set the maximum price indicated again by the demand curve. *The monopolist cannot set both the price and the quantity at her will.*

In the real world, there are few pure monopolies. However, it is still worth considering the monopoly market structure in some detail, because when there are a few firms in the market, they exercise some market power (i.e. act as price-setters), and we can get an insight into their strategies by analysing the monopoly case. In India, for example, the public sector has enjoyed monopoly or near-monopoly positions in electricity, postal services, and airlines.

4.2.1 The Profit-Maximizing Monopolist

As in the case of a perfectly competitive firm, we continue to assume that the monopolist tries to maximize profit. But unlike the perfectly competitive firm, the monopolist faces the downward-sloping industry demand curve. Let the equation of the (inverse) demand curve facing the monopolist be $P = P(Q)$, where $dP/dQ < 0$. The total cost function is $C = C(Q)$.

When the demand curve is downward sloping, the extra revenue from selling an additional unit will be different from price, because to sell more, the firm must reduce its price. The extra revenue, also called *marginal revenue* (*MR*), is the change in total revenue from selling an additional unit: $MR = dTR/dQ$. But $TR = P.Q$. Hence $MR = P + Q(dP/dQ) = P(1 - 1/e)$, where e is the price-elasticity of demand. For $e > 1$, $MR < P$; for $e < 1$, MR will be negative.

The monopolist tries to maximize $\Pi = TR - C$, where $TR = P(Q).Q$ and $TC = C(Q)$. The first order condition is

$$d\Pi/dQ = dTR/dQ - dC/dQ = 0,$$
$$\text{i.e. } dTR/dQ = dC/dQ.$$

The expression on the left hand side is the marginal revenue while the expression on the right hand side is just the marginal cost (*MC*). Hence the first order condition for profit-maximization can be written succinctly as $MR = MC$.[1] Once the monopoly selects its output the market price is determined at the corresponding point on the demand curve. Fig. 4.8 shows two (equivalent) ways of looking at the profit-maximizing monopolist's output. One can either draw the *TR* and *C* curves and then the resultant profit curve. The profit-maximizing output is reached at the peak of the profit curve, where the slope of the profit curve is zero. Otherwise, one can directly work with the MR and *MC* curves.

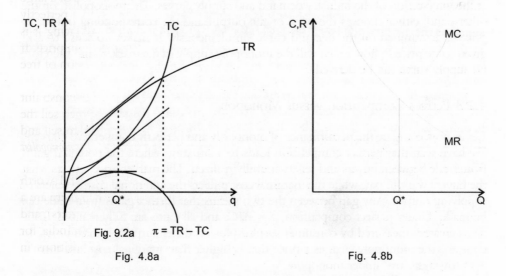

Fig. 4.8a   Fig. 4.8b

We should note here that the equality of marginal revenue with marginal cost is a quite general condition for profit-maximization. The same condition is used in the case of a perfectly competitive firm to derive the profit-maximizing output. However, since the demand curve facing a perfectly competitive firm is horizontal, $TR = p^*Q$, and hence $MR = p^*$.

The intuition behind the $MR = MC$ condition is the same as before. The firm has to examine whether an extra unit of output adds more to cost or to revenue. If it adds more to cost, that provides a signal to cut down on output. If it adds more to revenue, output should be expanded.

Example 4.2. Linear demand and cost curves. Let the equation of the inverse demand curve faced by the monopoly be $P = 100 - Q$, and let the cost function be $C = 2Q$. Then total revenue is $TR = PQ = 100Q - Q^2$. Then $MR = dTR/dQ = 100 - 2Q$. The *MR* curve will be a straight line, having the same *P*-intercept as the inverse demand curve and intersecting the *Q*-axis at the mid-point of the inverse demand

[1]The second order condition is that at the profit-maximizing level of output, the slope of the *MR* curve must be less than the slope of the *MC* curve. If we assume that the *MC* curve is upward sloping, then the second order condition is satisfied either if the *MR* curve is downward sloping, or if the *MR* curve is upward sloping but cuts the *MC* curve from the left to the right.

curve's intercept. $MC = dC/dQ = 2$. Equating the two, we get $100 - 2Q = 2$, or Q^* = 49. Note that we need the condition that the inverse demand curve must have an intercept that is higher than the marginal cost. From the equation of the inverse demand curve, $P^* = 100 - 49 = 51$. Note that the price is higher than marginal cost.

4.2.2 The Monopolist does not face a Supply Curve

One important difference between the competitive market and monopoly is that no supply curve exists in the latter case. Equilibrium in the competitive market is established at the intersection of the industry demand and supply curves. The monopolist, on the other hand, either chooses the price or the output and the corresponding output or price is determined on the demand curve simultaneously. It makes no sense to ask: given some price P, how much will the monopoly supply in the market? and therefore no supply curve can be derived.

4.2.3 Perfect Competition versus Monopoly

Let us now compare the performance of monopoly and perfectly competitive markets. We have seen that perfect competition leads to a situation where the potential gains from trade between buyers and sellers are fully realized. The market price reflects what the buyers want to pay, while the marginal cost reflects the additional cost to sellers of supplying output. Any gap between the two means that further gains from trade can be made. Under perfect competition, $p = MC$, and all gains are fully realized. Total value created, measured by consumer surplus plus producer surplus, is maximized. In contrast, the monopoly charges a price that is higher than marginal cost and there is a 'deadweight loss' under monopoly.

To show this, assume that conditions of constant cost prevail. The competitive industry long run supply curve is a horizontal straight line. The long run competitive industry equilibrium is established in Fig. 4.9 at E^* with price = p^* and quantity =

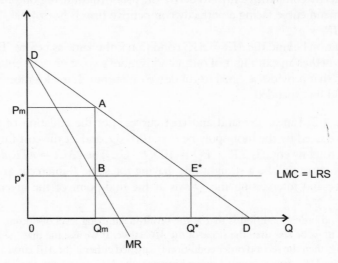

Fig. 4.9

Q^*, where $p^* = LMC$. Consumer surplus is equal to the triangle Dp^*E^*. Producer surplus is zero. Now, consider a monopoly with the same long run demand curve and marginal cost curve equal to LRS. The monopoly will select price and output using the $MR = MC$ condition. Hence it will produce Q_m amount of output and charge a price p_m. Consumer surplus is then the area DAp_m while producer surplus is equal to $p_m ABp^*$. Comparing with the aggregate social welfare under perfect competition, we find that there is a deadweight loss under monopoly equal to the area ABE^*. In other words, less value is created than under perfect competition.

However, note that under monopoly, *consumer surplus is lower while producer surplus is higher* than under perfect competition. The monopolist's ability to set its price enables it to appropriate more value than a competitive firm.

4.2.4 Sources of Monopoly Power

How can a firm attain the enviable position of a monopoly so that it can continue to earn supernormal profits without threat of competition from rivals? A monopoly can exist only if there are barriers to entry in the industry. Such barriers to entry can be classified into three categories: natural, policy-created, and strategic. Below, we give examples of each of these different types of entry barriers.

1. Natural entry barriers:

(a) *Economies of scale*. In the long run, the existence of economies of scale implies that the firm has a downward-sloping average cost curve. The more the firm produces, the lower its unit cost of production. This makes it difficult for newcomers to compete with the existing low-cost producer. Further, in such situations, the least costly way of serving the market is to have a single producer serve the market. In Fig. 4.10, if the entire output OQ' is produced by one firm, the average cost is AC. If, on the other hand, there are two firms each producing half the amount, the average cost for each is AC', which is higher than AC.

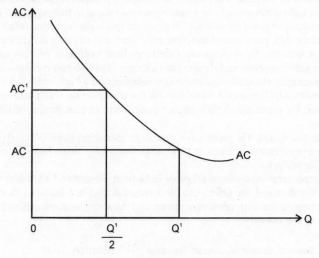

Fig. 4.10

(b) *Entry Lags*. In industries like steel, there is a huge gestation lag between the time the work starts on plants and machinery and the time when production begins. These gestation lags prevent new firms from entering the industry quickly in response to the existence of supernormal profits.

(c) *Switching costs*. A switching cost is a one-time cost incurred when an agent switches from one product to another. This may be the cost incurred by a buyer when she switches from one supplier's product to another. If switching costs are high, then buyers will not switch to products of other firms.

2. Strategic entry barriers:

(a) *Control over critical inputs*. If in an industry, an input is critical in the production process, and one firm controls the supply of the input, then that firm can become a monopoly. Other firms cannot enter the industry because they do not have access to the critical input.

The criticality of an input can be the result of technical requirements as well as the firm's success in establishing the uniqueness of a certain component in the eyes of the customers. An example of the former was the monopoly of the Aluminum Company of America (Alcoa) in the production of aluminum (aluminium) through its control over the supply of bauxite in the early part of the twentieth century. It signed long-term contracts with companies supplying bauxite and these contracts specified that the bauxite could not be sold to anyone else. An example of the latter is the almost sole control of the DeBeers Diamond Mines over most of the world's supply of raw diamonds. Even though synthetic diamonds are now produced in large quantities and such diamonds can sometimes fool even experienced jewellers, the public's preference for 'the real thing' enables DeBeers to exercise monopoly power in the diamond industry.

BOX 4.2 USING BETTER TECHNOLOGY TO RETAIN MONOPOLY STATUS

Electrosteel Castings makes cast iron (CI) and ductile iron (DI) spun pipes used mainly in transportation of water and sewage. The company pioneered the manufacture of DI pipes in India and continues to hold a near monopoly status in this segment. This should stand the company in good stead since DI pipes are gradually replacing other substitutes like CI, spiral welded, pre-stressed concrete, mild steel, and asbestos concrete pipes due to their superior features. By undergoing a different heat treatment process and having a different chemical composition, DI pipes have a longer life and better mechanical properties like greater strength, elongation, corrosion resistance, and a high level of resilience over other substitutes which makes it more suitable for transporting water and sewage.

However, DI pipes are slightly higher priced over certain grades of CI and spiral welded pipes.

All over the world, DI pipes have to a large extent replaced other type of pipes. However, the penetration in India at present has been low due to lack of awareness and a relatively higher price.

The low penetration levels of DI pipes in India at present and an export market will mean a healthy demand for DI pipes. Electrosteel is also not likely to face any major threat in the near future with unviable imports and the absence of any other manufacturer of DI pipes in the country.

Source: *The Business Standard*, 'Smart Investor', 1–7 February 1999.

(b) *Reputational effects*. Sometimes a firm may acquire a reputation for fighting aggressively any new firm trying to enter the market, and this prevents further entry.

3. Policy-created entry barriers:

(a) *Patents*. Most countries give an inventor sole control over the use of an invention for a certain number of years. In India, a patent is granted for seven years. Patents create monopolies, and as we have seen, monopolies lead to inefficiencies and deadweight losses. This static inefficiency is supposed to be balanced by gains to *dynamic efficiency*: it is argued that unless inventors and innovators are rewarded in this manner by creating time-bound monopolies, less effort would be put into invention and innovation and society would lose out on the technological progress front.

To take the case of Alcoa again, the monopoly position of the firm was maintained initially by the many patents that it had obtained for the different phases of the aluminium ingot production process. However, while giant firms like Alcoa can utilize the patent process to their own advantage, individual innovators often find it impossible to keep track of the many infringements of their patent rights and obtain legal redress.

(b) *Licences*. It is illegal to enter many industries without a government licence, i.e. a permission from the Government to set up the firm. In India, the Industries (Development and Regulation) Act, 1951, enabled the Government to direct industrial investments through a licensing system. An industrial license was required for setting up a new large-scale industrial undertaking or expansion of an old one or the manufacture of a new article. This was buttressed by a system of issuing licences for capital goods imports. Usually, licences are issued only to firms already in the industry, so that this effectively gives monopoly power to incumbent firms.

4.3 CONTESTABLE MARKETS: THE IMPACT OF POTENTIAL ENTRY

The existence of a monopoly depends on the inability of new firms to enter the market. If new firms actually enter the market, then the monopolist's market power is eroded. However, another equally powerful force can be the threat of potential entry. While in many markets, there may be significant barriers to entry, whether natural or artificial, there might be others where entry and exit is relatively easy. Baumol, Panzar, and Willig have characterized an extreme form of such markets as contestable markets. The main assumption they make is that such markets do not involve sunk costs of entry. Incumbents are subject to hit-and-run entry, meaning that potential entrants can costlessly enter and exit from the industry, and not have to wait until they generate sufficient revenues to cover the sunk cost of entry. This keeps the incumbents on their toes and if incumbents do not have any cost advantages over potential entrants, they can make only normal profit. Pricing that generates supernormal profit immediately attracts hit-and-run entry. The concept of equilibrium in contestable markets includes the provision that the incumbents must be using prices such that potential entrants cannot undercut the incumbents and at the same time make non-negative profits.

It is very hard to think of markets where there are no sunk costs of entry. It has been shown that in the presence of even tiny sunk costs, entry is deterred. It has also been shown that hit-and-run entry tactics will not work if the incumbent's rate of response is sufficiently rapid. The value of the concept of contestable markets seems to lie, like the concept of perfect competition, more in providing a benchmark than in a realistic characterization of markets.

4.4 THEORIES OF OLIGOPOLISTIC COMPETITION

In most markets, firms have to take into account the actual and potential responses from rival firms. We call these oligopolistic markets. An oligopoly is characterized by the presence of 'few' sellers in the market. The word 'few' does not refer to any number or range of numbers. We say that there are few firms in the industry if each firm must take explicitly into account reactions from rival firms.

Since firms can react in many ways and since in anticipating reactions, the beliefs, perceptions, and calculations become important, there is no single theory of oligopoly. We can, however, present a series of models that capture some of the main issues in the theory of oligopolistic behaviour.

We note here that there is a continuum of possible strategic/competitive relationships. Three distinct types of competitive relationships can be placed in this continuum:

- Independent
- Leader-follower behaviour
- Collusive behaviour

The degree of coordination increases as one moves from independent behaviour to collusive behaviour. Collusive behaviour will be taken up in Chapter 7.

4.4.1 Independent Behaviour

Firms can use many instruments to compete in the market place. These can be roughly classified according to the speed at which they can be altered.

Short Term	Medium Term	Long Term
Price	Technology Capacity Product Characteristics	Research & Development

We begin with price competition and then consider a model of quantity competition. From the point of value appropriation, the lesson from the subsequent discussion will be that price competition can be destructive for firms, while quantity competition is more benign.

4.4.2 Bertrand Competition in Prices

The Bertrand model focuses on price competition, i.e. situations where firms try to gain market shares by undercutting each others' prices. In the basic model, the surprising result that emerges is that even with a few firms in the market, price competition can lead to a duplication of perfectly competitive results. *The result of the Bertrand model highlights the dangers of engaging in price competition.*

Suppose that there are only two firms in the industry (so that the industry is a 'duopoly') that produce an identical commodity at a constant per unit cost of c. There is no fixed cost. Then $AC = MC = c$. The industry demand function is $q = D(p)$. The firms are denoted by subscripts 1 and 2.

In this model, we assume that the firm charging the lower price captures the entire market. If both firms charge the same price, then the market is divided up equally between the two firms.

The Bertrand equilibrium is a pair of prices chosen by the firms such that each chosen price maximizes the firm's profit, given the other firm's price. Thus, a Bertrand equilibrium is a pair of prices (p^*_i, p^*_j) such that

$$\pi_i(p^*_i, p^*_j) \geq \pi_i(p_i, p^*_j), \qquad i \neq j; i, j = 1, 2.$$

It should be easy to see that we are employing the concept of a Nash equilibrium here. The equilibrium is a Bertrand–Nash equilibrium in prices.

The Bertrand Paradox states that in equilibrium, firms will charge equal, competitive prices, and therefore make zero profits:

$$p^*_1 = p^*_2 = c.$$

It is quite easy to understand the proof of this result. The proof consists in showing that neither unequal prices nor prices that are equal to each other but not equal to c can form a equilibrium. In either case, at least one of the firms will have an incentive to change its price, more specifically, to undercut the other, to increase its profit. Moreover, if the prices are equal to each other and to c, such a pair will form a Bertrand–Nash equilibrium.

As an example of the reasoning employed, consider the situation where $p^*_1 > p^*_2 > c$. Then firm 1 makes zero profit. But it can do better by charging a price p'_2 that is slightly lower than p^*_2 but greater than c. Hence it can capture the entire market and make a positive profit. Obviously, the original pair of prices (p^*_1, p^*_2) could not have been an equilibrium pair, since at least one firm can do better with a different price p'_2 in response to p^*_1.

What happens if one firm is more efficient than another? Suppose that $c_1 > c_2$. Then firm 2 can exploit its cost advantage by charging a price of $c_1 - \varepsilon$, thus preventing firm 1 from being able to operate at a profit, and at the same time making a positive profit itself.

The Bertrand Paradox therefore highlights the competition engendered through price-cutting. Firms caught up in a price war would like to find ways of escaping from such a situation. There are various ways of resolving the Bertrand Paradox and we discuss them briefly next.

1. The Edgeworth solution: Edgeworth pointed out that the introduction of a capacity constraint can solve the Bertrand Paradox. Suppose that firm 1 has a productive capacity K such that $D(c) > K$, $D(c)$ denoting the quantity demanded at price $= c$. That is, even if the firm prices at marginal cost, it cannot meet the entire market demand. Then $p^*_1 = p^*_2 = c$ cannot be an equilibrium. At $p^*_1 = p^*_2 = c$, both firms

BOX 4.3. INTEL PRODUCT AND PRICE WAR

In 2001, the *New York Times* reported that Intel planned to use its newest, fastest microprocessor as a weapon against its chief rival, Advanced Micro Devices, in what could be a price war that would make consumers happy but cut into each company's bottom line.

Intel was expected to introduce its 1.7-gigahertz Pentium 4 microprocessor, the fastest chip yet for desktop personal computers, for less than half the introductory price of the chip's predecessor, which Intel released only five months earlier. The company also planned deep discounts on the rest of its Pentium 4 line.

Intel and Advanced Micro, which hold a virtual duopoly in the desktop PC microprocessor market, both said they wanted to avoid a price war. Yet neither appeared ready to back down.

Intel said it had improved its production efficiency and would continue to pass along those savings to customers, as it undertakes an aggressive rollout for the new chip in hopes of luring PC users to replace their older machines. For its part, Advanced Micro said that it intended to match or beat Intel's pricing at each speed level at which the companies compete.

Both proclamations spelt trouble for investors, who anxiously watched the companies' profit margins as the economy slowed. Indeed, in its forecast, Intel cited the accelerating rollout of its Pentium 4 line as a prime reason for shrinking gross margins.

Source: Chris Gaither, 'Intel product could set off a price war', *The New York Times*, 23 April 2001.

BOX 4.4. WHY PRICE WARS GET STARTED

Garda and Marn (The *Mckinsey Quarterly*, 1993) identify 'misreads' as one of the major reasons why price wars get started. According to them, companies rarely embark on price wars as part of a strategic programme. But firms often incorrectly identify innocent rival actions as price wars or misjudge how competitors will react to their own pricing manoeuvres.

Some of the reasons they advance for companies to avoid price wars are as follows:

1. Price elasticities may be such that very large increases in volumes will be required to compensate for even small price declines. In all probability, rivals will also cut prices, so that the required increase in volumes will not materialize.

2. Customers come to accept low prices as a matter of course and continue to demand low prices.

3. Customers become sensitive to price at the expense of value and benefits. This reduces the ability of providers of high-quality goods and services to charge premium prices for their products.

Source: R. A. Garda and M. V. Marn (1993), 'Price Wars', *The McKinsey Quarterly*, No. 3, pp 87–100.

make zero profit. Suppose that firm 2 raises its price slightly. Then all customers try to buy from firm 1, but it cannot meet the entire demand because of the capacity constraint. Then some customers are forced to buy from firm 2 which makes a positive profit. Therefore (p^*_1, p^*_2) such that $p^*_1 = p^*_2 = c$ is no longer a Bertrand–Nash equilibrium.

2. Product differentiation: It can be shown that if products are not identical, then a Nash equilibrium in prices may involve firms charging different prices and making positive profits.

4. Price-setting in a dynamic context: Even when a firm has an incentive to cut price, it may not do so if it can foresee that rival firms will retaliate with price cuts and everyone will lose.

4.4.3 Cournot Competition in Quantities

Consider now a duopoly where firms choose quantities rather than prices. Given the quantity choices q_1 and q_2, the market price adjusts to the level $p(q_1 + q_2)$ that clears the market; $p(q_1 + q_2)$ is the inverse demand function. We assume that $p'(q)$ (i.e. dp/dq) < 0 at all $q \geq 0$.

The Cournot–Nash equilibrium for this model consists of a pair of quantity choices (q_1^*, q_2^*) such that

$$\pi_i(q_i^*, q_j^*) \geq \pi_i(q_i, q^*_j), \qquad i \neq j, i, j = 1, 2.$$

We can solve for the equilibrium quantities by looking at the best response functions or the 'reaction functions' of the two firms. Firm 1's reaction function shows the quantities that firm 1 should produce to maximize its profit, for any level of output produced by firm 2. It can be obtained from the equation $\partial \pi_1/\partial q_1 = 0$, which yields the best output of firm 1 as a function of firm 2's output: $q_1 = R_1(q_2)$. Similarly, we can use the equation $\partial \pi_2/\partial q_2 = 0$ to get the reaction function for firm 2, $q_2 = R_2(q_1)$. The Cournot–Nash equilibrium quantities are obtained by solving the two reaction functions together. Graphically, the Cournot–Nash equilibrium is represented by the

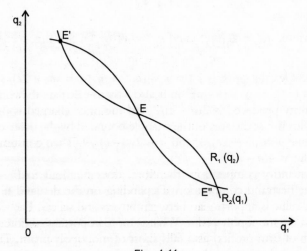

Fig. 4.11

point of intersection of the reaction curves. Further assumptions are needed to ensure that at least one Cournot–Nash equilibrium exists. On the other hand, Fig. 4.11 shows a situation where more than one Cournot–Nash equilibrium exist.

It will be instructive to analyse the Cournot–Nash equilibrium for the case where both demand and cost functions are linear. Suppose that the inverse demand function is $p = a - (q_1 + q_2)$, the cost functions are $C_i = cq_i$, $i = 1, 2$, and $a > c$. Then $\pi_i = [a - (q_1 + q_2) - c]q_i$, $i = 1, 2$.

The reaction function for firm 1 is obtained from $\partial \pi_1 / \partial q_1 = 0$. This yields $a - c - 2q_1 - q_2 = 0$, or $q_1 = (a - c - q_2)/2 = R_1(q_2)$. Similarly, $q_2 = (a - c - q_1)/2 = R_2(q_1)$.

These two reaction functions are downward sloping straight lines. The point of intersection is the quantity pair that constitutes the Cournot–Nash equilibrium.

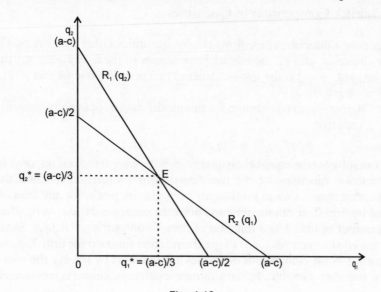

Fig. 4.12

In equilibrium, $q_1^* = R_1(q_2^*)$ and $q_2^* = R_2(q_1^*)$. Solving, we get

$$q_1^* = q_2^* = (a - c)/3.$$

The market-clearing price is $p^* = a - (q_1^* + q_2^*) = (a + 2c)/3$ and each firm earns a profit $\pi_i(q_1^*, q_2^*) = (a - c)^2/9$. It also easy to calculate the consumer surplus. The total quantity produced is $2(a - c)/3$ and the price charged is $(a + 2c)/4$. The consumer surplus is just the area of the triangle bounded by the inverse demand curve and the price line $p = (a + 2c)/3$, and it is $2(a - c)^2/9$. Then consumer surplus plus producer surplus is $4(a - c)^2/9$.

Cournot quantity competition, therefore, does not lead to the extreme result obtained under Bertrand competition. Depending on the demand function and the cost functions, value is apportioned between buyers and sellers. Each seller obviously makes less than the monopoly profit. What is more important to note is that industry profit (the sum of firm profits) also falls short of monopoly profit. This 'dissipation' in profit can be traced to the fact that the firms are acting noncooperatively in competing with each other.

If there are more and more firms, would all the supernormal profits be dissipated? Let us go back to the linear case to examine this. In general, if there are n identical firms, $n > 1$, in the industry, then the reaction function for firm i will be

$$(a - c) - [2q_i + \Sigma q_{-i}] = 0,$$

where q_{-i} refers to outputs of all firms other than the i-th firm. Since the firms are identical, we can consider the symmetric Cournot–Nash equilibrium in which all outputs are equal to q^*. Substituting in the expression for the reaction function, and solving, we get $q^* = (a - c)/(n + 1)$, and $p^* = a - nq^* = (a + nc)/(n + 1)$. As n becomes large, it is obvious that the output of each firm becomes negligible, and the industry output nq^* approaches $(a - c)$, the competitive level of output. Also, p^* tends to c, the marginal cost. Hence the Cournot–Nash equilibrium tends to the perfectly competitive equilibrium as the number of firms tends to infinity and all supernormal profits are competed away. So when there is quantity competition, large numbers is bad news for every firm in the industry.

4.4.4 Leader–Follower Models

Even when identical firms are choosing quantities, some firms may be in a position to extract higher value in the industry. They do this by exploiting their leadership positions in the industry.

We next turn to a consideration of some leader-follower models. In these models, one player decides its price or output first. Based on this choice, the second player decides its price or quantity. The first player is in an advantageous position because it can anticipate the effect of its actions on the second firm, and use this superior knowledge to appropriate more value.

4.4.5 The Stackelberg Model

In the Stackelberg model, one firm (the 'leader') gets to choose the quantity first and then the other firm (the 'follower') selects the level of its output. The leader then enjoys a *first-mover advantage* in that it can anticipate the actions of the follower and make its optimal choice accordingly.

The equilibrium concept that we employ is the subgame-perfect equilibrium. Remember that the subgame-perfect equilibrium is obtained by solving the problem backwards. We again consider the linear demand and cost function case. Let firm 2 be the follower. First, we derive firm 2's reaction function which is $q_2 = (a - c - q_1)/2$. Firm 1 realizes that for any q_1 it selects, firm 2's output will be chosen from the reaction function. Therefore, firm 1 maximizes its profit given the constraint $q_2 = (a - c - q_1)/2$. Given this constraint, $\pi_1 = [a - (q_1 + q_2) - c]q_1 = \frac{1}{2}(a - c - q_1)q_1$. The first order condition $d\pi_1/dq_1 = 0$ yields $q^s_1 = (a - c)/2$ and $q^s_2 = (a - c)/4$. The leader now produces *more* than the follower, unlike in the Cournot model, where both produced the same quantity in equilibrium. Next calculate the profits: $\pi_1 = (a - c)^2/8$, while $\pi_2 = (a - c)^2/16$. The leader's profit is higher than the profit earned in the Cournot model and also higher than the follower's. The follower is worse off than in the Cournot model.

The Stackelberg solution can also be derived in the following way. The reaction function of the follower is the constraint facing the leader. Given this constraint, the leader tries to maximize profit by finding out the highest *iso-profit curve* that just touches the constraint. The iso-profit curves are the loci of those combinations of q_1 and q_2 for which the firm earns a constant amount of profit. Let $\pi_1 = [a - (q_1 + q_2) - c]q_1 = K$, a constant. Setting, $d\pi_1 = 0$, we can solve for the equation of the slope of an iso-profit curve: $dq_2/dq_1 = (a - c - 2q_1 - q_2)/q_1$. The slope of the reaction function for firm 2 is $-(1/2)$. Setting $(a - c - 2q_1 - q_2)/q_1 = -1/2$ and employing the equation of the reaction function for firm 2, we find again that $q_1^s = (a - c)/2$ and $q_2^s = (a - c)/4$.

Diagrammatically, the Cournot–Nash solution is obtained at the intersection of the two reaction functions. But in the Stackelberg model, we have seen that the leader takes as given the follower's reaction function, and chooses to produce at the point where one of its iso-profit curves is tangential to the reaction function of the follower.

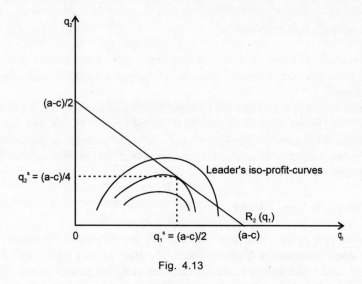

Fig. 4.13

4.4.6 Dominant Firm with a Competitive Fringe

Why should one firm be in a position where it can act as a leader? In the Stackelberg model, we assign leadership to one firm without trying to explain how it came to be accepted as a leader. Sometimes leadership is a natural consequence of size. Some firms are leaders because they are the 'dominant' firms. While it is difficult to find pure monopolies, examples of dominant firms are easy to come across. In India, Indian Airlines was at one time the dominant airline serving domestic routes, with 85 – 90 per cent of the market share, though its share in recent times has fallen to 45 per cent. In the car market, Maruti Udyog Ltd. for a long time had a market share between 75 per cent and 80 per cent. Pricing decisions of such dominant firms often seem to be accepted and closely followed by other firms in the market. For example, when Indian Airlines increases its fares, the smaller firms seem to immediately follow suit.

We now consider a model where there is a dominant firm in the market, as well as a competitive 'fringe', i.e. a number of small firms that act like price-takers, accepting the price set by the dominant firm as the market price. In this model, we again have a leader–follower type of situation. The dominant firm sets its price, fully anticipating the response from the fringe firms. While the dominant firm obviously is in a better position than the fringe firms, the existence of the fringe firms sets checks on its exercise of monopoly power. Moreover, this monopoly is further eroded if there is free entry by fringe firms into the industry.

a. No entry

First, let us analyse the case where there is a fixed number n of identical fringe firms. Their supply curve is merely the sum of the marginal cost curves. Let this be denoted by $S(p) = nq_f$. The demand curve facing the industry is $D(p)$. Then $D(p) - S(p)$ is the *residual demand curve* faced by the dominant firm. The latter sets a price; fringe firms meet a certain part of market demand given this price, and the dominant firm supplies the rest.

The situation is depicted in Fig. 4.14. The residual demand curve in the right hand side is derived by horizontally subtracting $S(p)$ from the $D(p)$ curve. Note that this is a kinked curve. If the market price is set below p', the fringe firms do not supply anything and the residual demand curve becomes the market demand curve. The MR curve has two segments, each related to the corresponding segment of the residual demand curve. The dominant firm equates MR with MC, and sets the price p^*. At this price, the fringe firms supply an amount Q^*_f, while the dominant firm supplies Q^*_d.

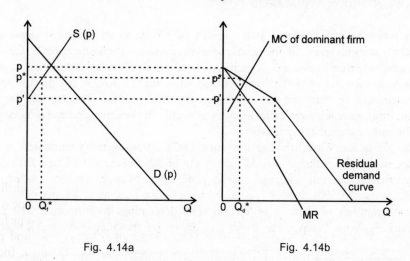

Fig. 4.14a   Fig. 4.14b

Several things can be noted here. First, unless the dominant firm enjoys a significant cost advantage over the fringe firms (its MC curve is much lower than the $S(p)$ curve), it loses some of its market share to the fringe firms. Secondly, it has to choose a lower price than a pure monopoly. Thirdly, if the dominant firm cuts its price, it is reflected throughout the industry.

b. Free entry by fringe firms

Let us consider an extreme case where new fringe firms can instantaneously enter the industry. Therefore, the $S(p)$ curve is horizontal. Whenever profits are made by existing fringe firms, entry takes place until profits are driven down to zero. The residual demand curve facing the dominant firm has a horizontal segment and this sets a ceiling on the price that the dominant firm can charge.

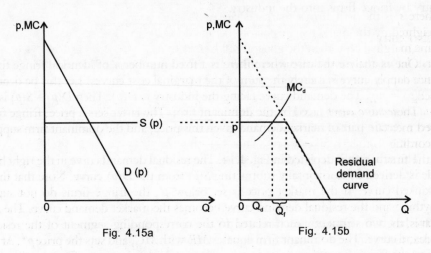

Fig. 4.15a   Fig. 4.15b

4.5 CONCENTRATION AND MARKET POWER

Market power may be defined as the ability of a firm to set its prices above cost, particularly marginal cost. Greater market power translates into higher profits. Creating and maintaining market power is, therefore, central to a firm's value-maximizing strategy.

We have seen that in perfect competition, firms do not possess any market power. Price is equated to marginal cost. Perfect competition is also characterized by zero concentration, since any firm in the industry is 'small'. At the other extreme is monopoly, with the most extreme concentration.

The Structure-Conduct-Performance (SCP) paradigm (mentioned in the introduction to this volume) would seem to imply that there would be a causal link between market concentration and market power. Structure determines conduct. For example, as discussed in chapter 7, collusive price-fixing is easier to achieve when there is a small number of firms. Conduct in turn determines performance. The more competitively firms behave, the lower the degree of market power and lower the profits.

If performance is a function of structure and conduct $[P = f(S, C)]$ and conduct itself is a function of structure $[C = g(S)]$, then we can simplify the above points as performance being determined by structure $[P = f(S, C(S)]$.

Since the degree of market concentration is one of the elements of the structure of an industry, we can try to see if higher concentration leads to greater market power. The Bertrand model, however, alerts us to the possibility that market concentration may not always accurately predict the degree of market power. As we noticed, when firms with identical marginal costs engaged in price-competition, even a duopoly led to the perfectly competitive results.

In empirical investigations of the relation between market concentration and market power, it is important to define these two concepts in a meaningful way. Market power is usually measured by the Lerner index: $(p - MC)/p$. If firms in the industry have different marginal costs, then we can use a generalized Lerner index L:

$$L = [\Sigma \, s_i(P - MC_i)]/p,$$

where s_i is the i-th firm's market share. Thus the price-marginal cost margins are weighted by the market shares before being added up. Note that if all firms have the same marginal cost, then the generalized Lerner index is the same as the Lerner index.

One of the most difficult problems in empirical investigations is to calculate L. Since data on marginal costs are not available, proxy measures such as average costs are used.

There are various possible measures of market concentration. The most commonly used measure is the m-firm concentration index C_m. Suppose firms are first indexed according to their market shares. Thus s_1 is the firm with the largest market share, s_2 is the firm with the second largest share, and so on. Then

$$C_m = \sum_i^m s_i \,,$$

that is, the sum of the market shares of the m largest firms. The four-firm concentration index, for example, is the total of the market shares of the four largest firms.

Another measure that is used is the Herfindahl index H:

$$H = \Sigma \, s_i^2.$$

The Herfindahl index is found by adding up the squares of market shares of all the firms. While it is a better measure of concentration than the m-firm concentration index, it requires data on the market shares of *all* the firms in the industry.

5 Product Differentiation

In the discussion so far, we have been assuming that all firms in an industry produce identical products. When products are identical, competition occurs on the single dimension of price competition. In an earlier chapter, we have also pointed out the dangers of price competition. Price wars can exhaust all players in the market and benefit none (except the consumers).

One way of avoiding this possibility is for firms to differentiate their products. Products within an industry are said to be differentiated if consumers treat the different products as close but imperfect substitutes. It is important to understand that even physically identical goods will be treated as different commodities if the buyers view them as such. The same drug paracetamol for paediatric use is sold as different brands, e.g. Crocin syrup, Metacin syrup, Zupar syrup, etc. They will be considered as different products since consumers perceive them as such. On the other hand, product heterogeneity *per se* does not ensure product differentiation. Consumers might treat even heterogeneous products as identical products. For example, consumers might find it difficult to compare two types of cars—one of which has a more powerful engine but less passenger space—and end up treating the two brands as equivalent.

Economists distinguish between vertical differentiation and horizontal differentiation. To understand the concept of *vertical product differentiation*, consider two types of cars. If all other attributes are the same, but one car has a more powerful engine, then *all* consumers will prefer the car with the more powerful engine. To put this differently, if the same price is charged for the two types of cars, everyone will agree on which product is preferred and will buy that one product. Therefore, roughly speaking, vertical differentiation makes one product better than another. This concept also applies frequently to differentiation that occurs over time. For example, over time, PCs are produced which use more advanced types of chips and offer a larger number of features. If two PCs are available at the same price, one of which is run on Pentium 4 chips while the other runs on Pentium 3 chips, then consumers will definitely prefer the former. Sellers of vertically differentiated products may charge different prices, since some buyers may be willing to pay more for the additional features.

Horizontal product differentiation is aimed at making a product distinctive from others It is based on the premise that different consumers have different tastes or preferences. Some firms will produce bath soaps that smell of rose or jasmine, while others will produce soaps that smell of popular antiseptic creams. Even if the prices are the same, consumers will not be able to agree on the relative desirability of the two types. Some will prefer the soaps with fragrances, while others will want to buy the second type of the soap to protect them from germs.

Box 5.1. Vertical Differentiation in the Indian car market

Hyundai Motor India Ltd. achieved large sales of its subcompact car Santro in a surprisingly short period of time in India. Santro was seen as a better car than Maruti 800 because of several features. Unlike the flimsy-looking 800, Santro looked tough and the engine delivered adequate 'torque'. The seating was high, which delivered 'road command'. Moreover, Santro had a multi-point fuel-injection engine (MPFI), the first small car to possess this relatively fuel-efficient and eco-friendly technology. The base LE model price, at Rs 3.1 lakh, was very competitive against the Maruti Zen. It also went in Santro's favour that the engine met Euro II emission norms. When the Supreme Court ruled in 1999 that all new cars selling in Delhi would have to meet this emission criterion, Maruti had to stop production of Zen to switch over to the new norms, while Santro and Matiz had a field day.

Source: *Advertising and Marketing*, 18 August 2001.

A number of models of product differentiation are presented below. Chamberlin's model of monopolistic competition demonstrates that even product differentiation cannot ensure supernormal profits in the long run, if entry conditions are relatively easy. The next three models show that with a fixed number of firms in the market, differentiation does allow a firm to earn supernormal profits. Finally, we look at the advertising decisions of a firm.

5.1 Monopolistic Competition

If products are not identical, what is the definition of the industry? In Chamberlin's model of monopolistic competition there is a clearly defined 'industrial group' which consists of a large number of producers of goods that are close but imperfect substitutes of each other. Chamberlin's model is, therefore, a preliminary attempt at capturing elements of both perfect competition and monopoly. Since there are many small producers and free entry and exit in the long run, this makes the model similar to perfect competition. Firms do not believe that they can influence market conditions nor do they react to each others' actions directly. However, firms produce goods that are imperfect substitutes for each other. Hence, each firm has a market niche, where it can act as a monopoly. In other words, the demand curve facing each firm is downward sloping. This market power diminishes as more and more firms enter the industry, since more and more substitute products are thereby made available to consumers. In other words, buyers of any firm's product find a larger number of firms selling similar products.

Chamberlin's model is a preliminary attempt to do away with the assumption of homogeneity of products. At the same time, it retains the assumption of a large number of sellers and free entry and exit in the long run.

A fundamental feature of Chamberlin's model is the perfect symmetry in the position of all individual firms in the industry. Each firm believes that other firms will not respond in any way to its price and quantity decisions. Yet, when one firm finds it optimal to alter its price, others also do so by symmetry. This changes the demand conditions facing the firm. In other words, each firm confronts two different demand curves: there is a *dd* curve that describes what happens when it alone changes its price and there is a *DD* curve that describes what happens when all the firms change prices together. Obviously, the *dd* curve is more elastic (flatter) than the *DD* curve. The firm makes its decisions on the basis of the *dd* curve, rather than the *DD* curve, because, as we have already noted, each firm believes that other firms will not respond in any way to its price and quantity decisions.

The long run monopolistic competition equilibrium, as envisaged by Chamberlin, involves two important components. First, each firm, acting as a monopoly, must be maximizing profit by equating *MR* with *MC*. Secondly, free entry and exit leads to a situation where each firm earns zero profit. If profit is negative, some firms leave the industry while if it is positive, firms continue to enter the industry. This requires $p = AC$ in equilibrium. The Chamberlinian equilibrium, with price p^* and quantity q^*, is shown in Fig. 5.1. Therefore, even when product differentiation is allowed, this does not enable the firms to appropriate value: the large numbers and free entry and exit assumptions are too strong to allow firms to earn any supernormal profits in the long run.

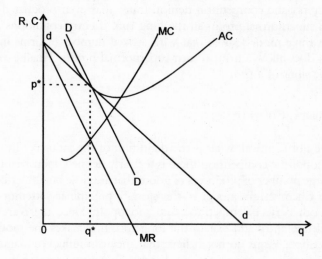

Fig. 5.1

Note that because the demand curve dd is downward sloping, the Chamberlinian equilibrium, which takes place at a point of tangency of the *AC* curve with the demand curve, occurs at a point to the left of the minimum point of the *AC* curve. Under perfect competition, the long run equilibrium takes place at the minimum point of the *AC* curve. Therefore, compared with perfect competition, it seems that monopolistic competition leads to higher per unit production costs. There are unexploited scale economies, in the sense that each firm is producing on the negatively sloped portion of its average cost curve, and not at the minimum point. This seems to point to waste and inefficiency under monopolistic competition.

However, consumers now have more variety and the higher average cost can be thought of as the price they pay for this variety. Increasing the number of differentiated products has two effects: (a) it increases the amount of excess capacity in the production of each product because there are more products competing for the same demand; (b) the increased product differentiation is better able to satisfy diverse tastes. Optimally, the number of products should be such that the marginal gain in consumers' satisfaction equals the loss from higher per unit cost.

In the real world, product differentiation is an universal phenomenon. But if there are many close substitutes in a market, one should not jump to the conclusion that there are many small firms and hence they neglect each other's actions. Often a few large firms each produce many differentiated varieties of the same product. An example is the cigarette industry in India, where only four firms produce all the different types of cigarettes that are available.

5.2   DUOPOLY MODELS

The Bertrand model yields the surprising result that even with a small number of firms in the market, it is possible to get competitive results. When firms produce homogeneous outputs, price competition leads to erosion of all supernormal profits. We next demonstrate that product differentiation helps the firms to escape this situation. We begin with a model of quantity competition, where firms choose volumes, and then convert the model to one of price competition. Next, an interesting spatial pricing model is considered.

5.2.1 Quantity Competition

Consider a duopoly producing two differentiated products indexed by $i = 1, 2$. There is no cost of production. Each firm produces a single commodity. Following Dixit (1979), we assume that the inverse demand functions for the two products are

$$p_1 = \alpha - \beta q_1 - \gamma q_2 \text{ and } p_2 = \alpha - \gamma q_1 - \beta q_2, \text{ where } \beta > 0, \beta^2 > \gamma^2.$$

The assumption $\beta^2 > \gamma^2$ implies that the price of a brand is more sensitive to a change in the quantity of this brand rather than to a change in the quantity of the rival brand.

A measure of differentiation will tell us how differentiated the two commodities are in the eyes of the consumers. If the commodities are close substitutes, then the own-price and cross-price effects will be almost the same, i.e. β^2 will be almost equal to γ^2. We can then use as a measure of differentiation the variable $\delta = \gamma^2/\beta^2$.

- The products are *highly differentiated* when δ *is close to 0*, i.e. γ^2 is close to 0. If δ is equal to 0, then the price of each product depends only on the quantity of that product, and not on the quantity of the rival product: $p_i = \alpha - \beta q_i, i = 1, 2$.

- On the other hand, when δ *is close to 1*, the goods are *close substitutes*. If it is equal to 1, there is only one inverse demand function, with the price depending on the total quantity of the two commodities: $p = \alpha - \beta q_1 - \beta q_2$.

Let us now examine the Nash equilibrium in the output levels. The i-th firm tries to maximize

$$\pi_i(q_1, q_2) = (\alpha - \beta q_i - \gamma q_j) q_i, \quad i, j = 1, 2, i \neq j,$$

with respect to q_i, treating q_j as fixed. The reaction functions are given by

$$q_i = R_i(q_j) = (\alpha - \gamma q_j)/2\beta, \quad i, j = 1, 2, i \neq j.$$

The reaction functions are downward sloping straight lines, and they are represented in Fig. 5.2. Note that as γ increases and approaches β, i.e. the products become more homogeneous, the reaction functions become steeper. If γ tends towards 0, the reaction functions tend to become vertical to the respective axes.

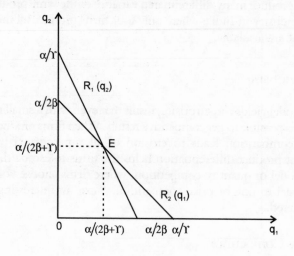

Fig. 5.2

From the two reaction functions, we can solve for the equilibrium quantities, prices, and profits. These are (by symmetry)

$$q_i^* = \alpha/(2\beta + \gamma), \ p_i^* = \alpha\beta/(2\beta + \gamma)$$

and $\pi_i^* = \alpha 2\beta/(2\beta + \gamma)2, i = 1, 2.$

We note an important result here: As γ falls and tends towards zero, the profit of each firm increases. That is, *as the products become more and more differentiated, the profits of both firms increase.* Interestingly, both firms can charge higher prices and sell more as the products become more differentiated. This explains why firms try their best to convince consumers that their products are unique. If products are highly differentiated, then each firm in effect becomes a monopoly and enjoys monopoly profits.

5.2.2 Price Competition

Instead of firms choosing their quantities, let us consider the case where firms choose their prices. We start with the inverse demand functions $p_1 = \alpha - \beta q_1 - \gamma q_2$ and $p_2 = \alpha - \gamma q_1 - \beta q_2$ as before. These two equations can be inverted to solve for the demand functions (we express the quantities as functions of prices, using Cramer's rule). The demand functions are

$$q_1 = a - bp_1 + cp_2 \text{ and } q_2 = a + cp_1 - bp_2,$$

where $a \equiv \alpha(\beta - \gamma)/(\beta^2 - \gamma^2)$, $b \equiv \beta/(\beta^2 - \gamma^2) > 0$, $c \equiv \gamma/(\beta^2 - \gamma^2) > 0$, by the earlier assumptions.

Now solve for the Nash equilibrium in prices. Each firm takes the other's price to be given and tries to maximize $\pi_i(p_1, p_2) = (a - bp_i + cp_j)p_i$, $i, j = 1, 2, i \neq j$. The reaction functions are given by $p_i = R_i(p_j) = (a + cp_j)/2b$, $i, j = 1, 2, i \neq j$.

The reaction functions in prices are represented in Fig. 5.3. Note that the reaction functions are now upward sloping.

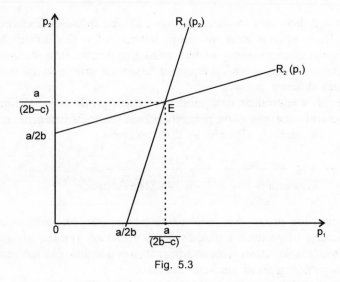

Fig. 5.3

Finally, from the reaction functions in prices, we solve for prices, quantities, and profits:

$$p^*_i = a/(2b - c) = \alpha(\beta - \gamma)/(2\beta - \gamma), \quad q^*_i = ab/(2b - c) = \alpha\beta/(\beta + \gamma)(2\beta - \gamma),$$

$$\text{and } \pi^*_i = a^2b/(2b - c)^2 = \alpha 2(\beta - \gamma)^2\beta/(2\beta - \gamma)^2.$$

How does a change in the degree of product differentiation affect profits? The profit for each firm can be written as $\pi^*_i = (\alpha^2\beta)[(\beta - \gamma)^2/(2\beta - \gamma)^2] = (\alpha^2\beta)[(\beta - \gamma)/(2\beta - \gamma)]^2$. It is easy to show that as γ increases, i.e. the products become less differentiated, the term $(\beta - \gamma)/(2\beta - \gamma)$ decreases, so that profits decrease. In the limit, when γ increases to the level of β, and the products become homogeneous, profits fall to zero and we get back the Bertrand result.

Therefore, whether there is quantity competition or price competition, increasing product heterogeneity increases the level of profit for both firms. This explains why firms try to differentiate their products from each other.

5.3 THE HOTELLING MODEL

The previous two models assumed forms of the demand and inverse demand functions. One fruitful way of thinking about product differentiation (of the horizontal variety) is to go back to the heterogeneity of preferences of consumers. It is because different people have different preferences that firms find it profitable to offer differentiated products. Further, in many instances, we see that products do not exist to satisfy the exact preferences of all consumers. Only a few products are available in the market. Some consumers are lucky enough to find their most preferred variety among the few available, but for others, it is more a question of selecting the product that comes closest to what they really want. Such a situation is captured nicely by the Hotelling model.

Suppose that there are two stores in a town located at two different points on the main street. Their different locations can be interpreted as product differentiation in the sense that customers prefer to buy from the nearby store because of lower transportation costs. This confers a degree of monopoly power on the two stores and they can charge different prices.

This model is equivalent to a model in which products are defined by their characteristics and consumers have preferences over these characteristics or attributes. An example is the ranking of pickles by their 'sourness':

Pickles — — A - — — — — — — — — — — — — —
     Less sour — — — — — ⟶ More sour

Some consumers like pickles that are less sour while others like pickles that are more sour. By deciding to produce a pickle with the level of sourness given by A (i.e. deciding to locate at A), a firm gains an advantageous position *vis-à-vis* consumers who prefer pickles with degrees of sourness close to A.

Another example comes from the field of politics. There is a political spectrum ranging from the Left (communists) to the Right (conservatives). Parties have to decide where to locate themselves on this spectrum, given that voters have preferences distributed in a certain manner along the spectrum.

To present Hotelling's model, we make the following assumptions:

1. There are two firms. They locate along a straight line (road) which is of length L. The location decisions are treated as exogenous in this model. They produce and sell commodities that are identical in all respects except for the location at which they are sold.

2. Consumers are distributed uniformly over the line and each has a unit demand. Demands are, therefore, perfectly inelastic. The only decision a buyer takes is which firm to patronize and this decision is based on the minimum price (including the transportation cost) at which the commodity is available.

3. To go to a store/firm, a consumer has to pay a transportation cost of t per unit of distance.

4. Cost of production is zero for both goods.

5. Finally, to present the model in a simple form, we assume that an equilibrium in which firms charge strictly positive prices always exists. For this, the firms must be located at a sufficient distance from each other, i.e. they should not be 'close' to each other.

```
Length L                          I
-----------------!--------------------!---------------------!-----------------------
         a      1        x          y        2        b
```

The firms are located at points 1 and 2 respectively. The distances from the end-points are *a* and *b*. Note that firm 1 has an intrinsic advantage *vis-à-vis* the consumers who are located to the left of point 1; unless firm 2's prices are significantly lower, these consumers will prefer to buy from firm 1. Similarly, firm 2 has an intrinsic advantage over consumers who are located to the right of the point 2.

I is the point where the consumer is exactly indifferent between 1 and 2. Therefore, for the consumer at I, $p_1 + tx = p_2 + ty$. Since we also know that $a + x + y + b = L$, we can solve for both x and y (and hence the point I), *given the prices*:

$$x = \tfrac{1}{2}\,[(L - a - b) + (p_2 - p_1)/t], \; y = \tfrac{1}{2}\,[(L - a - b) - (p_2 - p_1)/t].$$

Therefore, the market for firm 1 (the quantity firm 1 can sell) is

$$q_1 = a + x = a + \tfrac{1}{2}\,[(L - a - b) + (p_2 - p_1)/t],$$

and that for firm 2 is

$$q_2 = b + y = b + \tfrac{1}{2}\,[(L - a - b) - (p_2 - p_1)/t].$$

We now consider the Nash equilibrium in prices. The profit equations are

$$\pi_1 = p_1 q_1 = p_1[a + \tfrac{1}{2}\,\{(L - a - b) + (p_2 - p_1)/t\}],$$

and

$$\pi_2 = p_2 q_2 = p_2[a + \tfrac{1}{2}\,\{(L - a - b) - (p_2 - p_1)/t\}].$$

Setting the first partial derivatives equal to 0, we get

$$\partial\pi_1/\partial p_1 = a + \tfrac{1}{2}\,(L - a - b) + p_2/t - 2p_1/t = 0,$$

$$\partial\pi_2/\partial p_2 = a + \tfrac{1}{2}\,(L - a - b) - 2p_2/t + p_1/t = 0.$$

Solving from these two equations of reaction functions in prices, we finally obtain

$$p^*_1 = t\{L + (a - b)/3\} \text{ and } p^*_2 = t\{L - (a - b)/3\},$$

from which we can solve for the quantities:

$$q^*_1 = \tfrac{1}{2}\,\{L + (a - b)/3\} \text{ and } q^*_2 = \tfrac{1}{2}\,\{L - (a - b)/3\}.$$

- If the firms are located symmetrically from the two end-points, then $a = b$, and the firms charge the same prices and produce the same quantities: $p^*_1 = p^*_2 = tL$ and $q^*_1 = q^*_2 = \tfrac{1}{2}\,L$.
- However, in general, the firms charge different prices. For example, if $a > b$, we can see that firm 1 has a larger set of 'captive' customers and we expect it to exploit this advantage by charging a higher price. Since $a > b \Rightarrow a - b > 0$, we can see that $p^*_1 > p^*_2$ *and* $q^*_1 > q^*_2$. Firm 1's locational

advantage allows it to charge a higher price and also sell more than firm 2. That is, a firm which produces a commodity that satisfies the preferences of more consumers is in a position to exploit this advantage and charge a higher price, and at the same time sell more.

So far, it has been assumed that the locations are exogenously given. That is, the degree of product differentiation is fixed. What happens if the firms are allowed to choose both prices and locations *simultaneously*? Unfortunately, there will be no Nash equilibrium in this two-dimensional game. To show this, let us find out what firm 1's optimal location decision will be, given the price and location of its opponent. We see that $\pi_1 = \frac{1}{2} t[L + (a - b)/3]^2$ This means that $\partial\pi_1/\partial a > 0$: given any a and b, firm 1 can increase its market share and profit by moving toward firm 2 (this is called the *principle of minimum differentiation*). However, this leads to a contradiction, because when firms get too close to each other, an equilibrium will not exist.

The choice of the location is called *product positioning*. Product positioning is also a strategic decision since firms must position their products with respect to rival brands. Like capacity choice, location choice is a long-run variable (difficult to change) whereas price is a short-run variable (easy to change). Hence it is natural to think of models where firms first (simultaneously) choose where to locate their products and then (simultaneously) choose prices, given the location decisions.

The firms then choose locations in the first period, anticipating the second period price competition. There are essentially two effects that have to be taken into consideration. First, for given prices, the closer the two firms are located to each other, the greater the demands faced by each and therefore the greater the profits. This may be referred to as the *direct effect* of product positioning.

On the other hand, the assumption of given prices is incorrect. When firms are located closer to each other, their products are more similar and price competition is more intense. This is the *strategic effect* and works in the opposite direction to the direct effect. In the extreme case, when the firms are located in the same position, the Bertrand model reappears and prices are set equal to marginal cost.

We thus have two effects of opposite sign. The exact balance of these two effects is likely to depend on the value of transportation costs and on the distribution of consumers. In general we can conclude that when price competition is intense, firms will try to locate far apart to lessen the intensity of price competition.[1]

5.4 Advertising

One of the most important tools used to differentiate products is advertising. However, advertising can perform functions other than differentiation of products. In this section, we look at the different roles that advertising can play.

Economists classify goods into search goods and experience goods. A *search good* is one whose attributes can be ascertained by consumers before purchase. For example,

---

[1] d'Aspremont and others (1979) have shown that if we introduce quadratic transportation costs and consider a two-stage game where firms first decide where to locate and then choose prices, then a subgame-perfect equilibrium involves *maximum differentiation*: $a = b = 0$ and the firms locate at the end-points.

a customer can feel the texture of a trouser, see its colour and even try it on for comfort before buying it. Before selling his grapes, the vendor on the roadside sometimes allows customers to taste one or two pieces of grapes to determine whether they are sweet or sour. On the other hand, an *experience good* is one whose attributes can only be ascertained after purchase. No amount of test-driving can completely reveal the quality of a used car to the buyer. The durability of a piece of equipment is revealed only after it is bought and used for some time.

Corresponding to this distinction between types of goods, a parallel distinction can be made between two types of advertising. *Informative advertising* provides information about a product's existence, its attributes, and selling terms. It does not try to change preference structures. One would expect it to be more closely associated with search goods: since consumers can find out about the characteristics of a search good before purchase, advertising can only provide information about the product to the consumers.

Persuasive advertising aims at changing consumer preferences in favour of certain products. An advertisement may show that a certain perfume is being used by a popular actor. Such an advertisement usually says nothing about the perfume as such, nor will it provide information about the price of the product (it does provide information about the existence of the product). Its aim is to influence preferences of consumers—since their favourite actor is using the perfume, they might feel the urge to use the perfume, too.

One might argue that persuasive advertising also fulfills an information-providing function indirectly. Suppose time is divided into two periods—the present and the future. In the first period a number of products (of the experience goods type) are launched into the market. Some of these are of good quality, some are of poor quality. Consumers are unable to determine qualities before purchase, so some low quality goods also get sold. However, after purchase, consumers come to know which goods are of good quality and which are of poor quality. In the second period, they will not buy the poor quality products. Therefore, there will be no repeat purchase of poor quality products.

What role can advertising play to help buyers distinguish between poor and good quality products? Suppose that firms launch good quality products with expensive advertising campaigns. The implicit message is that such firms are sure that their products will have repeat purchases because they are of high quality, and hence they can afford to spend so much money on their advertising campaigns. Rational consumers should be able to realize this and buy these products, both today and tomorrow. Hence, advertising expenditures may serve as a *signal* of product quality.

5.4.1 The Optimal Amount of Advertising

Some industries spend more on advertising than others. One measure of advertising intensity is the *advertising-to-revenue* ratio. This ratio is generally low for an article of common consumption like salt, and high for products like shampoos and detergents.

Dorfman and Steiner have built a monopoly model that seeks to explain the differences in advertising in different industries. Let A be the advertising expenditure of a monopoly firm. A affects the position of the demand curve as a parameter: an increase in A shifts the demand curve to the right. The firm's profit is then

$$\Pi = pq(p, A) - c(q(p, A)) - A.$$

BOX 5.2. TOP ADVERTISERS IN INDIA

The top ten advertising spenders in India in 2000-1 in terms of absolute amounts spent on advertising were the following companies:

Company	Adspend (Rs crore)
1. Hindustan Lever	696.58
2. Colgate-Palmolive India	213.96
3. ITC	183.32
4. Dabur India	146.08
5. LG Electronics India	131.40
6. Nestle India	128.46
5. McDowell & Co.	118.94
8. Bajaj Auto	102.53
9. Maruti Udyog	88.20
10. Herbertsons	85.93

However, if we examine the advertising to sales ratio, then some of the leading companies were the following:

Company	Adspend/Sales Revenue (per cent)
Lakme Lever	19.34
Colgate-Palmolive India	18.18
Sara Lee-TTK	16.46
Artos Breweries	15.95
Dabur India	12.46
Emami	12.17
Marico Industries	12.12

While the total spending by Hindustan Lever Ltd. (HLL) was Rs 482 crore more than Colgate-Palmolive India Ltd. (CPIL), its nearest rival, the latter had a advertising-sales ratio of over 18 per cent while for HLL it was just 6.08 per cent. Till the late 1980s, Colgate was the dominant toothpaste in India in terms of market share. But then HLL moved aggressively to divide the market into two segments with its two brands—Close-Up, a gel paste for conveyable fresh breath (a youth need), and Mentadent (later Pepsodent), for strong gums and healthy teeth. As CPIL's market share slipped, it tried to find new strategies to counter this threat. It ultimately decided to undo the segmentation by harmonizing the two different needs. It therefore launched an advertising campaign that focused on the root cause of the problem, the germs that cause bad breath and infections too. Its advertisement drew attention to the Colgate brands available at all price levels to tackle this problem—Colgate Toothpowder, Colgate Cibaca Top, Colgate Herbal, Colgate Dental Cream, Colgate Sensitive Care, and Colgate Total. CPIL's strategy paid off and its market share rose to 51 per cent.

Source: *Advertising and Marketing*, 31 October 2001.

The monopolist tries to maximize profit by choosing the appropriate levels of p and A. The first order condition for maximizing profit with respect to p yields:

$$(p - MC)/p = 1/e,$$

where MC is marginal cost and e is the price-elasticity of demand.

The first order condition for maximizing profit with respect to A yields:

$$(p - MC)/p = A/\{(pq)k\},$$

where k is the advertising elasticity of demand: $k = (A/q)(\partial q/\partial A)$.

These two first order conditions together yield the Dorfman–Steiner condition:

$$A/pq = k/e.$$

In other words, the advertising intensity is equal to the ratio of the advertising elasticity of demand to the price-elasticity of demand. The advertising intensity or the advertising-to-sales ratio is greater (i) the greater is the advertising elasticity of demand and (ii) lower is the price-elasticity of demand.

One might argue that the full impact of advertising on demand is only realized over time. Current advertising affects not only current demand but also future demand. Current advertising contributes to a long-lived asset which may be called 'goodwill' which affects future demand.

The Dorfman–Steiner condition will then have to be modified. The monopolist will be trying to maximize the present-discounted value of cash flow instead of a single-period profit. She will then purchase advertising until the marginal cost of current advertising— 1 in this set-up—equals the present discounted value of marginal profit, over all future time, that results from a current increment to advertising.

5.4.1.1 Advertising in Oligopoly

In oligopoly situations, firms have to take into account the reactions from rival firms when they step up advertising. Consider two tobacco firms competing in a market. Each can choose to either advertise or not advertise. Their possible payoffs are:

		Firm 2	
		Not Advertise (cooperate)	Advertise (cheat)
Firm 1	Not Advertise	(30, 30)	(0, 55)
	Advertise	(55, 0)	(5, 5)

These (illustrative) figures reflect the fact that when at least one of the firms advertises, this shifts the market demand curve outwards, but there is also a large fixed cost involved in advertising. The firm that advertises gets all the customers it wants to, its rival gets nothing (a rather extreme assumption). On the other hand, if both advertise, there is no additional effect in terms of a shift in the demand curve. Since both bear the fixed costs of advertising, both make significantly lower profits.

This game illustrates a Prisoners' Dilemma situation. It is clear that for both firms cheating is the dominant strategy. Each firm advertises and earns a profit of 5. Both would have been better off if both had refrained from advertising. The dominant strategy equilibrium is not optimal from the point of view of the firms, since both firms could have earned more if they had not cheated.

The 'cheat, cheat' outcome occurs because each firm has to guard against opportunistic behaviour by the other. One cannot trust the other. If firm 1 tries to be 'nice' and not advertise, firm 2 will always find it advantageous to cheat and vice versa. However, both firms are fully aware of the payoffs involved and of the virtues of cooperation. But they do not have any way of entering into an agreement that will be respected by both parties. Can one firm take the lead and signal to the other firm its willingness to go back to a cooperative situation?

Suppose that firm 1 takes the initiative and stops advertising, hoping that firm 2 will follow suit. But till firm 2 also stops advertising, it will continue to enjoy a pay-off of 55 (rather than 30 from not advertising), while firm 1 is earning 0. Thus, firm 2 has every incentive to delay not advertising. Fear of further delays can convince firm 1 that it should restart its advertising campaign.

We know that one can get out of a Prisoners' Dilemma situation by changing the payoffs. Suppose that the Government, influenced by anti-tobacco lobbying, bans all tobacco advertising. Effectively then it will act as the policeman to supervise and enforce an implicit collusive agreement between tobacco manufacturers. Advertising will attract a penalty of 30 and the pay-off matrix becomes:

| | | Firm 2 | |
		Not Advertise (cooperate)	Advertise (cheat)
Firm 1	Not Advertise	(30, 30)	(0, 25)
	Advertise	(25, 0)	(−25, −25)

Now the dominant strategy of each firm is not to advertise.

To enrich this model, we will have to recognize that (a) firms' products are differentiated and (b) advertising as a means of product differentiation can have different types of effects in the market. We can distinguish between four possible cases:[2]

1. Advertising is *cooperative*: advertising by any firm shifts the demand curves for all varieties away from the origin, although a firm's advertising has a greater positive effect on its own demand that on demands faced by rivals.

2. Advertising is *perfectly cooperative*: advertising by any firm has an equal effect on the demand curves for all products.

3. Advertising is *neutral*: demand for the product of one firm is not affected by the advertising of any other firm.

---

[2]The reader is referred to Martin (2002) for a model incorporating these possibilities.

4. Advertising is *predatory*: a firm's advertising shifts its own demand curve away from the origin but shifts demand curves of rival firms towards the origin.

5.4.1.2 Price Competition and Advertising

Firms use both price and advertising to compete in the market. The advertising game that we presented earlier showed that advertising competition and price competition have certain similar features. In both types of games, firms can get trapped in a Prisoners' Dilemma situation. This effect is the strongest in the advertising game when (a) advertising is perfectly predatory—it does not expand the market but leads to a shift of market share in favour of the advertising firm and (*b*) the firm that advertises more gets the entire market. In this case, firms will be tempted to keep on increasing advertising until the entire profit is dissipated, a result that closely parallels the result of the Bertrand model.

However, there are also some significant differences between prices and advertisement as strategic instruments. The frequency with which advertising decisions are made is normally lower than pricing decisions. Prices can be changed almost on a day-to-day basis. But advertisement levels are determined only at infrequent intervals. Moreover, as we noted earlier, advertising has a long-term effect while price decisions mostly have short-term effects. Taking these two things into consideration, we would expect collusive agreements on advertising to be more difficult to reach and sustain than agreements on prices. Firms would anticipate that retaliation to cheating would be more difficult in the case of advertising.

We should also consider the interplay between pricing and advertising competition. Does advertising competition soften price competition or make it more intense? One can think of situations where either of the two might happen.

First let us try to visualize a situation where advertising competition will soften price competition. Think of the Hotelling model, with an element of uncertainty. Suppose that there are two firms producing two types of chocolates. Consumers have heterogeneous preferences. Some like their chocolates to be sweet while others like their chocolates to be bitter. This is an example of horizontal differentiation. However, consumers do not have any information about the relative sweetness/bitterness of the two brands of chocolates being produced, though they can observe the prices.

Since consumers cannot *a priori* distinguish between the two types of chocolates, they treat them as if they are identical. Then the only variable that determines demand is price: if the price of one brand of chocolate is lower than that of the other, then all consumers will buy this brand. Competition will force the firms to price at marginal cost and the Bertrand result is obtained.

If now the firms advertise their locations in product space, i.e. provide information about the degree of sweetness their respective brands of chocolates possess, then consumers can differentiate between the two products. As in the Hotelling model, firms can then set prices above their marginal costs by an amount that is proportional to the 'transportation cost' (i.e. the cost to consumers of buying a variety that is different from their optimal variety). In general, we can conclude that advertising product characteristics increases product differentiation and thereby softens price competition.

Even if advertisements contain no direct information about product attributes, they can help to soften price competition. Persuasive advertising creates brand loyalty that increases product differentiation and allows firms to charge different prices.

However, we can also think of situations where advertising competition intensifies price competition. Consider two stores selling a homogeneous product. Each consumer is willing to pay up to u for the product. But consumers do not have information about prices charged by both stores. Getting information about both prices is also quite costly (the stores do not quote their prices over the phone and the distance between them is substantial). Then a consumer will go to one of the stores at random, and if the price is less than or equal to u, buy the product. Knowing this, both stores will set their price at u.

Now, suppose that the stores advertise their prices and all consumers learn about the prices. Because the products are homogeneous, consumers will go to the store that quotes the lower price. The stores are then forced to lower their prices until $p = MC$. The Bertrand situation reappears.

If advertising prices intensifies price competition, why would firms advertise prices? Three explanations are possible:

1. Advertising, as we have already seen, may have the nature of a Prisoners' Dilemma game. Given that one store is charging u, the other firm has the incentive to inform consumers that it is charging a lower price, and capture all the demand. But this incentive works for both stores, and both end up with $p = MC$.

2. Consumers have positive search costs, and advertising prices is one way of reducing such costs. Advertising prices may be part of an equilibrium wherein some firms price lower and attract customers.

3. Even when prices are advertised extensively, retail prices seem to remain high and similar across retailers. One might argue then that implicit collusion keeps prices high, while advertising is used to remind consumers of the existence of a retail firm. Thus, in spite of advertising, consumers do not gain from low prices. All that they have to do is to choose a retailer and buy, and advertisements play an important role in this decision. Moreover, when profit margins are high, the marginal benefit of advertising is very high—even one additional consumer can significantly add to the profits of the firm.

6   Pricing Strategies

A firm in an imperfectly competitive market faces a downward sloping demand curve and can set its price, unlike a competitive firm that takes the market price as given. Firms with market power employ a variety of pricing strategies to try to extract more of the consumer surplus. In this chapter, we consider the pricing strategies that a firm might employ to appropriate a larger portion of the value it creates and boost its bottom line. We discuss the phenomenon of price discrimination, both at a point of time and over time, as well as tying and bundling, and auctions.

In practice, even a firm charging the same price for all units to all customers may not find it easy to determine the best price. This is because firms may not know the exact demand curves facing them; further, they have to anticipate possible responses from competitors.

Box 6.1. Maximum Price for Buyers

One way of thinking about a demand curve is to look at it as an indicator of the maximum prices that a buyer is willing to pay for various quantities of the product—the so-called 'values' created by the firm through its product for the customer. Firms must be able to evaluate correctly the value they have created for their customers (which may be quite different from the production cost). In the absence of adequate information about demand, firms often follow some rules based on past experience. This may lead to the firm passing up on profit opportunities. As an example consider Glaxo's pricing policy when it launched its ulcer medication Zantac. The conventional wisdom dictated that Glaxo price its product 10 per cent below the established incumbent Tagamet, since as the new entrant, it had to establish the quality of its product in the market. However, Glaxo's CEO realized that Zantac had fewer drug interactions and side effects than Tagamet. It, therefore, could potentially deliver greater value to its customers. This superiority was adequately communicated to the market place and Zantac was introduced at a significant price premium over Tagamet. Zantac quickly managed to gain the market leadership position.

Source: R. L. Dolan and H. Simon, 1996, 'Power Pricing', The Free Press, New York.

6.1 Price Inertia: The Kinked Demand Curve Model

In many industries, prices seem to be remarkably stable and do not change in response to even significant changes in cost conditions. What explains this inertia in prices? We use the kinked demand curve model to provide an explanation of this phenomenon.

Suppose that the ruling market price is p^*. A firm in the market then assumes the following:

1. If it raises its price above p^*, other firms in the market will not change their prices, and hence it will lose a lot of customers. Thus, for prices above p^*, its demand curve will be quite elastic.

2. On the other hand, if it lowers its price below p^*, other firms will do the same as a defensive measure. Hence it will not be able to get many more customers through price cuts. The demand curve below p^* will be rather inelastic.

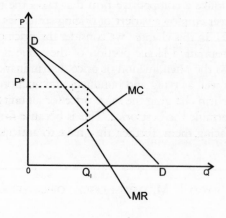

Fig. 6.1

Given a kinked demand curve, the MR curve facing the firm will have two segments, with a vertical segment in between. If the firm's MR curve is cut by the MC curve in this vertical segment, then the firm charges p^* to its customers. Moreover, even if the cost conditions change and the MC curve shifts a bit, it is possible that the same price will be charged. So this model seems to explain why observed prices remain sticky even under changing cost conditions. Obviously, a major shortcoming of this model is that it leaves unexplained how p^* was determined in the first place.

6.2 Cost-Plus Pricing

In practice, many firms seem to rely on the 'cost-plus pricing' method. Unit costs are determined and then a mark-up is employed to arrive at the price to be charged to consumers:

$$\text{Price} = (1 + m) \times \text{Unit Cost},$$

where m is the mark-up.

Mark-ups are based on factors like industry tradition, individual experiences, or rules of thumb. The mark-up reflects the return that the firm wants to gain on each unit sold.

The cost-plus method is simple and easy to apply. Since it is based on 'hard' cost data, it seems to provide a rigorous method for determining price. If firms in the industry have similar cost conditions, the cost-plus method can facilitate collusion.

However, the cost-plus method is a flawed method because it does not take account of demand conditions. In fact, the price customers are willing to pay depend on the perceived value of the product, and may have no relation to the price arrived at by the cost-plus method. Moreover, cost-plus is often based on 'full costs', i.e. fixed cost plus variable cost. The fixed cost does not affect the shape of the profit curve and should not be considered in setting the best price. This fundamental principle is ignored in cost-plus pricing.

6.3 Price Discrimination

We have been assuming that the monopolist sets $MR = MC$ and charges the same price to all customers. If the monopolist can set different prices for different customers, it can be immediately shown that this enables her to increase her profit. Consider the profit-maximizing output for the single-price monopolist in Fig. 6.2. At this output level, price p_m is greater than marginal cost. Thus, an extra unit sold can generate more revenues for the monopolist, if *only the last customer* can be charged a price slightly lower than p_m. Thus, while all other customers are charged a price of p_m, the monopolist gains by charging p' for the extra unit that is sold and making additional profit of AB. Therefore charging different prices to different customers can increase profit.

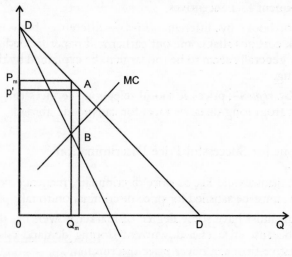

Fig. 6.2

For a single-price monopolist, this course of action is unattractive, because the lower price has to be charged to *all* customers and the consequent loss in revenue outweighs the gain from the last customer.

In the real world, different groups of buyers are often charged different prices for similar products. Sometimes such non-uniform pricing simply represents quality differences or transport costs. At other times, the same price charged to different buyers represents non-uniform pricing, e.g. if the buyers are located in different areas. The buyers who are located farther away are in effect having to pay less if the final price, including delivery charges, is the same for all buyers. To bypass such problems, we follow Stigler's (1987) definition: there is *price discrimination*, when different buyers are charged different unit prices for similar goods, and the prices are in different ratios to marginal costs.

Price discrimination seems to be ubiquitous. Some common examples of price discrimination are given below:

- Pricing of cinema hall tickets by *time of day*—usually matinee shows are priced lower than evening shows.

- Pricing of transport services by *age*—children and senior citizens typically are charged at lower rates for riding on buses or trains.

- Pricing of professional services by *income categories*—doctors often charge relatively wealthier patients more than poorer patients, sometimes even foregoing fees for the latter.

- The Government of India sets prices of motor spirit, high speed diesel, and aviation turbine fuel, which are used for 'luxury' purposes, above their respective costs, and prices of kerosene and LPG below their costs.

- Pricing of goods by *different degrees of recognition or frequency of purchase*— the neighbourhood grocer charges lower prices to nearby residents who purchase frequently and refuse to lower prices for casual customers; airlines offer frequent flier incentives.

- Pricing of books by different *editions*—differences between the prices of hardback editions that come out earlier and paperback editions that come out later generally seem to be too large to be explained by the relative costs of binding.

- Pricing by *region*—prices for local telephone services can be significantly different from long-distance rates for calls made abroad.

6.3.1 Conditions for Successful Price Discrimination

Even though all firms would like to price discriminate, many are not able to do so. Three conditions must be satisfied for price discrimination to take place successfully:

1. The firm must have some degree of market power, i.e. the ability to set prices because it faces a downward sloping demand curve. A perfectly competitive firm can never price discriminate.

2. The firm must be able to separate customers into two or more groups. Sometimes, the customers can be easily separated, e.g. they may be buyers living in different regions. or they may be distinguished by physical characteristics like age or sex. Sometimes the firm may try to induce buyers to reveal their types through their purchases, e.g. matinee shows will be attended by people who are not working full-time.

3. The firm must be able to prevent arbitrage by buyers, i.e. resale by buyers who paid the lower prices to buyers who are willing to pay higher prices.

The requirement that resale should not be possible can be satisfied for a number of reasons. See Carlton and Perloff (1994):

- Services: Most services, like doctors'services, once purchased, cannot be resold. The commodity is consumed in the act of purchase.

- Warranties: The firm can void a warranty if the object is resold. Warranties can often be used only by the original purchasers.

- Adulteration: Suppose that alcohol can be used for drinking purposes and for medicinal purposes. To prevent buyers for medicinal purposes from reselling alcohol to drinkers, the firm can adulterate the alcohol sold to the former to make it unfit for human consumption.

- Transaction cost: If consumers incur large transaction costs to resell the product, then resale is unlikely. Tariffs and transportation costs are examples of transaction costs that prevent resale at a profit. Sometimes, the firm can design a method of price discrimination that makes the transaction cost of resale prohibitively high. Suppose Pepsi places coupons in certain copies of a newspaper and these coupons can be used to get discounts from retailers. The buyers who get the coupons will have to find out buyers who did not get the coupons and bargain with them for resale. This process will generally be considered prohibitively costly in relation to the size of the discount available.

- Contractual remedies: As a part of the sale contract, the firm may prohibit the buyer from reselling the product. Companies sometimes provide low-rent housing to some of their workers. Tenants are prohibited from subletting their apartments, at the risk of being thrown out if they violate the contract.

- Vertical integration: A firm that produces more than one stage of production is said to be vertically integrated. Suppose that a steel producer sells steel parts at a higher price to car manufacturers than it sells to furniture manufacturers and these parts are easily interchangeable. There is then an incentive for furniture manufacturers to resell the parts to car producers. To prevent this, the steel manufacturer can decide to produce furniture itself, i.e. integrate forward into furniture production.

- Government intervention: The government can enact laws that prevent resale. Or it might raise the transaction costs of resale by requiring resales to be registered and hefty fees to be paid.

6.3.2 Different Degrees of Price Discrimination

The traditional classification of the different types of price discrimination is due to Pigou (1920), who distinguished between first, second, and third degree price discrimination. We will first consider these and then analyse other practices like tying and bundling that facilitate price discrimination.

6.3.2.1 First-degree or perfect price discrimination

The seller has perfect information about the demand curves of buyers and for each unit sold, charges the buyer an amount equal to the maximum willingness to pay for that unit.

Consider a case where there are five buyers, each demanding one unit of the commodity. The maximum prices they are willing to pay are given below. Let $MC = 8$.

Buyer	Maximum price buyer is willing to pay	Total market demand
A	10	1
B	9	2
C	8	3
D	7	4
E	6	5

The monopolist will go on selling as long as price > MC. Therefore, she will sell one unit each to buyers A, B, and C, charging them respectively 10, 9, and 8. In this way, the perfectly discriminating monopolist captures the *entire consumer surplus* (remember that the consumer surplus for any unit is the maximum price the buyer is willing to pay for that unit, less the price the buyer actually pays).

Next, suppose that each consumer wants one unit of a product, but consumers are willing to pay different amounts. By ranking the consumers according to their maximum willingness to pay and plotting the aggregate demands, we get a downward sloping aggregate demand curve. The firm then charges each consumer the maximum that the person is willing to pay and sells to any customer whose maximum willingness to pay exceeds or is equal to the marginal cost.

This is shown in Fig. 6.3. Assume that $MC = m$, a constant. In a perfectly competitive industry, the quantity produced would have been Q^* and each buyer would have been charged $p^* = m$. A perfectly price discriminating monopolist also produces Q^*. However, only the last (marginal) buyer is charged p^*. Everyone else is charged the price on the demand curve. The first unit is sold at the price p_1, the second at the price p_2, and so on. The demand curve facing the monopolist then becomes the *marginal revenue curve*: each extra unit is sold at the price on the demand curve. In this way, the monopolist appropriates the entire consumer surplus (equal to the area Dp^*A).

The results from the efficiency standpoint are the same for perfect competition and perfect price discrimination. Neither gives rise to any deadweight loss. However, the distributional implications are quite different since under perfect competition, consumer surplus is positive and under perfect price discrimination, consumer surplus is zero and *all the surplus is captured by the monopolist.*

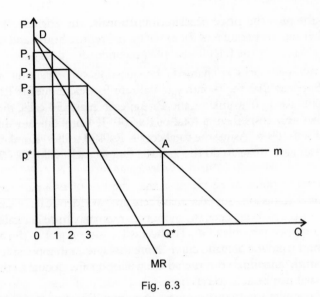

Fig. 6.3

6.3.2.2 Second-degree price discrimination

Second-degree or non-linear pricing occurs when buyers face non-linear price schedules, i.e. the price paid depends on the quantity or quality bought.

- An example is quantity discount. An individual who purchases one 500 gm pack of butter pays Rs 50 for the pack, while the individual who buys 5 packs of 100 gms pays Rs 12 per pack.

- Sometimes differences in quality, too, get reflected in a non-linear manner in prices. The price difference between a high quality and a low quality good is more than that can be explained by the difference in cost to achieve the higher quality. Proctor–Silex sells its top-of-the-line iron for $54.95, while the next-best iron is priced at $49.95. The manufacturing-cost difference between the two qualities is less than a dollar, as the top model only adds a small light to signal that the iron is ready for use.

- Software companies typically set non-linear prices for licenses, with the per head fee going down as the number of users increases.

- Health clubs may price exercise sessions in such a way that the per session charges go down as the number of sessions purchased increases.

Non-linear pricing takes many forms. A few of these are noted here:

- All-units quantity discount: If a certain quantity is exceeded, a lower price applies to all units. For example, suppose the price is Rs 4 for any quantity not exceeding 1000 units and Rs 3 per unit for all units if the quantity exceeds 1000.

- Two-part tariff: A two-part tariff consists of a fixed fee that buyers have to pay to be allowed to purchase the commodity (sometimes called the access fee) and a fixed per unit charge thereafter. Examples are membership fees for clubs plus the price of drinks and meals, the entrance fee to the zoo together with separate fees for entering the reptile house and other exhibits, monthly rentals for telephones plus payment for calls, etc.

When a two-part tariff is charged, the question of preventing resale assumes importance. Suppose that the monthly rental rate for telephones is Rs 300 and the charge per call is Re 1. If Kumkum and Pankaj each make 50 calls, then taking two telephones separately costs them a total of Rs 700. If Kumkum can subscribe to the telephone and sell calls to Asim, the total cost is Rs 400 to her. Kumkum and Pankaj can enter into an agreement to do this and the cost to each will be Rs 200 instead of Rs 350.

One interesting point to be noted is that the use of two-part tariffs facilitates perfect price discrimination. Suppose that there are two identical consumers and that the marginal cost is a fixed m. Then the monopolist can maximize her gains by charging each consumer a price per unit of m. The access fee is set equal to the corresponding consumer surplus from the demand curve. Note that if the monopolist sets a price that is different from the marginal cost, then there will be an area (equal to the deadweight loss) that she will not be able to capture.

Now suppose that the two consumers have two different demand curves. If the moonopolist knows each demand curve completely, again she can set a price to each equal to the MC and then set the access fee equal to each consumer's surplus. Thus the access fees and the prices differ from consumer to consumer (the prices will not differ when the MC is constant). In Fig. 6.4, consumer 1 is charged an access fee of CS_1 and consumer 2 is charged an access fee of CS_2. The per unit charge for each is m.

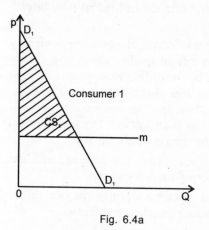

Fig. 6.4a

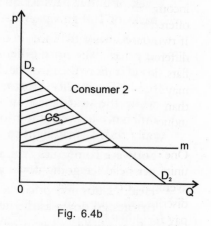

Fig. 6.4b

But if the monopolist has no way of distinguishing between different consumers, she must charge the same access fee and the same price per unit to all of them. The access fee she charges cannot exceed the minimum consumer surplus, if she is to sell to both the consumers. The firm then faces a dilemma. If she charges a low per unit price, she sells more of the product and can charge a higher access fee from each consumer. But her ability to charge a high access fee from the second consumer is constrained by the low willingness-to-pay of the first consumer. In some cases, the firm may make greater profits by concentrating on the second consumer and charging an access fee so high that the first consumer is priced out of the market and only the second consumer buys the product.

Two-part and multi-part tariffs are common in many public utilities and transportation services in India. For electricity supply, a household has to pay a lumpsum connection charge, and monthly rental and power consumption charges based on a declining block schedule. To get a telephone, one has to deposit a sum at the time of application, pay installation charges, and pay bimonthly rental and call charges.

• Two-block tariff: A price per unit is charged up to a certain quantity, and then a lower price is charged for all subsequent units. Thus a price of Rs 4 is charged for $0 < Q \leq 100$ and a price of Rs 3 for all units starting from the 101st unit.

6.3.2.3 Self-selection

Generally, the monopolist will not be able to identify the type of a particular buyer, though she may have a good idea about the distribution of buyer types. That is, the monopolist may know that 60 per cent of the buyers in the neighbourhood will be middle-income, 30 per cent low-income, and 10 per cent high-income types. But the income group to which a particular buyer belongs may be difficult to establish. The monopolist then constructs a price schedule in such a way that buyers reveal their types by choosing points on the schedule. For example, high income buyers choose flats with three bedrooms, middle income buyers choose flats with two bedrooms, and so on. It is important for the monopolist to ensure that buyers of a certain type do not find attractive a package that has been designed for a lower type. For example, suppose that all buyers are only interested in the floor space of the flats they buy and high income types want to buy flats with larger floor space. Only two types of flats are offered for sale—one with floor space of 500 sq. ft and the other type of 1000 sq. ft. If two flats of 500 sq. ft each are available side by side on the same floor, the price difference should be such that high income types are not tempted to book two smaller flats side by side rather than one larger flat. In some cases, informational constraints may be so acute that the monopolist offers a schedule where there is a *pooling*, rather than a *sorting*, of types: all buyers are offered the same deal and there is no attempt to induce the buyers to reveal their types through their purchases.

Why is non-linear pricing useful from the point of view of value appropriation? One reason is the simple fact that a buyer's willingness to pay decreases for additional units. The seller can then increase profit by using a declining price schedule so that the average price decreases for larger amounts purchased. Unlike the perfect price discrimination case, the seller is not aware of the exact amounts a buyer is willing to pay for different quantities. The choice of a point on the price schedule reveals the buyer types.

A second reason for adopting non-linear pricing is that large customers often have higher price-elasticity of demand. The large volumes make it worthwhile for large buyers to shop around and compare prices because the potential for savings is higher. They may also have procurement alternatives not available to small buyers. This higher price-elasticity makes it a better strategy to offer discounts to large buyers.

Non-linear pricing may also have strategic competitive implications. Take two-part tariffs. Suppose that I have paid the annual fee for a club. This entitles me to get certain services which I will forego if I decide to switch to a different club. Hence, the access fee constitutes a switching cost that creates exit barriers.

6.3.2.4 Third-degree price discrimination

Under third-degree price discrimination, different groups of buyers are charged different prices. Obviously, this presupposes that the different groups can somehow be distinguished. Based on observable characteristics, the firm decides on the price the buyer has to pay. Sometimes children are charged a lower ticket price for watching a movie. The ticketseller looks at the buyer to determine the age. Harvard Business School may make Casebooks available to academicians at a cheaper rate than to corporate customers. The buyer has to establish her academic credential by producing a certificate from the head of the academic institution.

Suppose that the buyers can be separated into two groups, with inverse demand curves $P_1(Q_1)$ and $P_2(Q_2)$, respectively. The monopolist's cost function is $C(Q_1 + Q_2)$. Then the monopolist tries to maximize the joint profit from the two groups of buyers:

$$\Pi = Q_1[P_1(Q_1)] + Q_2[P_2(Q_2)] - C(Q_1 + Q_2).$$

The first order conditions are

$$\partial\Pi/\partial Q_1 = \partial\Pi/\partial Q_2 = 0.$$

These yield the conditions $MR_i(Q_i) - MC(Q_1 + Q_2) = 0, i = 1, 2$. The conditions can then be written alternatively as $MR_1(Q_1) = MR_2(Q_2) = MC(Q_1 + Q_2)$. So long as any one of these equalities is violated, the monopolist is not maximizing profit. For example, if the MR from group 1 is higher than that from group 2, the monopolist can gain more by selling extra units to group 1. And if MR in any market is different from the MC of selling to that market, the monopolist can increase profit by increasing or decreasing production in that market.

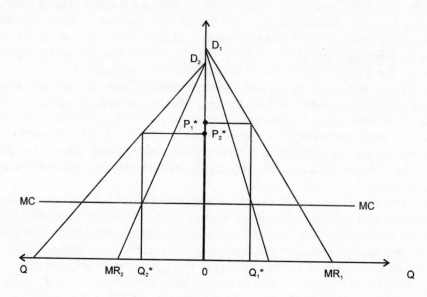

Fig. 6.5

The condition that the marginal revenues in the two markets should be equal to each other gives us one more piece of information. Remember that $MR_i = P_i(1 - 1/e_i)$, where e_i is the price-elasticity of demand in the i-th market. Then $MR_1(Q_1) = MR_2(Q_2)$ implies that $P_1/P_2 = (1 - 1/e_2)/(1 - 1/e_1) = (e_1e_2 - e_1)/(e_1e_2 - e_2)$. This shows that prices charged to the two groups of buyers are equal if the price elasticities are equal. Otherwise, $P_1 >$ or $< P_2$ according as $e_1 <$ or $> e_2$. That is, the higher price will be charged to that group of buyers which has a more inelastic demand.

The situation is graphically represented in Fig. 6.5 for linear demand curves (and hence linear MR curves). The MC curve is horizontal. The monopolist equates MC with MR in each market and produces Q_1^* and Q_2^* respectively for the two groups. Note that the higher price is set in the market with the steeper demand curve.

Example 6.1. Let $P_1 = 80 - 5Q_1$, $P_2 = 170 - 20Q_2$, and $MC = 10$. Then $MR_1 = 80 - 10Q_1$ and $MR_2 = 170 - 40Q_2$. Setting $MR_1 = MC$ and $MR_2 = MC$, we get $Q_1^* = 7$ and $Q_2^* = 4$. Then, from the inverse demand equations, $P_1^* = 45$ and $P_2^* = 90$.

6.3.3 Product Line Pricing

In many instances, we find firms selling a number of products. Sometimes the demand for the products are independent of each other, e.g. if the firm is in the business of selling drugs and cement. More often, there are demand interrelationships with respect to these products, i.e. the demand for product *A* directly affects the demand for product *B*. There are four possible types of interrelationships (see Dolan and Simon, 1996):

1. Potential traffic-building effects: A lower price for *A* attracts more buyers into the store who then buy *B*. An example is a store selling clothing for both adults and children. It can hold periodic 'sales' of the clothing for children, hoping that this will attract parents who will come to the store and then also purchase some items for themselves. The lower margin on *A* is compensated by the higher margin on *B*.

2. Product-line image: A firm can build up a reputation for producing high quality white goods items like TVs and refrigerators and then diversify into smaller household gadgets. Its brand image helps it to charge a premium price for the latter.

3. Complements: If an increase in the demand for *A* leads to an increase in the demand for *B*, they are said to be complementary products. Dolan and Simon use the example of a men's clothing store to explain how complementarity affects pricing strategy. In this store, the sale of a suit generated additional sales of shirts and ties. More specifically, the sale of a suit led on the average to the sale of 0.8 shirts and 1.2 ties. If the interdependency was not taken into account, then the best (stand alone) price to be charged for a suit was DM 350 per unit. At this price, 300 suits would be sold per day at a profit margin of DM 150 per suit, generating a total profit of DM 45,000 from the sale of suits alone. Shirts had a profit margin of DM 15 and ties of DM 10. The suit buyers would

purchase 240 shirts and 360 ties, so the total profits from the sales of suits, shirts, and ties came to about DM 45,000 + DM 240 × 15 + DM 360 × 10 = DM 52,200.

Given the price-elasticity of demand of 2.33, it was found that a price of DM 338 would lead to sales of 324 suits per day. This would mean that the profit from suit sales alone would be DM 44,712, slightly lower than DM 45,000. However, the number of shirts and ties sold now went up and added DM 7775 to profit instead of the earlier DM 7200. Overall, there was an increase in profit.

It was, therefore, worth sacrificing some profit from suits to generate additional profits from shirts and ties. Dolan and Simon make the following recommendations in this context. For complementary products, the optimal product-line price:

- is lower than the optimal isolated/stand-alone price;
- decreases with the strength of the complementary relationship (absolute magnitude of the cross-price elasticity);
- decreases with increasing margins of complementary products.

4. Substitutes: If an increase in the demand for *A* leads to a fall in the demand for *B*, they are said to be complementary products. There are two cases that need to be considered here:

   (i) The firm produces a range of products catering to diverse tastes. For example, the same model of car may be sold in different colours. Different purchasers have different colour preferences and will select the colour they like best. Suppose that the car dealer has run out of stocks of blue cars. Then buyers who want to buy blue cars can be persuaded to buy green cars only if the price is lowered to them. The prices will have to be determined depending on the relative demands for blue and green cars and the strength of these demands.

   (ii) The firm produces goods such that if the prices were the same, everyone would prefer one over the other. For example, everyone would want faster PCs rather than slower ones. So the price has to be such that the price differential would make it worthwhile for some consumers to buy the slower computers but not the others. If, suppose, the price of the slower computers is too low, even potential buyers of faster computers may be tempted to buy the slower ones. On the other hand, setting a lower price for the faster computers attracts the 'low income' types to buy these, but the firm loses profit it could have extracted from the 'high income' types. It is obvious that this is again a problem in non-linear pricing.

Dolan and Simon reach the following conclusions for substitute products:

- The optimal price for a product at the upper end of the price scale is higher than the best stand-alone price;
- The optimal price increases with the cross-price elasticity, i.e. the strength of the substitute relationship;

- The optimal price increases with the margins of the substitutes—the more profitable the substitutes are, the more costly cannibalization becomes,

- Typically (though not always), the optimal price for a product at the lower end of the price scale is lower than the best stand-alone price.

6.3.4 Durable Goods Monopolies: Price Discrimination over Time

Till now, we have been discussing the pricing of goods that are perishable through usage and that must be bought repeatedly. In contrast, durable goods do not perish even after repeated usage. Examples are 'white goods' like refrigerators that can be used for a long time. It follows that units of durable goods at different points of time tend to be substitutes. If I buy a TV this year, it is highly unlikely that I will buy a TV next year.

This raises an interesting possibility. If the monopolist seller charges the price that maximizes today's profit then a certain number of people buy the TV today. Tomorrow's demand curve then lies below today's demand curve (with an unchanged or slowly growing number of consumers). The monopolist is tempted to charge a lower price tomorrow. But if buyers can correctly anticipate this, then they will postpone their purchases today. The problem then is to work out the equilibrium time path of prices, given the expectations of the buyers about future price changes. Coase (1972) had conjectured that if the time periods are short enough and the consumers can rationally anticipate monopolist's actions, then the price might immediately drop down to the level of marginal cost and the monopolist forfeit all market power.

The monopolist has the option of either *renting* out the product or *selling* it. By renting the product to a consumer for a price p_r, the monopolist retains ownership of the product, but contracts with the consumer to let the consumer enjoy the services from the product for the period specified under the contract. The seller, on the other hand, will transfer the ownership rights to the consumer for a price p_s, say. Renting out the product avoids the Coasian problem. The monopolist who sells has an incentive to cut the price in the future, whereas such behaviour does not occur if the good is rented out. However, in certain instances, renting is not feasible. Then the monopolist must sell the product and intertemporal price discrimination can take place.

How can a durable-goods monopolist escape this predicament? The monopolist's task is to influence consumers' expectations by credibly committing to not lowering prices in the future. This can be done in a number of ways:

1. The monopolist can refuse to sell her product and only rent or lease it. However, for goods like cars, this is infeasible. Cars can be rented for short periods, but not on a regular basis, because the consumer renting the car is unlikely to be as careful in driving a rented car as he would be in driving his own car.

2. The monopolist can produce less durable goods, thereby limiting her ability to lower the price in the future.

3. The monopolist can ensure that future production is prohibitively costly, e.g. via capacity constraints that she sets herself. For example, an artist can destroy the plates used to make lithographs.

4. The monopolist can guarantee to buy back the good in the future from any consumer at the price he/she paid for it. This is sometimes not possible because consumer usage can change the nature of the good or lower its value. Alternatively, the monopolist promises consumers to give them the benefits of any future lowering of prices to any customers.

5. The monopolist can try to acquire a reputation for never lowering the prices of her goods. She can do this by sticking to her prices for a long time, even in the event of poor demand.

6.4 TYING AND BUNDLING

Tying refers to a situation where a consumer can buy one good only by purchasing another good as well. Someone who buys a polaroid camera must buy films from the same firm because other films cannot be used in a polaroid camera. Another example is when one has purchased a 'pilgrimage' package which involves paying for the hotels on the way as well as meals. Even if one chooses to eat outside, one has to pay for the meals.

Bundling is a special case of tying in which two or more commodities are sold only in fixed proportions. Shoes come with shoe laces, though one can purchase shoe laces separately, too. One buys a healthfood packet and finds that a 'free' pencil-box is included along with the packet. Another type of tying occurs through *requirements tie-in sales*, when buyers are required to purchase a minimum quantity of a second commodity, B, from the same seller, if they purchase a commodity A from him. *Exclusive dealing* is a special form of a requirements contract in which customers are required to buy all of a product or service from a firm. Exclusive dealing is not always a case of tying, since buyers may be required to purchase all of a commodity from a firm independently of the purchases of any other commodity. We first discuss some of the reasons why tying might occur. Then we examine bundling in more detail.

6.4.1 Reasons for Tie-in Sales

Tie-in sales can occur for a number of reasons that are unrelated to pricing strategy. We first discuss these briefly before considering how tie-in can be used to price-discriminate.

- *Efficiency*: In some cases, tying increases efficiency by lowering transaction costs. A radio consists of many individual components. It would be inefficient to sell these separately and then provide the buyer with a manual to help put the components together (some people like to do things themselves and might prefer to assemble the radio themselves, but for most people a completely assembled radio is better).

- *Evasion of regulations*: Suppose that there is a Rent Control Act that does not allow a landlord to charge more than Rs 2000 per month for a flat. The landlord thinks that the correct rent would be Rs 2500. The building has a garage which is otherwise unused. The landlord can then rent the flat only if the tenant agrees to rent the garage, too, for a rent of Rs 500 per month. In this way, tying helps a firm to evade regulations.

- *Quality assurance*: A firm can claim that it alone can assure the quality of certain accessories that consumers are required to buy from it. For example, Kodak claimed that it tied the development of its films to its film sales because it did not believe that independent developers could develop its films as well as it (Kodak) could.

Next we analyse how tie-in can be used as a pricing strategy. There are two main considerations here:

1. *Secret price discounts*: A firm may want to gain higher market share by cutting its price, but fears that this will invite retaliatory price-cutting by its competitors if they come to know about it. The firm can then use a tie-in to provide price discounts secretly. A bowl worth Rs 5 is provided along with each packet of cornflakes if the firm producing the cornflakes wants to give a price discount of Rs 5. A related reason may be that the firm wants to give a price discount without appearing to do so. Why? Because it thinks that the higher price on the packet signals higher quality to customers and any overt lowering of price will bring it directly into competition with a lower price, lower quality product.

2. *Price discrimination*: Tie-in sales can also be used for purposes of price discrimination, where price discrimination can be defined more broadly as a pricing strategy that enables a firm to capture a part of the consumer surplus and increase profit. We use a a simple example to show how the requirements tie-in sales can be used to price-discriminate between consumers.

Suppose that a firm has a machine that automatically stamps a person's name and other details on stick-on labels. Some people need lots of such labels, say 10,000 per year. Another type of people need only 1000 labels a year. The machine works for one year and then has to be replaced. Before the machine came on the market, labels had to be manually stamped and the cost was 10 paise per label. The price for the label paper in the competitive market is 50 paise per label paper. The first type of customer would therefore be saving Rs 1000 per year with the machine while the second type would be saving Rs 100 only.

Now suppose that the monopolist manufacturing the machine decides to give away the machine for free to a consumer provided that the latter buys all the stick-on label paper from it. It prices the paper at 60 paise—10 paise above the competitive price.

As a result, the type one consumers who accept the firm's offer effectively pay a higher price of Rs 1000 for the machine, while type 2 consumers pay Rs 100. The tie-in therefore allows the monopolist to charge buyers effectively different prices for the machine. Buyers who value the machine more pay more. The monopolist captures all the consumer surplus in this case.

The requirements tie-in sales is an extreme case of product complementarity. As we have seen earlier, when product complementarities exist, it makes sense to price low to push up sales on one item. In our example, the price of the machine was pushed down to zero.

6.4.2 Bundling

Companies selling a variety of products sometimes have to decide whether they want to sell the products separately or as a bundle. Such bundling may be either *pure* or *mixed*. Pure bundling occurs when a firm sells two or more products only in a bundle and not individually. Mixed bundling occurs when the commodities are made available both in bundles and individually. We will use a simple example to show how and under what circumstances pure bundling can add to a firm's profits.

Suppose that there is a monopoly selling shaving cream and toothpaste as a bundle. There are two types of customers, one type concerned more with presenting before the world a dazzling set of teeth, the other a clean-shaven look. Their reservation prices (i.e. the maximum amounts they are willing to pay for shaving creams and toothpastes) are given below in rupees per tube. It can be seen that there is a negative relationship between the reservation prices of the two types. Type 1 values toothpaste more and type 2 values shaving cream more. There are 100 consumers of each type. Cost of production is assumed to be zero to simplify the calculations. The firm therefore is concerned with total revenues only.

	Shaving Cream	Toothpaste	Total
Type 1	12	30	42
Type 2	13	25	38

If the firm were selling the commodities separately, and wanted to ensure that all customers bought both commodities, then it must price a tube of shaving cream at Rs 12 and a tube of toothpaste at Rs 25. Its total revenues will be Rs 7400 (Rs 12 × 200 + Rs 25 × 200).

However, suppose instead that the two commodities are always sold as a bundle. Type 1 consumers are willing to pay upto Rs 42 for a bundle and type 2 Rs 38. The firm charges Rs 38 for a bundle, thereby ensuring that both types buy the bundle. In this case, the total revenue is Rs 7600. The firm adds to its profit by selling the bundle rather than the commodities separately. However, even the bundling strategy fails to capture all of consumer surplus, which in this case happens to be Rs 4200 + Rs 3800 = Rs 8000.

Bundling will not work if the reservation prices are positively correlated, i.e. both types of consumers have similar preferences. An example is given below.

	Shaving Cream	Toothpaste	Total
Type 1	13	30	43
Type 2	12	25	37

It can be easily demonstrated that both the pure bundling strategy and the separate pricing strategy generate the same total revenue of Rs 7400.

6.5 Auctions

Auctions have been used as a method of selling goods from time immemorial. One of the earliest references to a regularly organized auction deals with the Babylonian marriage market, where brides were auctioned to Babylonian men. Since then auctions have been used to sell a variety of 'commodities', ranging from slaves to famous pictures to perishable goods like fresh fishes and cut flowers.

6.5.1 Different Types of Auctions

There are many different types of auctions, depending on the rules for submitting bids, choosing winners, determining the amount to be paid by the winner, and so on. Some of the major ways of differentiating auctions are given below.

* *Sealed bid versus open outcry bidding*: In sealed bid auctions, the potential buyers put their bids in sealed envelopes and these are opened simultaneously to determine the highest bid. The basic aim is to have an auction where bidders are not aware of rival bids when submitting their own bids. Therefore, the bids need not actually be put in sealed envelopes; however, they will be made known in front of all bidders at the same time. On the other hand, in open outcry auctions, buyers bid openly in front of each other. After anyone bids, another buyer is free to announce a higher bid and this continues till only one bidder remains.

* *English auctions versus Dutch auctions*: In an English auction, bidders announce or otherwise indicate their bids in an open manner. *Each successive bid must be higher than the previous one*, so this is an *ascending auction*. The bids are known to everyone participating in the auction; the auctioneer repeats the last bid a number of times to make sure that everyone is aware of the price that must be beaten. The process of bidding continues until only one bidder is left. The English type of auction is used when a unique object is being sold. This unique object may be a paintings by a famous painter or a particular head of cattle out of many.

In contrast, in a Dutch auction, the auctioneer starts with a high price. The price is then systematically lowered until one bidder accepts the bid, usually by pressing a buzzer. Thus a Dutch auction is a *descending auction*. Most Dutch auctions are run automatically. They use a clock-like device that ticks down every few seconds to a lower bid.

Dutch auctions are used for selling perishable goods like fishes. A variant of the Dutch auction is also used when the seller is not sure about the perceived value of a good to buyers. Some stores start with a high price for their products. If sufficient sales are not forthcoming, then the price is automatically marked down after a period. This is like a Dutch auction; the buyer weighs the benefit of waiting and getting a lower price with the risk that the product will be sold out in the intervening period. From the seller's point of view, pricing high initially and decreasing over time helps reveal the underlying valuation by customers and prevents the mistake of selling below the price that buyers are willing to pay.

- *First-price versus second-price auction*: In the first-price auction, the highest bidder pays her bid and takes the object home. In the second-price auction, the highest bidder wins, *but pays the second-highest bid*.

Thus, for example, in first-price sealed-bid auctions, each bidder submits a bid in a sealed envelope. The envelopes are opened at the same time and the highest bidder is selected. The method is generally used by governments and firms for selling items that have become redundant, old, or damaged, like old cars or computers. Sometimes the time of receiving the bids is stamped on the bids. If there is a tie between the highest bidders, the one who submitted the bid earlier is chosen.

What should be a buyer's bidding strategy in a first-price auction? Suppose that the value of the object to the buyer is V. If the buyer bids V and wins, she has to pay V and has no surplus left over. So she might want to bid less than V, say B. This is called *shading*. If the buyer wins, she now enjoys a surplus of $V - B$ rather than zero. So the buyer has an incentive to shade the bid. But there is a trade-off here: the lower is B relative to V, the higher is the potential surplus from the auction, but also the higher is the probability that somebody else will bid higher and the buyer will not be able to win.

In a second-price sealed-bid auction, *the winner pays the amount bid by the second-highest bidder*. We will have more to say about the second-price auction later.

Box 6.2. Auction design

Auctions have to be designed carefully. In 1990, New Zealand auctioned the spectrum for radio, television, and cellular phone companies using second-price auction. One company that bid NZ\$ 100,000 paid the second highest bid of NZ\$ 6. An Otago University student bid NZ\$ 1 for a television license in a small city and paid nothing as no one else bid.

Source: J. McMillan, 1994, 'Selling Spectrum Rights', *Journal of Economic Perspectives*, Vol. 8, No. 3.

- *Common-value versus private-value auctions*: In common-value auctions, the value of the object is the same for all bidders, but each bidder generally has only an imprecise estimate of it. For example, suppose companies are bidding for an oil drilling tract. If the amount of oil below ground could be precisely estimated, then every company would have exactly the same valuation of the tract. But if the amount of reserves is unknown, then each company will have its own estimation of the reserves and bid accordingly. In private-value auctions, each buyer places a different value on the object. For example, potential buyers may have different values for the same painting.

Box 6.3. Winner's curse

In a common-value auction, winning the auction may be a signal that the winner has bid too high. That is, a bidder winning the auction is likely to have paid more than it is worth. This phenomenon is known as the winner's curse.

The winner's curse is easy to illustrate in a slightly different context. Suppose that a raider bids for a target firm and wins. This is like an auction, with the management of the target firm acting as the auctioneer to choose between the bids. Let the winning bid be b. Then the value of the target firm under the present management is somewhere between 0 and b, otherwise the bid would not have been accepted. If all values between 0 and b are equally likely, then the raider expects the current value to be $b/2$. Under the raider, there will be, say, a 50 per cent increase in the worth of the company. So the value of the company under the raider is expected to be $1.5 \times b/2 = 075b$, which is less than the winning bid b. Hence the raider is going to pay for the target firm more than it is worth.

Source: Dixit and Skeath (1999).

An auction can be a very useful tool for appropriating value. This is because auctions are means for eliciting information about buyer valuations of an object and using the mechanism of competing bids to get the highest possible bid. A rather extreme example is the Vickrey-type auction, which is next described.

6.5.2 Truthful Revelations of Valuations

Suppose that an auction is being held for an object with private value, i.e. different buyers have different valuations for the object. William Vickrey showed that a second-price sealed-bid auction of this object will elicit bids reflecting true valuations on the part of buyers. In other words, the dominant bidding strategy for each buyer would be to bid the true valuation.

Suppose a particular buyer values the object at Rs V. Her bid is Rs B for the object, which may or may not be equal to V. The largest bid from among the rival buyers is Rs R.

If the buyer bids $B > V$, what happens?

 (i) If $R < V$, the buyer wins the object. Her surplus is $V - R$. She would have achieved the same result by bidding V instead of B.

 (ii) If $V < R < B$, the buyer wins the object but ends up paying R which is more than her true valuation of the object. She would have been better off bidding V and losing the bid, because then she would have made zero rather than a loss.

(iii) If $V < B < R$, the buyer loses the bid. She would have attained the same result by bidding V.

Similarly one can consider the possibilities under the condition $B < V$.

 (1) If $R < B$, the buyer wins the object and gets a surplus of $V - R$. She could have also won by bidding V.

(2) If $B < R < V$, the buyer loses the bid. She would have done better by bidding V and winning, so that her surplus would have been $V - R$.

(3) If $B > V$, the buyer cannot win the object. No harm would have been done by bidding V.

It can, therefore, be shown that truthful bidding is never worse than, and sometimes better than, bidding below or above the true valuation. Therefore, truthful bidding is the dominant strategy in the second-price sealed-bid auction.

6.5.3 The Revenue Equivalence Theorem

Since there are different possible auctions, the question arises as to which auction will fetch a higher return for the seller. We have seen that the Vickrey-type of auction elicits truthful bidding, but this is achieved at a price. The seller is giving the bidder a profit margin (the difference between the highest and the second-highest bid) to counter her temptation to shade down the bid.

Which auction is better will depend on bidders' attitudes towards risk and their beliefs about the object being auctioned off. Consider the simple situation where all bidders are risk-neutral and their (private) values are independent of each other. If these two conditions hold, then we get a powerful result, called the revenue equivalence theorem: sellers can expect to get the same average revenue from any of the four primary types of auctions—English, Dutch, first, and second-price sealed bid. There is therefore nothing to choose between these four types of auctions from the revenue point of view.

This result of course only means that if these auctions were held numerous times, then on average the same revenue would be generated. It does not mean that all the auctions will yield the same revenue every time for the same object sold. Further, the cost of holding the different types of auctions may be different, which can explain why one auction is used rather than other. Moreover, if either of the conditions of the theorem were violated, then there would be additional considerations for choosing one auction rather than another.

6.6 QUALITY AND PRICING

As the lemons problem highlights, there are a number of goods whose quality cannot be fully ascertained at the time of purchase. It would therefore seem that firms have an incentive to cheat, i.e. produce shoddy goods. What can deter cheating is the reputation effect: customers buy repeatedly and once they buy a shoddy product from somebody and find out that they have been cheated, they refuse to buy from this firm in the future. Thus a firm will have to weigh the short term gain from cheating against the long term loss of foregone profits.

Suppose there are many identical firms. Any firm can produce a good quality product at a unit cost of c_g and a bad quality product at a unit cost of c_b, $c_g > c_b$. The shoddy commodity can be detected, but only after purchase. The rate of discount is r.

In any period, if a firm does not cheat, then it makes $p - c_g$ per period from the buyer and the present discounted value of its profit is $\{(p - c_g)(1 + r)\}/r$. If it cheats, it gets $p - c_b$ this period and zero thereafter.

Therefore, the firm will not cheat if

$$\{(p - c_g)(1 + r)\}/r > p - c_b,$$

i.e.

$$p > c_g + r(c_g - c_b).$$

This shows that for cheating to be unprofitable, the good quality commodity must be sold at a price that exceeds marginal cost. The price–marginal cost differential will be higher the higher r is.

How does a new entrant in this market persuade customers that it is producing the high quality good? It can offer at a price below c_g. But if the price is above c_b, then any of the firms can produce the shoddy good and still make a profit. On the other hand, if it prices below c_b, then it sends out a credible signal of its quality. Only a firm that is producing the high quality good can afford to do this, because it can make up the first period loss through the repeat purchase that the first period's low price engenders; a producer of a shoddy good cannot do this, because first-time buyers will get to know about its quality and no repeat purchases will occur in the future. This explains why the introductory price of a product is sometimes so low as to involve losses.

7 Collusion, Entry Barriers, and Entry Strategies

In a perfectly competitive market, it is difficult for firms to keep on making supernormal profits in the long run. Firms then would like to operate in environments where competitive conditions do not obtain. We have seen that there are four main planks of perfect competition:

- Product homogeneity
- Large numbers
- Free entry
- Perfect information.

Firms can adopt the following strategies to make sure that these conditions do not hold together at the same time:

- Product differentiation
- Creation of entry barriers
- Collusion
- Use of proprietary information.

Creation of entry barriers and collusion are techniques to avoid the problems of large numbers and free entry. In a sense, entry condition is more critical, because entry barriers also solve the large numbers problem. Moreover, Chamberlin's model of monopolistic competition (see Chapter 5) demonstrates that even with product differentiation, firms may not be able to earn supernormal profits if entry into the industry is easy.

7.1 COLLUSION

In this section, we analyse collusive behaviour. In any market, monopoly profits represent the highest aggregate profits attainable. If more than one firm compete in the market, their output will be higher than the monopoly output and their joint profit is bound to fall short of the monopoly profit. It then makes sense for the firms to enter into a collusive agreement and restrict aggregate output to the monopoly level to earn monopoly profits, which can then be shared appropriately amongst themselves. In other words, if there are only a few similar firms in an industry and if these firms agree not to undercut one another, they can all make a profit by restricting output and charging a high price for their product. This profit is in the nature of a monopoly rent.

One would then expect to come across many instances of collusion (cooperative behaviour). However, collusion is usually very difficult to sustain. The classic case of collusion is the OPEC oil price *cartel*. This cartel had some initial successes in raising oil prices by enforcing production quotas amongst member countries, but since has been relatively ineffective in a number of years. We will examine two main reasons for cartel failures. One relates to the inherent problem of cheating faced by cartel members. The second relates to the fact that in many countries explicit cartels are illegal and cartels must find ways of coordinating actions of members that do not invite legal sanctions.

7.1.1 Explicit collusion

A cartel is an organization of producers who jointly decide how much to produce and how the total production is to be allocated between the different firms in the cartel. The joint decision means that the cartel can act like a multiplant monopoly, if it comprises all the firms in the industry, and if it can prevent non-members from entering the industry.

Let us consider the decision-making by a cartel. For simplicity, assume that the cartel faces a linear (inverse) demand curve $P = a - Q$, where $Q = \Sigma q_i$ is the aggregate output of the cartel. Let there be n firms in the cartel, each with the cost function $C_i = F + cq_i^2, F, c > 0$. Then the marginal cost function for each firm is $MC_i = 2cq_i$, and the average cost function is $AC_i = F/q_i + cq_i$.

The cartel's problem is to maximize the profit from the operation of all its members. It therefore must choose q_i, i = 1, 2, ... n, to maximize

$$\Pi(q_1, q_2,.... q_n) = PQ - \Sigma\{F + c(q_i^2)\}.$$

The first order conditions are $\partial\Pi/\partial q_i = 0$, i = 1, 2, ... n. In terms of marginal revenues and costs, $MR = MC_i$, i = 1, 2, ... n. These yield us the n conditions $a - 2\Sigma q_i - 2cq_i = 0$ for all i.

Since all firms have identical cost functions, we know that all firms will produce the same amount of output. That is, $q_i = q$ for all i. This tells us that $a - 2nq - 2cq = 0$, i.e.

$$q^* = a/2[n + c].$$

From the inverse demand curve,

$$P^* = a(n + 2c)/2(n + c).$$

It can be seen that an increase in n or c reduces each firm's output in equilibrium. What happens to total output $Q^* = nq^*$? $Q^* = na/2[n + c] = a/2[1 + c/n]$. As n increases, c/n falls and hence Q^* increases. This means that P^* falls, because the demand curve is downward sloping. The profit of each member of the cartel will fall as n increases: $\Pi_i = P^*q^* - (F + cq^{*2}) = a^2/4(n + c) - F$, which falls as n increases. Thus *members of a cartel have an interest in keeping the number of firms in the cartel as small as possible and discouraging new members from joining the cartel.*

Members of a cartel would also like to see few or no members outside the cartel, because the cartel may not have any control over the activities of non-cartel members.

Box 7.1. CARTEL IN THE CEMENT INDUSTRY

In 1998, the Monopolies and Restrictive Trade Practices Commission (MRTPC) launched a probe into consumer allegations that cement majors, including ACC, JK Cements, Indian Rayon, and Sri Cements, had forged a cartel to fix artificially high prices for their products.

Consumers had alleged that the 'artificially high prices' were not consistent with the cost of production incurred by the cement companies and the exercise was tantamount to unfair trade practice, said officials with the Commission.

The Cement Manufacturers Association of India, which is the representative body for the cement industry and includes all the top manufacturers in the country as its members, was asked to furnish relevant information to the Commission on the issue.

The charges of cartel-forging in the cement industry came close on the heels of an earlier allegation by the Directorate General (Investigation & Registration) (DGIR) that cartels were being set up in the domestic banking industry to fix steeper lending rates. The DGIR is an investigative arm under the Department of Company Affairs.

Source: *Business Standard*, 20 February 1998.

In practice, cartels find it difficult to survive because members of the cartel have an incentive to cheat. Consider the following game. Two firms have the options of either colluding and setting a high price for their products, or competing by charging low prices. Their payoffs are summarized in the pay-off matrix below.

		Firm 2	
		Charge High price (cooperate)	Charge Low price (cheat)
Firm 1	Charge High price	(2,2)	(0,3)
	Charge Low price	(3,0)	(1.5,1.5)

It is clear that for both firms cheating is the dominant strategy and the proposed cartel breaks down. Each firm charges a low price and earns a profit of 1.5. Both would have been better off if both had charged the high price. Note that this is a happy situation from the point of view of the customers who end up paying a lower price. The market outcome (3) is also higher than the monopoly outcome (2).

The 'cheat, cheat' outcome occurs because each firm has to guard against opportunistic behaviour by the other. One cannot trust the other. If firm 1 tries to be 'nice' and charge a high price, firm 2 will always find it advantageous to cheat and vice versa. However, both firms are fully aware of the payoffs involved and of the virtues of cooperation. But they do not have any way of entering into an agreement that will be respected by both parties.

Several steps are involved in the successful operation of a cartel:
• Reaching an agreement between members

- Implementation of the agreement which involves:
  - (i) Detecting cheating
  - (ii) Punishing cheating

7.1.1.1 Reaching an agreement

Reaching an agreement may not be a simple matter. In brief, the more heterogeneous the industry and larger the number of firms, the more difficult is it to reach an agreement. If, for example, cost conditions differ and product differentiation exists to a significant degree, different firms will have different expectations and it will not be easy to reach an agreement. Also, the *larger the number of items* on which firms have to agree, the greater the hurdles in the way of concluding successful negotiations. If conditions in the market are *uncertain*, agreements must be reached more often, thereby increasing negotiation costs. In addition, divergence of opinion about future conditions becomes likely.

7.1.1.2 Detection of Cheating

How can firms detect cheating? Other than spying on rival firms and trying to keep track of market trends, firms can also adopt innovative monitoring systems. For example, a firm can adopt a meet-the-competition (MCC) clause to detect cheating and make the threat of future punishment more credible. Under a MCC, the company promises to match any rival bids. If another firm sells the same item at a lower price, a customer has the incentive to report it to the firm to get the benefit of the lower price. This is a policing mechanism, in which the customers do the policing in their own interest.
What determines the period after which cheating is detected?

- Market concentration:
  - (a) the fewer the rivals, the less expensive it is to monitor prices and market shares
  - (b) with a smaller number of larger firms, cheating leads to larger effects on prices and market shares and such effects are easier to sort out from random shocks.
- Lumpiness of orders:
  Cheating becomes more attractive when orders are lumpy and infrequent, because the retaliation lag is then longer.
- Information about sales transactions:
  - (a) Are sales transactions public? (e.g. petrol pumps post their prices openly)
  - (b) Do transactions involve dimensions other than price?
  - (c) Are product attributes customized to buyers?
- Number of buyers:
  When each firm sells to many small buyers, cheating is more difficult. Buyers can report price cuts to receive even more favourable conditions.

- Volatility of demand conditions:

Firms can sometimes observe only their own prices and market shares. Then more volatile demand conditions will make it more difficult to detect cheating.

7.1.1.3 Punishment

Cheating can be deterred through the threat of future punishment in repeated interactions. 'Punishment' in this context does not necessarily refer to physical punishment; the possibility of punishment arises from the fact of repeated interactions between players. Cheating by one player leads to the breakdown of the agreement as soon as it is detected and the other players can then adopt a non-cooperative stance. In an earlier chapter, we have seen how Iran may be dissuaded from cheating by the prospect of non-cooperation from Iraq. When a firm adopts a *MCC* clause, it reacts to cheating by another firm by lowering its own price. If the rival firm reduces the price further, the firm comes back with a lower price and so on. This prospect of a price war can deter cheating.

Formally, suppose that the market demand in each period is given by $D(p)$. The cost functions are $C_1 = cQ_1$, where $Q = D(p)$.

First consider a non-cooperative equilibrium in the market, e.g. a Cournot equilibrium.[1] All n firms in the market charge the industry price p_0 and share the industry profit Π_0 equally, so that each earns Π_0/n.

If a cartel is formed, the industry profit is the monopoly profit Π_m and each firm earns Π_m/n. The monopoly price p_m will be greater than p_0 and $\Pi_m > \Pi_0$.

If a firm decides to cheat, then it lowers its price to p_0 and captures the entire industry profit Π_0; other firms earn zero profit. Assume that $\Pi_0 > \Pi_m/n$, so that there is an incentive to cheat. The cheating is detected next period after which all firms switch to non-cooperation and start charging p_0; hence each firm earns Π_0/n.

If a firm cheats, then the present discounted value of its profit stream will be

$$\Pi_0 + \Pi_0/\{n(1 + i)\} + \Pi_0/n\{(1 + i)\}^2 + \Pi_0/n\{(1 + i)\}^3 + \ldots$$
$$= \Pi_0 + \Pi_0/\{n(1 + i)\}\{(1+i)/i\} = \Pi_0 + \Pi_0/ni.$$

If the firm does not cheat, it expects to earn

$$\Pi_m/n + \Pi_m/\{n(1 + i)\} + \Pi_m/n\{(1 + i)\}^2 + \Pi_m/n\{(1 + i)\}^3 + \ldots$$
$$= \Pi_m/n + [\Pi_m/\{n(1 + i)\}]\{(1+i)/i\}$$
$$= \Pi_m/n + \Pi_m/ni.$$

Therefore, the firm is better off not cheating if

$$\Pi_m/n + \Pi_m/ni > \Pi_0 + \Pi_0/ni.$$

This condition can be written as

$$[(\Pi_m - \Pi_0)/n]/[\Pi_0 - \Pi_m/n] > i.$$

In this expression, the left-hand side is the benefit–cost ratio associated with not cheating. The numerator captures the net future benefit to cooperation compared with

[1]The discussion here follows that in Besanko, Dranove, and Shanley (1996), chapter 10.

non-cooperation while the denominator captures the extra profit in the current period from cheating.

This expression also shows that if i is sufficiently close to zero, then there will be no incentive to cheat. That is, if the future is not discounted too heavily, then the prospect of future loss from breakdown of cooperation will always outweigh any temporary gains to cheating.

The expression can also be used to see how the market structure affects the incentive to cheat. Let $X = [(\Pi_m - \Pi_0)/n]/[\Pi_0 - \Pi_m/n] = (\Pi_m - \Pi_0)/(n\Pi_0 - \Pi_m)$. It can be seen that as n increases, i.e. as the number of firms goes up, X becomes smaller and it becomes more likely that the incentive to cheat will be stronger. Why is this so?

In a more concentrated market,

(a) a typical firm has a larger market share, and therefore captures a larger fraction of overall benefit when price is moved from p_0 to p_m;

(b) a cheater who already has a larger market share can hope to steal a smaller amount of business by charging p_0;

(c) with a smaller number of firms, it is easier to move to a cooperative equilibrium.

Suppose that in the benefit–cost expression, the period is one week for detection of cheating. On the other hand, if the period had been one month, then the condition would become $X > 4i$, which would be more difficult to satisfy.

7.1.1.4 Sustaining Collusion

We can mention two other considerations that are important for sustaining collusion.
Firm asymmetries:

(a) Suppose firms face different cost conditions. Then each firm would like to charge a different price and there will be no natural 'focal point' which can be agreed on.

(b) Larger firms have less incentives to deviate from a cooperative pricing formula.

   (i) Larger firms gain more from collusive pricing because they capture a larger part of the additional industry profit.

   (ii) Larger firms have less incentives to punish smaller players. An example will clarify this. Suppose that a large firm is charging Rs 100 and selling $Q = 100$. Its marginal cost is a constant Rs 50. A small firm undercuts this price by 5 per cent and takes away z per cent of volume from the larger firm. If the larger firm matches the price cut, then its profit is $(95 - 50)100 = $ Rs 4500. If it does not match the price cut, then its profit is $(100 - 50)100(1 - z) = 5000(1 - z)$. Hence the larger firm will not match the price cut if $5000(1 - z) > 4500$, i.e. if $z < 0.1$.

Multimarket contact:
If firms compete in different markets, then a cooperative solution in one market is easier to attain through a threat of retaliation in other markets.

7.1.1.5 Punishment strategies

What characteristics should punishments have to deter cheating? How severe should they be? To take the second question first, one might think that the punishment should be as severe as possible. Then the mere threat of punishment will deter cheating and the punishment need never be employed at all. The problem with this line of thinking is that it ignores the possibility of mistakes. The detection process may fail, indicating cheating where there is none. If punishment is too big, such mistakes will be very costly.

An answer to the first question emerged from a computer tournament conducted by Robert Axelrod of University of Michigan, Ann Arbor. In 1979, Axelrod invited a number of professional game theorists to submit strategies to be used in a series of Prisoners' Dilemma games. He asked for strategies to be encoded as computer programmes that could respond to a 'C' (cooperate) or 'D' (defect, cheat) of another player, taking into account the remembered history of previous interactions with that same player. A programme should always reply with a 'C' or 'D', but its choice could be random. Fifteen strategies were entered, and each was made to play with every other programme and itself 200 times. The overall goal was to amass as many points as possible.

The programme that won is called TIT FOR TAT and its strategy is Cooperate on move 1; thereafter, do whatever the other player did the previous move.

A second and larger tournament was held later. Altogether 62 entries were received, including TIT FOR TAT. The result of the tournament surprised everybody: TIT FOR TAT was again the winner.

Axelrod argues that TIT FOR TAT embodies four principles that should be evident in any effective strategy: clarity, niceness, provocability, and forgiveness. TIT FOR TAT is as clear and simple as it is possible to get. It is nice in that it never initiates cheating. It is provocable, that is, it never lets cheating go unpunished. On the other hand, it is forgiving, because it does not hold a grudge and is willing to restore cooperation.

Dixit and Nalebuff, however, argue in their book *'Thinking Strategically'* that TIT FOR TAT is a flawed strategy because it does not allow for the possibility of misperceptions. The moment the player with the TIT FOR TAT strategy thinks that the opponent has cheated, he immediately switches to cheating, making no allowance for the possibility of a mistake being made. Moreover, it lacks a way of saying 'enough is enough', i.e. it never initiates a move towards cooperation. One should be more forgiving when a defection seems to be a mistake rather than the rule. Even if the defection was intentional, after a long-enough period of punishment it may be time to call it quits and try re-establishing cooperation.

7.1.2 Tacit Co-operation

Explicit collusion is often illegal. Nine OECD countries now have criminal penalties for cartels that fix prices, restrict output, submit collusive tenders, or divide or share markets. The US has obtained criminal convictions and record fines in several global cartel cases. An example is the global graphite electrode cartel. Nearly every major worldwide producer of graphite electrodes has pled guilty to participating in a 5-year cartel (1992-7) that fixed prices until the execution of search warrants in the US and 'dawn raids' in Europe. The cartel had raised the price of graphite electrodes in the US from $0.95 per lb in 1992 to $1.56 per lb in 1997—an increase of over 60 per cent. To date in the US, six corporations have been sentenced to pay fines in excess of US$ 300 million.

Firms that cannot explicitly collude can try to achieve co-operation tacitly, by employing *facilitating practices*. As an example, consider how third party intervention can help to convert the Prisoners' Dilemma type of situation to one where cooperation is a possible equilibrium. *Self-imposed penalties* can help to change payoffs and create monitoring of the cooperative outcome. Salop has suggested that the most favoured nation (MFN) clauses offered to customers fulfill this function.

A MFN (also sometimes called a most-favoured-customer clause—MFC) is a contractual arrangement between a firm and its customer, that guarantees the customer that he will always get the best price offered by the firm to anyone. Consider a retroactive MFN: the firm agrees to match all future price reductions to customers. Every time it lowers its price, it must refund the price difference to customers who had bought from it earlier. This reduces its pay-off by 1.25. The pay-off matrix now becomes:

		Firm 2	
		High Price	Low Price
Firm 1	High Price	(2, 2)	(0, 1.75)
	Low Price	(1.75, 0)	(0.25, 0.25)

Cheating is no longer the dominant strategy for the players. The existence of a MFC changes the incentive to lower the price. The firm can withstand pressure from its customers to lower the price by pointing out that any price reduction has to be passed on to all customers.

One problem with giving MFCs is that it might create a disadvantage *vis-à-vis* competitors. If firm 1 has adopted a policy of MFC and firm 2 has not, then firm 2 can poach on firm 1's customers, knowing full well that firm 1 cannot retaliate by charging lower prices. If, on the other hand, both firms adopt the MFC policy, as we assumed they did in our example, then this becomes a viable way of keeping prices high in the market.

There are other means of coordinating pricing decisions among rival firms. One is price leadership. One firm in the market is looked upon as a price leader, perhaps because of its dominant position in the market. The price this firm sets is followed by the other firms in the industry.

Sometimes, a number of prices are possible and it is important to tacitly select one of these. This is done through the mechanism of focal point pricing. 'In a variety of problems, when behavior must be coordinated tacitly—that is, without direct communication—there is a tendency for choices to converge on some such focal point.'[2]

---

[2]Scherer and Ross (1990), p. 266.

Focal points are prominent points. Examples are shoes being priced at Rs 99.97. The focal point chosen might owe its prominence to analogy, symmetry, custom, etc.

7.2 ENTRY BARRIERS AND LIMIT PRICING

If the fewness of firms leads to high profits, should we not expect more and more firms to enter the industry, so that the industry supply curve gets flatter and flatter until it becomes horizontal and no monopoly profits can be made? The reason why there are only a few firms in some markets is that new firms are prevented from entering these markets by what economists call entry barriers. An entry barrier is a cost that has to be borne by new entrants, but not by firms that are already established in the market.

The pioneering analysis of how entry barriers arise and how they can be exploited by the established firms to prevent new entry is provided by Bain (1956). He argues that the structural (i.e. the inherent demand and supply) characteristics of some industries are such that the incumbent firms have some advantages over the new entrants. This allows the incumbents to forestall new entry by producing a limit output at a limit price, which allows the incumbents to make a profit but does not leave enough demand for a new firm to make a profitable entry. Thus, new entry is prevented by a combination of two things: entry barriers or the advantages incumbents have over new entrants and the limit price which exploits these advantages to pre-empt the market.

Bain identifies three types of entry barriers: absolute cost advantage, product differentiation advantage, and economies of scale. We discuss below how they arise and how they can be exploited to forestall new entry. In each case, the advantage enjoyed by the incumbent allows it to set a *limit price* and produce a *limit quantity*, which makes entry unprofitable.

7.2.1 Absolute Cost Advantage

An established firm has an absolute cost advantage over a potential entrant if it can produce the same volume of output at a lower cost of production. Even if the two firms are equally efficient, the former may have an absolute cost advantage over the latter for two reasons.

First, the established firm may have a preferential access to inputs like materials and components, skilled manpower, patented knowledge, or financial capital, etc. The suppliers may incur a higher transaction cost by dealing with new entrants owing to the uncertainties involved in dealing with new parties or the need to terminate old contracts and finalize new contracts, and the higher transaction cost may get reflected in higher input prices for new entrants. This effect tends to be particularly strong when established firms have to make market transactions possible by finalizing long term contracts with suppliers.

Second, in many industries the unit cost of production falls as cumulative output rises. This relationship can be shown in the form of a downward sloping 'experience curve', where the cost of production is measured on the vertical axis and cumulative output on the horizontal axis. Underlying the experience curve is the so-called 'learning effect': by producing the same product repeatedly, a firm becomes more and more adept at producing it, so that its unit cost of producing the product falls over time.

An obvious reason for this is labour learning. But even organizations as a whole learn with experience, because by doing the same thing again and again, they devise better and better methods of doing it. Clearly, other things being equal, an established firm by virtue of its accumulated production experiences and greater learning would have an absolute cost advantage over a firm that is new to the field. This advantage tends to be especially strong in technologically complex industries.

Figure 7.1 shows how the incumbent firm can exploit its absolute cost advantage to set a limit price and forestall new entry. We assume that there is one incumbent, I, and one potential entrant, E. I's unit cost of production is constant and is represented by $C_i C_i$. E's unit cost of production is higher than I's, also constant and represented by $C_e C_e$ which lies parallelly above $C_i C_i$. Both I and E, face the same industry demand curve DD. But I, being the first in the market, sets a limit price $P_1(C_e)$ and produces a limit output Q_1, leaving a residual demand D^*D for E. At P_1, E makes a profit, because $P_1 > C_i$. But E finds it unprofitable to enter the market: faced with a demand curve D^*D and a cost curve $C_e C_e$, at no volume of output can it get a price that covers its cost of production.

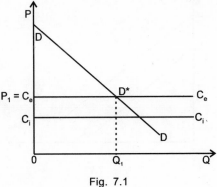

Fig. 7.1

7.2.2 Product Differentiation Advantage

The product differentiation advantage of the incumbent firm envisaged by Bain flows not from any functional superiority but the structural characteristics of the market. Customers who have been used to buying a particular product from an existing supplier incur a switching cost if they buy the same product from a new supplier.

The switching cost may arise from learning. For example, a customer who is used to a computer manufactured by one firm may have to do a certain amount of delearning and relearning if he switches to very similar computer manufactured by another firm. The switching cost may also arise from acquired taste. Consumers often get attached to the products they use (e.g. cigarettes, perfumes) and switching to another product, though very similar, has a psychological cost attached to it.

The customer may also incur some additional transaction costs by switching to a new product. These result from the uncertainties involved in trying out a new product, the cost of terminating an old contract and entering into a new contract (e.g. closing an old bank account and opening a new one), the losses due to an unsuccessful trial, the embarrassment involved in going back to the old supplier if the new supplier fails to deliver, etc. To compensate for these switching costs, the consumer will pay a lower price for an identical product produced by a new and untried supplier. This explains why 'me-too' products command a lower price than the pioneering brand.

Figure 7.2 shows how the incumbent firm can exploit its product differentiation advantage to set a limit price and forestall new entry. We assume that there is one incumbent, I, and one potential entrant, E. Since I has a product differentiation advantage, E has to offer a fixed discount on I's price to sell the same quantity as I. Thus D_eD_e, the industry demand curve facing E, lies parallely below D_ID_I, the industry demand curve facing I, and the vertical distance between the two is the discount E has to offer on I's price. Both I and E have the same unit cost of production which is constant and is represented by CC. I produces a limit quantity Q_l, the quantity at which the price available to E is equal to his cost of production, at a limit price P_l, leaving a residual demand of $D^*_eD_e$ for E. Since $P_l>C$, I makes a profit. But E finds it unprofitable to enter the market. Faced with a demand curve $D^*D^*_e$ for E, and cost curve CC, at no volume of output can it get a price that covers its cost of production.

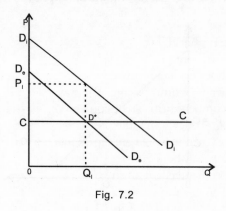

Fig. 7.2

7.2.3 Economies of Scale

In industries where economies of scale are substantial and the minimum economic scale (*MES*) is high in relation to the competitive output, the established firm may be able to forestall new entry by producing in excess of the *MES*. The established firm makes a profit, but the potential entrant faces a dilemma. If it enters on a large scale, it adds so substantially to the industry output that the industry price falls to an unprofitable level.

Figure 7.3 shows how the established firm can take advantage of economies of scale to prevent new entry. As before, there is one incumbent, I, and one potential entrant, E. DD is the industry demand curve faced by both I and E. They also have the same average cost curve, AC. AC falls until the output is Q_m, which is the *MES*, and becomes constant thereafter. The competitive output, Q_c, and the competitive price, P_c, of the industry are at N, where DD meets AC and $P_c = AC$. I sets his output at $Q_I = Q_c - Q_m$ and sets his price at P_I which is the market clearing price for Q_I. This leaves a residual demand P_ID_e for E which lies parallelly below DD, so that the horizontal distance between the two is Q_I. Since $MN = Q_c - Q_m + Q_I$, P_ID_e touches AC at M.

At all other points $P_I D_e$ lies below AC. I therefore cannot find any output at which entry is profitable.

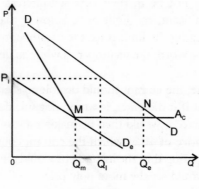

Fig. 7.3

7.2.4 The Limit Pricing Model

Even if an incumbent does not enjoy any cost advantages over an entrant, it can still try to deter entry by means of limit pricing. We now use limit pricing to refer to the practice whereby an incumbent firm can discourage entry *by charging a low price before entry occurs*. If the entrant believes that the post-entry price would be as low or lower than the pre-entry price, then it would anticipate making losses and hence not enter.

A numerical example can be used to show how limit pricing works. Consider a market with an inverse demand curve given by $P = 80 - Q$ in each period. The market lasts for two periods. The incumbent has a constant marginal cost of 20 and there is a fixed cost of 300. If there is no danger of entry, the incumbent would set $20 = 80 - 2Q$. It would produce $Q = 30$ and charge $P = 80 - 30 = 50$. Its profit would be 600 in each period.

Now suppose that there is another firm E which has the same cost function and which is considering entering the market in the second period. When it observes a price of 50, it believes that the incumbent would not be an aggressive competitor and would accommodate entry. If Cournot competition is likely to prevail post-entry, then each firm would produce 20, price would be 40, and E's profit would be $(40 - 20)20 - 300 = 100$. The incumbent's total profit over the two years would be $600 + 100 = 700$.

The incumbent instead can charge a lower price in the first year. It would be making lower profit in the first year, but if it can deter entry, then it can do better in the second year. Thus, for example, it can set a price of 30 in the first year. The entrant then reasons that price can at best be 30 after entry. Total market demand would be 50 and if this is divided up equally, the entrant's profit would be $(30 - 20)25 - 300 = -50$. Firm E then would not enter. The incumbent makes a profit of $(30 - 20)50 - 300 = 200$ in the first year, since it serves the entire market. In the second period, it earns the monopoly profit of 600, and therefore a total of 800.

The limit pricing model provides a good starting point for analysing how established firms deter new entry, but requires both the incumbent and the potential entrant to act in a manner which may not be in their best self-interest. Unless the incumbency advantages are very significant, the limit price is lower than the profit maximizing price. Therefore, by charging the limit price the incumbent incurs a cost. If this cost is very high, it may not be worth the incumbent's while to deter entry by charging the limit price.

In the above example, the entrant should be able to see through the incumbent's ploy and understand that if it did enter, it would not suit the incumbent to continue charging a price of 30, since it would then be making a loss. It would be rational for it to charge the higher price of 40 at which the entrant could make a profit. Firm E would then enter. Anticipating this, the incumbent would see no point in charging less in the first period and would set the monopoly price.

Therefore, the incumbent may not even be able to deter new entry by charging the limit price. The potential entrant is deterred by the limit price only if he believes that the incumbent will maintain his pre-entry output even after he enters the market (this is the so-called Sylos postulate, named after Sylos Labini, an Italian economist). He, therefore, believes that his entry will raise the industry output and depress the industry price to a level where it is no longer profitable for him to enter. But this by no means is the only outcome possible. Since the fall in price hurts the incumbent also, the incumbent may find it more profitable to keep the price high by reducing his own output and accommodating the new entrant. If the potential entrant believes that this is how the incumbent will respond to his entry, he will enter the market, regardless of the pre-entry price or output of the incumbent. In that event, the incumbent cannot deter new entry by charging the limit price.

This argument can be rephrased in more familiar game-theoretic terms. Consider the following game in normal form. Firm 1 is a monopoly and firm 2 is a potential entrant. If firm 2 does enter the market, firm 1 has the option of 'fighting' (e.g. by flooding the market and hence lowering prices) or 'sharing' the market. The hypothetical payoffs are shown below (the second number in each pair gives the entrant's payoff):

		Firm 2	
		Not Enter	Enter
Firm 1	Fight	(100, 0)	(30, –50)
	Share	(100, 0)	(40, 60)

At first sight, it seems that there are two Nash equilibria in this game—(Not Enter, Fight), (Enter, Share). If firm 1 'fights', it is best for firm 2 to not enter. If firm 2 does not enter, firm 1 is indifferent between fighting and sharing, so we can say that 'fight' is the best strategy for firm 1. Similarly for the other pair of strategies.

However, let us assume that firm 2 gets to move first, i.e. it gets to decide whether to enter or not. Then firm 1 decides whether to fight or share. This sequence of moves can be represented in an extensive form game by means of a game tree:

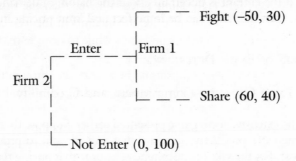

We know that the way to analyse this game is to go to the end and work backward. Suppose firm 2 has already made a choice and firm 1 is sitting on one branch of the game tree. If firm 2 has chosen to stay away, firm 1 will earn 100. But if firm 2 has entered, then the sensible ('rational') thing for firm 1 to do is to 'share' and the payoffs are (60, 40). Firm 2 will, therefore, enter and earn 60.

Firm 1 can of course threaten to fight if firm 2 enters. If this threat is taken seriously, it will be better for firm 2 not to enter, since firm 2 will get –50 if it enters and 0 if it does not. However, firm 2 realizes that this threat is an empty threat given that firm 1 is a rational player: if it does enter, given the payoffs, firm 1 will find it optimal to share in the event of entry (and get 40 instead of 30). Knowing this, firm 2 will enter and earn 60. The subgame-perfect equilibrium is one in which entry is accommodated. *In other words, the threat to fight does not give us a subgame-perfect equilibrium.*

7.2.4.1 Rescuing limit pricing

How can we rescue the concept of limit pricing as a barrier to entry? In general, the entrant must be uncertain about some characteristic of the incumbent firm or the market demand if limit pricing is to work. This is because the incumbent uses limit pricing to influence the entrant's perception of the post-entry price. If there is no uncertainty, the entrant should be able to calculate the incumbent's pay-off in all post-entry scenarios and correctly forecast the post-entry price.

Various types of uncertainty can exist. One is uncertainty about the incumbent's objectives. Is the incumbent completely rational and therefore its actions predictable based on payoffs only? Or is it swayed by some irrational factors like a desire to monopolize the market even at the expense of some profit?

Another uncertainty may exist with respect to the cost of the incumbent. The entrant would know only with some probability that the incumbent is a low-cost producer and hence a tough competitor. A high-cost incumbent would then try to signal that it is a low-cost type by charging a low price. A low-cost incumbent would have to charge a price that is sufficiently low to distinguish itself from a high-cost type. But if it does this, then the entrant would be able to infer the incumbent's true marginal cost from its price. Limit pricing by the high-cost type will not deter entry and, therefore, its best strategy would be to charge the monopoly price in the first period and allow entry in the second period. If limit pricing is to work, the entrant should not be able to perfectly infer the incumbent's cost from the limit price. Saloner has showed that if the entrant is uncertain about the nature of demand as well as the incumbent's cost, then inference can be imperfect and limit pricing may work.

7.3 OTHER MODES OF ENTRY DETERRENCE

7.3.1 Building Extra Capacity: Commitment and Credibility

Let us return to the extensive form game presented earlier. Suppose that the incumbent can purchase some extra productive capacity that will allow it to produce more at a lower marginal cost. For the sake of concreteness, assume that buying the extra capacity adds 10 to the fixed cost of the firm and lowers variable cost by 20 if extra output is produced (this also includes the effect of a fall in the price). The payoffs are now given in the figure below.

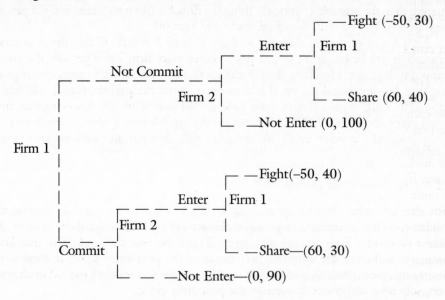

Building the extra capacity dramatically changes the complexion of the game. If firm 1 commits by purchasing the extra capacity, it becomes rational for firm 1 to fight rather than share, and this makes its threat to fight *credible*. Recognizing this, firm 2 will decide not to enter, and firm 1 will earn a monopoly profit of 90. On the other hand, in the absence of any commitment, firm 1 will accommodate entry and earn 40. Therefore, by backward induction, firm 1 should invest in the excess capacity and earn a monopoly profit of 90. Note that firm 1 does not need to actually use the excess capacity. The presence of the excess capacity represents a *commitment* to fight on the part of firm 1, because by incurring the expenditure on the excess capacity, the incumbent has denied itself the (rational) option of sharing the market.

7.3.2 Plant Proliferation as a Deterrent to Entry

To understand how new entry can be deterred by pre-empting geographical markets, we consider a simple arithmetic example. We assume that at a given ex-factory price P there is a total demand for 100 units of a homogeneous product from 100 consumers, each consuming 1 unit. These consumers are distributed equally over the geographical space which can be represented by the circumference of a circle (see Fig. 7.4). All consumers pay the ex-factory price P, but have to incur an additional cost to transport the product from the factory to the point of consumption. This cost increases with the distance over which the product is to be transported. Each consumer, therefore, prefers to buy his product from the plant nearest to him. To enter this market, a producer has to sink the fixed costs of setting up a plant. At price P, a plant cannot break even until it reaches an output of 20 units (or 20 per cent of the market). Beyond this point, the higher the output, the higher are the profits.

The first mover into this market could earn a monopoly profit in the short run by meeting the entire market demand of 100 units from one plant, located at say point A. But in that event, the prospect of earning high profits would attract other firms into the market. In long run equilibrium, there would be four more firms located at points Q, R, S and T, so that each of the five segments AQ, QR, RS, ST, and TA represent 20 per cent of the circumference. Each of the 5 plants would then meet 20 per cent of the market demand and earn a normal profit.

The first mover could, however, deter entry by pre-empting the market. He could do so by sinking the fixed costs of setting up two more plants at points B and C, so that each of the three plants meets $33\frac{1}{3}$ per cent of the total demand. In this situation, the best that a new entrant could do is to establish a plant midway between any two of the existing plants. But in that event, he could expect to get only $16\frac{2}{3}$ per cent of the market for his plant, compared to the break-even level of 20 per cent. Since the first mover has already made a commitment by sinking the fixed costs of his three plants, he cannot be expected to close any of these down, even if they cannot recover the full costs after new entry. On the other hand, the potential entrant, for whom all costs are avoidable, is deterred by the prospect of making losses. The first mover continues to make a profit because each of his plants produces $33\frac{1}{3}$ per cent of market demand, compared to the break-even level of 20 per cent. However, because of the pre-commitment made by him, his profit is lower than the short term monopoly profit that could be earned by meeting the entire market demand from one plant.

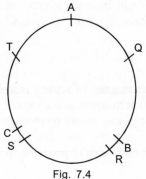

Fig. 7.4

7.3.3 Product Proliferation as a Deterrent to Entry

We can understand how product proliferation can act as an entry deterrent by using exactly the same analysis as above, with three minor modifications to the underlying assumptions. First, we assume that all consumers in the market want the same basic product, but vary in terms of the detailed product characteristics demanded by them. Consumers are distributed equally along the product characteristics space (rather than geographical space) which can be described by the circumference of a circle. Second, although all consumers are prepared to pay the same basic price for the product, they incur a psychological cost (rather than a transportation cost) if they have to use a product whose characteristics differ from those of their most preferred product. Therefore, of the products available to each consumer, she chooses the one that is nearest to her most preferred product in terms of its characteristics. Third, the seller has to incur some sunk costs to position a product at a particular location in the characteristics space (rather than to set up a new plant at a particular location) and a product cannot be re-positioned costlessly. Given these assumptions, we can use exactly the same analysis as before to see how the first seller can pre-empt the market by so locating his products in the characteristics space as to leave insufficient room for other sellers to enter.

7.3.4 Reputation as a Deterrent to Entry

In the strategic entry deterrence model, entry is deterred not by low prices but by the threat of a price war, should entry take place. In the models described above, the threat is made credible by making a commitment. But since commitment is expensive, a cheaper alternative may well be not to make a commitment but build a reputation for fighting a price war. If the potential entrant does not know for sure if the incumbent is committed or not, he may mistake an uncommitted opponent who fights for a committed opponent. In this situation, an uncommitted incumbent may be able to deter entry by misleading the potential entrant and earn high profits by fighting a price war during the initial phase of the game. However, the less convinced the potential entrant is of the incumbent's commitment, the more repeatedly will he confront the incumbent and the more inclined will the latter be to accommodate and share. It has been shown that as the entrant's assessment of the probability of meeting a committed incumbent falls, the number of last games in which the uncommitted incumbent has to share increases, but very slowly. In other words, even a small probability of facing a committed incumbent can make a lot of reputation building activity profitable.

7.3.5 Predatory Pricing

Predatory pricing refers to the practice of setting prices to drive out firms that have already entered the market. If often involves the idea of setting price below cost, with the expectation that the resulting loss would be recouped once competitors have been driven out of the market.

There are three major sets of models of predatory pricing and we examine these in turn.

7.3.5.1 Long purse models

According to these models, the primary means of forcing rivals to exit consists of waging a price war that inflicts losses on the rival until its resources are exhausted. For this to happen, the predator must have a 'deep pocket' or a 'long purse', i.e. more resources than its rival. In Telser's model, for example, the rival's ability to raise equity and debt financing is limited and the potential predator is aware of this limitation. However, in such models, there is often no convincing explanation for the asymmetry in the financial conditions faced by the incumbent and the rival.

7.3.5.2 Predation for reputation

Does predatory pricing in one market create a reputation that deters entry in another? Suppose there are a finite number of markets. For concreteness, suppose that the incumbent operates in 12 markets and faces the threat of entry in each in different months. Should it lower prices in January to deter entry in successive months?

In December, it would make no sense to keep prices low, since there is no further entry to deter. The entrant in the twelfth month will realize this and enter. But then the incumbent can entirely disregard the twelfth market and consider the eleventh market as the last market to consider. Similar considerations dictate that prices should not be slashed in November. Reasoning in this manner, we reach the striking conclusion that predatory pricing would be ineffective and never take place if the incumbent is rational.

It can be shown that if there are an infinite number of periods, then there can be one equilibrium where predation takes place. However, the assumption of an infinite number of periods is rather unsatisfactory. Another way of rescuing predatory pricing would be to plant a small doubt in the rivals' minds about the rationality of the predator. That is, there is a small possibility that the predator would engage in predation even if the payoffs are lower. In this situation, the incumbent will fight to generate a reputation for toughness.

7.3.5.3 Signalling predation

If the rival entertains some doubts about the incumbent's cost condition, then the conclusion might change. Suppose that the incumbent can be a low-cost or a high-cost type. If the incumbent is low-cost, then it is a 'tough' competitor and the rival will make losses and have to exit. Then the incumbent has an incentive to signal that it is in fact a low-cost type.

7.3.6 Strategic Groups and Mobility Barriers

Caves and Porter provide an interesting extension of the entry deterrence model to explain how the extant firms in an industry earn a profit not only by preventing new firms from entering the industry but also by competing amongst themselves.

Standard models of entry deterrence assume that entry into an industry can be deterred by all incumbents making a pre-emptive and irrevocable investment along one key dimension like capacity, product proliferation, etc. In effect, they act in unison to put up a common entry barrier against all potential entrants. This may be a reasonable approximation to reality in some industries. But in some others, although the industry is well defined, in that all firms produce a very similar product, heterogeneities in demand and technology make several types of entry-deterring investments possible. Since firms are differently endowed and cannot hope to beat the median firm along all dimensions, different firms adopt different strategic postures by concentrating on different types of entry deterring investments. For example, in the pharmaceutical industry, some firms concentrate on producing new molecules by investing in R&D, some on creating a brand equity for their over-the-counter (OTC) products by investing in promotional activities, and some on enlisting professional support by investing in medical representation.

This has three implications. First, although different firms in an industry adopt different strategic postures, some of them resemble one another quite closely. For example, in the pharmaceutical industry, we may have several firms concentrating on new drugs and several others on OTC products. Thus, they form subgroups within an industry, or what Caves and Porter call strategic groups. Firms within each strategic group recognize their interdependence more closely than those outside. Second, each strategic group erects its own special variety of entry barriers, or what Caves and Porter call mobility barriers. Since these mobility barriers vary from one strategic group to another, they deter not only firms outside the industry, but also firms from other strategic groups within the industry. Third, these mobility barriers are erected jointly by all firms in a strategic group for their common benefit. Each firm's decision to invest in these depends on its assessment of its own share in the increase in group profits resulting therefrom. In an uncoordinated oligopoly, this may lead to an over-provision of mobility barriers in some strategic groups because of excessive rivalry between the firms, and an under-provision in others because of free riding. Consequently, firms belonging to strategic groups with high mobility barriers earn a higher profit than those belonging to groups with low mobility barriers, although they are all in the same industry.

7.4 Entry Strategies: Four Modes of Entry[3]

Just as incumbents would try to deter entry by setting up entry barriers, new firms would try to surmount these barriers. In general, one can distinguish between four generic modes of entry: (i) 'build', i.e. set up a new firm in the industry, (ii) 'buy', i.e. purchase an existing firm (through mergers, amalgamations, or 'friendly' takeovers), (iii) 'acquire control' via hostile takeovers, and (iv) enter via the 'joint-venture' (JV) route.[4,5]

[3] This section follows Anindya Sen, 'Entry Strategies: A Survey', *Economic and Political Weekly*, M-99 to M-106, 29 November–5 December 1997.

[4] We are abstracting from licensing possibilities because we assume that the entrant is directly involved in production decisions.

[5] In clubbing 'friendly takeovers' along with mergers and acquisitions, we are relying on Morck, Shleifer and Vishny's (1988) analysis of the characteristics of hostile and friendly takeovers. According to them, hostile takeovers are 'disciplinary takeovers, the purpose of which seems to be to correct the non-value-maximizing (NVM) practices of managers of target firms'. On the

(Contd on the next page)

If all these possibilities are taken into account, then the game tree must be expanded in the following manner. In this game tree, the entrant has to take two decisions—whether to enter the market or not and the mode of entry. (A third choice relates to the scale of entry, which will be discussed later.)

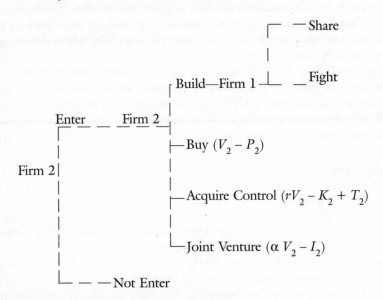

The payoffs to firm 2 are discussed below:

- 'Buy' decision: Here the pay-off to firm 2 is V_2, the discounted stream of profits, less the price P_2 that is paid for acquiring the existing firm.

- 'Acquire control': The firm has to pay K_2 to some of the existing shareholders to buy their shares and gain a controlling interest in the firm. The takeover process is also likely to involve substantial transaction costs that are denoted by T_2. The term r denotes the share of profits the firm 2 will get on the basis of the shares held by it.

- 'Joint venture': α represents the share of firm 2 in the payoffs from the joint venture while I_2 denotes the investment made by it. It is likely to be less than the fixed costs of new entry under the 'build' decision, since the partner firm will bear a part of the costs of setup.

---

other hand, 'the second class of takeovers can be loosely called synergistic, since the motivating force behind them is the possibility of benefits from *combining* the businesses of the two firms'. The authors admit that the distinction is not clear-cut. Some diversification-related takeovers undoubtedly run into resistance from managers of the targeted firms, who are unhappy either with expected changes in operations or with the compensation they receive for giving up control. Similarly, some takeovers whose aim is to change the target's operating strategy proceed with the consent of the target's managers. However, the main point is that in one case the target firms' operations are merged with the acquiring firms, while in the other case the entities retain their individual identities.

The entrant's decision to enter, therefore, involves two types of comparisons. First, the resources used to enter a market have alternative uses and the opportunity cost in an alternative use *outside* the industry must be calculated. This opportunity cost may be, for example, the foregone interest from buying risk-free government bonds, or the expected stream of revenues in another market (e.g. a MNC deciding between investing in India vs. China). Secondly, the best mode of entry and the associated stream of returns in a particular entry mode have to be determined and this return then compared with the opportunity cost of entry.

One important factor determining the returns from various modes of entry will be existing government policies. For example, in India, when there was a ceiling on equity-holding in Indian firms by MNCs, joint-venture was a preferred route of entry for many MNCs. However, after the abolition of the ceiling, the 'build' or 'buy' modes seem to have become attractive options.

7.4.1 Some General Issues

7.4.1.1 Post-entry Profits

The level of V is likely to be affected by the existence, extent, and nature of commitment on the part of the incumbent firm. However, economists have often assumed that commitment by existing firms do not affect the payoffs to the entrants directly, but only through the enhanced competitiveness of incumbents.[6]

How can commitment by the incumbent affect the entrant's pay-off directly? As an example, note that when the incumbent decides to 'commit' by way of building up excess capacity, this makes the threat to 'fight' more credible and diminishes the entrant's incentive to enter via the 'build' route. But it also reduces the entrant's incentive to enter via the other modes, because if the entrant comes in by these modes, in the post-entry situation it may be left with excess capacity on its hands (assuming that the incumbent is a monopoly in the pre-entry situation and the entrant must purchase it or enter into a JV with it); post-entry profit would definitely be lower when compared with the no-commitment case and this will have a negative effect on the entrant's incentive to enter. On the other hand, if the incumbent has invested in (say) cost-reducing R&D, this might make it a more attractive target for takeover or acquisition.

7.4.1.2 Uncertainty

In case the entrant decides to enter via the 'buy' or 'JV' route, a period of bargaining will follow. There will be inherent uncertainty about the outcome of this bargaining process. In case the entrant wants to stage a takeover, it will usually have to overcome resistance from the existing managers. In any of these decisions, the 'expected' stream of future payoffs will be the relevant criteria, because (a) the outcome of the negotiating process or the takeover attempt is uncertain and (b) the payoffs will accrue over an uncertain future.

---

[6]See Shapiro (1989), p. 384. He writes, '... the strategic aspect of the investment K in this model is not that it alters firms 2's incentives or opportunities, but rather that investment by firm 1 alters the firm's own incentives at a later date'.

As an example of (a), consider Eicher's proposed tie-up with Volkswagen (VW) to produce cars for the Indian market. The proposed venture was called off *two years* after Eicher signed a memorandum of understanding with VW to conduct a feasibility study as a prelude to launching VW's passenger car in the country.

Secondly, the static one-shot depiction of the game conceals the fact that there will be a process of learning and revisions of payoffs in this stage of the game. For example, suppose the entrant starts out with very little knowledge of the market, which seems initially to rule out the 'build' option. It considers the other options with some prior beliefs about relative bargaining strengths and possible gains. But as it begins to negotiate with the incumbent, it might face unforeseen difficulties (e.g. the incumbent might overestimate the entrant's eagerness to acquire or enter into a JV and quote too high a price or too high a share for itself). These force the entrant to revise its estimates of the relative gains from the different outcomes, and it might even think that the risk of entering a market on its own is worth taking.

Again, the Eicher case is worth considering. In the two years that passed after the signing of the initial Memorandum of Understanding ((MoU), the passenger car market in India witnessed radical changes. There were more players in the market, and demand conditions were slack, so that the proposed joint venture looked much less attractive to VW.

7.4.1.3 Sunk Costs

The decisions of the incumbent and the entrant firm will then have to be taken in the light of all such possibilities. The interesting thing about the 'buy' or 'JV' options is that the entrant might be able to avoid some of the sunk costs of entry. For example, if it decides to buy, then to the extent the assets possessed by the incumbent are not 'specific' to the firm, the entrant's cost will not be sunk.

On the other hand, these two decisions involve substantial transaction costs in the bargaining process and in the process of drawing up contracts. Such transaction costs can form a large part of the sunk costs the entrant must bear. Interestingly, the incumbent will also have to bear part of these costs and hence the entrant and the incumbent are on a more similar footing in this respect. Moreover, to the extent that the incumbent has been in the market for some time and has assets that have become partly obsolete economically, the entrant's sunk costs via the routes of 'buy' or 'acquire control' will be higher. The process of takeover also involves substantial transaction costs.

7.4.1.4 Bargaining Powers

In the 'buy', 'acquire control', and 'JV' decisions, the bargaining power of the firms come into play. One way of improving one's bargaining position is to increase the value of the 'threat point', i.e. the value of the next best non-cooperative outcome. Getting a bid from a third party is one way of doing this. As an example, the analysis by Brandenburger and Nalebuff (1995) can be cited. They show how, faced with a hostile takeover attempt, a firm can get a new offer from a new, friendly source, thereby pushing up the price of takeover. Similarly, the entrant may simultaneously start joint venture talks with different incumbents to get a stronger bargaining position *vis-à-vis* any one of them.

7.4.1.5 Multimarket Entry

Potential entrants may be existing firms in related markets, which may be regional markets of a homogeneous good or different product markets that are related technically or by goodwill. One then must analyse the feedbacks from the entry market to the home market and vice versa. In order to deter entry an incumbent firm may, for example, shift the battleground from his own market to that of the entrant.

7.4.1.6 Product Differentiation

Firms rarely produce identical products. In general, firms produce differentiated, substitutable brands, so that entry is likely to lead to a direct confrontation only on a subset of the incumbent's existing brands. For example, Indian Airlines faces competition from private airlines only on a subset of the routes its operates. In some cases, the entrant may not even directly compete with the incumbent. When Nirma entered the cheaper segment of the detergent powder market, it did not pose any direct threat to the established producers who were concentrating more on the higher end of the market.

The nonhomogeneity factor links up with the question of multi-market operations. To get a flavour of the issues involved, let us consider Judd's 1985 model. Suppose an incumbent firm has two products that are substitutes, call them cornflakes and oatmeal. Entry in the market for cornflakes can drive down the price of cornflakes. Consumers then have a tendency towards switching to cornflakes, so that the incumbent is forced to lower the scale of its operation in the market for oatmeals and concentrate on cornflakes.

We now turn to the various modes of entry in turn and consider them in some detail.

7.4.2 The 'Buy' Decision

In the bargaining process relating to the 'buy' decision, the willingness of the incumbent firm to sell is critical for the success of the outcome. The decision to sell may not reflect the local market conditions at all. If the incumbent is a subsidiary of a MNC, its decision may reflect a global strategy of the parent body.

Hall has suggested a framework of three equations for analysing the 'buy' decision. If we let $V_j(X_i)$ be the increment in firm j's value that results from the purchase of firm i's assets (X_i), then Hall assumes that firm j purchases firm i if

(a) $V_j(X_i) - P_i > V_j(X_k) - P_k$ for all possible firms k, and

(b) $V_j(X_i) - P_i > 0$, with

(c) $P_i = V(X_i)$,

where P_i is the price of firm i. The logic underlying equations (a) and (b) is that if firm j purchases firm i, the increment in firm j's value from this particular purchase must be both greater than the increment in value from any other purchase and greater than zero. Equation (c) states that the price of firm i depends only on its own assets.

This framework has been criticized on a couple of grounds. First, j acquires i when it is profitable for j to do so but only when it is not more profitable for some other firm k to acquire i. Further, the potential acquisition price might depend on j's characteristics. Pakes has suggested an alternative model:

(a') $V_j(X_i) = max_k V_k(X_i)$

(b') $V_j(X_i) > P_i > V_r(X_i)$

with

(c') $V_r(X_i) = max_{(k \neq j)} V_k(X_i)$,

where max refers to the operation of taking the maximum. Equation (a') states that if j purchases i, the value of i to j must be at least as the value of i to any other potential buyer. Equations (b') and (c') state that the price paid for i will lie between the two highest valuations of i.

The question of course is what will determine the Vs and how the entrant can change the V term to its own advantage. V is not certain—it depends critically on perceived market conditions. In a concentrated industry, a firm that offers a serious *de novo* entry threat has bargaining leverage that can be used to secure advantageous terms for a buy-out of an existing firm. An established firm's pre-takeover market value should reflect the probability that direct entry may occur, which would have negative consequences for profitability and hence for the firm's pre-takeover value. *The entrant then will have an interest in taking actions that credibly commit it to new entry in case the bargaining falls through.*

Acquisition is more likely to be the preferred mode of entry in industries that are natural oligopolies with only a few firms since direct entry into such industries is disadvantaged by large sunk costs and a large negative impact of another competitor on industry profits.

In India, recent sales of businesses have a lot to do with the history of licenses and controls. In an era when licenses protected local businesses from domestic as well as foreign competition, firms had the incentive to set up businesses irrespective of the nature of such businesses and their relations with the parent firms. When liberalization began, many firms found themselves saddled with unrelated, unprofitable entities and tried to downsize through divestiture. The small size of many firms in the pre-liberalization era, again a result of government policies, also prevented these firms from reaping economies of scale and aggravated the situation. Moreover, some acquisitions have been the direct result of policies adopted by the parent MNC worldwide. For example, in 1994, the American foods conglomerate H. J. Heinz & Co. bought pharmaceutical major Glaxo's foods business for Rs 210 crore, after which Glaxo decided to exit from foods business worldwide and put up its Indian foods division for sale.

7.4.3 Joint Ventures

A JV refers to the creation of a new business entity by partner firms, in which partners have shares in both ownership and control. A JV is fundamentally different from the other modes of entry because the return to each firm depends on the extent of cooperation elicited from the other firm in the venture. Kay distinguishes between 'wholehearted cooperation' and 'holding back' in a JV and points out that a Prisoners' Dilemma type situation emerges in JVs: both partners have an incentive to hold back, even though each understands that wholehearted cooperation will enlarge the total pie. The problem then is to devise a contract that will lead to wholehearted cooperation, and Kay's argument is that 'relational contracts' rather than legal contracts are needed for this.

The benefits of joint ventures come from the 'synergy' effects, including more efficient use of complementary assets, the avoidance of wasteful duplication of effort, and risk sharing. These benefits must be weighed against the potential costs, including the administrative and transaction costs of establishing and maintaining cooperative relationships and the potential erosion of competitive position by helping one's rivals. According to Porter, 'alliances are frequently transitional devices', primarily because they involve too many costs in strategic and organizational terms, including the problems of coordination and the creation of potential competitors. Other writers point out that there are situations in which JVs might confer significant benefits on the partners.

One must remember that a JV combines several features at once:

- A JV is a form of *ex ante* cooperation. Before the project is undertaken, a JV agreement typically spells out the members' commitments and responsibilities for financial and other contributions to the project.

- A JV is a mechanism for mutual monitoring. A JV agreement may set up a structure that increases its members' abilities to monitor one another's actions.

- A JV gives partners stakes in the outcome. Partners have financial stakes as well as share in the risks.

- A JV has a particular status with the government.

The payoffs from a JV can be viewed as the outcome of a bargaining process (game), where the division of the pie is made on the basis of the relative 'bargaining strengths' of the partners. In the simplest scenario, the outcome is efficient, i.e. the partners maximize the *size* of the pie, and then it is divided up according to the bargaining strengths of the partners. The bargaining strengths depend on (a) the alternatives available to the players, i.e. what they will get if they walk away from the bargaining table and (*b*) the criticality of the resources the respective players contribute. A partner gains bargaining power to the extent the resources contributed by it cannot be replaced/duplicated by the other partners.

From (b) it follows that the size of the pie might be dependent on the proper use of the critical resources. Thus bargaining powers determine the extent of managerial control over the JV exercised by the respective partners and ultimately the performance of the firm. If the more inefficient partner has greater bargaining power in the beginning and more say in the running of the enterprise, this can affect the firm's performance adversely.

A case in point is the tussle between Suzuki and the Government of India over the control of Maruti Udyog Ltd. After the retirement of the former Managing Director (MD), Mr Bhargava, the Government of India (GOI) put its own nominee as the MD, overruling objections from Suzuki. In the Maruti venture, the Government of India (GOI) now seems to be the partner with the greater bargaining power. It remains to be seen whether it will also run the company efficiently.

In terms of our model, partners in a JV may have other options of entry. Each partner agrees to set up a JV only after evaluating the costs and benefits of alternative modes of entry. Sometimes, however, local laws may not permit a MNC to enter a country via the routes of setting up wholly-owned subsidiaries or taking over existing firms.

In a JV, the 'hold-up' problems may become especially acute. The transaction costs of negotiating and enforcing contracts make it prohibitively costly to write long-term contracts which specify all obligations under all contingencies. Since contracts cannot be complete, agents will try to behave opportunistically when unanticipated events arise. In such situations, there must be institutions to settle disputes. Such institutions may be external (e.g. the legal system) or internal ('governance structures'). The relative efficiency of the different types of institutions may determine which one shall be adopted in any particular context.

In a broader sense, asset specificity refers to the assets, whether tangible or intangible, that a partner in a JV commits to the venture and those that represent sunk costs if the need for withdrawal from the JV arises. These contributions may also be a form of hostage exchange—where each party is contributing assets that will have value only if the partnership is conducted successfully.

If the hold-up problem is perceived to be acute, there will be a greater reluctance to enter into joint ventures. Also, as these problems come to the fore in a JV, there will be a tendency for a partner to buy out the other and the JV converted to a single-ownership firm.

The first step for a local partner in a JV with a MNC is to assess the reason why the international firm wants to enter a JV. It is important to know where the proposed JV fits into the international firm's global strategic vision. If the local partner realizes that the MNC is only interested in using it as an instrument for initial entry, it can still enter into the venture if (a) it is confident of being able to maintain market power at a later stage, (b) it will have to commit small amounts of specific capital to the venture, and (c) its perceived gain from the JV, either from the learning process or from the entry into a new market, is expected to be high.

7.4.4 Hostile Takeovers

Economists have generally viewed hostile takeovers as the market's instrument for disciplining errant managers. The argument goes something like this: the inefficient functioning of the firm is reflected in poor share prices since poor dividends are declared. A raider will then buy out the low price shares, gain control over the firm and replace the existing team of managers by a more efficient team. As the performance of the firm improves, so does its share price, and the raider can then make a profit by selling off the shares acquired earlier at the new, higher price.

This argument of course assumes that the existing managers will react passively to the threat of a takeover. Incumbent managers have been known to fight takeover bids tooth and nail if such bids jeopardized their position. A host of weapons with rather fanciful names like greenmail, poison pills, etc. are available to managers.

In addition, Grossman and Hart pointed out an inherent free-rider problem in the takeover process. Suppose that after takeover, the value per share will rise to v given that the firm will be managed more efficiently. The raider will be prepared to pay a price $p < v$ for the takeover. In fact, given that costs per share of successfully concluding the takeover process is k, the raider can only pay $p \leq v - k$. However, (a) if each shareholder is 'small', so that no one's action individually determines the success of the takeover process, and (b) the shareholders correctly expect the share price to rise to v after the takeover is over, then no shareholder will want to sell shares at price p. The takeover attempt will fail. The raider will lose out and so will the shareholders who refused to sell, because they will be saddled with the existing inefficient management.

Takeovers can still take place if there is a divergence between the valuation of the raider and current shareholders (say, v_s) so that $v - k > v_s$. But this is a matter of chance. Grossman and Hart argue that the existing shareholders should recognize the free-rider problem and voluntarily undertake a commitment that will overcome the problem by driving a wedge between v and the value that the free-riding shareholders place on their shares. This can be done by incorporating provisions that allow a successful raider to reduce the value of the post-raid company by a certain amount, which the raider is permitted to pay to himself. There are different ways of doing this. 'For example, the raider can be allowed to pay himself a large salary or issue a number of shares to himself.' The raider might also be allowed to sell the target firm's assets or outputs at an artificially low price to another firm owned by the raider. The end-result in each case is the same: the value to shareholders of not tendering their shares to the raider and of becoming minority shareholders in the raider-run firm is reduced. If, in this way, v_s is made sufficiently small relative to v, then takeovers can take place.

7.4.5 Scale of Entry

Once the entry decision has been taken and the mode of entry decided, the entrant still has to choose the scale of entry. The alternatives are to enter in a small way (the 'puppy dog' ploy) or to enter as a substantial competitor. Gelman and Salop (1983) showed that a firm may succeed in entry by committing itself (if possible) to remaining small and thereby evoking a less aggressive response on the part of its rival. Adopting such a strategy of judo economics involves investing in only limited capacity so that the entrant's scale of entry is restricted and therefore its potential market share is also restricted. It might then be in the incumbent's interest to accommodate entry and not to fight. Such strategy often involves 'toe-hold' entry and might also occur because the entrant simply does not have the requisite network or knowledge about the new market. In dealing with toehold entry, the incumbent must gauge the entrant's future intentions. If the entrant is serving a niche market which fits in with its current line of business, then there is less chance that it will have plans to expand substantially in the future. If it is serving a generic market, then its intentions should be suspect.

Malueg and Schwartz (1991) point out that growing markets are especially vulnerable to toehold entry. To deter all toehold entry, the incumbent would have to install a prohibitively costly level of capital ahead of market expansion.

A related point is that advances in technology often facilitate entry into particular segments of the market. Clemons (1997) points out that large incumbent firms often charge uniform prices to all customers, thereby implicitly cross-subsidizing one set of customers from the profitable transactions with other customers. The latter are particularly vulnerable to entry, since by definition the price charged to them is substantially higher than the cost of serving them. New advances in technology, particularly Information Technology (IT), reduce economies of scale and enable firms working on a small scale to be cost competitive with large firms and attack the profitable segments. The incumbent firms are often unable to use the same technologies because of commitment to old technologies.

The role of infrastructures and institutions can be quite crucial. In India, banking habits and the law and order situation is such that it would be difficult to set up ATMs all over the country. Cheque-based transactions are also few in number. Hence foreign banks tend to concentrate in a niche market.

A further point is that the initial entry may be small-scale because the entrant's bargaining power is small. Over time, as the entrant learns more about the market, its bargaining power grows and it demands a higher and higher share of the pie in a bargaining context. This dynamic effect of 'learning by doing' is different from the usually considered effect on a firm's costs.

Can there be large-scale entry? Bagwell and Ramey (1996) provide a model of large-scale entry. Their essential point is that large-scale entry makes aggressive action on the part of the entrant credible and if the incumbent firms have large avoidable fixed costs (which can be avoided by shutting down operations, not necessarily by exiting from the industry), then the incumbent responds optimally by shutting down. Thus, with significant avoidable fixed costs, the market-capturing strategy becomes easier to employ and more profitable for the entrant. Again, having less options is actually better for the incumbent.

The process of cost reduction through learning from experience is important in many industries where organizational efficiency in production and management can significantly reduce costs. Because of learning effects, potential entrants in these industries anticipate that they will initially face a higher cost structure than incumbent firms. Then one possible strategy for the entrant is to adopt a learning process *beginning before entry* and continuing afterwards, for example, by setting a small-scale firm. Although such a strategy loses money in the beginning, its learning effects might enable the entrant to enter in a bigger way later if costs are sufficiently reduced. The question here is why does the incumbent not continue with the learning process. One reason might be sheer inertia. Another might be that the incumbent has already exhausted the possibilities of cost reduction. Further, if cost reduction requires investment in new assets, the incumbent firm might be unwilling to undertake the huge cost of replacing its existing assets.

7.4.6 Entry by Foreign Firms

Finally, one must remember that entry into a market by *foreign firms* raises a host of issues. Governments react in different ways to such entry and potential foreign investors must take account of such reactions. As an example, consider the nature of the foreign direct investment (FDI) flowing into Central and East European economies in the 1990s. East Germany witnessed large sales of existing assets (the 'buy' route for entry) to West Germans, and this did not create any resentment. But sales of assets on a large scale (bringing down asset prices) to foreigners in other countries has created strong resentment and governments are actively discouraging such sales. Sinn and Weichenrieder (1997) suggest that joint ventures with governments owning these assets would be one way of overcoming such resentments.

8 Firm as the Source of Profit

We have assumed so far that all firms are identical. Some of them make a profit only because they operate in markets that are structurally imperfect and are protected by entry barriers. But very often, two firms in the same market make dissimilar profits, and this happens because the firms themselves are dissimilar. In fact, several studies show that the firm is a more important source of profit than the market.[1] To understand how the firm can be a source of profit, we have to first understand the economic role of the firm.

8.1 THEORY OF THE FIRM

8.1.1 What is a Firm?

If I want to build a house, I could hire an architect, a civil engineer, and a few masons, carpenters, electricians, plumbers, and painters, and ask them to build the house by interacting with one another. Alternatively, I could give the entire job to a firm of building contractors. In the former case, I build the house by transacting with the experts and artisans through the market. I go to the market, hire the experts and artisans, and leave them to work on their own. If I find that some of them are not performing satisfactorily, I discipline them by threatening to terminate their contracts or by withholding payments. In the latter case, I build the house by routing all the transactions through a firm. I transact with the firm and the firm transacts with the experts and artisans. Thus, a firm is an *institution that organizes production by internalizing the transactions* required to produce an output.

8.1.2 Why Do We Need a Firm?

I shall use a firm only if it meets my requirements more efficiently than the market. If I need to get a leaky tap fixed, I shall probably choose to call a plumber directly, because by going through a firm of building contractors, I will have to contribute towards its overheads and may end up by paying much more. But when I want to build a house, I am likely to entrust the job to a firm. The reason for this is that when production requires the cooperative effort of a number of owners of productive resources,

---

[1]See Rumelt (1991) and Roquebert, Phillips, and Westfall (1996).

three problems arise and the firm can often deal with them more efficiently than the market.[2]

The first is the problem of *mobilizing, coordinating, and motivating resources*. By using a firm, I can avoid the hassles of finding suitable experts and artisans, negotiating terms with each of them individually, monitoring their activities, resolving conflicts among them, measuring their work, and paying accordingly. The firm deals with these problems by establishing an *architecture* that brings multiple owners of productive resources into long-term relationships with one another.

The second problem is one of *information asymmetry*. The experts and artisans I hire know what kind of work they are capable of. But as I do not build a house everyday, I am unlikely to have used them before and do not know what kind of work they will deliver in the end. This is not a major problem when I call a plumber to fix a tap. Because even if he does a bad job, the cost of this from my point of view may not be very high. But the problem becomes quite acute when I have to hire a large number of people, because it may not be possible for me to check their credentials individually and if they fail to perform, the resultant loss for me can be very high. Rather than risking these losses, I may even decide not to build a new house at all, and buy or rent an existing house instead. However, if I can find a reputed firm of building contractors to do the job for me, I may build a new house, because I then have some assurance of the kind of work I can expect from them, although this way I may pay a little more. In other words, the firm solves the problem of information asymmetry by building a *reputation* that bridges the information gap between the firm and those who have not dealt with it before, and makes possible transactions that may not take place otherwise.

Finally, there is a problem of *know-how*. Even if the experts and artisans I hire are very good at their own work, none of them can be expected to have complete knowledge of how to build a house. By appointing a firm of building contractors, I can take advantage of its collective *knowledge* of how a house should be built.

We may now draw the following general conclusion. When two or more owners of productive resources have to work together to produce an output, a firm often becomes a more efficient alternative to the market, because its architecture, reputation, and knowledge enable the firm to use these resources more efficiently than the market. The architecture of a firm reduces the production losses that may arise if the owners of these resources transact with one another through the market. Its reputation minimizes the production losses that would arise if production does not take place at all, because of an information asymmetry between buyers and sellers. And the firm's knowledge of how production should be carried out enables the productive resources to produce more than they would otherwise.

8.1.3 The Concept of Proprietary Assets

As the economist sees it, the firm is an institution that produces or *adds value*, by *transforming* a set of inputs into a product, or a form considered valuable by the buyer,

---

[2]Alchian and Demsetz (1972) explain why cooperative effort provides the basis for a firm. Kay (1993, chapters 4 to 8) spells out how the firm promotes cooperation by developing three 'distinctive capabilities', namely architecture, reputation and innovation.

and *marketing* or reaching the product from the firm to the buyer. The firm does so by using three types of productive resources: its architecture, reputation, and knowledge, or what Richard Caves calls its *proprietary assets*[3]; its *strategic assets*; and *non-proprietary factors of production*, like land (the ultimate source of all material inputs), labour, and general purpose physical and human capital.

- The defining characteristics of proprietary assets are that they are intangible, created by the firm itself, unique in the sense that no other firm has them, and available for the exclusive use of the firm.

- Strategic assets are similar to proprietary assets in that they are also unique and available for the exclusive use of the firm. But they are also dissimilar in that they` may be tangible or intangible, and are not created by the firm, but acquired by buying or hiring them from the market. Examples are a bauxite mine owned or taken on lease by an aluminium producer, or a patent or trademark bought by an Indian firm from an MNC.

- Non-proprietary factors are not unique, in that they are the same for all firms and are equally available to all firms who can buy or hire them from the market. We call these factors non-proprietary to distinguish them from proprietary assets, although they may in fact be owned by a firm legally (e.g. an office building, or a computer, or a motor vehicle).

A firm is distinguished from other firms by its proprietary assets. These assets do not participate in the production process directly, but work through the non-proprietary factors employed by the firm. Together, they determine the *technology* of the firm, or the distinctive way in which it uses non-proprietary factors to produce an output. They also determine the firm's *capabilities*, or the kind of things it can do, like producing an aeroplane, or selling in rural markets, or organizing fashion shows. Most importantly, they can generate an *economic profit* for the firm, even when it is not protected by structural or any other externally imposed entry barriers.

8.1.4 A Resource-based View of the Firm

The idea that internal resources and capabilities, or the proprietary assets, of a firm enable it to earn a profit was first propounded by Edith Penrose,[4] developed by a number of other authors, and is known as the *resource-based view* of the firm.[5] The argument very simply is that even if a firm is not protected by structural or any other externally imposed entry barriers, it can use its proprietary assets to build a protective shield around itself that deters competition and enables it to earn a profit.

However, this is possible only if the proprietary assets meet four conditions.

- First, they must be *valuable*: they should be able to create value, or generate a surplus, by enabling the firm to use non-proprietary factors more productively than the market.

[3]See Caves (1996), pp 3–5.
[4]See Penrose (1995), pp 24–6.
[5]Two excellent expositions of the resource-based view are Barney (1991) and Peteraf (1993).

- Second, they must be *superior*, or capable of creating more value than the proprietary assets of competing firms, and *scarce*, or available only to the extent the firm chooses to make them available. This would enable the firm to restrict the supply of the services of its superior assets and convert a part of the value created by these assets into a rent that can be shared by the firm and its proprietary assets.
- Third, the assets must be *imperfectly imitable*. Otherwise, this rent cannot be sustained. Competitors will copy these assets as soon as they notice their rent-yielding capacity and compete the rent away.
- Finally, the assets must be *imperfectly tradable*, in the sense that they should create more value within the firm than outside it. This would ensure that the assets themselves cannot appropriate the entire rent and a part of it accrues to the firm as a profit.

We develop these points more fully below.

8.2 ARCHITECTURE

8.2.1 How Does Architecture Create Value?

When production requires the participation of a number of owners of productive resources, it involves a series of transactions, or transfer of goods and services, among them. This is illustrated by Table 8.1 which shows, in the form of a standard profit-and-loss account, how customers, vendors, manual workers, knowledge workers, creditors and risk capital providers have to transact with one another to produce an output and share it among themselves.

Table 8.1. Transactions involved in the production process

	Rupees	Represents Transactions	
		With	For
Gross Output	100	Customers	Sale of output
Cost of Material Inputs	50	Vendors	Purchase of inputs
Value Added	50		
Wages	15	Manual workers	Supply of physical effort
Salaries	5	Knowledge workers	Supply of mental effort
Interest Cost	10	Creditors	Supply of debt capital
Profit	20	Risk capital provider	Supply of risk capital

These transactions may be *one-off* or *repetitive*. Repetitive transactions may be based on a series of *spot contracts* or one *long-term contract*. A long-term contract may be *explicit* or *implicit*. In an explicit contract, all the rights and obligations of the contracting parties are spelt out and can be enforced legally. A lease agreement between a landlord and his tenant is an explicit contract. Quite often, however, a contract cannot specify these rights and obligations completely, because the contracting parties cannot comprehend or foresee all the contingencies that may arise while the contract is in force. In that event, contracts have to be *implicit*.[6] The parties know the nature of their rights and obligations. But these cannot be specified precisely and, therefore, remain implied. The contract that I have with my cable TV operator is, for example, an implicit contract. We both know that in return for the money I pay him, he has to keep my channels running. But we cannot list precisely everything he may have to do to keep my channels going. Therefore, his obligations are not fully specified, but implied by the contract. Because implicit contracts are incomplete, they cannot be enforced in a court of law. They have to be enforced by the parties themselves.

When several owners of productive resources transact with one another on the basis of implicit contracts to produce an output, they may take advantage of the incompleteness of contracts and try to gain at the expense of one another. This may lead to avoidable production losses, or what economists call transaction costs. What is more, since the partners in production act individually, and not as a team, they fail to enhance the productivity of one another. A firm deals with these problems by forging long-term relationships with and among risk capital providers, manual and knowledge workers, customers, vendors, and other partners in production, on the basis of implicit contracts. These relationships constitute the architecture of the firm. Architecture creates value by getting the partners in production to transact with one another through the firm. This *minimizes the transaction costs* that would be incurred if the partners were to deal with one another directly, and enhances their productivity by *promoting teamwork*.

To see how architecture creates value, consider the following situation. A trucker and four container loaders come together on the basis of market transactions to offer a container service to customers. The service involves carrying some material from the warehouse to the truck at the point of origin; loading it into the truck; transporting it to the destination; unloading it from the truck; and carrying it from the truck to the warehouse at the point of destination. A contract has to be finalized with the customer by agreeing on a price that factors in things like load characteristics, the amount of material handling involved, the distance and terrain to be covered, etc. Customers can hire a container truck from one of several truck owners by paying a standard hiring charge of Rs 100 per hour. The market for container service is competitive and they can pick up any amount of business at the going market price. Assume that the five associates get an assignment at a price of Rs 40,000. We can measure the cost of completing the assignment by the time taken to complete it. This is because they can find any number of assignments at the going market price. The quicker they complete an assignment, the larger is the number of assignments they can handle in a given period of time, and the higher are their earnings.

To complete the assignment, the trucker and the loaders have to spend time not only to carry out the productive activities listed above, but also transact with the

---

[6] See the discussion on transaction costs in Chapter 1 and the discussion on asymmetric information in Chapter 3 which provide the framework for what follows.

customer and the truck owner, and among themselves. Before they get the assignment, the five of them have to negotiate five contracts with the customer. After they get the assignment, they have to negotiate five contracts with the truck owner to finalize hiring arrangements, and ten two-way contracts with one another to specify how the work and rewards should be shared. Suppose they agree eventually that when the assignment is completed, the trucker will get a third of whatever is left after paying the truck owner and the rest will be shared equally by the loaders. The time expended to negotiate and finalize all these agreements is the *cost of contracting*.

When they start working together, they may find that some of the associates are not as competent as they had claimed to be. The extra time that is required to complete the assignment as a result of this is the *cost of adverse selection*. This cost arises because the market cannot distinguish between good and bad workers and pay the same average price for both. At that price, there is an undersupply of good workers and an oversupply of bad workers in the market, and the probability of picking up bad workers from the market is higher. The associates may also find that one or two of the loaders are shirkers and their work has to be monitored by the others. Some of the heavy loads may have to be carried by all the four loaders together. In such cases, the output is the result of *team effort* and cannot be apportioned to the loaders individually. If the shirkers put in less effort than the others, it becomes difficult to detect the culprits, and the time required to detect the culprits and monitor their work may not be worth spending. But the work of the entire team slows down. The time that is lost because of shirking, the need to monitor the shirkers, and the slowing down of production owing to undetected shirking, comprises the *cost of moral hazard*. This cost arises because once a contract is finalized conferring a pre-specified benefit on a contracting party, the latter's incentive to honour the contract is reduced.

Once the loaders start carrying and loading materials, they may find that some of the loads are heavier than they had thought. They may then demand a higher share of the rewards than agreed originally and stop work to press their demand. Similarly, the trucker may find the terrain rougher and the road more congested than he had anticipated, demand a higher share of the reward, and stop driving to press his demand. Since there is *asset specificity*, in that the trucker needs the loaders and vice versa, both parties have to bargain and negotiate a settlement. *Hold-up costs* are, however, incurred in the process.

Suppose that if all members of the team had worked at their peak capacity and did not spend any time on non-productive activities, they would have completed the assignment in 50 hours. But as a result of the various problems mentioned above, they actually take 100 hours to complete the assignment. Then the transaction costs incurred to complete the assignment are 50 hours, valued at Rs 20,000. After paying the truck owner Rs 10,000 at Rs 100 per hour, the amount left for sharing is Rs 30,000. The trucker gets Rs 10,000 and the rest is shared equally by the loaders. Per man-hour put in, the trucker and the loaders earn Rs 100 and Rs 50, respectively.

Now consider how the situation changes if the trucker becomes the sole owner of the business and runs it as a firm on the following basis. He enters into long-term contracts with the loaders, whereby he agrees to pay each loader Rs 60 per man-hour, regardless of the time it takes to complete this or any other assignment. The loaders become his employees and have to work under his authority. He has the right to instruct the loaders, and to sack or fine them if they do not perform to his satisfaction. The loaders accept this arrangement for two reasons. First, under the earlier arrangement their hourly earnings were lower by 20 per cent. Second, there was a risk that these earnings would be even lower if the assignment took more than 100 hours to be completed. Now their hourly earnings are guaranteed, because the risk that the assignment may take longer is absorbed by the trucker who is the owner of the business.

The trucker also negotiates a long-term contract with one of the truck owners, whereby the latter gets 20 per cent of the total amount paid by the customer. The truck owner accepts this arrangement, because he expects a steady flow of business from the trucker. He also expects that the new arrangements will enable the trucker to complete assignments more quickly and his hourly earnings will be more than Rs 100. The agreement that the truck owner has with the trucker is an implicit contract. The implicit understanding is that the trucker will feed the truck owner with a steady flow of business and complete assignments quickly. But this understanding cannot be enforced in a court of law.

The new arrangement is potentially advantageous to the trucker also. After paying the loaders and the truck owner their due, the residual earnings will come to him as payment for his own services and profit. He, therefore, has the opportunity to increase his earnings by using his authority over the loaders to reduce delays and complete the assignment in less than 100 hours. The trucker is in a position to reduce delays in many ways. Earlier, 20 two-way contracts were required. Now only six two-way contracts have to be negotiated, between the trucker on one side and the customer, the truck owner, and the four loaders on the other. What is more, the trucker enters into long-term contracts with the truck owner and the loaders, so that each time a new assignment comes, new contracts do not have to be negotiated with them. There can thus be a substantial saving in contracting costs. The trucker can also avoid the cost of adverse selection by observing the performance of the loaders over a period of time and replacing the incompetent loaders. Since the trucker now monitors the material handling operations when he is not driving, he can detect shirking more effectively, discourage it by imposing penalties, relieve the non-shirkers of the burden of monitoring shirkers, and thus minimize the cost of moral hazard. The new regime brings down the hold-up costs too. Since the loaders are paid by the hour, they do not gain by holding up, while the trucker loses by holding up.

Apart from reducing transaction costs, this arrangement has another positive effect. It enables all the partners in production to exceed themselves by promoting teamwork. *Coordination* improves, because all members of the team work to a common plan, as set by the trucker. *Cooperation* also improves. Since the members have a continuing association with one another, they get to know the strengths and weaknesses of one another. By exploiting the strengths and eschewing the weaknesses of individual members, the team as a whole produces more than the total of what the members would produce by working on their own. Finally, the long-term association creates *commitment*. The trucker, loaders, and the truck owner develop team-specific knowledge and other assets (e.g. a specially designed truck) that are worth more within the team than outside. They, therefore, have a vested interest in maximizing the performance of the team.

Suppose, as a result of all this, the assignment is now completed in 75 hours. This means that by internalizing the transactions, the firm generates a surplus of 25 hours, valued at Rs 10,000. The truck owner is paid 20 per cent of Rs 40,000, i.e. Rs 8000. If he were paid at Rs 100 per hour, he would have got Rs 7500. The extra Rs 500 that he gets now is his share of the surplus. If the loaders were paid at the old rate of Rs 50 per hour, they would have received Rs 15,000. At the new rate of Rs 60 per hour, they get Rs 18,000. The difference of Rs 3000 is their share of the surplus, paid to them as wages. At the old rate of Rs 100 per hour the trucker would have got Rs 7500. Now as the owner of the business he gets Rs 14,000, the residue after paying the truck owner his hiring charges and the loaders their wages. The extra Rs 6500 that he gets now is his profit.

8.2.2 Internal and External Architecture

The surplus has been generated by establishing an architecture, or a *nexus of implicit contracts* that binds the trucker, the loaders, and the truck owner in a long-term relationship with one another. The contracts that bind the trucker and the loaders together constitute the *internal architecture* of the firm. The distinguishing feature of these contracts is that the trucker enforces them by using his *authority* over the loaders. The *external architecture* of the firm consists of the contract that brings the trucker and the truck owner into a long-term relationship with each other. The distinguishing feature of this contract is that it is *self-enforced*, or enforced by the parties themselves. The trucker and the truck owner abide by the contract themselves, because they gain by continuing to do business with each other.

8.3 REPUTATION

8.3.1 How Does Reputation Create Value?

While the architecture of a firm creates value by reducing transaction costs, its reputation creates value by making possible transactions that would not take place otherwise due to an information asymmetry between buyers and sellers.[7]

Suppose that only two varieties of basmati rice can be produced—superior and inferior. All producers have the same production cost. The cost of producing superior basmati (C_s) is higher than the cost of producing inferior basmati (C_i), i.e. $C_s > C_i$. Consumers are prepared to pay a higher price for superior basmati (P_s) than for inferior basmati (P_i), i.e. $P_s > P_i$. The market is competitive, so that $P_s = C_s$ and $P_i = C_i$. However, both types of basmati are visually identical and the producers cannot be identified. Therefore, at the time of purchase, the consumer has no way of knowing if the product she buys is actually superior or inferior. The producer, on the other hand, knows what he is selling. If he takes advantage of the consumer's ignorance by giving her inferior basmati when she asks for superior basmati, he makes a profit of $P_s - C_i$. If he does not cheat, he makes a profit of $P_s - C_s = 0$. The profit-maximizing producer

---

[7] This part of the discussion is based on Klein and Leffler (1981).

will, therefore, cheat. However, when the consumer actually tastes the rice, she will find out that she has been cheated. Therefore, the next time she goes to the market, she will avoid the risk of being cheated by asking for inferior basmati and paying P_i for it. Over a period of time, all buyers will stop buying superior basmati, the market for superior basmati will disappear and even the honest producer will stop producing this variety. Thus, in equilibrium, the producer does not make a profit, the consumer does not get cheated, but only inferior basmati is supplied.

Because of information asymmetry, the market has failed to generate a transaction in superior basmati, although it is in demand and can be produced. In other words, we are faced with the *lemons problem* discussed in Chapter 3. The buyers cannot tell differences in product quality at the time of purchase, so that the market price reflects the inherent risk of a low quality product being supplied. At that price, the sellers find it profitable to sell a low quality product, but unprofitable to sell a high quality product. Therefore, low quality products dominate the market.

An enterprising producer, however, can break this impasse by charging a *quality assuring price* (P_a) that is higher than C_s and discourages cheating. Since $P_a > C_s$, by not cheating the producer makes a perpetual stream of profits of $P_a - C_s$. By cheating, he makes a one-time profit of $P_a - C_i$. If the value of P_a is so chosen that the net present value of the perpetual stream of profits that can be made by not cheating is at least equal to the one-time profit that can be made by cheating, then the producer has no incentive to cheat. Algebraically, P_a should be such that $(P_a - C_s)/R \geq P_a - C_i$, where R is the discounting rate. Although $P_a > P_s$, there will be some consumers who will have enough consumers' surplus to buy superior basmati at the higher price.

However, why should the consumer pay P_a, unless she can be assured that she will get superior basmati in return? This assurance is provided by the producer investing in building a reputation that identifies, is specific to, and represents a sunk cost for the producer. The consumer will then reason that by cheating, the producer makes a one-time profit of $P_a - C_i$, but loses his reputation, the value of which is the net present value of the stream of profits it generates, or $(P_a - C_s)/R$. She will reason further that $(P_a - C_s)/R$ is unlikely to be lower than $P_a - C_i$, the one-time profit he can make by cheating, because he would not have incurred the cost of reputation building otherwise.

To sum up, reputation identifies a producer, signals his commitment to quality, and gives the consumer the opportunity to punish him specifically, should he cheat. This enables the producer to generate a surplus by giving the consumer what she wants. One part of this surplus goes to the consumer as consumer's surplus and the other to the producer as a price premium. What applies to the product market also applies to the input market. Reputation also differentiates a buyer from his competitors in the input market and enables him to generate a surplus by giving his potential employees, creditors, investors, and vendors the opportunity to sell their services and products to a reputable buyer. His share of the surplus is the price discount he gets from his input suppliers in return for assuring them a fair deal.

8.3.2 Is Reputation the Prerogative of a Firm?

We have argued that buyers and sellers would rather deal with a firm than an individual transactor in the market, because the former has a reputation. Does this mean that individual transactors cannot have a reputation? This is obviously not the case. We often go to a doctor or a lawyer because he has a reputation. However, a firm has two advantages over an individual transactor. First, when a group of individuals have to join hands to produce an output, it is more important for the group to have a reputation than the individuals comprising it. Second, even when an individual can work fairly independently, it may be cheaper for him to build and share a collective reputation with other individuals than build an individual reputation. When a lawyer practices as a partner of a law firm rather than as an individual, he benefits not only from his own reputation, but also from the reputation of his partners. What is more, all the partners can invest jointly in reputation-building activities like advertising, public relations, etc. and share the benefits. For an individual lawyer, this can be a very expensive proposition.

BRAND IMAGE AND CORPORATE IMAGE

In 1991, there was practically no market for high quality potato wafers in India. A few local sellers did supply small quantities of pre-packaged wafers at higher prices than loose wafers. But the difference in quality was not very significant and very few consumers were willing to pay the price premium.

Enter Frito Lay, the Snacks Division of Pepsi Foods, with a recognizably superior product. It delivered a superior product by managing the supply chain—from the procurement of potatoes to the retailing of wafers—effectively, instituting strict quality control measures, packaging the chips scientifically, and nitrogen-flushing the packages. It charged a quality-assuring price that was some 30 per cent higher than the price of loose potato wafers. It signalled its commitment to quality by building a reputation for its product. It did so by giving its product a brand name, putting the product in a package that identified the brand, and communicating what the brand stood for through extensive consumer promotion and TV advertising. Frito Lay promised to deliver potato wafers that were much fresher, crisper, and tastier than what was available in the market, by charging a reasonable price premium. The brand name initially chosen was Ruffles. The product took some time to establish itself, because consumers needed some time to try out the product and convince themselves that the product was worth the premium. Over a period of time, as more and more consumers tried out the product and found it satisfactory, sales picked up. Meanwhile, the brand name was changed to Ruffles Lays, and then to Lays. Branded potato wafers now enjoy a sale of Rs 150 crore and account for 30 per cent of the tonnage of all potato chips sold in India. Lays has a 40 per cent share of the branded product market and is the brand leader. Frito Lay has created a market for high quality potato chips in India by building a reputation for its product, which involved making a credible promise to supply such chips and living up to this promise consistently.

Frito Lay built a reputation for its product by giving it a brand name, and did not try to build a reputation for the firm as a whole. In the language of Business Policy literature, it built a *brand image* for its product. It did so because it wanted to establish its credibility with consumers, and consumers were interested in the product and not the firm as a whole. However, when a firm wants to establish its credibility with a wider public, consisting of suppliers, investors, potential employees, and other associates, it has to build a reputation for the firm as a whole, or what Business Policy literature calls a *corporate image*. In principle, building a corporate image is not very different from building a brand image. Instead of making a credible promise about its product, the firm has to make a credible promise about its own conduct and establish its credibility by living up to its promise, consistently and throughout the firm.

To understand what this involves, it will be useful to look at an image building exercise undertaken recently by Dr Reddy's Laboratories (DRL), a successful pharmaceutical company. DRL was founded by Dr Anji Reddy, an exceptionally competent technocrat. Through new product launches and mergers, the firm grew rapidly and achieved a turnover of about Rs 1000 crore in 1999. Being an export-oriented company, it also listed itself on the New York Stock Exchange. It was generally perceived that DRL owed its success to the technical and entrepreneurial strengths of its founder, but was not very quality conscious or professionally managed. This was also the time when the management of the firm was passing on from the founder to his heirs. The latter felt that DRL should make a conscious effort to project itself as a professionally managed company.

To this end, DRL retained a well-known firm of image consultants and with its help, took a number of steps.

- They talked to various customers to find out what *attributes* they wanted to see in DRL.
- This led to a *statement of promises*, made by DRL to its various customers.
- To give *tangible expression* to the kind of company it wanted to become, DRL adopted new house colours, a new logo, a code of conduct for its employees, a catchy company anthem, and a new slogan.
- With a view to ensuring that its *actual conduct* conforms to its promises, DRL made extensive changes in its organization structure, management practices, value systems, and leadership styles.

Source: The Economic Times, Mumbai, 'Brand Equity', 24–30 November 1999 and 5 September 2001.

8.4 KNOWLEDGE

8.4.1 How Does Knowledge Create Value?

How a firm's knowledge enables it to create value is best explained by using the concept of *production function*. The production function is a technical relationship that tells us the maximum output that can be produced with each and every set of inputs, given a certain state of knowledge. If the state of knowledge improves, the maximum output that can be produced with the same set of inputs increases, and we move to a higher production function. Assume that if 10 software engineers agree among themselves to work together, by working full steam for 100 hours together they can produce 100 software programmes of a particular type. The knowledge that they have at their command is the total of the knowledge each has individually. Now assume that the same 10 engineers can also work together as employees of a software firm and produce the same type of software programmes. The firm has worked on similar programmes before and has documented the knowledge it has acquired thereby in the form of an instruction manual. If the engineers work together as employees of the firm, their state of knowledge improves, because they can now use not only their own knowledge but also the instruction manual that enables them to avoid a few pitfalls and take a few shortcuts. Consequently, by working together for 100 hours, they can now produce more, say 125 programmes. The extra 25 programmes that they can now produce is the surplus generated by the firm's knowledge.

We can use the same example to see how the surplus generated by the firm's knowledge is different from the surplus generated by its architecture and reputation. Suppose that if the engineers work on their own and coordinate their activities by transacting among themselves, production losses due to costs of contracting, moral hazard, and hold-ups are 40 per cent, so that by working for 100 hours together they can actually produce only 60 programmes (60 per cent of 100). If they work as employees of the firm and their activities are coordinated by the authority of the firm, these losses are only 20 per cent, so that they then produce 100 programmes (80 per cent of 125). The surplus generated by the firm's architecture is the surplus generated by its knowledge and architecture (40 programmes) less the surplus generated by its knowledge alone (25 programmes), or 15 programmes. Suppose further that the firm has a good reputation and can sell these 100 programmes at a 20 per cent higher price than what the engineers would get if they were to sell them on their own. Then, the value of these programmes, in terms of what the engineers can get for them, is 120 programmes, and the surplus generated by the firm's reputation is 20 programmes. To sum up, 10 engineers working together for 100 hours produce 60 programmes if they work on their own, and the equivalent of 120 programmes if they work as employees of the software firm. The difference of 60 programmes is the value created by the proprietary assets of the firm—25 by its knowledge, 15 by its architecture, and 20 by its reputation.

8.4.2 The Theory of Organization Capital

The defining characteristic of knowledge is that it resides in the minds of individuals. This is as true of knowledge embodied in individuals as of knowledge encapsulated in formulae, recipes, drawings, blueprints, computerized data banks, etc., because even the latter becomes productive only when it is assimilated and used by individuals. We have seen, however, that knowledge creates a surplus for the firm, because its collective knowledge is greater than the sum of the knowledge of all individuals comprising the firm. How is this possible, if all knowledge resides in individuals?

One explanation is provided by the theory of organization capital, propounded by Prescott and Vischer.[8] By creating a pool of knowledgeable individuals and using them repeatedly on various assignments, the firm creates for itself an *organization capital*, consisting of three distinct types of knowledge. These are knowledge about the suitability of specific individuals for specific tasks, knowledge about how well specific individuals gel together as a team, and knowledge that individuals themselves acquire about their colleagues and the firm. The organization capital of the firm enables it to assign the right persons to each job and get the right people to work together as a team. Thus, the collective knowledge of the firm is greater than the sum of the knowledge of its constituents, not because it has more knowledge about how to do a job, but

[8]See Prescott and Vischer (1980).

because it knows how to harness the knowledge of individuals more productively than the individuals themselves.

8.4.3 The Knowledge-creating Firm

More recently, several authors have pointed out that a firm can use its organizational resources not only to harness the existing knowledge of its constituents more productively, but also create new knowledge for their use.[9] It can do so by managing the process of acquisition, preservation, and propagation of knowledge in a planned and systematic manner.

By setting up a mechanism for *capturing* the knowledge of each of its constituents and *transferring* it to other constituents, it can increase the stock of knowledge at its disposal. By making the same stock of knowledge available to a larger number of people, it multiplies its total stock of knowledge. What is more, as one individual leaves the firm and is replaced by another, the firm's stock of knowledge increases. While the knowledge of the departing individual is passed on to others and stays with the firm, the in-coming individual brings with him some new knowledge.

An individual acquires new knowledge by undergoing formal training and by learning from experience. The latter kind of knowledge can be *explicit* or *tacit*. The defining characteristic of explicit knowledge is that it can be expressed unambiguously and represented in the form of instruction manuals, operating procedures, drawings, formulae, recipes, etc. Explicit knowledge can, therefore, be transferred to others without much difficulty. Tacit knowledge, on the other hand, consists of subjective insights, intuitions, hunches, etc., cannot be articulated clearly, and is much more difficult to disseminate to others. It can be disseminated widely if it is *externalized*, or converted into explicit knowledge. Sometimes, tacit knowledge can be externalized by helping the knowledge provider to articulate his knowledge with the use of metaphors, analogies, and models. Sometimes, the knowledge provider cannot articulate his knowledge, because he knows how to do a job but does not know why his method works. In such cases, it may be possible for another person to externalize his knowledge by observing him at work, analysing his methods, and conceptualizing the underlying principles. When tacit knowledge cannot be externalized at all, it has to be transferred through *socialization*, or a close interaction between the provider and recipient of knowledge, by using methods such as apprenticeship, on-the-job training, workshops, brainstorming sessions, etc.

A firm can supplement the stock of its internally generated knowledge by *acquiring knowledge from outside*. It can do so by hiring knowledgeable people as consultants or employees, buying proprietary knowledge like patents, and entering into an alliance with knowledgeable firms or individuals. The firm can multiply the knowledge so acquired by transferring it to multiple individuals within the firm.

A firm can also create knowledge by *re-configuring existing knowledge*, available within the firm or outside.[10] A simple way of doing this is to apply the knowledge acquired in one context to a new context. For example, the knowledge acquired by

[9]See, for example, Nonaka (1991) and Teece (1998).
[10] See Kodama (1992).

marketing fast-moving consumer goods is now used extensively for marketing financial services at the retail level. A more complex method is to *fuse* or combine two or more strands of existing knowledge to create a new strand of knowledge. For example, the knowledge for producing fibre optics communication systems has been created by a group of Japanese companies by fusing glass, cable, and electronics technologies.

Finally, a firm can create completely *new knowledge* by undertaking or sponsoring R&D. The knowledge created by fusing existing knowledge or achieving new breakthroughs is usually the result of the effort of brilliant individuals. But the firm may facilitate the creation of this knowledge by providing organizational and financial support. The latter is especially important, because the outcome of R&D projects is uncertain and individuals are often unable to raise the required funds from the capital market that tends to be shortsighted and risk-averse.

BOX 8.1. THE KNOWLEDGE-CREATING FIRM: INFOSYS TECHNOLOGIES

Infosys Technologies Limited, a very successful IT firm in India, is a good example of a firm that creates knowledge. It creates knowledge by establishing a *knowledge management system* that tries to capture, consolidate, and store the new knowledge acquired by its employees in the course of their work, so that it may be re-used by its other employees, present and future.

This knowledge can be accessed and downloaded from the company's intranet and takes several forms.

- The *knowledge shop* catalogues what is available in the firm by way of technical documents, continuing education facilities, seminars and workshops, and personal skills of employees.

- The technical knowledge acquired by the firm's employees by doing various assignments is stored in a central repository called the *body of knowledge*.

- The project management tools developed and used in the past, like project and management plans, requirement and design documents, test plans and standards, checklists, causal analysis reports, etc., are stored as the *process assets* of the firm.

- The *people-knowledge map* provides a directory of who knows what. It enables the knowledge user to establish direct contact with the knowledge provider and elicit tacit knowledge.

Infosys operates its knowledge management system by making a number of organizational arrangements.

- A *steering group* consisting of senior people sets the knowledge management agenda.

- This agenda is implemented on the ground by *working groups*, set up specifically for that purpose.

- Employees are encouraged to record and share their knowledge through a system of *rewards and incentives*.

- The acquisition, recording, and dissemination of knowledge are the responsibility of all departments. In addition, a central *Education and Research Department* collects, consolidates, and reconfigures the knowledge generated by other departments, educates professionals, evaluates new technologies, and conducts research with a view to creating new knowledge.

Source: A case prepared by Prof. R. Srinivasan and Prof. Archana Shukla, Indian Institute of Management, Lucknow.

8.5 How Proprietary Assets Create a Rent

8.5.1 Asset Superiority and Competitive Advantage

We now know how the proprietary assets of a firm can create value by organizing production more efficiently than the market. If all firms have equally efficient assets, then under conditions of free entry, the firms themselves will not gain anything by creating value. More and more firms will enter the market and bid product prices down and factor prices up, until the entire value created by their assets accrue to consumers and factor owners, and no surplus is left for the firms.

However, the entire point of the resource-based view is that the assets of different firms are dissimilar in terms of their capacity to create value. This means that the assets of some firms are *superior*, in the sense that they enable these firms to create more value than their competitors with the same input of non-proprietary factors. Put differently, a firm that has superior assets has an advantage over its competitors, or what in Business Policy literature is referred to as a *competitive advantage*. Competitive advantage can be of two types—*cost advantage* and *differentiation advantage*.[11] The former arises when a firm is enabled by its proprietary assets to produce the same output of a particular product at a lower cost of non-proprietary factor inputs than its competitors. The latter arises when these assets enable the firm to sell something different from its competitors, something that buyers value and are prepared to pay a premium for.

8.5.2 Asset Scarcity and Quasi-rent

By definition, proprietary assets are scarce, in the sense that they are available only to their owners and their services are available in the market only to the extent their owners choose to supply them. By restricting the supply of the services of its superior assets, a firm can avoid paying out as lower product prices and higher factor prices some of the extra value created by its assets by virtue of their superiority. The value so retained is a *rent* that accrues to the proprietary assets of the firm and can be shared by the firm and its proprietary assets. Thus, even under conditions of free entry, the firm is able to generate a surplus after paying non-proprietary factors their market price, because its assets are superior and scarce.

The rent that accrues to the superior proprietary assets of a firm is in the nature of a scarcity rent, similar to the Ricardian rent that accrues to a superior piece of land. However, there is an important difference. Land is scarce because its supply is fixed by nature. Proprietary assets are scarce because their supply is *quasi-fixed*, or fixed only to the extent their owners choose not to supply them. Economists have coined the term *quasi-rent* for the rent that accrues to the proprietary assets of a firm, to distinguish it from the *pure rent* that accrues to land and other non-proprietary factors (like an unusually strong man capable of exceptional physical effort), the supply of which is fixed naturally. We, however, use the terms rent and quasi-rent interchangeably.

[11]Porter (1985) provides a comprehensive treatment of cost and differentiation advantage.

BOX 8.2. COST VS. DIFFERENTIATION ADVANTAGE

The difference between cost and differentiation advantage can be illustrated by considering the competitive advantages of two major players in the Indian ice cream market.

The organized ice cream market in India is estimated at around Rs 600 crores per annum at present. Hindustan Levers Limited (HLL), the Indian subsidiary of the Anglo-Dutch multinational Unilever Plc, has a 50 per cent share of this market. HLL entered the market by acquiring the ice cream businesses of Jagatjit Industries (Milkfoods) and Cadbury Schweppes India (Dollops) and three family-owned companies producing Kwality brand ice creams.

HLL can differentiate its products from its competitors in a number of ways.

- Its brand name Kwality Walls has a strong following. Kwality has been a strong brand name all over India for many years. Walls, available to HLL because of its Unilever connection, is an internationally admired brand name for ice creams.

- It can use the technical and marketing experience of Unilever to offer a wide range of flavours and tastes.

- Thanks to its acquisitions, it can distribute its products in a variety of locations and in a variety of ways, like pushcarts, retail outlets with refrigeration facilities, ice cream parlours, and institutional sales.

- HLL uses these advantages to differentiate its products by image, tastes and flavours, geographical markets, and modes of distribution, and charge a hefty price premium for its ice cream.

The other important player is the Gujarat Milk Marketing Federation (GMMF), a very large producer of liquid milk and milk products, even by world standards. GMMF entered the ice cream market recently as an extension of its product line and sells under the brand name Amul, which is the umbrella brand for all its products. By using an umbrella brand and selling standard flavours, GMMF economizes on marketing costs. In addition, its architecture, or the way it has organized the production and distribution of liquid milk gives it a strong cost advantage in terms of access to low cost milk. Its cost advantage allows GMMF to not only make a profit at going market prices, but also maximize volumes by lowering prices and expanding the consumption of ice cream in India. Currently, the per capita consumption in India is 100 ml per year, compared to 22 litres in the USA. GMMF's medium term objective is to increase this figure to 1 litre. GMMF has already become a major player in Western and Southern India. It is currently in the process of launching its products in Northern and Eastern India. Its ambition is to become the largest producer of ice cream in the world.

Source: The Times of India, Mumbai, 17 May 2002.

8.5.3 Proprietary Assets and Cost Advantage

How does a cost advantage arise? Recall how the proprietary assets of a firm enable it to produce an output at a lower cost than the market. Its knowledge reduces the input of non-proprietary factors by increasing the maximum output that can be produced with any given set of inputs. Its architecture reduces the production losses that arise because the owners of non-proprietary factors do not work together in a perfectly harmonious manner. Its reputation reduces the cost of non-proprietary factors by persuading their owners to sell their services at a discounted price. A firm has a cost advantage if its proprietary assets can perform these functions more efficiently than the proprietary assets of its competitors.

8.5.4 Cost Advantage and Quasi-rent

To understand how a firm converts its cost advantage into a quasi-rent, we consider two cases. In the first case, its assets are *embodied* in physical entities like human beings or capital goods, and in the second, the assets are *disembodied* in that they reside in the firm, which is an amorphous entity. We can see the difference by comparing the working of a small firm of management consultants run by a reputed professional with two or three assistants, with that of a large decentralized firm of management consultants. In the former, knowledge and reputation reside in the consultant himself and the architecture consists of one-to-one interactions between the consultant and his assistants. In other words, the proprietary assets are embodied in the consultant. In the latter, reputation resides primarily in the firm itself. Knowledge resides partly in documented models, manuals, files, etc. and partly in a large number of professionals, and is collected, processed, and disseminated through a knowledge management system. The architecture consists of a nexus of contracts, organization structure and systems, shared values, etc. In other words, the proprietary assets are largely disembodied.

8.5.4.1 Case 1: Embodied Assets

When the proprietary assets of a firm are embodied, they become *rivalrous*: if they are used by one non-proprietary factor, their physical availability to other non-proprietary factors is reduced. If the small firm of management consultants expands its output by increasing the number of assistants it employs, with each addition the time that the consultant can devote to each of his assistants is reduced progressively. Consequently, the amount of knowledge, supervision, and marketing support that he can provide to each of them also diminishes, leading to a progressive diminution in their productivity. Put differently, as output increases, the marginal cost of producing one unit of output increases, the average fixed cost of proprietary assets per unit of output falls, and the average total cost falls until marginal cost equals average total cost and rises thereafter. In other words, when the proprietary assets of a firm are embodied, its marginal cost curve is upward sloping and its average cost curve is U-shaped.

How the superior assets of a firm with a rising marginal cost curve earn a quasi-rent under conditions of free entry is shown in Fig. 8.1. In panel A, AC_1 and MC_1 are the average and marginal cost curves of firm 1 which is the most efficient firm in the industry. P_1 is the lowest price at which firm 1 can break even. Therefore, the supply curve of firm 1 is MC_1 at P_1 and above. Firm 1's supply curve is shown as P_1S_1 in panel B, on the assumption that the minimum economic quantity of firm 1 is so small in relation to the industry output that P_1S_1 starts virtually from the vertical axis. The next most efficient firm is Firm 2 whose average and marginal cost curves are AC_2 and MC_2 and supply curve is MC_2 at P_2 and above. As long as the industry price is less than P_2, firm 1 is the only supplier in the industry and P_1S_1 is the industry supply curve. But when the industry price reaches P_2, firm 2 also starts supplying and the industry supply curve shifts to P_1S_2. Thus, as the industry price increases, less efficient firms enter the industry, so that the industry supply curve is an upward sloping curve, which has been shown as P_1S in Fig. 8.1. DD is the industry demand curve. Industry demand balances industry supply at price P and output Q. At P, firm M, whose average and marginal cost curves are AC_m and MC_m, just breaks even and is the marginal firm. Firms 1 and 2 set their outputs at q_1 and q_2 by equating P with MC_1 and MC_2, respectively, and their proprietary assets earn a quasi-rent because at these levels of output, P, is higher than AC_1 and AC_2.

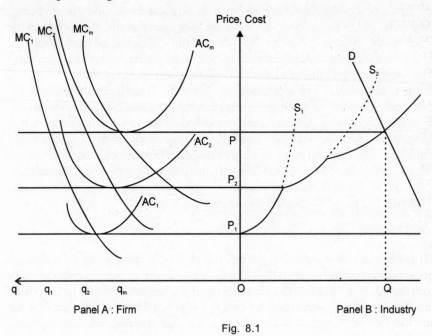

Panel A : Firm   Panel B : Industry

Fig. 8.1

The assets of firms 1 and 2 earn a quasi-rent for two reasons. First, they are superior to the assets of firm M, so that the production costs of the two firms are lower than firm M's. Second, these assets are scarce, because their owners choose not to meet the industry demand fully and allow less efficient firms to enter the industry. Because superior assets are scarce, they coexist with less efficient assets. Product and factor prices are determined by the productivity of the assets of the marginal firm. And at those prices, a firm that has assets superior to the assets of the marginal firm earns a quasi-rent.

8.5.4.2 Case 2: Disembodied Assets

We now turn to the other situation, where the proprietary assets of a firm are disembodied. When the proprietary assets are disembodied, they are *non-rivalrous*: their use by one non-proprietary factor does not reduce their physical availability to other non-proprietary factors. If the large decentralized firm of management consultants expands its output by employing new professionals, the new professionals can use the firm's knowledge, architecture, and reputation without reducing their availability to the professionals already in the firm. They can access the firm's documented knowledge or attend in-house training programmes without denying others these facilities. They can dovetail their work with that of their colleagues' by using the firm's organization structure, systems and procedures, etc. without reducing their availability to others. They can look for new business by using the firm's reputation, without diminishing its availability to other professionals. The recruitment of new professionals does not, therefore, reduce the productivity of the existing professionals in the firm. What is more, after a brief period of orientation the new professionals become as productive as the existing professionals, because they can use the firm's proprietary assets to the same extent as the latter. Therefore, the firm's marginal cost of producing one unit of output remains constant, regardless of the volume of output. The average fixed cost of proprietary assets and, therefore, the average total cost falls as output increases. In other words, when the proprietary assets of a firm are disembodied, its marginal cost line is a straight line parallel to the horizontal axis and its average cost curve is downward sloping.

In Fig. 8.2, DD is the industry demand curve. MC_1 and AC_1 are the marginal and average cost curves of firm 1, the most efficient firm in the industry. MC_2 is the marginal cost curve of firm 2, the second most efficient firm. MC_2 lies above MC_1 because firm 1's proprietary assets are superior to that of firm 2. The residual demand curve facing firm 1 is P_2ED. Firm 1 cannot charge a price higher than $P_2 = MC_2$, because if the price is higher than P_2, firm 2 enters the market and bids the price down to P_2. At any price below P_2, firm 2 does not enter and the demand curve facing firm 1 is the same as the industry demand curve. The marginal revenue curve corresponding to P_2ED is P_2EMN. Firm 1 maximizes its profit by choosing a price P and output Q, that equate marginal revenue with MC_1. At Q, $P>AC_1$ so that firm 1's superior assets earn a quasi-rent. But since $P<MC_2$, firm 2 does not enter the market. Thus, although entry into the market is free, firm 1's proprietary assets earn a quasi-rent for two reasons. Being superior, they shut firm 2 out of the market. And by becoming scarce, i.e. by firm 1 not expanding its output until the price equals MC_1, they extract a rent from the market.

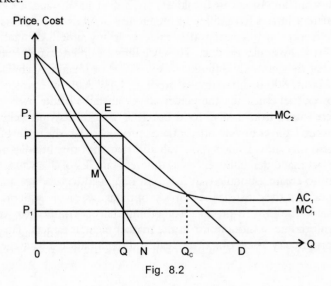

Fig. 8.2

If firms compete freely, firm 1 cannot charge a price higher than P_2. It may, however, be more profitable for the firm to charge a price higher than P_2 by coming to a tacit or explicit agreement with firm 2 and one or two other low cost firms in the market, and sharing the demand available at that price with the other firms in accordance with an agreed formula. The superior and scarce assets of the firm will then enable it to create an oligopolistic market and exploit it in the manner discussed in Chapter 4.

8.5.5 Proprietary Assets and Differentiation Advantage

Chapter 5 provides a detailed account of product differentiation. We may link it up with our discussions here by restating some of the salient conclusions.

Products within an industry are differentiated if buyers regard them as close but imperfect substitutes of one another. There are two kinds of models of product differentiation. In the *location* model, product differentiation arises because different buyers have different preferences and each buyer buys a product that satisfies her preferences best. For example, all buyers may buy a motor car for personal use because they want mobility, comfort, and speed. But beyond these basics, each buyer may have preferences that are different from those of other buyers. An elderly buyer may prefer a sober colour like white or grey. A young buyer may prefer a flashy colour like pink or orange. The elderly buyer may prefer manoeuverability to size. The young buyer with a large family may prefer size to manoeuverability. The elderly buyer may want her car for city driving and prefer low fuel consumption to speed. The young buyer may like to go out on long drives over weekends and prefer speed to low fuel consumption. If there are different models of cars available in the market, the elderly buyer will choose a model that meets her preferences best. For exactly the same reason, the young buyer will choose another.

The distinctive characteristic of the location model is that each buyer sticks to one type of product. In the *representative consumer* model, product differentiation arises because the same buyer buys different types of products, as she likes variety. She may, for example want an American breakfast, an Indian lunch, and a Chinese dinner. Whether different buyers have different preferences at all times or the same buyer has different preferences at different times, there is at any time a demand for different variants of a basically similar product. These variants are differentiated from one another by the fact that they embody different mixes of real or imaginary characteristics. For example, a Maruti 800 is differentiated from an Opel Astra in terms of size, driving comfort, power, fuel efficiency, the perceived social status of the owner, etc. Chinese food is differentiated from Indian food in terms of taste, flavour, richness, etc. This means that when a buyer buys a differentiated product, what she really buys is a *bundle of characteristics* that she considers more valuable than the other bundles available in the market. The fact that different buyers value different bundles of characteristics differently allows a firm to create a bundle that it is best equipped to produce and sell it those buyers who value it the most. If the firm's proprietary assets are superior, in the sense that they enable the firm to produce something that its competitors cannot match, then the firm becomes a monopolist in the market niche it targets. This in a nutshell is how the proprietary assets of a firm create a differentiation advantage for the firm.

A detailed account of how firms use their proprietary assets to create a differentiation advantage is more in the realm of Business Policy than Economics. But we may, by way of illustration, note the broad linkages here. Basically, there are four ways in which a firm can differentiate its product. First, the *physical attributes* of the product may be different. A shirt may be differentiated by its styling, colour, the material it is made of, etc. Second, the product may be the same, but accompanied by different packages of *services*. One seller of refrigerators may emphasize pre-sale buyback arrangements and loan facilities. Another may emphasize post-sale repair and maintenance services. Third, there may be differences in the method of *distribution* of the product, in terms of stock availability and turnover, geographical locations served, types of outlets covered, etc. Finally, the product may be differentiated by the subjective *image* it creates in the minds of the buyers. For example, two brands of wheat flour may be qualitatively the same. But one may be projected as more tasty and the other as more nourishing. If a buyer is looking for taste, she will buy the former. If she is looking for nourishment, she will buy the latter. In either case, she prefers one brand to the other, because she *thinks* that it is more valuable in terms of its ability to meet her specific preference. This means that even if a product actually offers more value, it will not be bought unless the buyer thinks that it offers more value. Conversely, even if the product actually does not offer more value, it will be bought if the buyer thinks that it offers more value.

The seller, therefore, has to create an image for his product by communicating with the buyers, with three things in view. If the buyer knows her utility function (or what she wants), the seller *informs* her that he can offer a bundle of characteristics that would satisfy her requirements. If the buyer does not know her utility function fully, the seller *persuades* her to buy his product by telling her that the bundle of characteristics he has to offer is really what she wants. If the buyer knows both her utility function and the bundle of characteristics that would satisfy her utility function, the seller *assures* her that if she buys his product, she will get exactly what is promised.

A firm that is knowledgeable about the needs of buyers, inputs, and processes will probably find it easier to differentiate its product in terms of physical attributes. Similarly, it may be easier for a firm with a strong internal and external architecture to differentiate its product in terms of service and distribution, while a firm with a good reputation may be able to differentiate its product in terms of image more easily. But the linkage is by no means so straightforward. A firm with a strong architecture may be able to differentiate its product in terms of physical attributes by accessing knowledge from its customers, dealers, vendors, or allies. A firm with a good reputation may be able to do the same by buying knowledge or recruiting knowledgeable people from outside. Similarly, a firm with a strong knowledge base may succeed in differentiating its product in terms of service or distribution by devising innovative methods of providing service or distributing to its buyers. A firm with a good reputation may do the same by enlisting the support of good dealers and franchisees or recruiting good sales and service personnel. Likewise, a knowledgeable firm may be able to create a distinctive image for its product by packaging it in an innovative manner. A firm with a strong architecture may do the same by using its sales and service staff to project an appropriate image for its product. There are no limits to such permutations and combinations. But the basic point is that a firm's capacity to differentiate its product in a certain manner or to target a certain market niche depends on the nature and quality of its proprietary assets.

8.5.6 Differentiation Advantage and Quasi-rent

By definition, a differentiated product cannot be substituted by other products perfectly. The demand curve facing the producer of a differentiated product is, therefore, downward sloping. The higher the degree of differentiation (or the lower the substitutability), the more inelastic is the demand curve. At one end of the scale, we may have a seller who differentiates his product so strongly that he becomes a virtual monopolist in the market niche he targets. Examples of such products are special purpose machines or custom-built motor vehicles. At the other end of the scale, we may have a seller who differentiates his product so weakly that he has to compete with a large number of producers of fairly similar products. Examples of such products are packaged sugar or toilet products. In either case, the seller can fix his output and price by equating marginal revenue with marginal cost, because he does not have to consider the reaction of his competitors to his output and price decisions. More commonly, we have the intermediate case of a producer differentiating his product fairly strongly and competing with only a few other sellers. In this situation, he has to consider the reaction of his competitors to his own output and price decisions, and ends up by fixing his price and output at levels that are acceptable to his competitors. Most branded consumer durables and fast moving consumer goods would come under this category.

A crucial decision from the seller's perspective is how strongly he should differentiate his product. The more strongly he differentiates, the less elastic is the demand for his product, and the higher is his profit margin. On the other hand, the less strongly he differentiates, the greater is his ability to substitute competitors' products by his own, and the larger is the market available to him. Thus, there is a trade-off between margin and volume. The seller makes a profit only if he so differentiates his product that his total operating surplus (margin × volume) exceeds the fixed cost of his proprietary and other assets.

The profit earned by a firm by differentiating its product is a quasi-rent that accrues to its proprietary assets. Being superior, these assets enable the firm to differentiate its product from that of its competitors. Being scarce (i.e. available for the exclusive use of the firm), they allow the firm to restrict output and earn a monopoly rent.

8.6 How the Rent is Sustained and Appropriated

8.6.1 Imperfect Imitability of Assets and Sustainability of Rent

The rent earned by the proprietary assets of a firm is not *sustainable* if other firms notice the rent-yielding capacity of these assets and can replicate them. If, for example, a firm earns a profit by using a new process that reduces costs, it cannot sustain this profit if other firms are also able to reduce their costs by copying the new process. We can see why this is so by going back to Figs. 8.1 and 8.2. If all firms can replicate the superior assets of firm 1, they all become as efficient as firm 1. Under conditions of free entry, the industry supply curve then becomes horizontal at P_1, the industry output increases to Q_c, the industry price falls to P_1, and all firms in the industry make a normal profit. The reason for this is that imitability increases the supply of superior assets and erodes their scarcity value.

Firms are able to sustain the rent earned by their superior assets, because they are protected by what Rumelt calls *isolating mechanisms*[12] or barriers to imitation. In principle, isolating mechanisms are no different from entry or mobility barriers, except that while isolating mechanisms are internal to the firm and protect individual firms, entry and mobility barriers are external to the firm and protect all firms and groups of similar firms in an industry. Business Policy literature identifies an impressive array of isolating mechanisms. We consider below three—causal ambiguity, the asset accumulation process, and social complexity—which seem to us to be more basic than the others.

Causal ambiguity[13] arises when a profitable firm has several rent-yielding assets and it is difficult to identify the exact contribution made by each asset to the overall profitability of the firm. This discourages other firms from imitating these assets, because imitation involves a sunk cost, and the pay-off is uncertain. For example, the profitability of a firm like Hindustan Levers is the result of its distribution network, the quality of its marketing staff, the strength of its brand names, its technological and managerial strengths and a whole host of other assets. One reason why other firms do not try to replicate these assets is that they do not know for sure which of these are most worth replicating.

It has been suggested that causal ambiguity can be an effective barrier to imitation only if even the firm that owns the rent-yielding assets does not know the exact contribution made by each of its assets to the overall profitability of the firm. Otherwise, potential imitators could buy this knowledge and imitate the assets that are worth imitating. It is quite plausible for a firm to suffer from causal ambiguity about its own assets, if these are complex, interdependent, and not subject to explicit analysis. Managers may have various hypotheses about the value of each asset, but are not in a position to test these out rigorously, so that the causal link between the assets and the firm's profitability remains ambiguous.

Some assets, like a firm's knowledge base or reputation for quality, have to be accumulated incrementally over time. These cannot be imitated easily because of the difficulties in repeating the *process of asset accumulation*.[14] These difficulties are threefold. First, there are *time compression diseconomies*: it may be expensive or infeasible to crash the accumulation process. For example, in the automobile market where only a limited number of customers buy a new car every year, a new firm may not be able to match the customer base of an established firm by crashing its marketing programme. Second, there is a problem of *asset mass efficiency*. A firm that has a large stock of a particular asset may be able to add to it more cost effectively than another firm which has only a small stock of that asset. To go back to our earlier example, an automobile manufacturer who has accumulated a large customer base already may be able to expand it in a more cost-effective manner than a new producer who has to promote his product more

---

[12]See Rumelt (1984).

[13]Lippman and Rumelt (1982) develop a formal model to show how causal ambiguity can lead to uncertain imitability and inter-firm differences in profitability under conditions of free entry. Reed and DeFillippi (1990) discuss the sources and effects of causal ambiguity.

[14]See Dierickx and Cool (1989)

vigorously. Finally, the imitability of a particular asset may also be limited by the *interconnectedness of asset stocks*: it may not be possible to accumulate one asset without accumulating another. It may, for example, not be possible to build a large base of customers without building a wide service network. Consequently, a would-be imitator who does not have a large service network cannot replicate the large customer base of another firm.

Some assets defy imitation, because they are *socially complex*, in that they are based on complex social relations. Examples are the culture of a firm, the interpersonal relations of its managers, its reputation amongst customers and suppliers, etc. The reason why such assets cannot be imitated with any degree of accuracy is that each firm is a unique social entity and the social relations that characterize one firm cannot be faithfully reproduced in another. The more complex these social relations, the more difficult it is to replicate them.

8.6.2 Imperfect Tradability of Assets and Appropriability of Rent

The rent earned by an asset does not translate into a profit for the firm, unless the firm can appropriate a part of this rent. The firm can do so if the asset earns a higher rent within the firm than outside. Because, in that case the firm can retain the asset by paying it a little more than what it would earn in its next best use (the opportunity cost) and keep back the rest as profit. The difference between the rent earned by the asset within the firm and the rent it would earn in its next best use is the rent that is *appropriable* by the firm. It arises because the asset is imperfectly tradable, in the sense that it does not command the same price in all its uses.[15]

We can illustrate this by considering the case of a chemist who works for a pharmaceutical firm and is specially trained to produce the firm's products. Being specially trained to produce the products of his present employers, he can produce more in his present firm than he would in any other firm. The difference between what he produces in his present firm and what he would produce in another firm is the rent that accrues to his employer's proprietary knowledge, which is embodied in him. His employer can retain his services by paying him a little more than what he would earn in his next best employment and keep back the rest of the rent as profit. The position does not change substantially if the asset is owned and not hired by the firm. Assume, for example, that the rent-yielding asset is a superior process owned by the firm and designed specifically to meet the production requirements of the firm. The appropriable rent is still the difference between the rent earned by the process within the firm and the royalty that can be earned by renting the process to the highest bidder outside the firm. The firm's revenue from using the process internally is the gross revenue earned by the process and the firm's cost of using the process is the royalty it foregoes by not renting it out to the next best user. The difference is the appropriable rent or profit. There is one difference, however. If the firm owns the asset, it can appropriate the entire quasi-rent. If the asset is hired, the quasi-rent may have to be shared with the owner of the asset (i.e. the chemist). While the asset owner needs the firm, the firm

---

[15] See Klein, Crawford, and Alchian (1978).

also needs the asset owner and the firm's share of the quasi-rent depends on its bargaining power *vis-à-vis* the asset owner.

An asset may be more productive within the firm for three main reasons.

- First, the asset may be *firm-specific*, or designed specifically to meet the idiosyncratic requirements of the firm. The scientist in the pharmaceutical firm who has been specially trained to produce the firm's products is an example of a firm-specific asset.

- Second, the asset may be *embedded* in the firm and be non-transferable, so that its productivity outside the firm is zero.

- Third, the asset may be *co-specific*. Even if it can be separated from the firm and transferred to another, it may produce most only when it is used in conjunction with other assets that are embedded in the firm.

8.7 STRATEGIC ASSETS

Earlier in the chapter, we had introduced briefly the concept of strategic assets. Below, we elaborate on it further.

The strategic assets of a firm are productive resources that are similar to proprietary assets, in that they are capable of earning a quasi-rent, but dissimilar, in that they are not created by the firm but acquired from the market. Strategic assets can be bought or leased from government authorities, e.g. the exclusive right to offer telecom facilities in a state; or from another firm, e.g. the patents and trademarks of a multi-national corporation; or from individuals, e.g. a site for locating a petrol pump.

Strategic assets are capable of earning a quasi-rent for the same reasons as proprietary assets. First, they create value. When they are intangible, they create value in the same way as proprietary assets. For example, a patent or a trademark acquired from an outside party generates a surplus in exactly the same way as the knowledge or reputation created by a firm internally. When these assets are tangible, they create value in the same way as non-proprietary factors. For example, a shop site is what economists would classify as 'land'. Second, they can be superior and scarce. A shop site owned or leased by a retailer is superior if it is more optimally located than sites owned or leased by other retailers. It is also scarce, because it is available for the exclusive use of the retailer who can decide how long his shop should be kept open every day. Third, they can be imperfectly imitable: a particular shop site cannot be imitated unless an identical site is available next to it. Finally, they can be imperfectly tradable. The shop site becomes imperfectly tradable, if the retailer acquires the necessary knowledge and other co-specific assets to use it more productively than other retailers.

However, the firm does not create the strategic assets and often has to acquire them from parties with a strong bargaining power. This limits the firm's capacity to appropriate as profit the rent generated by these assets. For example, when a valuable patent or commercial site is offered for leasing, a number of potential lessees may bid for it and push the rental up to a point where the lessor appropriates most of the rent. Even if the firm is able to get a lease on terms that are favourable initially, the lease may not be renewed on expiry.

Box 8.3. Valuation of intangible assets

The capital value of intangible assets of a firm is the present value of the stream of incremental cash they generate. But this figure is difficult to estimate, because it is difficult to segregate the cash flows that can be attributed to intangible assets alone. However, we can arrive at a *summary estimate* as follows. The market value of a firm's assets, tangible and intangible, is equal to the market value of its liabilities (equity plus debt). The market value of the firm's tangible assets is the replacement cost of these assets. The difference is the market value of the firm's intangible assets. Often, the net book value of the firm's assets is used as a surrogate for the market value of its tangible assets.

From the shareholders' point of view, a more important number is the value of the firm's proprietary assets, or the intangible assets that generate an appropriable stream of cash for shareholders. We can obtain a rough estimate of this figure by calculating the so-called *market value added* (*MVA*). *MVA* is the difference between the cash that shareholders have put into the firm since its start-up and the cash that they can get out of it now by selling their shares. The cash that shareholders can realize by selling their shares represents the market value of all assets *owned* by the firm, proprietary and non-proprietary. The cash that they have put in represents the historical cost of non-proprietary assets, or assets acquired by the firm from the market. The difference, therefore, is the value of proprietary assets, or assets created by the firm exclusively for its own use. Clearly, the firm has to maximize its *MVA* to maximize shareholders' wealth.

To manage the acquisition and utilization of its intangible assets, a firm has to estimate the values of specific intangibles. It can do so by using one of three basic approaches. In the *cost approach*, the present value of all build-up and support expenses incurred in the past for a specific intangible is treated as the value of that intangible. The problem with this approach is that it ignores the earning capacity of the asset. In the *market approach*, the market value of an intangible is estimated by using benchmarks or valuation multipliers available from transactions in similar intangibles. The problem with this approach is that the benchmarks or multipliers are not fully reliable, because no two intangibles or transactions are exactly similar. In the *income approach*, the value of an intangible is calculated by estimating the present value of future incremental cash flows that would result from using that intangible. The problem with this approach is that estimation of future cash flows and apportionment of it to a particular intangible tends to be highly judgmental.

It is quite common for Indian companies nowadays to value and report the values of three intangibles, namely human capital, brands, and customer relations. Human capital is usually valued by using the *Lev & Schwartz method*, in which the present value of the future earnings of employees is used as a surrogate for the human capital they embody. Brands are usually valued by using the *brand earnings multiple method*, developed by Interbrand. In this, brand earnings are calculated by deducting from the total cash flow accruing to a brand a 'normal' return on the capital used by the brand. The brand earnings are then converted into a brand value by using a valuation multiplier. The valuation of customer relations is usually based on an analysis of the so-called *remaining useful life* of the existing portfolio of customers. This involves an estimation of the rate at which the existing portfolio may *decay* and its impact on future cash flows. It should be clear from our discussions in the previous paragraph that all these methods are subject to a number of problems.

Source: Ashwani Puri, 'Intangibles in Action', *The Economic Times*, Mumbai, 28 December 1998.

9 Multi-market Operations I: Vertical Integration and Conglomerate Diversification

In the last chapter it was seen that a firm operating in a single market makes a profit either by exercising market power or by becoming more efficient than the marginal firm. In reality, most large firms operate in more than one market, for two basic reasons. First, by extending its operations to more than one market, a firm may be able to increase its efficiency or market power and earn a higher profit than it would by remaining a single market firm. Second, by operating in multiple markets, the firm may be able to make some strategic gains, although there may not be any immediate increase in its profits.

We consider three common types of multi-market operations: vertical integration, conglomerate diversification, and internationalization. In this chapter, we consider vertical integration and conglomerate diversification. Internationalization and strategic motives for multi-market operations are taken up in the next chapter.

9.1 Types of Multi-market Operations

Vertical integration involves an expansion in the firm's market portfolio without any expansion in its product portfolio. The final product is the same, but the firm expands its market portfolio by becoming a supplier of its own inputs or a customer of its own output. When it moves into the production of an input for its existing product, the firm is said to have *integrated backward*. When it moves into the production of a product that uses its existing product as an input, it is said to have *integrated forward*.

Conglomerate diversification (or simply diversification), on the other hand, involves an expansion in the firm's market portfolio through an expansion in its product portfolio. The firm enters a new market by producing a product that it did not produce earlier. When the new business shares a distinctive expertise acquired by the firm in its existing business, the firm is said to have engaged in *related diversification*. When no such commonality is apparent, the firm is said to have engaged in *unrelated diversification*.

Internationalization involves an expansion in the firm's market portfolio by the firm entering into geographical markets outside its own home country with its existing products. When the firm does so by exporting its products from the home country, it is said to have engaged in *international trade*. When it does so by producing abroad, it is said to have engaged in *international production*.

9.2 VERTICAL INTEGRATION

9.2.1 The Efficiency Motive of Vertical Integration: Economies of Vertical Coordination

Economies of vertical coordination exist, if a firm can reduce its cost of production by coordinating the activities of the various links in the vertical chain. When these economies are substantial, the firm has an incentive to integrate vertically.

Early theories of vertical integration have focused on how, in some situations, the input of materials or services required for producing a product can be minimized by locating a few vertically linked activities in close *physical proximity* of one another.

- First, by integrating several stages in the production process for some products, it may be possible to avoid the *repetitive use* of the same input at each stage. By integrating the production of iron, steel, and hot rolled coil, and feeding molten iron into steel-making and molten steel into hot coil rolling, the repetitive use of energy for heating of the metal at each stage can be avoided.

- Second, by locating the successive processing of some materials at the same place until they undergo a significant loss of weight or volume, it may be possible to achieve substantial *transportation economies*. Cement producers locate all processes from the mining of limestone to the production of clinkers at one place precisely for this reason.

- Third, by locating the processing of perishables near their point of production, *losses due to perishability* can be minimized. This is why fruits and vegetables processors often set up their plants near the farms.

Firms often integrate backwards to ensure *reliability of input supplies*, in terms of quality, quantity, or timeliness. Unreliable input supplies can become costly in many ways. The firm may miss out on revenue opportunities. Alternatively, it may have to carry an inventory of inputs to guard against supply failures. If multiple inputs are required to produce the final product, a failure in the supply of one may lead to an underutilization of the others. These costs can be particularly high if the input is critical in the sense that it cannot be substituted easily.

In recent years, firms have become aware of the large savings that can be effected by *integrating the planning of production* at various stages in the vertical chain. Each link in the chain, instead of planning its own production independently of the others, derives its production plan from the production plan of the link that buys from it. The main advantage is that it reduces capital requirements by way of inventories. An inventory of the final product has to be carried to take care of variations in its demand. But the integrated approach eliminates any mismatch between demand and supply in the intermediate stages of production, facilitates a continuous flow of materials through the vertical chain, and minimizes the need to carry an inventory of intermediate products.

Finally, by coordinating the *dissemination of technological information*, it may be possible to increase productivity in the vertical chain as a whole. There are two reasons for this. First, the superior technology developed for one product may be equally applicable to other vertically linked products. For instance, farmers may be able to increase farm productivity by adopting the post harvest crop management techniques developed by the processors of agricultural commodities for their own use.

Second, some links in the vertical chain tend to have a higher technological capability than others and the entire chain can benefit by sharing this capability. The processors of farm produce the world over have used their technological capability to improve not only processing technology, but farming technology also.

NEW TOOLS OF VERTICAL COORDINATION

The success of new IT-enabled management tools like supply chain management, enterprise resource planning, and business process re-engineering shows just how significant the economies of vertical coordination can be. In the last 3–4 years, scores of Indian firms have started using these tools and are reported to have effected cost savings up to 1 per cent of their sales turnover.

Supply chain management (SCM) consists of planning, tracking, and controlling the flow of materials from the supplier to the customer across all the links that connect the two. The objective is to so integrate supply and demand that all links in the supply chain respond to changes in demand as they arise, in a coordinated manner. In a large firm, this is not easy to accomplish, because there are many links in the chain. Materials come from many suppliers. The final product goes to many customers. Within the firm, transformation of the materials into the final product involves many processes, undertaken by many different people and at many different locations.

SCM has been facilitated by the development of *enterprise resource planning* (ERP) systems like SAP, PeopleSoft, Baan, Oracle, etc. These are ready-made software systems, designed for different functional modules like materials management, production planning, sales and distribution, human resource development, finance, management information, etc. All modules use the same information and dovetail into one another. When put together, they integrate all the activities of a firm. Customers place orders through the net, specifying their requirements. Enterprise resource planning collects these orders, sifts them, allocates them to different production centres, checks inventories, places orders for materials, tracks the flow of materials through the supply chain, maintains financial and other records, and generates management reports. Since all links in the chain use the same information and access it in real time, they can respond to changes in demand as soon as they arise and in exactly the same way.

Being a ready-made package, an ERP system is based on pre-defined business processes, which reflect the software producer's idea of 'best practices'. A *business process* may be defined as a set of value adding activities, performed in a certain manner and in a certain sequence. The business processes on which an ERP system is based are unlikely to be exactly the same as the existing business processes of a firm that wants to adopt that system. Therefore, when a firm adopts an ERP system, either the ready-made software has to be adapted to its existing business processes, or its existing business processes have to be adapted to the ready-made software. The former requires *customization*, or rewriting of some of the software. The latter requires *business process reengineering* (BPR), or redesigning some of the business processes of the firm. Usually, there is a bit of both.

SCM, ERP, and BPR have the potential to reduce costs in a number of ways. By integrating demand and supply, they minimize underutilization of production capacity. By speeding up the flow of materials through the supply chain, they reduce working capital requirements. By re-engineering business processes, they facilitate the adoption of best practices, improve efficiency, and reduce manpower costs. However, these tools are expensive. Also, as they make fundamental changes in the way a firm works, they attract resistance and have to be introduced cautiously.

9.2.2 The Efficiency Motive of Vertical Integration: Transaction Costs

However, the existence of economies of vertical coordination alone does not explain vertical integration. A firm can exploit these economies in one of two ways. It can undertake the vertically related activities in-house and establish an internal authority structure to coordinate these activities within the firm. By doing so, it incurs a *cost of internalization*, or the costs of starting and running some additional activities within the firm. Alternatively, it can remain a specialist producer and coordinate closely with its suppliers and customers. By doing so, for reasons explained below, it incurs a *cost of market transactions*. It pays the firm to integrate vertically only if, to achieve the same level of vertical coordination, its cost of market transactions is higher than its cost of internalization. Its additional profit from vertical integration is the saving in input costs due to better vertical coordination less the cost of internalization. More formally, the firm engages in market transactions if

$$\Pi^* > C_i > C_t, \tag{9.1}$$

where Π^* is the potential profit that can be earned by the firm through a saving in input costs because of better vertical coordination, and C_t and C_i are the costs of achieving this coordination through market transactions and internalization respectively. On the other hand, the firm integrates vertically if

$$\Pi^* > C_t > C_i, \tag{9.2}$$

and by integrating vertically, the firm realizes an additional profit

$$\Pi = \Pi^* - C_i. \tag{9.3}$$

Under what circumstances would we expect the transaction costs to exceed the costs of internalization? Typically, a firm incurs a high cost of market transactions when its suppliers or customers have to make a *transaction-specific investment*.[1] There is *asset specificity* when the suppliers or customers have to invest in physical or intangible assets or human capital that are designed to meet the specific requirements of the firm. Soft drink manufacturers, for instance, require their bottlers to invest in company specific bottling plants, train their staff in company specific bottling and distribution techniques, and promote the principal's brand names. There is *site specificity* when the suppliers or customers are required to locate their assets at sites specified by the firm. These assets, even if they are general purpose, become specific to the firm's requirements, because they cannot be used for requirements at other sites. For example, by locating itself next to a steel mill so that it may buy molten steel and save energy costs, a hot rolling mill

---

[1]For an authoritative exposition of this view, see Willamson (1981).

engages in site specific investment, because it can buy molten steel only from the steel mill located at that particular site.

When such transaction specific investments are called for, the firm does not have a ready market where it can go for its purchases or sales. It has to create these markets by identifying potential suppliers or buyers, assessing their suitability, negotiating terms, finalizing contracts, and equipping them suitably. All this involves a substantial one-time *contracting cost*. Maruti Udyog, for example, incurred a substantial one-time contracting cost when it first established its vendor network in India.

Asset specificity has three other implications. First, the firm has to deal with a *few* suppliers or customers, because transaction specific investments become uneconomic if a large number of parties make such investments. Second, the firm has to enter into *long-term contracts* with its transaction partners. Otherwise, neither the firm nor its partners can recover the one time costs of market creation, nor can they reduce costs over time by 'learning' about one another. Third, these contracts remain *incomplete*. They cannot specify all future contingencies because the human mind, being *boundedly rational*, cannot comprehend all possible contingencies.

The need to enter into long-term, incomplete contracts with a few suppliers and buyers results in the firm having to incur some recurring transaction costs also. First, since the firm's transaction partners run the risk of not being able to utilize their transaction specific assets fully, they have to be paid a *risk premium* which is built into the price paid or received by the firm. Second, asset specificity and the fewness of the firm's partners give rise to a bilateral monopoly situation. Since the contracts are incompletely specified, new contingencies arise from time to time. The sharing of the gains or losses arising therefrom has to be negotiated each time and the ability of either party to get a fair deal depends on its bargaining power, rather than its contribution to these gains or losses. This may lead to *hold-ups* and production losses. Third, the firm may also suffer some losses due to *negative externalities*. When the firm allows its partners to use its proprietary assets which have the property of 'public goods', it exposes itself to the risk of these being abused, leading to an erosion in their competitive value for which the firm is not compensated. For example, the know-how passed on by Maruti Udyog to its component suppliers may be used by the latter to supply Maruti's competitors also, without Maruti being compensated for the resultant erosion in the competitive value of this know-how.

To sum up, asset specificity and its attendant consequences lead to two types of transaction costs: a one-time cost of market creation and the recurring costs of risk premium, opportunism, and negative externalities.

TRANSACTION COSTS AND VERTICAL INTEGRATION: COCA-COLA INDIA

Coca-Cola came back to India after the liberalization of economic policies in 1991. In line with its international practice of franchising its bottling and distribution activities, it started by entering into an alliance with the Chauhans of Parle in 1993, who at that time had a 60 per cent share of the soft drinks market in India. Under the terms of this alliance, Coca-Cola bought over Parle's brands (Thums Up, Gold Spot, Limca, Citra, and Maaza) by paying $40 million upfront. Parle's was given an exclusive bottling franchise for Mumbai, 50 per cent of the franchise for Delhi, and the right of first refusal on the franchises for Pune and Bangalore. In addition, Coca-Cola and Parle would float a 50:50 joint venture to invest in new bottling plants as required. The Chauhans would also be paid a consultancy fee of $1 million over a period of five years.

Coca-Cola also appointed a large number of other bottlers as its franchisees. Coca-Cola Beverages, a 100 per cent subsidiary of Coca-Cola, would produce and sell to all franchisees (including Parle's) concentrates for all the brands owned by Coca-Cola, including those acquired from Parle. The franchisees would be responsible for bottling, transportation, distribution, and local promotion, while Coca-Cola would be responsible for the supply of concentrates, marketing, brand management, and technological development.

The agreement with Parle broke down within a year. Parle was found to be producing the concentrates for their erstwhile brands. For Coca-Cola, not only did this mean a loss of concentrate sales, but a dilution of its most important proprietary asset, namely its brand equity. It retaliated by pulling out of its commitments to float a joint venture with the Chauhans, give them the first refusal on Pune and Bangalore franchises, and pay them a consultancy fee. The dispute was settled eventually by Parle paying Coca-Cola Rs 4.27 crore as compensation for failing to buy the concentrates from Coca-Cola and Coca-Cola paying the Chauhans a further $3 million to buy up their bottling plants and their claim to the joint venture and consultancy fees.

Coca-Cola took two other steps towards assuming direct control over its bottling and distribution operations in India. To service areas where it did not have any franchisees, Coca-Cola established two bottling companies of its own. In other areas, it invited its existing bottlers to merge their companies into, and become minority shareholders of, one of two other bottling companies of which Coca-Cola would have majority control. After much negotiations, the company has now put in place an integrated bottling and distribution network by taking over most of its 54 bottling units and merging these as well its own four bottling companies into a fully owned bottling subsidiary called Hindustan Coca-Cola Holdings. The bottling units in Uttar Pradesh and the Punjab have been allowed to continue as franchisee-owned bottling operations, because Coca-Cola is happy with their performance.

In the soft drinks business, the economies of vertical coordination between marketing on the one hand and bottling and distribution on the other are obviously very high, because without adequate bottling and distribution all marketing inputs would be wasted. But why did Coca-Cola integrate into bottling and distribution in India, when elsewhere in the world they leave these functions to their franchisees? The reason evidently is that it considered the cost of transacting with its franchisees higher than the cost of establishing and running its own bottling and distribution activities.

Coca-Cola had been complaining about three kinds of transaction costs.

- It thought that its franchisees were using sugar and water inefficiently.
- It believed that it did not benefit fully from the rent that accrued to its proprietary assets, because of free riding by its bottlers. As the Parle experience showed, there was a risk of violation of its brand rights. Several bottlers were reported to be entering into franchising arrangements with other soft drink companies, directly or clandestinely, resulting in a dilution of Coca-Cola's bottling and distribution know-how. Coca-Cola's national promotions did not always lead to higher consumer sales, because benefits like free gifts or price discounts were not passed on to consumers. The bottling, distribution, and local promotion of many bottlers were inadequate, but they rode on Coca-Cola's goodwill.
- It felt that its own efforts to create a market for soft drinks in India were not matched by its bottlers' efforts to create a bottling and distribution infrastructure,

leading to lost market opportunities. This happened, because the strategic perceptions of Coca-Cola and its bottlers were quite different. Coca-Cola believed that the market potential for soft drinks in India was very large, given the hot climate, the large population, low per capita consumption of soft drinks, and changing lifestyles. The bottlers, on the other hand, took a more conservative view of the market, leading to frictions. Coca-Cola, for example, wanted to stimulate demand by adopting a low price, high volume approach. This, however, squeezed the bottlers' profit margins and was resisted by them. Similarly, the bottlers did not want to expand and upgrade their bottling, transportation, and distribution facilities at the rate desired by Coca-Cola, because they thought that Coca-Cola's demand projections were over-optimistic.

9.2.3 The Market Power Motive for Vertical Integration

A firm with market power in one market may be able to increase its profits through vertical integration by eliminating a monopoly in or extending its own monopoly into a vertically related market. To see how this works, we examine three cases. In all the cases, only one input is required to produce the final product. In the first case, both the output and input markets are monopolistic. In the second, the input market is monopolistic, the output market is competitive, and a fixed quantity of the input is required to produce one unit of output. In the third, the input market is monopolistic, the output market is competitive, and the quantity of the input required to produce one unit of the final product can be varied.

9.2.3.1 Case 1: Successive Monopolies

When both the input and output markets are monopolistic, monopoly rent is extracted in both the markets, leading to excessive output restriction. In such a situation, vertical integration eliminates monopoly mark-up at the input stage and allows the integrated monopolist to increase total profits by extracting his monopoly rent from an expanded output.

In Fig. 9.1 we assume that X is the final product, A its only input, and one unit of A is required to produce one unit of X. The production of both X and A is monopolized. The producer of X is not a monopsonist (the only buyer of A) and has no control over the price of A. The marginal cost of producing A is C, which is constant . The demand function for X is linear and is shown as D_x. Prior to integration, the marginal cost of producing X is the price of A charged by the monopoly producer of A. The monopoly producer of X sets his price and output by equating MR_x, the marginal revenue corresponding to D_x, with the price of A. Put differently, the price that the producer of X would be willing to pay for A at any given quantity of A demanded by him is equal to the marginal revenue he gets by selling the same quantity of X. Thus, MR_x becomes the demand curve D_a for A faced by the producer of A. The latter sets his price and output at P_a and A_1 respectively, by equating MR_a, the marginal revenue corresponding to D_a, with C, his marginal cost of production. The producer of X sets his output and price at $X_1 (=A_1)$ and P_{x1} respectively, by equating MR_x with P_a. The output monopolist's profit is $X_1 \times (P_{x1} - P_a)$ and the input monopolist's profit is $A_1 \times (P_a - C)$.

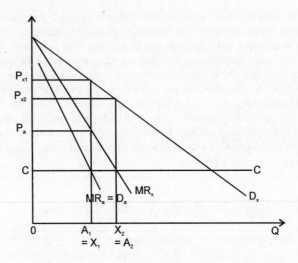

Fig. 9.1

Now consider what happens if the input monopolist buys up the output monopolist (forward integration) or the output monopolist buys up the input monopolist (backward integration). The integrated monopolist is interested in maximizing his total profits and not in the higher profit margins that result from the double mark-up. He, therefore, equates MR_x with C, so that the new price and output of X are P_{x2} and X_2 respectively. His profit is $X_2 \times (P_{x2} - C)$ which is higher than the combined pre-integration profits of the input and output monopolists. The drop in profit margin has been more than made up by the increase in volume. Although we have obtained this result by making a number of simplifying assumptions, it can be shown to hold good even if these assumptions are dropped.

9.2.3.2 Case 2: Vertical Integration by a Monopolist into a Competitive Market: Fixed Input Proportions

We now consider what happens if a monopolist in one market integrates into an adjacent market which is competitive, by making the following simplifying assumptions. The final product X uses two inputs, A and B. One unit of X can be produced by using one unit of A with one unit of B and there is no scope for substituting one input by the other. The production of A is monopolized. The markets for X and B are competitive. The marginal cost of producing one unit of A is C which is constant. The cost of buying one unit of B is W, which is also constant.

In Fig. 9.2, D_x is the market demand function for X, which is assumed to be linear. D_a is the market demand function for A, and can be derived from D_x as follows. At any output of X, $Q_x = Q_a$ and $P_x = P_a + W$, where Q_x and Q_a are the output, and P_x and P_a the price, of X and A respectively. The former equation follows from our assumption that one unit of X requires one unit of A. The latter equation holds, because we assume that X is competitively produced and its price equals the cost of production. Thus, D_a

lies below and is parallel to D_x, and the vertical distance between D_x and D_a is W. The marginal revenue curve corresponding to D_a is MR_a. The monopoly producer of A so sets Q_a and P_a that $MR_a = C$ and his profit is $Q_a \times (P_a - C)$.

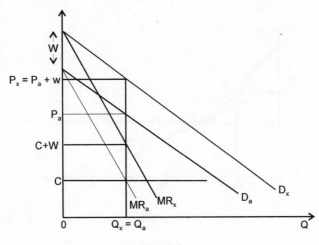

Fig. 9.2

If the monopoly producer of A now integrates forward and monopolizes the production of X also, he will be faced with a marginal revenue curve MR_x (corresponding to D_x) and a constant marginal cost of $C + W$. The integrated monopolist will maximize his profits by setting $MR_x = C + W$, and his profit will be $Q_x \times [P_x - (C + W)]$.

Since at any output of X, $Q_x = Q_a$ and $P_x = Pa + W$, it follows that $Q_x \times [P_x - (C + W)] = Q_a \times (P_a - C)$. In other words, the integrated monopolist earns exactly the same profit as the monopoly producer of A. When the inputs have to be combined in fixed proportions, the input monopolist can extract the entire monopoly rent at the input stage and does not have to integrate forward.

9.2.3.3 Case 3: Vertical Integration by a Monopolist into a Competitive Market: Variable Input Proportions

To see what happens if the two inputs can be combined in variable proportions, we retain all our previous assumptions except that we now assume that it is possible to substitute A by B and vice versa. This relationship is represented in Fig. 9.3 in the form of an isoquant curve XX which shows the different combinations of A and B that can be used to produce one unit of X. The isoquant is convex to the origin, because each successive unit of either input has to be substituted by a larger and larger quantity of the other because of diminishing marginal rate of substitution. To identify which precise combination of A and B will be used by the producer of X, we also have to draw a family of isocost lines which represent the varying combinations of A and B that can be bought by him with the same total outlay. Each isocost line is a straight line, which connects one point on the vertical axis with another on the horizontal axis. The distance of the point on the vertical axis from the origin measures the quantity of B that can be bought with a given total outlay if no A is bought. Similarly, the distance of the point on the horizontal axis from the origin measures the total quantity of *A* that can be bought with the same total outlay if no *B* is bought. Thus, each isocost line represents a given total outlay and has a slope of P_a/P_b, where P_a and P_b are the prices of *A* and *B* respectively.

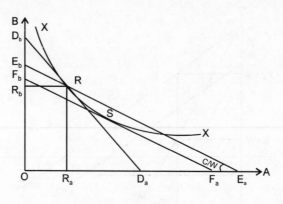

Fig. 9.3

The producer of *X* will produce one unit of *X* by choosing the least-cost combination of *A* and *B*. For the non-integrated producer this is represented by *R*, the point where *XX* touches the lowest possible isocost line with a slope of P_a/P_b. Thus, he will produce one unit of *X* by combining OR_a units of *A* with OR_b units of *B* at a total cost represented by the isocost line D_aD_b. Since all points on D_aD_b represent the same total cost, the total cost incurred by him to produce one unit of *X* is equal to OD_b units of *B* multiplied by P_b. This is also the price he charges for one unit of *X*, because *X* is competitively produced. Since *B* is also competitively produced, $P_b = W$. Therefore, the price of *X*, expressed in terms of number of units of *B*, is OD_b.

If both *A* and *B* were to be priced at cost, the isocost lines faced by the producer of *X* would have a slope of *C/W*. These lines would also represent the varying combinations of *A* and *B* that can be produced by the producers of the two inputs at the same total cost. E_bE_a is one such isocost line with a slope of *C/W*, which has been drawn through *R*. Since all points on this line represent varying combinations of *A* and *B* that can be produced at the same total cost, the total cost of producing OR_a units of *A* and OR_b units of *B*, expressed in terms of number of units of *B*, is OE_b. The difference between OD_b and OE_b (or D_bE_b) is the monopoly profit of the producer of *A*.

If the producer of *A* now integrates forward and becomes a monopoly producer of *X* also, the isocost line facing him will have a slope of *C/W*. This is because while $P_b = W$, for *A* he will charge himself a transfer price of *C*. His least cost combination for producing one unit of *X* will be represented by *S*, the point where *XX* touches F_aF_b, which is the lowest possible isocost line with a slope of *C/W*. In terms of the number of units of *B*, his total cost of producing one unit of *X* will fall to OF_b and his profit will increase to D_bF_b. Thus, when the inputs can be combined in variable proportions, by integrating vertically the integrated monopolist can increase his profits by choosing a more efficient input combination. He can do so because he can extract his rent from the output market and does not have to distort the input combination by extracting a rent at the input stage. Indeed, he is likely to do better because, in addition to using the most efficient input combination, he will so set the output and price of the final product as to extract the full monopoly rent from the output market. If prior to integration the final product was priced competitively, the post integration price will be higher and output lower. This will enable the integrated monopolist to increase his profits by increasing both efficiency and market power.

WHY DO FIRMS INTEGRATE BACKWARDS?
THE CASE OF RELIANCE INDUSTRIES LIMITED

Perhaps the most striking example of backward integration in India is provided by Reliance Industries Limited (RIL).

In the early 1960s, Dhirubhai Ambani, the founder of RIL, was engaged in buying textile fabrics in India, exporting them to West Asia, importing rayon and nylon with the replenishment licences, and selling them to fabric manufacturers in India. In terms of purchasing power parity, the rupee was highly overvalued at that time. As a result, fabric exports were unprofitable, but the high profits from the sale of imported rayon and nylon more than made up for the export losses. The low export prices, however, made it difficult to obtain export supplies from the market. Mr Ambani, therefore, set up his own fabric manufacturing facility at Naroda in Gujarat in 1966. In the late 1960s, when polyester fabrics became popular in India, he started importing polyester staple fibre for both captive consumption and commercial sale in India.

Rising domestic demand led to a change in RIL's business focus in the late 1970s, from exports to domestic sales. Soon, RIL became the market leader in India. thanks to its state-of-the-art technology and marketing innovations, like a design studio to create new designs, branding and advertising to create a consumer preference for its fabrics, and a chain of exclusive retail outlets to bypass an archaic wholesale trade. Through technology upgradation, capacity expansion, and the acquisition of a sick mill, RIL became the largest producer of textiles in India.

By the early 1980s, demand for polyester-based yarns in India had outstripped supply and both domestic and foreign suppliers were exploiting the shortage by charging high prices. RIL responded by becoming a polyester producer. It started producing polyester filament yarn (PFY) in 1981 and polyester staple fibre (PSF) in 1984 at a new unit in Patalganga, near Mumbai. The company ensured that the new facility was globally competitive by obtaining state-of-the-art technology from Du Pont (USA) and establishing a capacity, which was large even by global standards. Since its own captive requirements would not have utilized this capacity fully, RIL sold PFY and PSF to other fabric producers in India and exported PSF under its own and Du Pont's brand names. It was able to do so, because by combining global scales, modern technology, and cheap Indian manpower, RIL had become the lowest cost producer of polyester in the world. It increased its hold on the market further by acquiring the polyester units of ICI, India Polyfibres, J.K. Synthetics, and Raymond Synthetics. In the process, in RIL's portfolio, PFY became a more important product than fabrics.

Between 1988 and 1991, RIL integrated backwards from polyester into two of its basic inputs, namely purified terepthalic acid (PTA) and monoethylene glycol (MEG), and further from PTA to paraxylene (PX). By then, the company was into petrochemicals in a big way and diversified into a range of other petrochemicals which were unrelated to textiles, but offered high growth potential, namely linear alkyd benzene (LAB), an intermediate for detergents, polyethylene (PE), polyvinyl chloride (PVC), and polypropylene (PP). RIL now has two petrochemical complexes. At Patalganga, it produces PX, PTA, PSF, and PFY from naptha, and N-paraffin and LAB from kerosene. At Hazira, it produces MEG, PE, PP, and PVC from naptha.

RIL continues to integrate backwards. It has promoted a new company, Reliance Petrochemicals Limited (RPL), which has set up a 27 million tonne refinery at Jamnagar. Among other things, RPL will supply RIL's requirements of naptha and kerosene. RIL also plans to enter oil and gas exploration in a big way.

To what extent can we use the standard theories of vertical integration to explain RIL's evolution?

- As predicted by theory, the initial motivation for backward integration from fabric exports to fabric manufacture and from fabric manufacture to the manufacture of PFY and PSF appears to have been efficiency, in terms of reliability and cost-effectiveness of input supplies.

- By integrating backwards into polyester, RIL also increased the profits from its textiles business by creating a market power advantage. Fabric manufacture is highly competitive, because there are no major economies of scale attached to it. On the other hand, the markets for PFY, PSF, and their intermediates are oligopolistic, because their production is subject to substantial economies of scale. By becoming a large and efficient producer of PFY and PSF and integrating further into PTA and MEG, RIL was in a position to extract a monopoly rent from the vertical chain as a whole.

- Once RIL became a major player in petrochemicals, further integration and diversification was driven less by the compulsions of its textiles business than by an entrepreneurial urge to exploit emerging business opportunities in petrochemicals and hydrocarbons in India.

VERTICAL INTEGRATION VS. OUTSOURCING

In recent years, many vertically integrated firms in India have broken up their production chain, retained critical activities in-house, and outsourced the rest. For example, automobile producers like Telco and Mahindra & Mahindra, who were highly integrated not so long ago, buy most of their non-critical components and sub-assemblies from external suppliers. Asian Paints, Reckitt Benckiser, and Carrier Aircon no longer maintain their own fleet of cars, but outsource fleet management services from specialist fleet managers like Maruti Udyog and Lease Plan Fleet Management. Mutual Funds like Templeton, Alliance Capital, and Standard Chartered entrust routine servicing of their clients to external service providers like CAMS and Karvy Consultants. ICI, Pfizer, and Phillip Carbon Black have started buying management services like leave administration, payroll management, recruitments, and exit interviews from specialist firms like India Life Hewitt and Ma Foi Management Consultants.

A recent survey of outsourcing with a sample of firms in Europe and the USA brings out the following points.

- For European companies, the main motivation for outsourcing is cost savings, resulting from economies of scale.

- For American companies, the main motivation is access to best practices and the latest technology.

- Another important motivation is improved service quality, which arises because supplier companies are more focused than user companies on their own products and services.

- Increasingly, firms are outsourcing not just parts or components, but entire value adding systems like customer response handling or supplier relationship portfolio.

- User firms prefer long term associations with supplier firms with a proven track record and sector experience.

But why is it that firms who found vertical integration an efficient arrangement not so long ago are now discovering the advantages of outsourcing? Economists offer three possible explanations.

- When an industry is small and has an uncertain future, it cannot attract suppliers of industry-specific inputs and has to integrate vertically. When it grows to a certain size and becomes stable, suppliers emerge and make outsourcing possible. This may explain why automobile manufacturers have started outsourcing now.

- An industry producing specialized inputs can sell its products or services to other industries only if it can produce these more economically than the user industries. This happens when the supplier industry attains a certain size and competence level and has a substantial scale or efficiency advantage over the user industries. This may explain why the outsourcing of specialized services like IT or Human Resource Management (HRM) services are being increasingly outsourced in India.

- Recent innovations in industrial organization have reduced transaction costs and made it possible for firms to work together on the basis of a mutuality of interests. We shall deal with this point more fully when we discuss external architecture in Chapter 12.

Sources: 1 Kakabadse and Kakabadse (2002).
2 See Stigler (1951) and Levy (1984).

9.3 CONGLOMERATE DIVERSIFICATION

9.3.1 The Concept of Synergy

Firms engage in conglomerate diversification primarily with a view to exploiting what Business Policy literature calls synergy between businesses. There is *synergy* between two businesses if their combination gives rise to profit opportunities not available to either of them separately. From the economist's point of view, this could happen for two reasons. The firm may be able to reduce costs and increase profits by spreading its input costs over two products. We call this the *efficiency motive* of conglomerate diversification. Alternatively, if the demand in two markets is related in some way, a monopolist in one market may be able to increase its profits by diversifying and extending his market power into the other. We call this the *market power motive* of conglomerate diversification.

9.3.2 The Efficiency Motive of Conglomerate Diversification: Economies of Scope

Economies of scope exist when a firm can reduce its input costs by spreading them over more than one product, so that the cost of producing two or more products together is sub-additive (i.e. less than the total cost of producing them separately). More formally, if the firm produces two products, 1 and 2, with outputs of Q_1 and Q_2 respectively,

$$C(Q_1, Q_2) < C(Q_1) + C(Q_2), \tag{9.4}$$

where $C(Q_1, Q_2)$ is the cost of producing Q_1 and Q_2 together, and $C(Q_1)$ and $C(Q_2)$ are the costs of producing Q_1 and Q_2 separately. If the two products are competitively priced,

$$P_1 Q_1 = C(Q_1), \text{ and} \tag{9.5}$$
$$P_2 Q_2 = C(Q_2). \tag{9.6}$$

Replacing $C(Q_1)$ by $P_1 Q_1$ and $C(Q_2)$ by $P_2 Q_2$ in (eqn 9.4) and re-arranging terms, we get

$$\Pi^* = P_1 Q_1 + P_2 Q_2 - C(Q_1, Q_2), \tag{9.7}$$

where Π^* is a positive number and is the potential profit that can be earned by the firm because of economies of scope.

The sub-additivity of input costs may arise for three reasons:

- The first is what economists call *cost complementarity* between two products: the input cost of one product falls as the output of the other rises. This usually happens, because the input for one product is a by-product of the other. For example, vegetable oil is produced by extracting oil from oilseeds and the de-oiled seeds are converted into animal feeds. If one firm produces both vegetable oils and animal feeds, it can use the same oilseeds for both products. If one specialist producer uses some oilseeds to produce vegetable oils and another specialist producer uses some more oilseeds to produce animal feeds, their total cost of producing the two products separately will obviously be higher.

- The saving in input costs may also result from two or more products sharing the services of an *indivisible physical asset*, which cannot be utilized by any one of them fully. The under-utilization may arise because the demand for the asset from any one product is less than the minimum economic size of the asset. For example, one visit by a salesman of a soap-manufacturing firm to a retail outlet is indivisible. If the salesman's capacity to sell to the retailer during this visit is not utilized fully by selling soaps alone, the firm can also use him to sell detergents without a proportionate increase in costs. Alternatively, an asset may be underutilized because the demand for it from one product is seasonal and its utilization can be increased by using it for other products off season. This is why many food processors use their plant for processing mangoes during summer and tomatoes during winter.

- Finally, a firm can often spread the cost of its *intangible assets* over more than one product, because these assets have two important characteristics.[2] They are *fungible*. They represent general capabilities, which lie upstream from the end product and can have multiple product applications. The are also *privately owned public goods*. Once acquired for the production of one product, they can be used for the production of other products also, without

[2]Teece (1982) provides a comprehensive treatment of these points

any reduction in their availability for the product for which they were acquired in the first instance. The fungibility of intangible assets makes them shareable and their publicness makes the cost of sharing them sub-additive. For example, being fungible, much of the technology for producing fine chemicals developed by a drug manufacturer can be used for making pesticides also. And being public, this technology can be used for making pesticides without having to forego its use for making drugs. Consequently, by producing both drugs and pesticides, the drug manufacturer can produce both products more cost-effectively.

How is it that the intangible assets of a firm are like public goods and yet they earn a scarcity rent? The answer, as we have seen in Chapter 8, is that these assets are specific to a firm and scarce in a particular market, because the firm does not find it profitable to meet the entire demand in that market. Being superior to those of the marginal firm, they earn a scarcity rent in that particular market. Yet, being privately provided public goods, they can be made available for deployment in other markets, if it suits the firm to do so.

9.3.3 The Efficiency Motive of Conglomerate Diversification: Transaction Costs

However, as in the case of vertical integration, the efficiency motive of conglomerate diversification cannot stand on the plank of economies of scope alone, because a firm can also utilize its shareable inputs more fully by selling them to specialist producers. The vegetable oil producer can, for example, sell de-oiled cake to animal feeds producers. The soap manufacturer can sell his salesman's services to detergent manufacturers. The drug manufacturer can sell his fine chemicals technology to pesticide manufacturers. As in the case of vertical integration, by selling its shareable inputs to other firms, the firm incurs a cost of market transactions. On the other hand, by expanding its product portfolio to use the shareable inputs in-house, the firm incurs a *cost of diversification*, or the costs involved in starting and running a new business. The firm finds it profitable to diversify, only if the cost of market transactions is higher than the cost of diversification. More formally, the firm sells its shareable inputs if

$$\Pi^* > C_d > C_t, \tag{9.8}$$

where C_d is the cost of diversification. On the other hand, the firm diversifies if

$$\Pi^* > C_t > C_d, \tag{9.9}$$

and by diversifying the firm realizes an additional profit

$$\Pi = \Pi^* - C_d. \tag{9.10}$$

Under what circumstances should we expect the transaction costs to exceed the cost of diversification? As in the case of vertical integration, typically the cost of market transactions would be high if the buyers of shared inputs have to make some transaction-specific investments before they can use them. To go back to our earlier examples, the producer of animal feeds may have to locate his plant near the vegetable oil producer's plant, so that he can process the de-oiled cake before it rots. The detergent manufacturer may have to train the soap manufacturer's salesman specifically in the art of selling detergents. The car manufacture may have to spend money to adapt the truck manufacturer's technology for making cars. The need for transaction-specific investment leads to the same two types of transaction costs as we have noted in the context of vertical integration: a one-time cost of creating a market for these inputs and the recurring costs of risk premium, small numbers bargaining, and opportunism.

When a firm sells its intangible assets to another firm, it faces three other problems. First, as we have noted earlier, these assets are *imperfectly tradable*: they are worth more within the firm than outside it. Second, the market tends to undervalue these assets, because the so-called *fundamental paradox of information* puts the buyer at an advantage. The buyer is unwilling to pay for an intangible asset like technology or reputation until he has verified its usefulness by actually using it in his own specific context. But if he is allowed to use it before making a payment, he has in effect acquired the asset without having to pay for it. Third, being public goods, these assets generate *externalities* for which the seller is not compensated. We can illustrate this point by going back to the drug manufacturer who sells his fine chemicals technology to a pesticide manufacturer. The two may agree that the pesticide manufacturer should use this technology for producing pesticides only. But the pesticide manufacturer may use the same technology for making drugs also, without reducing its availability for making pesticides. If he does so, he generates a positive externality for himself in the form of an additional benefit from his technology purchase, and a negative externality for the seller in the form of a probable reduction in his drug sales. But the seller is not compensated for these externalities.

9.3.4 The Market Power Motive for Diversification

A monopolist in one market may diversify into another market to increase his profitability in both markets, if there are significant demand spillovers between the two markets. We can see why this is so by considering a simple example.

An increase in the price of tea reduces the quantity of tea demanded. The decrease in the quantity of tea demanded also tends to reduce the quantity of sugar demanded, because tea and sugar are *complementary* products, i.e. they are consumed together. On the other hand, the increase in the price of tea tends to increase the quantity of coffee demanded by encouraging some consumers to switch from tea to coffee, because the latter is a *substitute* for, i.e. can be consumed in place of, the former. Thus, an increase in the price of a product causes a decrease in the demand for its complementary products and an increase in the demand for its substitutes. The extent of demand spillover from one market to another depends on the *cross-elasticity of demand*, i.e. the percentage change in demand for one product as a result of a one per cent change in the price of another. The cross elasticity is negative if the products are complementary, positive if they are substitutes, and zero if they are unrelated.

When the demand for several products are linked, the profit maximizing behaviour of a monopolist producing two or more of these products tends to be different from that of a monopolist producing only one of them. To see this difference, we compare the profit maximizing behaviour of three firms: a monopolist producing only tea, a monopolist producing tea and coffee, and a monopolist producing tea and sugar. In Fig. 9.4, D_t, MR_t, and C_t represent the demand, marginal revenue, and marginal cost of tea alone. The tea-producing monopolist sets his price and output at P_t and Q_t

respectively by equating C_t with MR_t. For the monopolist producing tea and coffee, however, the marginal revenue schedule lies somewhere below MR_t, at MR_{tc} say. This is because, every decrease in the price of tea not only reduces the marginal revenue from tea sales, but also results in a revenue loss owing to a reduction in coffee sales, because lower tea prices encourage some coffee consumers to switch to tea. The tea and coffee monopolist, therefore, sets the price of his tea higher and output lower than the tea monopolist, at P_{tc} and Q_{tc} respectively, by equating C_t with MR_{tc}. For the monopolist producing tea and sugar, on the other hand, the marginal revenue schedule lies somewhere above MR_t, at MR_{ts} say. Although each decrease in the price of tea reduces the marginal revenue from the sale of tea alone, it also brings in some additional revenue through increased sale of sugar, because lower tea prices, by increasing the sale of tea, also increases the sale of sugar. The tea and sugar monopolist, therefore, sets the price of his tea lower and output higher than the tea monopolist, at P_{ts} and Q_{ts} respectively, by equating C_t with MR_{ts}. More generally, if the products are substitutes, the multi-market monopolist tends to set his price in each market higher and output lower than the single market monopolist. If the products are complementary, the former's price tends to be lower and output higher than the latter's. The higher the inter-market demand spillovers, the greater is the divergence in the profit maximizing behaviour of single and multi-market monopolists.

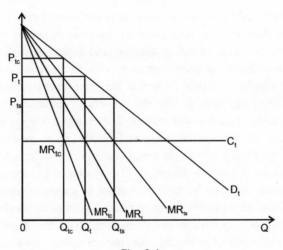

Fig. 9.4

Clearly, this divergence can become an important motivation for conglomerate diversification, if the demand spillovers are high, and the price-output behaviour of the monopolist in one market has a significantly adverse effect on the profitability of the monopolist in another. For example, if the tea monopolist finds that his profitability is very low because coffee prices are very low, he has an incentive to buy up the coffee monopolist and coordinate pricing in both markets. Likewise, if he finds that he is losing a lot of revenue because of high prices and output restrictions in the sugar market, he has an incentive to buy up the sugar monopolist and coordinate the pricing of tea and sugar.

9.3.5 The Case for Related Diversification

Exploitation of synergy calls for diversification into businesses that are related through shared inputs or demand linkages. It is, however, usual to define related diversification more narrowly, as diversification into a business, which shares the distinctive expertise acquired by a firm in the context of its existing business. Put differently, a firm is said to have diversified into a related business, if its new business shares the proprietary assets that are specific to the business it is already in. It is argued that the benefits of synergy can be substantial only if the firm's new and existing businesses are related in this narrower sense of the term.[3]

To understand the logic behind this argument, we go back to (eqn 9.7), which says that the potential extra profit from economies of scope

$$\Pi^* = P_1Q_1 + P_2Q_2 - C(Q_1, Q_2). \tag{9.11}$$

But, if all single product firms could produce both the products equally efficiently, then under conditions of free entry they would all become two product firms and drive down prices until P^* is competed away. Put algebraically, under these conditions,

$$P_1Q_1 + P_2Q_2 = C(Q_1, Q_2), \text{ and} \tag{9.12}$$
$$\Pi^* = 0. \tag{9.13}$$

The reason why Π^* does not become zero for some firms is that some of the inputs shared by their diverse businesses are proprietary assets which generate an appropriable rent, by virtue of being superior and scarce, imperfectly imitable, and imperfectly tradable. Now, the assets that are specific to the firm's existing business are likely to generate a higher rent than those that are generalizable across many businesses. This is because, being business specific, these assets are more scarce, more difficult to imitate, and less easily traded in the market. For example, a generalizable asset like a firm's ability to use information technology efficiently can be used in many businesses. But it is unlikely to yield a very high rent, because other firms either have the same ability or can acquire it easily by hiring an IT consultant. On the other hand, a firm that has acquired an expertise in rural marketing by engaging in its existing line of business can use the same expertise to generate a high rent in another business where it is a critical input. This is because not many firms have this expertise, nor can they buy it readily in the market. On the flip side, the specificity of this expertise limits the diversification options open to the firm.

Thus, the rent yielding capacity of related diversification is higher, because it capitalizes on the firm's business specific assets, which are more scarce and less easily imitated than general purpose assets. With related diversification, the cost of converting this rent into actual profits is also lower, because the cost of diversification, especially the cost of learning, is also lower. On the other hand, lower benefits and higher costs make unrelated diversification relatively unattractive, often unprofitable.

---

[3]For an exposition of this view, see Prahalad and Hamel (1990).

TELCO'S INDICA: A CASE OF RELATED DIVERSIFICATION

The production of passenger cars in India was static until the early 1980s. There were basically two producers, Hindustan Motors and Premier Automobiles, who between them produced 60–70 thousand cars every year and recovered cost increases by raising prices. Production picked up with the entry of Maruti Udyog, a joint venture of the Government of India with Suzuki Motors of Japan and reached 163,000 in 1992–3. After the liberalization of economic policies in 1991, a number of Korean, American and European companies started producing cars in India, and production increased by 20–25 per cent per year to 640,000 cars in 1999–2000. Even with this kind of growth, less than 1 per cent of all households in India owns a car. With increasing penetration, the Indian market for cars is expected to grow at 15–20 per cent per year.

Meanwhile, the sales of Tata Engineering Company (Telco), the biggest producer of commercial vehicles in India, were growing slowly and fluctuating from one year to another. In 1993, Mr Ratan Tata, the chairman of Telco, announced his intention to bring out an indigenously developed 'people's car', driven partly by business compulsions and partly by national pride. He backed this project personally against heavy odds. In 1999, Telco's first passenger car, Indica, rolled out of the factory. Interestingly, Maruti Udyog saw it as a major threat and introduced stripped down versions of two of its most popular models at reduced prices in 1998. Based on market feedback, Telco has made some improvements in its original product and brought out Indica V2, available in both diesel and petrol versions.

The initial market acceptance of Indica seems to be quite good. In 1999–2000, the first year of its launch, 55,000 cars were sold. In the last nine months of 2001–2, Indica was the largest selling car in its segment, ahead of segment leaders like Maruti Zen and Hyundai Santro. Even in 2002–3, it continues to be one of the three largest selling models in its segment, although absolute sales have fallen because of a general recession in the car market. Meanwhile, Telco has started exploring the export market. It may use the Indica platform to produce an 'Arab' car in Egypt in collaboration with the Egyptian government, for sale in the Middle East and North Africa. It may get a local producer to assemble its cars in Iran for the Iranian market. It is also talking to M.G. Rover of the UK about using Rover's dealer network to export its cars to Europe.

Although it is too early to come to any definite conclusion, there are signs that Indica has started making a positive contribution to Telco's profit. In 2000–1, Indica made a huge cash loss and Telco made a record loss of Rs 500 crores. In 2001–2, Indica made a cash profit. As a result, Telco's operating margin rose from 5 per cent to 8 per cent and its loss came down substantially.

Indica is a good example of related diversification, because it has allowed Telco to benefit from economies of scope in a number of ways.

- Some of the physical facilities and human capital created for commercial vehicles could be used for passenger vehicles.

- The basic knowledge and R&D facilities acquired for commercial vehicles needed to be upgraded incrementally, by purchasing new technology in gap areas, conducting trials, and recruiting knowledgeable people from outside (like the R&D chief who now heads the car division).

- The supplier network established for commercial vehicles was adapted for passenger vehicles.

- Telco's reputation as a reliable producer of automobiles has attracted customers for its cars. This has been strengthened by its proven commitment to the Indian market. Customers know that, unlike some assemblers of imported models, Telco will not quit at the first sign of losses, leaving them with enormous spares and servicing problems.

• Its external architecture has helped Telco build a dealer and service network, purchase technology, attract trained manpower, and manage the project expeditiously.

As the following table shows, thanks to these economies of scope, Telco has launched its car project more economically than its competitors (except Maruti, whose project costs are incremental to costs incurred on its Maruti 800 project). Consequently, at full capacity utilization, Indica has the lowest capital cost per car. It also has the highest local content among comparable models.

	Indica	Maruti (Zen/Alto/ Wagon R)	Daewoo (Matiz)	Hyundai (Santro)
Project cost (Rs crore)	1700	800	3500	2100
Capital cost per car (Rs lakh)	1.13	1.14	2.33	1.84
Local content (first year)	99	—	70	80

Source: *Business India*, 26 June 1998.

Because of these advantages, Indica should become more and more competitive as volume builds up and the rupee depreciates. It has one other advantage. It has been designed with the Indian consumer in mind. It is so priced that it competes with cars in the so-called 'B' segment of the market. But it offers some of the advantages of a bigger car. Indica is sturdy, which is an advantage given that typically Indian roads are in a bad condition. At 980 kg, it is 40 per cent heavier than other cars in its segment. The Indian consumer has a large family, travels with a lot of luggage, is often driven by a chauffeur, and sometimes wears a turban. Therefore, Indica is 30 per cent more spacious than other cars in its segment and has a 'tall boy' look. To cope with a heavier and bigger body, Indica is powered by a 1400 cc engine, while other cars in its segment use a 1000 cc engine.

9.3.6 SURPLUS CASH AND UNRELATED DIVERSIFICATION

Yet many firms seem to engage in businesses that seem unrelated and some do so very successfully. How do we explain this?

One reason why firms diversify outside their main line of business is to utilize their *surplus cash* profitably. If a firm's existing business yields a return on capital (R) which is higher than its rate of growth (G), by re-investing its profits in the same business the firm suffers an erosion in its profitability. If the firm ploughs back its entire profit, its R in times $t1$ and $t2$ are:

$$R_{t1} = M.Y_{t1}/K_{t1}, \text{ and} \tag{9.14}$$

$$R_{t2} = MY_{t1}(1 + G)/(K_{t1} + M.Y_{t1}), \tag{9.15}$$

where M is a constant margin of profit on output Y and K the capital stock of the firm. Replacing $M.Y_{t1}$ by $R_{t1}.K_{t1}$ in (eqn 9.15) and rearranging terms, we get

$$R_{t2}/R_{t1} = (1 + G)/(1 + R_{t1}). \tag{9.16}$$

If G is lower than R_{t1}, R_{t2} is lower than R_{t1}.

Faced with this situation, the firm could either return its surplus cash to the capital market as dividends, loans, or portfolio investments, or invest it in a new line of business. The latter becomes a more profitable option if the firm finds a more profitable outlet for the cash than the capital market, i.e. the *internal capital market* of the firm is more efficient than the external capital market. It is not unusual for the internal capital market to be better informed about investment opportunities which are related to the firm's own line of business. But under some circumstances, it may also enable the firm to take advantage of profit opportunities outside the firm's business more efficiently than the external capital market. For example, the external capital market, being risk averse, tends to under-finance potentially profitable projects with an uncertain outcome or a long gestation period, e.g. new technologies, emerging markets or infrastructural projects. An entrepreneurial firm may be able to capitalize on such opportunities better by taking a longer view and drawing on its internal capital market. A firm may also be able to use its surplus cash to enter high profit, high growth businesses by under-cutting and predating its rivals. The firm can borrow from its internal capital market to finance the temporary losses involved. But its rivals, even if they are equally efficient, cannot survive a prolonged price war because the external capital market is unwilling to lend to a loss-making firm.

9.3.7 Inefficient Markets and Unrelated Diversification

Surplus cash becomes a motivation for unrelated diversification if the firm uses cash more efficiently than the capital market. More generally, a firm may find it profitable to diversify into unrelated businesses, if its general-purpose proprietary assets like architecture and reputation can earn a high rent by mobilizing and allocating non-proprietary factors of production like finance, general-purpose human capital, or natural resources more efficiently than the markets.[4] In some markets, especially the so-called emerging markets, there may be a latent demand for a product that is yet to be introduced. The capability to produce the product may also exist. Yet transactions do not take place because of market failures. Production may not take place because the suppliers of financial or human capital or specialized inputs do not see the market potential and make the necessary investments. Buyers may not be willing to buy because they are not familiar with the product and do not know what utility they will get by using it. Even if suppliers are willing to supply and buyers are willing to buy, transactions may be blocked by institutional bottlenecks, unhelpful government regulations or an inefficient legal system making contract enforcement difficult. An established firm may, however, be able to make transactions possible by using its internal capital and labour markets, reputation, long-term relationships, and lobbying power to provide the required capital and trained manpower, attract suppliers and buyers, and remove external hurdles. The firm can then make a profit by using its general-purpose assets to correct market failures, because in these circumstances, even these assets are scarce and superior, and not easily imitated or traded. The 'chaebols' in Korea, or the 'business houses' in India, or the 'groupos' in Latin America engage in a wide variety of unrelated businesses, because they operate as a more efficient alternative for the product and factor markets.

---

[4]For an excellent presentation of this point of view, see Khanna and Palepu (1997).

Inefficient Markets and Unrelated Diversification:
Indian Business Groups

Economic liberalization threw open to private industry several sectors that were earlier reserved for the public sector. Three such sectors are power, telecommunications, and petroleum refining. A Study by the Centre for Monitoring Indian Economy (CMIE) study shows that in 1998 the top ten business groups in India had plans to implement new projects involving a total investment of Rs 180,000 crores. As much as 70 per cent of this investment was slated to go into these three sectors: 33 per cent in power, 25 per cent in petroleum, and 12 per cent in telecom. What is more, as the table below shows, practically all the groups, regardless of what businesses they are in now, were planning to enter two or more of these sectors.

Group	Main Businesses	New Projects
Tata	Diverse	Telecommunications
Aditya Birla	Textiles	Power
	Fertilizers	Petroleum refining
	Aluminium	
Reliance	Textiles	Power
	Petrochemicals	Petroleum refining
		Telecommunications
Ispat	Steel	Power
		Telecommunications
Essar	Steel	Power
		Petroleum refining
BPL	Consumer durables	Power
		Telecommunications

This seems a bit paradoxical. Many of these groups are currently in the process of shedding businesses that do not use their 'core competence'. Yet they are going into these three sectors which are not related to their existing lines of business. The reason for is that while these sectors, being basic to the economy, offer a high potential for growth, they require heavy investments with a long gestation lag. Therefore, although long term prospects are good, new projects in these sectors are unlikely to be very profitable in the short run. These sectors are also unattractive from another point of view: because of their importance to the economy, firms in these sectors will be monitored very closely by the government. It is, therefore, unlikely that the markets can mobilize and allocate financial, human, and other resources to the extent required to exploit the growth potential of these sectors. Large business groups, on the other hand, may be in a position to do this more efficiently than the markets. They should be able to use their reputation and architecture to mobilize government support, technology from abroad, financial and human resources from the capital and labour markets, and put them together to get the projects going. Although these businesses are unrelated to the existing businesses of the groups, not many firms would have the reputation or the architecture to handle projects of this magnitude. Therefore, the rent accruing to these general purpose proprietary assets should, over a period of time, be high enough to more than make up for the cost of learning about, starting, and running a completely new business.

9.3.8 MANAGERIAL MOTIVATIONS FOR UNRELATED DIVERSIFICATION

However, much of the unrelated diversification that takes place seems to be driven by a desire to maintain a steady rate of growth and a stable rate of profit, rather than earn a very high rate of profit. A firm in pursuit of growth has an incentive to diversify if its existing markets are not expanding fast enough. If the related businesses are also saturated, it tends to diversify in unrelated fields, even if this entails some loss of profitability.

The link between unrelated diversification and profit stability is much more direct. By diversifying, a firm can reduce the variability of its expected profits, if the profits from its different businesses are not perfectly correlated, i.e. they do not all rise or fall together by exactly the same percentage. More formally, if a firm has two businesses, each with an expected mean profit P and a variability (of the actual profit from the expected mean) V, the expected mean profit of the firm as a whole is $2P$ and its variability $V\sqrt{2(1 + R)}$, where R is the correlation coefficient of the expected profits of the two divisions and can have any value between $+1$ and -1. If R is less than 1, $V\sqrt{2(1 + R)}$ is less than $2V$: if the profits of the two divisions are not perfectly positively correlated, by combining the two the expected mean profit is doubled, but the variability of the profit is less than doubled. The lower the value of R, the lower is the value of $V\sqrt{2(1 + R)}$. In fact, when $R = -1$, $V\sqrt{2(1 + R)} = 0$: if the profits from the two divisions are perfectly negatively correlated, the variability of the firm's profit is zero. Clearly, a firm seeking profit stability will try to combine businesses that are affected differently by the same change in the business environment. Since unrelated businesses tend to be affected differently by environmental changes, profit stability constitutes an important motivation for unrelated diversification.

But why should a firm pursue growth or profit stability, if by doing so it has to sacrifice some profits? The ordinary shareholder is not interested in the growth or profit stability of individual firms in his portfolio. He wants his firms to maximize profits and give him as high a return on his investment as possible. He can achieve growth and stability in his portfolio by investing in a suitable mix of firms, directly or through mutual funds. If he finds that some of his firms are too static or unstable, he can shift his funds to other firms that meet his requirements better. The reason why a firm pursues growth and stability, even by sacrificing profitability to some extent, is that it is controlled by its majority shareholders, managers, and employees who have a different utility function. To the latter, the firm represents a sunk cost. They look upon it as a source of livelihood, status, and power, and cannot switch to another firm easily. For them, growth is important, because unless the firm grows, their own monetary and non-monetary rewards cannot increase. Profit stability is also important, because it ensures job security and income stability.

Thus, for the majority shareholders, managers, and employees of a firm, growth and stability may be more important than profit maximization. Since they have control over the surplus cash generated by the firm, they tend to use it to diversify into any business, even if it is unrelated to the firm's other businesses, as long as it enables the firm to maintain a steady rate of growth and profitability. This sometimes means that the firm earns a lower rate of profit than it would by sticking to its moorings. Non-profit maximizing diversification of this kind can continue until the firm's profitability falls so low as to risk a take over. There is some empirical support for this view. Research shows that there is a systematic tendency for firms to earn less on their retained earnings than on equity or loans.[5]

---

[5]Mueller (1972) and Amihud and Lev (1981) explain why managers seek growth and stability respectively, even at the expense of profits.

10 Multi-market Operations II: Internationalization and Strategic Motivations

In this chapter, we complete our discussion on multi-market operations by looking at internationalization as a means of expanding the market portfolio and the strategic motivations for multi-market operations.

10.1 Motives and Methods of Internationalization

A firm seeks markets abroad for one of two reasons. The home country of the firm has a *comparative advantage* in the product produced by the firm. Therefore, by selling abroad the firm gets a higher price for its product. Alternatively, the production process exhibits *economies of scale*. Therefore, by selling abroad and producing more, the firm is able to reduce its unit production costs. The firm can access markets abroad in one of two ways. It can engage in *international trade*. It can produce at home and export its product. Alternatively, it can engage in *international production*. It can set up production facilities abroad.

10.2 International Trade

10.2.1 Comparative Advantage and International Trade: A Brief Review

A country is said to have a comparative advantage in a product if the price of that product, in terms of other products, is lower in that country than in other countries. The basic rationale of international trade based on comparative advantage is that by exporting one unit of a product in which it has a comparative advantage, the country gets more of other products than it would by trading it within the country.

A product may fetch less at home than abroad because, relative to other products, it is less in demand at home than abroad. Alternatively, the country may have a comparative cost advantage in producing the product. Why does a country have a comparative cost advantage in producing some products? One explanation is international differences in *factor endowment*. A country has a comparative advantage in producing a product, if it is relatively well endowed with the factor of production that is used intensively to produce that product. This is because, other things being equal, a factor that is in abundant supply commands a low price relative to other factors. The other explanation is international differences in *factor productivity*. Even if two countries have similar factor endowments, one has a comparative advantage in a particular product because it can produce it with lower factor inputs.

International differences in factor productivity arise, because each country uses its factor endowments in conjunction with some *created common assets* like infrastructure, human capital, etc. These assets have some important characteristics. Like proprietary assets of firms, they increase the productivity of the factors with which they are used. Unlike proprietary assets, they can be used by all firms operating within the country. Finally, these assets are often created to increase the factor productivity in specific industries. This *industry specificity* of a country's created common assets makes the country relatively more productive in some industries, in which it develops a comparative advantage.

As Krugman[1] points out, an important reason for the industry specificity of these created common assets is that they are created to meet the specific requirements of a cluster of firms engaged in a particular industry. Three such assets are identified: industry specific productive assets acquired by input suppliers, industry specific human capital, and industry specific technology that spills over from one firm to another through interaction and imitation.

User firms cluster together, because the larger the number of user firms in a cluster, the lower is the cost of providing the services of these specialized assets. By pooling the requirements of a large number of customers, the providers of these assets are able to take advantage of economies of scale, diversify the risks of asset underutilization, and reduce the costs of market transactions. An initial cluster may arise to meet a large domestic demand or to take advantage of factor endowments. As the number of firms in the cluster increases, the cost of providing the services of these assets falls and more user firms are drawn to the cluster. Thus, the comparative advantage of a country based on created common assets tends to be self-reinforcing. In recent decades, several countries have created a comparative advantage in certain 'target' industries by reversing the above sequence as a matter of deliberate policy. By subsidizing the provision of industry specific common assets, they have created industry clusters, which in turn have made the provision of these assets a viable proposition.

It has been suggested that another important industry specific common asset is the way a country organizes work.[2] Social institutions like schools, training institutes, trade unions, consumer bodies, governments, etc. play an important role in shaping national patterns of work organization. Since these vary from one country to another, different countries evolve their own methods of organizing work and these methods tend to become particularly efficient in specific sectors where there is a close affinity between the social institutions and the task environment. Examples are the auto industry in Japan or the machine tool industry in Germany or the computer industry in the USA. International competition leads to a diffusion of the organizing principles from one country to another. But diffusion is slow because these principles are embedded in

---

[1] See Krugman and Obstfeld (1991), chapter 6, pp 120–51.
[2] Several articles in Kogut (1993) are of interest in this context.

firms and social organizations, so that the way a country organizes work becomes a source of comparative advantage over long periods of time.

10.2.2 Comparative Advantage and International Trade: How Does the Firm Gain?

How does a firm increase its profits by exporting on the basis of the home country comparative advantage? Panel A of Fig. 10.1 shows the home demand (DD) and supply (SS) of a product in which the home country has a comparative advantage. Without trade, production is Q_1 and price P_1. Panel B shows the demand (D^*D^*) and supply (S^*S^*) conditions abroad. Without trade, production abroad is Q_1^* and price P_1^*, so that $P_1^* > P_1$. If trade between home and abroad is now opened, a firm will initially be able to buy the product at P_1 at home and sell it abroad at P_1^* and make an arbitrage profit of $P_1^* - P_1$. However, if trade is free and costless, more and more firms will do the same, until the two prices equalize and the opportunity for arbitrage profits disappears. At a price of P_1 or less, there is no exportable surplus, because home demand equals or exceeds supply. But at a price above P_1 domestic supply exceeds demand and the difference is available for export. The home country's supply of exports at different prices (which is the difference between domestic supply and demand at each price) is shown as $S_x S_x$ in panel C. Similarly, at a price of P_1^* or more, there is no demand for home country exports, because the demand abroad can be met by supplies abroad. But at prices below P_1^*, demand abroad exceeds supply abroad and the difference is available as demand for the home country's exports. The demand for the home country's exports at different prices (which is the difference between demand and supply abroad at different prices) is shown as $D_x D_x$ in panel C. Given $S_x S_x$ and $D_x D_x$, the home country exports a quantity Q_x at price P_x. Post trade, the price in the home country rises from P_1 to P_2 and the price abroad falls from P_1^* to P_2^*, so that $P_x = P_2 = P_2^*$. With P_2 as the new price, home production rises from Q_1 to Q_2, home consumption falls from Q_1 to Q_2, and the difference between Q_3 and Q_2 is exported. Similarly, with P_2^* as the new price, production abroad falls from Q_1^* to Q_2^*, consumption abroad rises from Q_1^* to Q_3^* and the difference between Q_3^* and Q_2^* is imported.

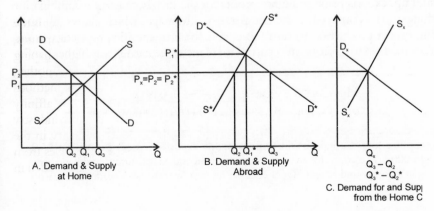

A. Demand & Supply
at Home

B. Demand & Supply
Abroad

Q_x
$Q_3 - Q_2$
$Q_3^* - Q_2^*$
C. Demand for and Sup|
from the Home C

Fig. 10.1

If trade equalizes domestic and international prices and eliminates arbitrage profits, how does a firm gain by exporting? The firm gains in two ways. First, the industry price increases from P_1 to P_2 and, for reasons explained below, a part of this increase accrues to the firm as an increase in its profit margin. Second, the industry output increases from Q_1 to Q_2, so that the firm has an opportunity to increase its profits further by increasing its output also.

If the productive resources in the home economy are fully employed and competitively priced, the increase in the price of the product would lead to an increase in the unit reward of all factors and created assets engaged in its production. Each product uses two types of inputs: *mobile factors and created assets* that are not specific to any product and can move freely from one product to another (e.g. general purpose transport equipment, unskilled workers, accountants, etc.), and *specific factors and assets* that can be used for producing that particular product only (e.g. special purpose machines, specialized human capital, etc.). Since all resources are fully employed and the stock of specific factors and assets cannot be increased quickly, the exporting firms expand output by attracting non-specific factors and assets from other uses and combining them with a fixed stock of specific factors and assets. This brings into play the law of diminishing returns. Since a larger quantity of non-specific inputs is combined with the same quantity of specific inputs, the marginal physical product of the former falls, while that of the latter rises. Under competitive conditions, the price paid to each input is equal to its marginal revenue product, i.e. its marginal physical product multiplied by the product price. Trade, by raising the product price, raises the price of all inputs. But the price of mobile inputs increases less than the product price, because the increase in the product price is partly offset by a fall in the marginal physical product of these inputs. The price of specific inputs, on the other hand, increases more than the product price, because the product price increase is reinforced by an increase in the marginal physical product of these inputs.[3] The increase in the price of the non-proprietary inputs are appropriated by the owners of these inputs, while the increase in the rewards accruing to the proprietary assets of the exporting firm is appropriated by the firm as an increase in its profit margin. Since by definition proprietary assets are specific to the firm and its products, the increase in the profit margin is higher than the increase in the product price.

To sum up, exports result in higher profits for the firm because of a combination of two things: (a) a country-specific comparative advantage, which allows all inputs engaged in export production to earn more, and (b) firm-specific proprietary assets, which allow the firm to appropriate a part of these increased earnings as higher profits.

How does exporting on the basis of comparative advantage benefit the firm?

The computer software industry in India is highly export oriented. Exports, at $6.2 billion in 2000–1, account for over 70 per cent of the industry's output and have been growing at a compound rate of 50 per cent per annum over the last decade. The reason

---

[3]Neary (1978) gives a formal account of why specific inputs gain more than mobile inputs.

for this basically is that India has a comparative advantage in computer software: the cost of producing it is much lower in India than in North America, Europe, and Japan, which account for 90 per cent of India's exports. This is because India is relatively well endowed with software engineers, thanks to an abundance of high quality manpower, widespread knowledge of the English language, and the training facilities available all over the country. Since software engineers are mobile, their services are to some extent accessed by software users abroad hiring and moving them across the borders, directly or through body shoppers. However, the Indian engineers that go abroad cannot be paid much less than the local engineers. To avoid this, and thanks to the advances in telecommunication technology, software users abroad prefer to import software products from India.

As predicted by theory, exports have led to a very significant increase in the price of software products in India. Also, as predicted by theory, the tendency towards product price equalization has started a tendency towards factor price equalization. Since the prosperity of the software industry is based largely on a country level comparative advantage, a large number of firms have entered the industry. (In 2000–1, the top 10 exporters together accounted for 40 per cent of industry exports and the share of the tenth exporter was less than 2 per cent.) These firms compete vigorously amongst themselves for the key resource, namely skilled manpower, by outbidding one another. Consequently, the annual turnover of professional staff in the software industry is 20-30 per cent and the annual increase in their wages has been a staggering 20–30 per cent in recent years.

If all software firms were equally efficient, by competing amongst themselves, they would have passed on the entire increase in software prices to the software engineers as higher wages. In reality, the exporters are not equally efficient. The marginal exporter ends up by passing on the entire increase in his price realization to his professional staff. But those exporters who are more efficient (i.e. the exporters whose proprietary assets are superior to those of the marginal exporter) are able to appropriate a part of the price increase as a rent accruing to their proprietary assets. Thus, by exporting on the basis of comparative advantage, not only do they get a higher price for their products, but they are also able to retain a part of the price increase as higher profits. To understand how this is achieved, we consider how Infosys Technologies, a very successful exporter of software, goes about its exports.

Like most Indian firms, Infosys does not try to compete abroad on the basis of technology or reputation. Technological innovation requires heavy investment. Development of a reputation requires size and marketing skills. In both these areas, Indian firms are at a disadvantage *vis-à-vis* their competitors in more advanced countries. Infosys competes by leveraging India's advantage of skilled manpower. It does so by developing the capability to use known but advanced technologies to provide complex solutions. To achieve this, it has created an architecture which enables and motivates its professional staff to handle complex tasks and produce more within Infosys than they would in other firms or on their own.

Some of the more interesting aspects of this architecture are as follows. Infosys has established a network of marketing offices located near the customers and software development centres located at or near the home towns of its software engineers. Thus it connects its software engineers with the customers without having to move them about too much. To the extent possible, Infosys recruits its professionals on campus, imparts to them complex firm-specific skills through in-company training programmes, and keeps them updated through a continuing education programme. To ensure that the output of project teams is higher than the total of individual outputs, Infosys emphasizes teamwork. It selects people who like to work in teams and inculcates team spirit in them through attitude conditioning. Infosys tries to assign each individual to projects where he or she is likely to perform best in terms of skills and interest. To this end, it maintains a dossier on each individual.

The reward system is designed to motivate and retain people and has two interesting features. There is a cafetaria approach: within an overall limit, each individual is free to structure his or her salary package to suit his or her specific needs. And the company has a stock option scheme, which enables all employees to share the prosperity of the firm. As much as 10 per cent of the firm's equity is available for distribution to its employees.

Source: Press reports.

10.2.3 ECONOMIES OF SCALE AND INTERNATIONAL TRADE: A BRIEF REVIEW

The other main reason why a firm sells abroad is to expand output and reduce costs by exploiting economies of scale. These economies of scale are of two types. They may be *external to the firm*. The increase in the industry output as a result of exports may be achieved by new firms entering the industry. As we have noted earlier, as the number of firms in the industry increases, the cost of providing some common inputs like industry specific physical and human capital, technology, materials, and components falls. Consequently, the increase in the industry output leads to a fall in the production costs of all firms in the industry, even if the output of individual firms may not increase. Alternatively, the economies of scale may be *internal to the firm*. The increase in the industry output as a result of exports may be achieved by the existing firms in the industry expanding their output, enabling them to spread their fixed costs over a larger output.

Whether the economies of scale are internal or external to the firm, a country can achieve a cost advantage over its trading partners by producing more of the same product, even if it has no inherent advantage in it. At the same time, the country can produce more of a product by differentiating its product, i.e. by specializing in a particular type of the same product, pooling the demand for it in several countries. A lot of the exchange of similar products between different countries, or what economists call *intra-industry trade*, takes place because different countries differentiate their products to take advantage of economies of scale. Intra-industry trade based on product differentiation and economies of scale benefit all trading partners, because they all get a wider variety of products at a lower cost.

10.2.4 Economies of Scale and International Trade: How Does the Firm Gain?

How does the firm gain from this kind of trade? When the economies of scale are external to the firm, the reduction in costs is common to all firms and does not confer any special benefit to any of them. However, by engaging in intra-industry trade, all firms get a higher price for their products, in the same way as in the case of trade based on comparative advantage. When the economies of scale are internal to the firm, by exporting and expanding its output, it soon reaches a size when it can no longer remain a price taker and has to reduce its price to expand output further. We cannot, therefore, predict the effect of economies of scale on a firm's profitability without considering the market structure within which it operates.

When the economies of scale are significant, an oligopolistic market structure is the most likely outcome. The industry is dominated by a few large firms who act in an interdependent manner. In setting their prices and outputs, not only do they consider the likely buyer response, but the likely response of their rivals too. Prices tend to be rigid and market shares tend to be stable. Since there are economies of scale, firms with high market shares make high profits. To protect their margins and market shares, the incumbent firms deter entry by erecting strategic entry barriers.

Faced with these barriers, a newly internationalizing firm could adopt one of two approaches. It could become a fringe supplier in the international market by restricting its overseas sales, so that it does not invite predatory action from the established sellers. By expanding its output, the firm would reduce its costs and increase its domestic profitability. On the other hand, by remaining a fringe supplier, it is unlikely to reduce its costs sufficiently to make a profit at the ruling international prices. Thus, when the economies of scale are substantial, a marginal entry into the international market is unlikely to be profitable. Alternatively, the firm could try to enter the international market in a big way. This way, it will make some initial losses, because it will have to fight a battle of attrition to overcome the entry barriers put up by the established sellers. But should it manage to break in and become internationally competitive by carving out a sizeable share of the international market, the firm's profits would increase substantially. In the 1960s and 1970s, several Japanese and Korean firms followed the latter approach successfully, thanks to a large domestic market, strategic support from their home governments, and superior efficiency.

The other type of market structure which has received much theoretical attention in recent years as an explanation for intra-industry trade between countries is monopolistic competition.[4] Monopolistic competition differs from oligopoly in two ways. First, each firm in the industry can take its price and output decisions independently of its rivals, because it sells a differentiated product, which is the preferred choice of some buyers. Therefore, by increasing (reducing) its price in relation to its rivals, the firm loses to (gains from) its rivals some but not all of its (their) sales. Second, new firms can enter the industry freely. Therefore, a newly internationalizing firm can enter a foreign market without having to contend with entry barriers.

To understand how a firm can exploit product differentiation and economies of scale to increase its profits by selling abroad and how this leads to intra-industry trade between countries, we assume that there are N firms in the industry, each selling a differentiated product. Since our firm produces a product which is the preferred choice of some buyers, it can get a market share of $1/N$ by charging a price P which is equal to the average price P^* for the industry as a whole. If it charges a higher (lower) price than the industry average, its market share falls (rises) by B-times the amount by which its price exceeds (falls below) the industry average. In other words, the firm faces a downward sloping demand curve which can be expressed as:

$$Q = S(1/N - B(P - P^*)), \qquad (10.1)$$

where Q and S are the sales of the firm and the industry respectively. On the cost side, we assume that C, our firm's average cost of producing one unit of output, consists of

---

[4]See Krugman and Obstfeld, (1991).

a constant marginal cost M and its fixed cost F, spread over its output Q. Algebraically,
$$C = M + F/Q. \tag{10.2}$$
There are increasing returns to scale, because as Q increases, F/Q falls and C falls. The firm maximizes its profits by equating its marginal revenue R with its marginal cost, so that the firm is in equilibrium when
$$R = M. \tag{10.3}$$

If our firm sets a price which is higher than its average cost, price would exceed average cost for the industry as a whole, because no other firm with a price lower than average cost can survive in the long run. In that event, since entry is free, more firms would enter the industry and bid down the price charged by our firm, so that in the long run,
$$P = C. \tag{10.4}$$
Combining (eqn 10.2) and (eqn 10.4) we get,
$$P - M = F/Q, \tag{10.5}$$
which is the margin the firm gets by differentiating its product. The total margin earned by the firm is $F \,(=Q.F/Q)$. Since a part of F is the cost of the firm's proprietary assets, the firm appropriates a part of F/Q as profit.

Figure 10.2 shows diagrammatically how, given the above assumptions, the profitability of our firm increases as a result of exports. D_1 and R_1 are the demand and marginal revenue curves facing the firm in the home market. The firm sets its price and output at P_1 and Q_1 respectively, so that $M = R_1$ and $P_1 = C_1$. Since the firm's product is differentiated, it is also the preferred choice of some buyers abroad. Therefore, by selling abroad the firm expands its demand and marginal revenue curves to D_2 and R_2 respectively. Assuming trade is costless, the firm now sets its price and output at P_2 and

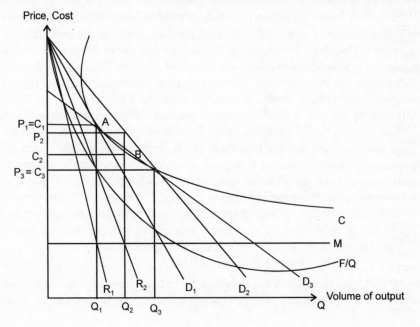

Fig. 10.2

Q_2 respectively, so that $M = R_2$. Although the expansion in output leads to a fall in price from P_1 to P_2, because of economies of scale the average cost falls even more from C_1 to C_2, and the profit margin increases by $P_2 - C_2$. If another firm, located abroad and producing a similar but differentiated product, exports to the home country of our firm, home and abroad engage in intra-industry trade based on product differentiation and economies of scale.

The implication of the free entry assumption is that the increase in the firm's profit would disappear over time. The high profits encourage more firms to enter the industry with a wider variety of substitute products. Consequently, the demand curve facing the firm not only moves downwards, but also becomes flatter (more elastic) and shifts from D_2 to D_3. The new long run equilibrium of the firm is reached at price P_3 and output Q_3, where $P_3 = C_3$. In reality, however, entry is never completely free, nor do new firms detect and respond to international profit opportunities quickly, nor can they match the product differentiation advantages of the established firms easily. Consequently, by exporting on the basis of product differentiation and economies of scale, firms are often able to achieve profit increases which persist over long periods of time.

BOX 10.1. PRODUCT DIFFERENTIATION, ECONOMIES OF SCALE, AND
INTRA-INDUSTRY TRADE

The pharmaceutical industry in India illustrates how product differentiation and economies of scale lead to intra-industry trade and how exporting firms benefit from it.

Pharmaceutical products can be divided into two broad categories: bulk drugs or the active ingredients that go into a product and fomulations or the dosage forms (tablets, liquids, etc.) into which the bulk drugs are converted. India's pharmaceutical exports in 1995–6 were worth Rs 2337 crore, accounting for 21 per cent of the the industry's total output and 60 per cent of the output of bulk drugs. India also imported Rs 1867 crore worth of pharmaceuticals in that year. Thus, the Indian pharmaceutical industry is not only export-oriented, but also characterized by a two-way, or intra-industry, trade.

The intra-industry trade in pharmaceuticals is the result of two things. First, Indian exporters have differentiated their product by specializing in generic drugs and drug delivery systems, and leaving the *R&D*-intensive patented drugs to exporters in advanced countries. In fact, individual firms have specialized further. For example, Ranbaxy's main products are anti-bacterials like cephalosporins, amoxycillin, ampicillin, and ciprofloxacin. Lupin concentrates on cephalosporins and anti-TB drugs like ethambutol, rifampicin, and pyrazinamide. Wockhardt is a major international producer of dextropropoxyphene, a bulk drug for analgesics. Second, their competitiveness in generic drugs and drug delivery systems is primarily the result of external economies of scale. India has no major comparative advantage in pharmaceuticals. Pharmaceutical production is not particularly labour-intensive, nor does India have any supply advantage in the basic chemicals that go into the production of bulk drugs. The plant level internal economies of scale are also not very significant. During the 1970s and 1980s, pharmaceutical production in India grew at a compound rate of 15 per cent per annum and more than half this growth came from an increase in the number of firms in the industry. The main reason for India's competitiveness in bulk drugs is that the growth in the number of firms in the industry has led to an expansion and upgradation in the external infrastructure catering to the industry as a whole. This has enabled all firms in the industry to become cost effective.

Perhaps the two most important elements of this infrastructure have been the availability of trained manpower and the expertise in developing low cost production processes. The latter has spilled over to a large number of firms through the CSIR laboratories and the movement of scientific manpower from one firm to another.

How have individual firms gained from this intra-industry trade? All exporters, large and small, have realized a higher price for their products and, depending on the quality of their proprietary assets, some have retained a part of the price increase as higher profits. The larger exporters like Ranbaxy, Dr Reddy's, Lupin, etc. have also gained from a reduction in costs by exploiting internal economies of scale. Although the plant level economies of scale are not very high, marketing and technology-intensive firms have been able to, by exporting, spread their costs of process development, marketing and sales promotion, quality assurance, good manufacturing practices, etc. over a larger volume of output.

Source: Press reports.

10.3 INTERNATIONAL PRODUCTION

10.3.1 International Production as an Alternative to International Trade

The basic rationale for a firm engaging in international trade may now be summarized as follows. By producing in its home country and exporting, the firm exploits either the comparative advantages of the home country to get a higher price for its product, or the internal economies of scale to increase the productivity of its factor inputs. Some of the gains that result therefrom accrue to consumers as lower product prices and to non-proprietary factors as higher factor prices. The rest is appropriated by the firm as higher profits.

However, when the barriers to trade in the finished product are high, the firm may be able to capture the gains from comparative advantage and economies of scale more fully by exporting critical inputs and combining them with local inputs to the finished product abroad. Four such situations can be identified.

- First, it may not be possible to export the finished product because it is immobile, but it may still be possible to export the inputs that go into its production. For example, the services of a hospital located in Chennai cannot be exported, but the doctors and nurses can.

- Second, even when the finished product can be moved, it may be cheaper to transport the inputs than the finished product. For example, it is possible to export freshly cooked Indian delicacies from Delhi to London by air. But it may be cheaper to produce the same food in London by exporting the cooks, recipes, and ingredients.

- Third, it is usual for importing countries to encourage local value addition by imposing steeper tariff and non-tariff barriers on finished products than on inputs.

- Finally, it often becomes necessary to incur some additional costs in the importing country before the product reaches the final consumer. These may be transaction costs incurred to identify, access, and strike deals with the consumer, or reprocessing costs (e.g. finishing, re-packing, branding, etc.) to ensure that the product conforms to the local regulations, preferences, and other local requirements. Often, these costs can be minimized by locating final production near the point of actual consumption.

Three kinds of inputs are commonly exported: proprietary assets like technology or reputation which are usually very mobile; mobile, non-proprietary factors of production like financial and human capital; and intermediate goods which embody home country comparative advantages (e.g. labour-intensive engineering components from India) or economies of scale (e.g. semi-conductors from the USA). By using its proprietary assets to produce abroad, a firm exploits both economies of scale and comparative advantage: the former because the same assets can be used to produce more, and the latter because they increase the productivity of local inputs abroad. By exporting non-proprietary assets that are in abundant supply at home, the firm transfers home country comparative advantages to its operations abroad. And by exporting intermediate goods that embody home country comparative advantages or economies of scale, the firm transfers these advantages to its operations abroad.

Thus, from the firm's point of view, international production is an alternative to international trade. When the barriers to trade in the finished product are high, the firm gains more by producing abroad. On the other hand, by producing abroad it also incurs some additional costs by way of shipment of inputs, setting up facilities abroad, using more expensive local inputs, managing operations abroad, etc. The firm prefers international production to trade, if the additional gains outweigh the additional costs.

10.3.2 The Theory of the Multinational Enterprise

The story is not yet complete. If international production means the export of inputs rather than the finished product, why does the firm not save the additional costs of international production by selling these inputs to producers abroad? The answer to this question is that by selling inputs on an arm's length basis, the firm incurs two kinds of transaction costs. First, if the market for these inputs is narrow, the firm faces the problems of asset specificity, small numbers bargaining, and opportunism. Second, because of problems relating to transfer, valuation, and imitation of its proprietary assets, the cost of renting these assets to an outsider may be very high. When the cost of selling these inputs through the market is higher than the cost of producing abroad, the firm uses the inputs in-house by engaging in international production.

We are now in a position to summarize the modern theory of the multinational enterprise. For the same firm to produce the same product in more than one country, three conditions must be fulfilled. First, the firm must have an *ownership (O) advantage*: it must have some proprietary assets that enable the firm to appropriate a part of the gains from its international operations. Second, there must be a *location (L) advantage*: the gains from international operations must be higher by producing in multiple locations than by producing in one location and exporting from there. Finally, there must be an *internalization (I) advantage*: the firm must earn more from its export of inputs by using them in-house than by selling them to other firms on an arm's length basis. This theory was originally propounded by John Dunning[5] and is known as the OLI paradigm.

Box 10.2. The OLI paradigm: EIH Limited

EIH Limited (formerly East India Hotels), which runs the Oberoi chain of hotels, went into the hotel business in the 1950s by acquiring a few hotels in India. Over a period of time it developed two important assets: an expertise in running hotels and a strong brand name. The company soon started using these assets to run not only its hotels but also properties owned by others. In 1996, there were 24 Oberoi hotels, of which 11 were owned by the company and the rest owned by others.

From the mid-1960s, the company started setting up hotels abroad, for two reasons. First, room tariffs in India were only about a quarter of those prevailing abroad. Second, the Indian government considered 5-star hotels an avoidable luxury and discouraged their growth through high taxes and other measures. In 1996, 11 of EIH's 24 hotels were located in 6 countries abroad. However, until the 1990s there were restrictions on how much Indian firms could invest abroad and EIH's international operations were initially based on their managing properties owned by local partners. Post 1991, these restrictions have been relaxed considerably and there has been a change in EIH's strategy. Between 1991 and 1996, the company has acquired 5 properties abroad.

EIH provides a classic example of how the OLI paradigm works. First, as we have noted earlier, the company has two important 'ownership' advantages, an expertise in running hotels and the Oberoi brand name, which are mobile across international borders. The business expertise can be moved by moving people who have the expertise. In recent years, it has also been packaged in the form of written manuals and performance standards that all employees and hotels in the chain must follow. The brand name travels across the borders through Indians going abroad, non-resident Indians, and the word of mouth. Second, there is also a 'location' advantage. Since the hotel services cannot be provided to customers abroad by exporting them from India, EIH can service its markets abroad only by locating its hotels near the points of consumption. Third, instead of setting up its own hotels abroad, EIH could conceivably have cashed in on its expertise and brand name by leasing these out to hotel owners abroad. But experience shows that the royalty earned through this route tends to be short-lived. As soon as new hotels start running smoothly, acquire a reputation and become profitable, the owners try to avoid paying royalty by terminating the lease agreement. EIH does not, therefore, accept a management contract for a hotel unless it is given a 26 per cent equity stake in it. In fact, the company is switching increasingly from minority to majority control over its hotels. In other words, there is also an 'internalization' advantage: it is more profitable for EIH to transfer its expertise and brand name internally than by entering into a market transaction with another party.

Source: Press reports.

10.3.3 Organization of International Production

International production involves centralizing the production of some inputs and decentralizing the production of the others. At one end, a firm can tailor the product

[5]See Dunning (1988), Chapters 1 and 2, pp. 13–70.

for the local market by engaging in what Michael Porter[6] calls *multi-domestic production*. Most of the production activities are decentralized in the countries where the product is consumed and only the proprietary assets and a few other key inputs are produced centrally. At the other end, the firm can achieve a high degree of cost effectiveness by engaging in *global production*. Most of the productive activities are undertaken centrally and very few are decentralized in the countries where final consumption takes place. The other feature of global production is that all centrally produced inputs need not be produced in the home country of the firm. Different inputs are centralized in different locations, depending on their comparative advantage, and products and inputs are exchanged amongst the various locations. This way, the firm combines the economies of scale with the comparative advantages of the countries in which it operates.

Each firm organizes its international production differently from its competitors, based on its own assessment of costs and benefits. There are three key dimensions of this difference. The first is the *degree of centralization*, or the extent to which the firm undertakes its production at certain central locations. The second is the *configuration* of the firm's activities worldwide, or the way the firm locates each of its productive

---

BOX 10.3. GLOBAL PRODUCTION NETWORK: THE ADITYA BIRLA GROUP

Although many Indian firms have set up operations abroad, they have done so to exploit market opportunities available locally, rather than establish a cost effective global production network. A notable exception is the Aditya Birla group.

Aditya Birla, who started his manufacturing operations abroad in the 1970s, was one of the earliest Indian entrepreneurs to look for business opportunities outside India. His initial motivation was to circumvent the policy-induced constraints to business growth in India. He exploited his entrepreneurial flair and international technology to establish very large units for the manufacture of simple products like palm oil, textiles, carbon black, etc. in a number of South East Asian countries like Malaysia, Thailand, Indonesia, and Vietnam. More recently, his group has moved into other territories like the Philippines, Egypt, and Canada. The group is the world's largest producer of viscose staple fibre, the largest single plant refiner of palm oil, third largest producer of insulators, and sixth largest producer of carbon black. One half of the group's profits comes from its international operations.

The overseas operations of the group have evolved in response to business opportunities available in various countries, and not necessarily with a view to developing an efficient global production network in a planned and systematic manner. However, in recent years, there has been an attempt to optimize textile production on a global basis. The group has recently taken over a large pulp mill in Canada which supplies dissolving grade chemical wood pulp to its textile mills in India, Thailand, and Indonesia. This enables the group to exploit Canada's comparative advantage in wood pulp (because of her rich forestry resources). The company in Thailand converts the wood pulp into viscose staple fibre not only for its own use, but also for the Indonesian company, enabling the group to take advantage of economies of scale.

Source: Press reports.

---

[6]See Porter (1986), Chapter 1, pp. 16–61.

activities in specific countries. The third dimension is *coordination*, i.e. the way the firm coordinates similar and related activities which are performed in different countries. Clearly, an important determinant of the profitability of a firm's international production is the distinctive way in which it deals with each of these three dimensions. In other words, the way a firm organizes its international production becomes a proprietary asset of the firm.

10.4 Strategic Motivations for Multi-market Operations

10.4.1 Strategic Motivation Defined

Higher profits constitute one motivation for multi-market operations. However, for reasons explained below, a firm may sometimes wish to enter new markets with a view to *gaining a strategic advantage*, or strengthening its position *vis-à-vis* its competitors, even if this does not lead to an immediate increase in its profits.

10.4.2 Predation and Entry Deterrence

It is sometimes argued that multi-market operation increases a firm's ability to predate (drive out) or deter the entry of its rivals by threatening a price war. The latter oblige if they find the threat credible and do not expect to win. It is argued that even if a multi-market firm and its single market rival are equally strong, the threat held out by the former is more likely to succeed, because it can use its strengths in one market to fight a price war in another. There are several versions of the story. We discuss three of them below.

The *long purse* version says that the multi-market firm is in a better position to win a war because it can finance the temporary losses in one market by using its profits from other markets. We should note, however, that the long purse works not because the firm operates in multiple markets, but because capital markets are imperfect. While the loss-making division of the multi-market firm can borrow from the internal capital market with a promise to repay when the prices are restored to profitable levels, the external capital market may not be willing to lend to a loss-making single market firm, even though it may have an equal chance of winning the price war.

The *shared cost* version suggests, on the other hand, that the multi-market firm does in fact have a better chance of winning precisely because it operates in multiple markets. It assumes that to make its threat credible, the firm has to sink some of its costs so that it becomes cheaper for the firm to fight than share. What is more, some of this sunk cost has to be in the form of excess capacity of its assets which normally remain underutilized. The firm has to carry some excess capacity when prices are profitable, so that supplies can be expanded and prices driven down to unprofitable levels when necessary. This puts the diversified firm at an advantage. Its sunk cost of carrying excess capacity is lower, because some of this excess capacity can be switched from one market to another as required. Thus, even if the multi-market and single market firms are otherwise similar, by sharing its sunk costs in more than one market, the former reduces its cost of fighting a price war and can hold out longer.

The *multi-market reputation* version is similar to the shared cost version except that it assumes that to make its threat of price war credible, a firm has to acquire a reputation for fighting by carrying out the threat if necessary. Since fighting a price war is expensive, there is a cost attached to reputation building. The multi-market firm is at an advantage, because once it has acquired a reputation in one market, its reputation spills over to other markets also and it does not have to incur the cost of reputation building in every market it operates in. In other words, while the multi-market firm can spread its cost of reputation building over multiple markets, the single market firm cannot make its threat credible without incurring the cost of reputation building in the specific market it operates in.

10.4.3 Multi-market Contact and Oligopolistic Consensus

It is sometimes argued that if rivals meet in more than one market, it becomes easier for them to co-operate. Therefore, one reason why firms diversify is to be able to meet one another in multiple markets so that they may earn high profits through oligopolistic consensus. There are two views on how this happens, one building on the symmetry between sellers and the other building on their asymmetry.

The *symmetry-based view*[7] holds that if firms with similar strengths and strategic compulsions diversify purposively, i.e. in pursuit of economies of scope or market power, they tend to diversify into the same markets. They exhibit other similarities also, like similar cost structures, similar strategic approaches, etc. This symmetry between the sellers facilitates oligopolistic consensus in two ways. First, by meeting one another more frequently and playing the same game more often than they would in one market alone, the multi-market rivals become more familiar with one another and are more likely to hit upon a cooperative-like accord in the markets they operate in. Second, once such an accord is reached, they are more likely to be able to sustain it, because they behave in a symmetric manner. For example, it can be shown that if the rivals in a market have identical costs and the price set by one is matched by the others, each firm will assume its market share to be constant and its profit-maximizing price will be the same as the monopoly price for the industry as a whole.

The *asymmetry-based view*[8] says that two firms may meet in two markets by design or by accident. But when they do, they value the same market differently, because they are different. Each firm develops, or is allowed by its rivals to develop, the market it values most as its own sphere of influence, where its rivals become its followers. Firms collude because of a mutual hostage position. No firm undercuts its rival in the latter's sphere of influence, because this invites retaliation where it hurts most, in its own sphere of influence.

To see the importance of asymmetry in this scheme of things, first consider a single market situation where price setting firms follow a simple trigger strategy. The monopoly price is sustained by each firm adhering to it and sharing the monopoly profits. Any one firm can appropriate the entire monopoly profit temporarily by setting its price just below the monopoly price and undercutting its rivals. But as soon as he

[7]See Scott (1993), Chapter 2, pp. 19–31.
[8]See Bernheim and Whinston (1990).

does so, his rivals react by undercutting one another until all firms return permanently to the single period Bertrand–Nash equilibrium, i.e. the zero profit price. By cheating, the firm's one-time pay-off is $Q(P - C)$, where P and C are the monopoly price and cost per unit of output and Q the industry output. By not cheating, its pay-off is the present value of its share of a perpetual stream of monopoly profits made by the industry. This can be written as $S \times Q(P - C)/D$, where S is the firm's share of the industry's profits and D the rate at which the firm discounts its future profits. The firm will not cheat if $S \times Q(P - C)/D > (P - C)Q$, or $S > D$. If there are two equally strong firms, A and B, in the market, each with $S = 0.5$, both will adhere to the monopoly price if $D < 0.5$ for both. But if for either of them $D > 0.5$, it gains by cheating and the monopoly price cannot be sustained.

Now consider a two-firm, two-market situation with perfect symmetry. Markets 1 and 2 are equally large and profitable. Both A and B operate in both markets. For both firms, $D = 0.55$ and $S = 0.5$ in both markets. Clearly, the monopoly price cannot be sustained in either market. But suppose B agrees to restrict its output and settle for a market share of 0.4 in market 1 in return for A doing the same in market 2. Now A and B have a vested interest in maintaining the monopoly price in markets 1 and 2 respectively, because $S < D$. They collude in both markets, because if B undercuts in market 1, A retaliates by undercutting in market 2. The outcome changes because the two firms now value the two markets asymmetrically, as their market shares are different. The same thing happens if the asymmetric valuation of the two markets by the two firms is reflected in an asymmetry in their discount rates. Assume, for example, that A discounts its future profits at a lower rate of 0.4 in market 1 which is its home market, and B does the same in market 2 for the same reason. Monopoly prices then become sustainable in both markets, even if both firms share both the markets equally.

10.4.4 Follow Thy Competitor

Finally, consider a situation similar to the above, in that the rivals are equally strong and recognize their interdependence. But unlike in the previous case, they lack sufficient consensus to coordinate their activities closely. It is argued that in such a situation, if one firm diversifies into a particular market, its rivals would follow him into the same market to deny him any cost or strategic advantage that he may gain from it. Consequently, no firm gains by expanding its market portfolio. There is excess capacity in all markets and the rivals try to keep afloat by keeping prices rigid and engaging in non-price competition.[9]

[9]See Knickerbocker (1973).

11 Architecture I: Internal Architecture and the Organization Structure

We introduced the concept of architecture in Chapter 8. To recapitulate, a firm's *architecture* consists of the long-term relationships it forges with and among risk capital providers, knowledge and manual workers, creditors, customers, vendors, and other partners in production, on the basis of implicit contracts. The contracts that bind risk capital providers and knowledge and manual workers constitute the *internal architecture* of the firm. The distinguishing feature of these contracts is that they are *enforced by the authority of the firm*. The contracts that bring the customers, vendors, creditors, and other partners in production together make up the *external architecture* of the firm. The distinguishing feature of these contracts is that they are *self-enforced*, or enforced by the parties themselves, because they benefit by doing business with one another.

In this chapter, we develop the concept of internal architecture more fully and deal with one of its components, namely the organization structure. The other aspects of architecture are discussed in the next chapter.

11.1 INTERNAL ARCHITECTURE

11.1.1 Authority Relationship in Internal Architecture

A firm uses both debt and risk capital to acquire its productive assets. But while it has an obligation to pay an interest and repay its debts to its creditors, it has no such obligation to the provider of risk capital. The provider of risk capital authorizes the firm to convert the finance provided by him into productive assets. His principal is kept in the form of the productive assets of the firm and the return that he gets on his principal is a stream of profits, or the residual income of the firm after meeting its obligations to its creditors, vendors, and employees. Thus, the risk capital provider is the owner of the firm's assets and the recipient of the firm's profits. In other words, he is the owner of the firm.

To acquire this privilege, the risk capital provider has to put at risk both his capital and the return that he gets on it. The return on his capital is at risk because the creditors, vendors, and employees have to be paid at a predetermined rate and any fluctuations in the firm's income are reflected fully in the profit that accrues to him. His capital is at risk, because he can recover his capital only by selling his claim to the firm's assets and the price he can get for it may exceed or fall short of his original investment, depending on how the market views the profit earning potential of these assets. If the firm goes bankrupt, he has the liability for meeting all outstanding obligations of the firm to its creditors, vendors, and employees. Depending on how the ownership of the firm is structured, this liability may be limited to the amount that can be raised by selling the firm's assets or unlimited in the sense that it has to be met by liquidating the risk capital provider's personal assets, if necessary. The risk capital provider takes these risks because he is risk-neutral and expects the firm to give him a higher return on his capital than less risky investments like bank deposits, government or corporate bonds, or real estate. Typically, the large investor is risk-neutral because he is entrepreneurial, while the small investor is risk-neutral because he diversifies his risks over a number of firms.

The knowledge or manual worker enters into a contract with the firm, whereby the firm has the authority to ask him to do anything and in any way it likes, unless prohibited explicitly by law or the contract itself. The contract is long term, because typically it is valid until terminated by either party. It is also implicit. Only a few things like remuneration, leave entitlement, and termination conditions are specified, while many other things like job responsibilities, increment and promotion norms, future postings, etc. are left unspecified. The knowledge or manual worker accepts the authority of the firm, primarily because he is risk averse. If he sells his services in the spot labour market, he exposes himself to the risk of fluctuations in his income because of personal exigencies (e.g. illness) or vagaries of demand or uncertainties in the availability of complementary inputs. He avoids this risk by entering into an employment contract with the firm that guarantees him a steady but lower income than what he would earn by selling his services in the spot market. The difference between what he would earn in the spot market and what his employer pays him is the premium he pays for insuring himself against the risk of his actual income deviating from his mean income.

The firm is in a position to insure him against this risk for two reasons. First, the risk faced by the firm is lower than the risk faced by individual workers, because the firm can to some extent diversify its risk across employees and businesses. In this sense, the firm is like an insurance company. Second, and far more important, the risk is absorbed by the provider of risk capital who is risk neutral. Consequently, the firm can insure its employees against the risk of fluctuations in their income by charging a lower premium than an insurance company. Thus, the individual worker gains by becoming an employee of the firm, rather than by selling his services in the spot market and using the services of an insurance company to insure himself against the risk of fluctuations in his income. In return, he accepts the authority of the firm.

Since the provider of risk capital is the owner of the firm, the authority of the firm over its employees rests with him. Thus, he has control over both the firm's assets and its employees. In other words, the *ownership and control of the firm are integrated* in the provider of risk capital. Typically, the risk capital is provided by the provider of risk finance, because the firm's assets are acquired either with the finance provided by him or by raising debts on the strength of the finance provided by him. However, in a knowledge-intensive firm, the main profit-yielding asset may be the knowledge that resides in knowledge workers. If this knowledge is specific to the firm, then the main capital at risk is not financial capital, but the knowledge of the knowledge workers. When this is so, knowledge workers may have a greater incentive to ensure efficient utilization of the firm's assets than the providers of risk finance and to gain control over the firm by also providing risk finance to the extent required. This is why law and accounting firms are usually owned and controlled by lawyers and accountants themselves.

11.1.2 Separation of Ownership and Decision-making

The arrangements described above are efficient. The risk capital provider, being the recipient of the residual income of the firm, has a vested interest in maximizing the productivity of the resources at the firm's disposal. He can avoid production losses due to hold-ups, because he is the sole owner of all the productive assets of the firm. He can also minimize production losses due to shirking and free riding by employees, because he has the authority to tell them what to do and how to do it.

However, these arrangements create some new problems by separating the ownership of a firm from the making of decisions on how the firm's affairs should be run. This separation takes place, because the owner does not have the *specific knowledge* required for making all the decisions. Typically, this knowledge resides in individual employees, who acquire it through *training* (e.g. an R&D scientist), *learning* (e.g. a production supervisor), or *proximity* to the scene of action (e.g. a salesman), and can be acquired by the owner at a considerable cost. Efficiency demands that the owner authorizes the employees who have the appropriate knowledge to take decisions on his behalf. In the economist's jargon, the owner should become the *principal* and use knowledgeable employees as his decision *agents*. Because if he did not do so, he would either have to incur the cost of acquiring the required knowledge or take suboptimal decisions in the absence of this knowledge.

The separation of decision-making from ownership leads to two kinds of problems. First, the agents may be guided by their own self-interest, rather than the owner's objective of profit maximization, and use the productive resources of the firm suboptimally. This is what economists call the *agency problem*. Second, since different types of specific knowledge are required to take different types of decisions, there are multiple decision agents in a firm. If these agents are not fully aware of the compulsions, plans, and actions of one another, they may work at cross-purposes and end up by taking decisions that use the productive resources of the firm wastefully. This is what economists call the *coordination problem*.

11.1.3 AGENCY PROBLEMS

The firm enters into a contract with an employee, whereby they agree, at least implicitly, that the employee will put in the effort required to maximize the firm's profits and the firm will compensate the employee suitably. The principle of delegating decision-making to those who know best would imply that the employee who has to do a certain job should decide how much effort he should put in. For example, since the salesman knows his customers best, he should decide how much effort he should put in to persuade them to buy the firm's products. However, Leibenstein[1] points out that this results in the employee putting in less than the profit maximizing level of effort. He argues that if we plot the amount of effort put in by an individual on the horizontal axis and the utility he derives from it on the vertical axis, we will get a curve that looks like an inverted 'U'. Initially, as he puts in more effort his utility increases, because he prefers some activity to no activity. But after a point, he prefers leisure to work and if he puts in more effort, his utility starts falling. If he is in a position to decide how much effort he should put in, he will adopt an effort position that maximizes his own utility, rather than the profit of the firm. Typically, the former will fall short of the latter. What is more, once he adopts a certain effort position, he will develop a set of work routines around it and resist any changes in his work routines and the effort position adopted by him. Thus, if he is allowed to decide how much effort he should put in, he is likely to *shirk*, or put in less effort than is required for profit maximization, and the firm's actual profit is likely to fall short of the maximum profit that could be achieved. The profit lost by a firm because its employees do not put in the optimal amount of effort is a measure of what Leibenstein calls the *X-inefficiency* of the firm.

Economists usually define shirking more broadly, as any action of employees that increase their own utility at the expense of the firm's profit, and X-inefficiency as the profit lost by the firm as a result of their shirking. Shirking may take many forms. Managers may 'shirk' by siphoning off profits to buy luxury cars for their personal use, or entertain personal friends lavishly. Typically, the remuneration and status of managers depend on the size of the firm they work for. They may, therefore, try to maximize the size, rather than the profits, of the firm. Baumol[2] argues that managers try to maximize sales rather than profits, so that at the margin, sales yield negative profits. Marris[3] argues that they try to maximize growth rather than profits, so that at the margin, the firm's capital is invested in loss-making projects. Being risk averse, they may also try to ensure job security by avoiding projects that are risky, even if they are potentially very profitable.

When the owner delegates decision making to his agents, typically we have a situation where a number of agents are involved in the decision making process. Each agent has his own objectives and the objectives of one may clash with those of another. For example, the agent in charge of sales may want the firm to produce products that can be sold easily and keep selling prices low to avoid buyer resistance. The agent in charge of production may on the other hand want the firm to sell a different set of products that can be produced easily and want selling prices to be kept high to avoid pressure on costs. Cyert and March[4] hypothesize that the firm resolves these conflicts by setting goals in various areas (like sales, market shares, production, inventories, and profits) that *satisfice*, or lay down minimum acceptable standards, rather than maximize profits. Each agent pursues the goals set for him by following certain *standard operating procedures*, or generally accepted decision rules, without necessarily considering the effects of his actions on the others. If this results in the non-fulfilment of some goals,

[1]See Leibenstein (1966).
[2]See Baumol (1958).
[3]See Marris (1963).
[4]See Cyert and March (1963), pp. 29–43.

then a *problemistic search* takes place to identify the underlying problems. Each problem is solved sequentially, by maintaining an *organizational slack*, or keeping some resources idle, so that the deployment of additional resources in one problem area does not create new problems in other areas. Thus, the firm ends up by producing less than its resources are capable of, because it sets its goals in terms of acceptable minima and maintains an organizational slack to achieve these goals.

11.1.4 Coordination Problems

Information asymmetry among decision agents can lead to a variety of coordination problems. Here we note three.

If all agents do not so formulate their own action plans that they dovetail into a common action plan for the firm, then they may end up by spending their effort and resources wastefully. For example, if the Press Shop Manager produces components that the Assembly Shop Manager does not want, then the effort and resources of the former are used wastefully.

Sometimes, decisions taken by one agent may in fact have a deleterious effect on the activities of another. If, for example, a Territory Manager sells a product at a discounted price in his territory, the prices in other territories may also get depressed, leading to a loss of profits for other Territory Managers.

Information asymmetry may also lead to a failure to share common assets and wasteful duplication of assets. For example, if a Factory Manager is unaware of the availability of an important piece of technical knowledge with another Factory Manager, he will try to rediscover that knowledge when he needs it, instead of getting it from his colleague.

11.1.5 Separation of Decision Control and Decision Management

Thus, when the firm undertakes production by organizing transactions internally, it is faced with a dilemma. If the owner takes the decisions, there are no agency problems, because he has an incentive to use the firm's resources optimally. There are no coordination problems also, because he takes all the decisions. But he has to incur the cost of acquiring the specific knowledge required to take these decisions, or of taking suboptimal decisions in the absence of this knowledge. If, on the other hand, the owner's agents take the decisions, the cost of acquiring specific knowledge is avoided, but there may be production losses owing to agency and coordination problems.

The firm resolves this dilemma by separating *decision management* from *decision control*.[5] The decision process has four basic elements: *initiation* of alternative proposals for action, *selection* of proposals that deserve to be acted upon, *implementation* of the selected proposals, and *monitoring* of the activities of the decision agents to keep them on the right track. Decision management consists of initiation and implementation; decision control consists of selection and monitoring. To take advantage of specific knowledge, decision management is delegated to the point of action. To minimize agency and coordination problems, decision control is exercised at a higher level.

[5]See Fama and Jensen (1985).

11.1.6 Components of Internal Architecture

The separation of decision management and decision control is achieved by establishing an *organization structure* that creates a decision hierarchy and assigns decision management and decision control rights to the appropriate agents at various levels in the hierarchy. The decision agents are made to fall in line with the principals' objectives by establishing a *control system* that has two parts. A *performance evaluation system* is used to measure the performance of the decision agents, and a *compensation system* is used to reward them in accordance with their performance. Thus, the basic components of internal architecture are an organization structure, a compensation system, and a performance evaluation system.[6]

Business Policy literature quite rightly adds a fourth component, namely corporate culture. Many firms make a conscious effort to create a distinctive *corporate culture* that tries to influence the behaviour of its employees by propagating norms of behaviour through the adoption and promotion of certain values, customs, rituals, taboos, slogans, role models, etc. People for example work hard or behave honestly, if it is customary for others in the firm to do so. Thus, the corporate culture of a firm tends to reinforce the behaviour pattern that its organization structure and performance evaluation and reward systems try to enforce. However, a detailed discussion of corporate culture is beyond our scope.

11.2 DESIGNING THE ORGANIZATION STRUCTURE

11.2.1 Bundling of Tasks into Jobs

The basic building block of an organization structure is the job. Production requires the performance of a number of tasks. At a very basic level, these consist of designing the product, purchasing inputs, acquiring productive assets, hiring knowledge and manual workers, using the productive assets and the workers to transform the inputs into a saleable output and reaching the output to the consumers. These broad tasks can be divided and further subdivided into a large number of smaller tasks. The first step in structuring an organization is to make a comprehensive list of the tasks to be performed and bundle them into jobs in such a way that each job occupies a suitably qualified worker fully. Thus, each job is a *bundle of tasks*.

Each job may be so designed that it becomes either a bundle of *complementary tasks* or a bundle of *specialized tasks*. To understand the difference, assume that a factory has four production lines. At any time, each line can produce only one type of product. Production requires the performance of four tasks: setting the machines for a particular type of product, actual production, quality control, and machine maintenance. The volume of work is such that one worker can perform either all the tasks pertaining to one production line or one task pertaining to all the production lines. We could so bundle the tasks into a job that one worker handles all the tasks relating to one production line. We would then create four similar jobs, by assigning to each of them

[6]For an exhaustive account of the three components of internal architecture, see Brickley, Smith, and Zimmerman (1997), Chapters 8 to 14.

the same set of complementary tasks. The advantage of this approach is that it would minimize any production losses that may arise owing to lack of coordination. Since the same worker handles all the activities that have to go together, he can ensure that none of them suffers because of the non-performance of the others. Alternatively, we could ask one worker to perform only one of the four tasks, but for all four production lines. We would then create four specialized jobs, by assigning to each of them one of the four specialized tasks involved. The advantage of this approach is that the specialist is likely to be more knowledgeable, and therefore more productive, in his job then a generalist. He may be specially trained for his job or develop an aptitude for it by doing the same things over and over again.

Obviously, we would choose the approach that offers greater benefits. The balance of advantages will depend on a whole host of factors, like the nature of the job, the kind of business the firm is in, the way it perceives the benefits of coordination *vis-à-vis* the benefits of specialization, etc.

11.2.2 ASSIGNMENT OF DECISION RIGHTS TO A JOB

To perform any task, and therefore any bundle of tasks, a number of decisions have to be taken. Take for example the case of a machine operator who has been assigned the job of operating a machine that can produce several products. He cannot perform his job without taking a decision on what should be produced and how the machine should be operated in terms of speed, sequence of operations, etc. He may take these decisions by proposing to his superior what should be produced and how, getting his proposals ratified and implementing them, under the supervision of his superior. In that case, he has the decision management rights relating to the job assigned to him.

Alternatively, he may have to check with his superior what should be produced, but have the authority to decide on how the machine should be operated, as long as he abides by certain standard norms and practices. In that case, he has only decision management rights relating to what should be produced, but both decision management and decision control rights relating to how the machine should be operated. The decision control rights have been assigned to him by *pre-ratifying* some basic decisions on how the machine should be operated, converting these decisions into a set of standard norms and procedures, and using these norms and procedures to set a *limit to his decision-making authority*. Thus, the machine operator is free to take any decisions relating to his own job within the limits of his decision-making authority. If, in addition, he has a helper, the latter has to refer proposals relating to some aspects of his job to the former for ratification. Typically, the machine operator can ratify or reject some of these proposals himself and has to refer the others to his superiors for a decision. In either case, the helper has to implement the ratified decisions under the supervision of the machine operator. In other words, the machine operator also has the right to control some of the decisions managed by his helper.

The general conclusions that follow from the above example are as follows. The holder of a job has the right to manage all decisions relating to his own job. He also has the right to control some of the decisions managed by himself and his juniors. What these decisions are is determined by the limits to his decision-making authority.

The *level of empowerment* of the jobholder is the extent to which he can control the decisions managed by himself and his juniors.

11.2.3 The Decision Hierarchy

The separation of decision management from decision control requires that some of the decisions managed at a certain level should be controlled at a higher level. This in turn requires the creation of a multi-tiered *decision hierarchy*. The person who controls the decisions is the boss and the person who manages the decisions is the subordinate, because the decisions ratified by the former have to be implemented by the latter. At the top of this hierarchy are the owners of the firm, because in the ultimate analysis they have the power to control all the decisions taken by the firm.

The optimal number of tiers in the decision hierarchy is determined by the optimum *span of control* of the average decision controller, or the optimum number of jobs he can control. The job of a decision controller is basically that of an information processor and communicator. He receives, from his superiors, information about the firm's objectives and strategies in the form of targets and action plans set for him. He processes this information into targets and action plans for his subordinates and passes these down the line. He receives, from his subordinates, proposals for action and evaluates these in the light of the objectives and strategies of the firm. He ratifies some of these proposals and rejects some others. He processes and refers the rest to his superiors for their consideration, and processes and conveys his superiors' decisions to his subordinates. He also receives from his subordinates information about their performance in relation to the targets and action plans set for them, processes and consolidates this information into information about his own performance, and passes it up to his superiors.

If we plot the number of jobs controlled by the decision controller on the horizontal axis and the corresponding average cost of controlling one job on the vertical axis, we would get a U-shaped curve, as in Fig. 11.1. If the decision controller controls only a

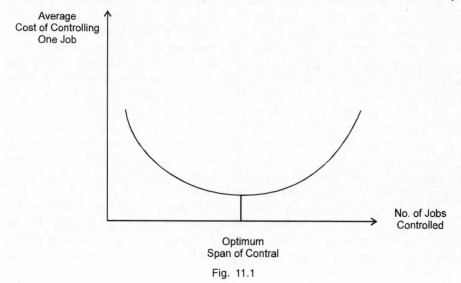

Fig. 11.1

few jobs, his capacity to process information and communicate is not fully utilized. As the number of jobs controlled by him increases, the average cost of controlling one job falls. But once his capacity to process information and communicate is utilized fully, the problem of 'bounded rationality' sets in. Beyond a point, as the number of jobs controlled by him increases further, the saving in cost resulting from one person controlling an increasing number of jobs is more than offset by production losses due to his failure to process information and communicate efficiently. The optimum span of control of the decision controller is reached when the average cost of controlling one job is at its lowest.

To understand how the optimum span of control determines the number of tiers required in the decision hierarchy, consider a model proposed by Oliver Williamson.[7] Williamson assumes that the optimum span of control is the same for all decision controllers, regardless of their personal ability or the jobs they control. He also assumes that the only 'productive' workers are those at the lowest level, like production workers or salesmen in the field. Thus, if tier 1 of a firm has 1000 'productive' workers and the optimum span of control is 10, then we will need 100 decision controllers in tier 2 to control the 1000 workers. Similarly, we will need 10 decision controllers in tier 3 to control the 100 tier 2 controllers and 1 decision controller in tier 4 to control the 10 tier 3 controllers. In other words, we will need to have 4 tiers in the decision hierarchy. Algebraically, if L is the number of 'productive' workers and S the optimum span of control, then the number of tiers required in the decision hierarchy is $N = \ln L / \ln S + 1$, where ln stands for natural logarithm.

11.2.5 Placing Decision Control Rights in the Hierarchy: Centralization vs. Decentralization

Other things being equal, a firm with a large number of employees (L) will have a large number of tiers (N) in its decision hierarchy. At which one of these tiers should the right to control a particular decision be placed? A decision is *centralized* if it is controlled at or near the top tier of the hierarchy. A decision is *decentralized* if it is controlled at or near the tier at which it is managed. Therefore, we may pose the same question by asking: to what extent should a particular decision be decentralized?

To answer this question, we have to go back to the trade-off that leads to a separation of decision management and control in the first instance. If we centralize decision making, we have to incur the cost of acquiring the required specific knowledge. What is more, it may not be cost effective for us to acquire all the specific knowledge required, so that we may still be left with a residual loss of production on this account. Thus, the *cost of centralization* may be defined as the cost of acquiring specific knowledge plus a residual production loss. If, on the other hand, we decentralise decision making, we have to incur the cost of setting up and running a system for controlling agency and coordination problems. What is more, it may not be cost effective for us to control agency and coordination problems fully, so that we may still be left with a residual loss of production on this account. Thus the *cost of decentralization* may be defined as the cost of setting up and running a control system plus a residual production loss. Now,

---

[7]See Williamson (1967).

consider a situation where A is the highest tier in the decision hierarchy of a firm, followed by B, C, D, E, F, etc., in that order, and a particular decision is managed at tier E (vide Figure 11.2). If the decision is also controlled at tier E, the cost of centralization is zero, because all the required specific knowledge is available at that level.

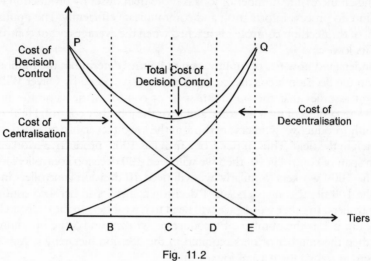

Fig. 11.2

As decision control is moved up the ladder from E to A, the cost of centralization rises, because at each higher level the total number of decisions that can be taken, and therefore the opportunity cost of acquiring the specific knowledge required to take a particular decision, is higher. This can be represented by PE, which shows how the cost of centralization increases as decision control is moved up from tier E to tier A. On the other hand, if the decision is controlled at tier A, the cost of decentralization is zero, because there are no agency or coordination problems at that level. As decision control is moved down the ladder from A to E, the cost of decentralization rises, because employees' knowledge of and commitment to the firm's overall objectives and strategies fall, leading to an increase in coordination and agency problems. This is represented by AQ, which shows how the cost of decentralization rises as decision control is moved down from tier A to tier E. If we add the two curves, PE and AQ, we would typically get a U-shaped curve, PQ which shows how the *total cost of decision making* changes as we decentralize decision making from tier A to tier E. At tier A, the cost of decision making consists only of the cost of centralization. At tier E, the cost of decision making consists only of the cost of decentralization. At the intermediate tiers, the cost of decision making is a combination of the two. The right to control this particular decision should obviously be assigned to tier C, where the cost of decision making is the lowest.

Different decisions managed by the same jobholder are often controlled at different levels in the hierarchy, because the balance of advantages is different. For example, the decision to procure cutting tools for a machine shop may be managed by the shop supervisor and controlled by the production manager who is his immediate boss. The cost of centralization is high. The cost of keeping the top management informed about the status of cutting tool supplies on a day to day basis is high and any delay in decision making leads to a disruption in production. On the other hand, the cost of decentralization is low. Coordination problems are minimal, because the procurement of cutting tools by the machine shop is unlikely to have any major implications for the rest of the firm. Agency problems are also not very serious, because cutting tools account for a small proportion of total production costs and the cost of suboptimal procurement of this item is not very high. Therefore, the balance of advantages will lie in decentralizing the control of a decision of this kind (see Fig. 11.3).

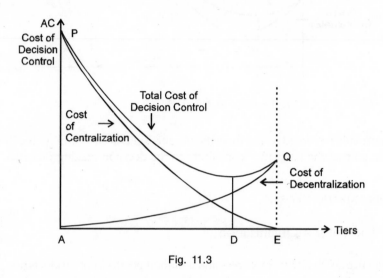

Fig. 11.3

The decision to buy a new machine tool may also be managed by the shop supervisor, in that he may have the right to propose the purchase of a new machine tool for his machine shop and implement the proposal after approval. However, the right to control such a decision is likely to be assigned to somebody more senior than the Production Manager, say the Production Director. The cost of centralization is low, because the Production Director will probably have as much specific knowledge about new machine tools as the shop supervisor and a delay in decision making will not lead to any immediate disruption in production.

On the other hand, the cost of decentralization is high. Coordination problems are significant, because the decision to buy a new machine tool for the machine shop may mean that a new piece of equipment cannot be bought to meet another, and perhaps a more pressing, requirement elsewhere in the firm. Agency problems can also be quite serious. Since a machine tool is an expensive item, any suboptimal decision with regard to its purchase may mean a substantial loss for the firm. Therefore, the balance of advantages will lie in centralizing the control of a decision of this kind (see Fig. 11.4).

When more than one tier separate the manager and the ultimate controller of a decision, communication between the two is usually routed through and vetted by the intermediate tiers. For example, the proposal and decision to buy a new machine tool

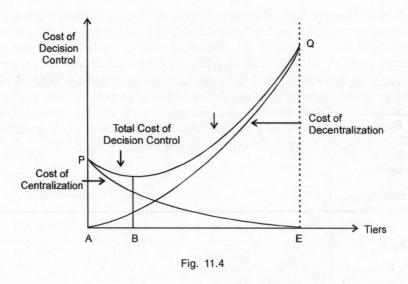

Fig. 11.4

would normally be routed to and from the Production Director through the Production Manager, so that the latter may contribute to the decision making process.

11.3 Organization Forms

11.3.1 The U-form Organization

In a small firm with a few employees and a limited portfolio of products and markets, application of the optimization principles discussed above is likely to result in a *unitary structure*, or what Williamson[8] calls a *U-form organization*. The basic features of the U-form organization are best explained by using a simple example.

Suppose that, an entrepreneur runs a business in ready-made garments with 25 'productive' workers and five supervisors, the optimum span of control of a supervisor being five employees. He could organize production in one of two ways. He could form five groups, each consisting of five workers and a supervisor, and ask each group to buy yarn, weave the yarn into fabric, cut and stitch the fabric into garments, sell the garments, keep an account of their purchases, production and sales, and manage the cash involved. This way, he would in effect run five production units. Alternatively, he could integrate these units into a single production unit and have five functional departments, one buying yarn, another weaving the yarn into fabric, another cutting and stitching the fabric into garments, another selling the garments, and the fifth keeping accounts and managing cash. The latter arrangement illustrates the U-form organization, so called because it treats the entire firm as one production unit. Figure 11.5 shows what the organization structure would look like under this arrangement.

---

[8]See Williamson (1975).

THE U-FORM ORGANIZATION

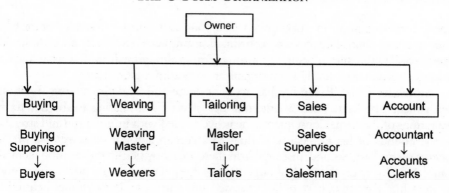

Fig. 11.5

The U-form organization has four important characteristics.

- First, the activities of the firm are departmentalized functionally. Instead of everybody doing everything, we have five types of functional specialists, namely buyers, weavers, tailors, salesmen, and accounts clerks.

- Second, the decision hierarchy is also functional. The decisions managed by the buyers, weavers, tailors, salesmen, and accounts clerks are controlled by the Chief Buyer, the Weaving Master, the Master Tailor, the Sales Supervisor, and the Accountant respectively.

- Third, the first four of the five functions are *line functions*. They are directly involved in the production process and take decisions that affect the volume and method of production. The other, namely Accounts, is a *staff function*. It supports and advises the line functions, but does not take any decisions that would affect the volume and method of production directly.

- Fourth, while the head of a functional department coordinates activities within his department, the owner himself coordinates the activities of the various functional departments on a day to day basis. This is the *operational* part of his job. There is also a *strategic* component to his job. He has to keep his business healthy over time, by changing and adding to his product-market portfolio and productive assets.

The U-form organization has a number of advantages. First, it increases productivity by maximizing the use of specialized knowledge. People in each function become adept at doing the jobs assigned to them through formal training as well as division of labour and learning by doing. Second, costs can be minimized by exploiting economies of scale. To go back to our example, we need only one set of looms, cutting and stitching machines, and computers, instead of five. Third, by dealing through only one set of buyers and salesmen instead of five, the firm is able to increase its bargaining power with suppliers and customers and get better terms from them. Finally, since the owner (or a Chief Executive who thinks like the owner) coordinates the activities of the functional departments on a day to day basis, he can exercise tight control over the affairs of the firm and minimize production losses because of agency and coordination problems.

11.3.2 Problems with the U-form Organization

The U-form organization works quite well as long as the firm is so small that the Chief Executive can control agency and coordination problems effectively and still has the time to deal with issues relating to the long term health of the firm. But when the firm reaches a certain size, the U-form organization becomes inefficient.

Since the Chief Executive has to coordinate the activities of the functional departments, he has to take a large number of decisions relating to the day to day operations of the firm. Consequently, he is overloaded with information and stretched to the bounds of his rationality, leading to a certain amount of *suboptimal decision making* on his part. Second, in a large firm there are many tiers in the decision hierarchy (since $N = \text{Ln } L/\text{Ln } S + 1$, N is large if L is large). Therefore, the instructions given by the Chief Executive have to be processed and reprocessed many times before they reach the 'productive' workers on the ground. Similarly, the feedback from these workers is also processed and reprocessed many times before it reaches him. Each time information is processed, some of it is lost or distorted. This loss and distortion of information impairs the Chief Executive's ability to control agency and coordination problems and leads to a *loss of control*. Third, the concentration of firm-specific knowledge in monolithic functional groups gives these groups the power to 'hold up' production with a view to fulfilling their own sub-goals. This makes it necessary for the Chief Executive to carry a *large organizational slack*, so that functional sub-goals can be reconciled without any loss of production. This, as we have noted already, leads to inefficient use of productive resources. Finally, the Chief Executive gets so involved with the operational problems of functional coordination and conflict resolution, that he does not have much time for addressing issues that do not have an immediate impact on the profitability of the firm. Consequently, there is a *neglect of strategic issues*, affecting the long-term health and prosperity of the firm.

11.3.3 The M-form Organization

The *multi-divisional structure*, or what Williamson[9] calls the *M-form organization*, tries to circumvent the problems associated with the U-form organization, without sacrificing its advantages. Figure 11.6 shows what the typical M-form organization looks like.

THE M-FORM ORGANIZATION

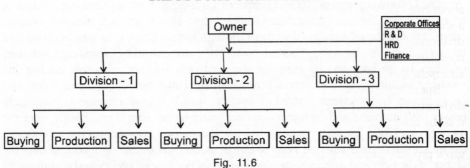

Fig. 11.6

[9]See Williamson, (1975).

The basic characteristic of the M-form organization is that it breaks the firm up into a number of mini firms, or *divisions*, or what strategic literature calls *strategic business units* (SBUs). A division should be so demarcated that it meets two criteria. It should be *separable* from the other divisions in terms of the product-market segments it serves and most of the productive assets it uses. And it should be *large* enough to give an adequate return on the assets it uses. If a division meets these criteria, it can become an independent *profit centre* and be run like a small firm. Usually, in a large firm it is possible to demarcate divisions that meet these criteria, because a firm becomes large in one of two ways. It may exploit economies of scale by selling more and more of the same product to an expanding range of customer groups or geographical regions. Or it may exploit economies of scope by selling an expanding range of products to the same or an expanding range of customer groups and geographical regions. Therefore, a division may be demarcated by the customer groups it sells to, or the geographical regions it sells in, or the products it sells.

Within a division, the U-form structure is retained. The *divisional head* is the chief executive of the division. The structure below him is functionally specialized. His job is to coordinate and control the activities of the functional departments in his division, optimize the use of productive assets and employees allocated to his division, and maximize the profits of his division. Typically, he has the authority to propose, but not decide, what assets and people his division should have. Thus, his job is cross-functional, but largely operational.

The divisional heads report to the *Chief Executive* of the firm. The Chief Executive's job is to maximize the profits of the firm as a whole. At the operational level, he has to ensure that the shareable resources and assets of the firm are allocated to the divisions, and used by them, optimally. This requires several things. First, when a resource is in limited supply, it must be so allocated that the profits of the firm as a whole are maximized. For example, if an automobile firm has a car division and a truck division as well as a central press shop that has a limited capacity and supplies stampings to both divisions, then the press shop capacity must be so allocated that the marginal profits in the two divisions are equalized. Second, product and market specific knowledge, reputation, and physical assets, created by one division for its own use and capable of yielding a rent in another division, must be pooled and used by both. If, for example, the car division knows petrol engines better and the truck division knows diesel engines better, and both divisions use both types of engines, then their knowledge about engines should be pooled and shared. Third, no division must be allowed to use a shared resource in a way that has a deleterious effect on the profitability of other divisions. If the truck division, for example, becomes so unresponsive to customer complaints that it affects the reputation of the firm and the sales of the car division adversely, then the Chief Executive must intervene.

But more important is the strategic aspect of the Chief Executive's job. Since the divisional heads are concerned primarily with the maximization of short term profits, it is the chief executive who has to ensure that the firm remains profitable over time. He has to decide what new assets are required by the firm to remain competitive and grow profitably in its existing lines of business. Given the firm's assets, he also has to decide what existing businesses should be dropped and what new businesses should be added. Once these decisions are taken, he has to implement them by making the necessary investments. For this, not only does he have to raise funds from the capital market, but also allocate the funds generated internally by the firm in an optimal manner. The latter requires that the funds should flow from the divisions that generate more funds than they can use profitably to the divisions that generate less than they need. To go back to our earlier example, if the truck division generates more funds than it can use profitably and the car division generates less than it needs, then some of the funds generated by the former should flow to the latter.

The chief executive is supported by a *corporate office*, consisting of a number of functionally specialized divisions, such as R&D, Human Resources Development (HRD), Finance, Secretarial, Legal, etc. These are purely *staff divisions*, in the sense that they have no line responsibility or authority. They help the chief executive perform his operational duties by providing him with consolidated information about the firm as a whole and advising him on how the shareable resources of the firm should be allocated. They also help the chief executive perform his strategic functions by providing him with information and advice, and creating or acquiring the shareable assets of the firm. For example, the R&D division would create or acquire technical knowledge, the HRD division would create or hire from outside trained manpower, the Finance division would mobilize funds from the capital market, and so on.

The M-form organization retains the advantages of the U-form organization. Since the divisional head is responsible for maximizing the profits of his division, his performance and rewards can be linked to the profit made by his division. This gives him an incentive to think and operate like the owner of his division. The advantages of the functional structure are also retained by departmentalizing the divisions functionally. At the same time, the problems associated with the U-form organization are circumvented. Most of the communication relating to the day to day operations of the firm stops with the division heads. This shortens the line of communication and reduces suboptimal decision-making and loss of control because of communication overload. The breaking up of the monolithic functional hierarchies into functional hierarchies at the divisions reduces the organizational slack. Finally, the devolution of functional coordination and conflict resolution to the divisional heads leaves the chief executive free to devote more time to his strategic duties.

From U-form to M-form: O&M's Project Columbus

Post liberalization, many firms in the Indian manufacturing sector have moved from the U-form to the M-form organization, for precisely the reasons discussed here. An interesting example of a similar move in the service sector is a recent initiative by Ogilvy & Mather (O&M), a leading advertising agency, to reorganize itself.

Typically, marketing or 'client servicing' in an advertising agency is done by its branch offices, which are located near the clients. Clients brief client service or 'accounts' executives of their requirements of advertising and other services. Accounts executives get these services produced by the appropriate functions in the agency and deliver them to the clients. These services are produced centrally by specialist functions like art, copy, media, direct marketing, customer relationship management, etc. Thus, the agency is treated as one production unit and has a U-form organization. O&M's present organization is not very different from this model.

Of O&M's billings, 85 per cent come from advertising, on which it gets a commission. The rest comes from other services like direct marketing, public relations, event management, etc., for which it charges a fee. O&M would like to increase its revenue by looking beyond advertising and widening the range of its fee-paying services. For this, it should be able to identify clients' new requirements as they arise and develop new services to meet them. This in turn requires that the firm should have an intimate knowledge of consumers, who are its clients' customers. As the managing director of O&M puts it, his company has to be in the business of not just 'managing brands', but 'managing the needs, wants and desires of a billion consumers via branded goods and services'.

With this in view, O&M has launched an initiative to reorganize itself, which it calls 'Project Columbus'. The firm plans to group all the brands it manages under 14 'clusters', each cluster being defined by a specific consumer need, like food and drinks, health and hygiene, transportation, travel and leisure, education, entertainment, etc. GlaxoSmithKline and Novartis will, for example, be grouped under the 'health and hygiene' cluster, and Cadbury and Coca Cola will be grouped under the 'food and drinks' cluster. Each cluster will be headed by a business director, who will be supported by functional specialists in strategy, art, copy, media, public relations, direct marketing, etc. Each cluster will be responsible for identifying and meeting the requirements of clients in its cluster. As O&M executives put it, the clusters will be responsible for 'knowledge application'. To keep abreast of developments in technology, O&M plans to create a central 'knowledge acquisition' cell, consisting of specialists in not only existing functional areas, but also new areas like rural marketing, retailing, identity design, etc. These specialists will collect information on technological advances in their own areas of specialization and feed it to specialists in the clusters.

Thus, what O&M has in mind is an M-form organization. The 'clusters' are business divisions and the central 'knowledge acquisition cell' is the corporate office. By delegating the responsibility for identifying and meeting client requirements to the clusters, O&M expects to minimize the dilution of focus that takes place in the process of accounts executives receiving briefs from clients, transmitting these briefs to the centre, and delivering the services produced by the centre.

Although the plan is interesting, its implementation is faced with a few problems. If a multi-product client like Hindustan Levers has brands that should be grouped in more than one cluster, it will have to be serviced by more than one set of people. Since communication will not have to move up and down as much as it does now, the number of tiers in the organization will be reduced. The staff that will be rendered surplus as a result will have to be retrained and redeployed, or taken care of in some other way. O&M is currently grappling with problems like this. If it does implement the project successfully, the new model will be extended gradually to O&M organizations in other parts of the world.

Source: 'Work in Progress', Brand Equity, *Economic Times,* Mumbai, 25 April 2001.

11.3.4 The Matrix Organization

The M-form organization assigns the task of short run profit maximization to the divisions. Consequently, the functional departments in a division tend to be judged by their contribution to the division's short run profits and have an incentive to maximize their contribution by eschewing sound functional policies and practices. The Purchase department may, for example, try to reduce input costs by compromising on the quality of inputs. The Production department may try to increase production by hiring casual workers or foregoing preventive maintenance of machines. The Marketing department may neglect markets that are potential winners, but do not offer high profits in the short run. In other words, the M-form organization may lead to a *loss of functional focus*, to the detriment of the long term health of the firm.

Many firms try to solve this problem by creating a structure that requires the head of a functional department in a division to report to the Divisional Head as well as the head of the appropriate functional division in the corporate office. A structure based on this kind of dual reporting is called a *matrix organization*, because the lines of authority run both vertically and horizontally. Figure 11.7 shows what the typical matrix organization would be like in a consumer product firm, which has three operating divisions.

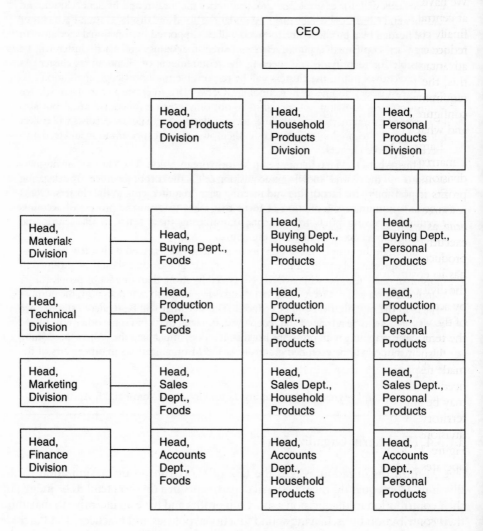

Fig. 11.7: The Matrix Organization

The functional heads at the corporate office are responsible for ensuring functional excellence at both the corporate office and the operating divisions. To this end, they lay down norms and standards, institute systems and procedures, conduct quality audits and upgrade the functional skills of employees by arranging training programmes, workshops, seminars, and conferences. They also have an important say in the recruitment and performance evaluation of employees in their own functions. The advantage of the matrix organization is that it captures the benefits of both functional and divisional organizations. But the disadvantage is that the dual reporting system may lead to conflicts and a dilution of accountability.

11.3.5 The Matrix Organization in a Multinational Corporation (MNC)

We have seen in Chapter 10 that an MNC carries out a part of its production process at central locations and decentralizes the rest to the countries in which the product is finally consumed. By centralizing a part of the production process, the firm is able to reduce costs by exploiting the economies of scale and scope as well as the comparative advantages of the countries in which the production is centralized. But as a result of this, the firm may lose some business, because it cannot respond fully to the local requirements of customers, dealers, governments, etc. The firm, therefore, has to so configure its production chain that it strikes an optimal balance between *cost efficiency* and what Prahalad and Doz[10] call *local responsiveness*.

Large MNCs try to combine cost efficiency with local responsiveness by creating a matrix organization that has the following broad characteristics.[11] The operating divisions are specialized by products and territories. They are responsible for maximizing profits in their product–territory segments by optimizing the use of the productive resources allocated to them. The head of each operating division reports to a *territory head* as well as a *product head*. The territory and product heads report to the chief executive of the firm, are responsible for the overall profitability of their territories and products, and have the authority to acquire and allocate resources. The territory head has to ensure local responsiveness by acquiring and allocating sufficient resources to the divisions operating in his territory. The product head has to ensure cost effectiveness by acquiring the right kind of resources and locating them optimally in different parts of the world. The responsibility for resolving any conflict between the requirements of the territory and the product heads rests with the chief executive of the firm.

Usually, an MNC like this is so large that the territory and product heads can be made responsible for ensuring functional excellence, and the Chief Executive does not need to have a large complement of functional staff. For example, each product head may be supported by a central R&D function for his group of products, while each territory head may have a central marketing function to ensure that the operating divisions in his territory are following sound marketing practices and procedures. Figure 11.8 shows what this kind of organization would look like in a firm that operates globally and produces three types of products.

---

[10]See Prahalad and Doz (1987), p. 15.
[11]For a detailed discussion of this kind of organization, see Bartlett and Ghoshal (1993).

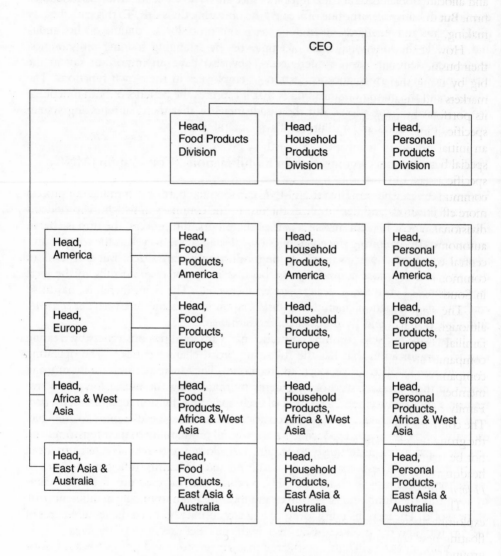

Fig. 11.8: The Matrix Organization in an MNC

11.3.6 The H-form Organization

Under the M-form organization and the matrix organizations that flow from it, the heads of operating divisions are subject to a fair amount of operational control and play an advisory, and not a decisive, role in the formulation of the business strategies of their divisions. This becomes necessary, because when the divisions share business-specific assets and resources, maximization of the economies of scale and scope for the firm as a whole becomes very important. Therefore, the responsibility for acquiring and allocating shared assets and resources has to rest with the Chief Executive of the firm. But this lengthens the line of communication and may lead to suboptimal decision-making, loss of control, and loss of local responsiveness.

However, as we have noted in Chapter 10, not all firms become big by applying their business-specific assets to an expanding range of businesses. Some of them become big by using their general-purpose assets to correct failures in product and factor markets and engaging in unrelated diversification. When a firm adds a new business to its portfolio by using its general-purpose assets, rather than those that are business-specific, it may be more efficient to spin the new business off into a separate firm, after an initial period of incubation. Since there are no economies of scale or scope, no special benefits can be derived by centralizing the creation and allocation of business-specific assets. On the other hand, by not centralizing and thus shortening the line of communication, the quality of decision making improves, operational control becomes more effective, and there is greater local responsiveness. Thus, instead of a large multi-divisional firm, we have a *group of firms*, with a fair amount of operational and strategic autonomy devolving on the chief executives of these firms, but a certain degree of central control on the general-purpose assets of the group. Such groups are quite common in developing countries and are known as 'business houses' in India, 'chaebols' in South Korea, and 'grupos' in Latin America.

The same entrepreneurial family or families control the firms within a group, although the shares of these firms may be publicly traded. Typically, but not always, familial control is exercised through one or more *holding companies*. The holding companies are fully owned by the families and have a controlling interest in the group companies. The families also hold shares in the group companies directly. Often, family members act as chief executives and other senior executives of the group companies. Family control is further strengthened by financial interlock among these companies. The companies are allowed to operate fairly independently within the overall limits of the group policies. The group policies are set at the *group headquarters* that may or may not be structured formally. Quite often, the holding companies operate as the group headquarters. This has prompted Williamson[12] to christen the group structure as the *H-form organization*.

The group headquarters identify new business opportunities, formulate plans for exploiting them, and implement these plans through the existing companies or by floating new companies. They help the group companies to get new projects off the ground by providing them with finance, trained manpower, project management skills, and the use of the group's reputation, relationships, and lobbying power. They exercise some control over the strategic decisions of the group companies to ensure that they enhance, or at least do not undermine, one another. This may mean anything from friendly competition to the development of complementary lines of business. They exercise control over the operations of group companies by participating in Board meetings. Most importantly, they nurture and enhance the group assets, especially reputation and relationships, on an on-going basis.

---

[12]See Williamson (1975).

H-FORM ORGANIZATION IN THE TATA GROUP

Business groups in India differ in the way they control and coordinate the activities of their group companies. The model followed by the Tata group is particularly interesting. Family shareholding in many of the group companies is small. Yet, while other groups are breaking up, companies in the Tata group have stayed together for 128 years. Most of them have also done quite well.

Before independence, the group's founder, Jamshetji Tata, and his successor, J. R. D. Tata, took upon themselves the task of industrializing India. They went into basic consumer goods like textiles, soaps, and vegetable oils, infrastructural industries like steel, cement, and power, and essential services like technical research and education, airlines, hotels, and insurance. After independence, with the government of India assuming 'commanding heights' over the economy, the group was not allowed to expand in many of these areas. Some, like airlines and insurance, were nationalized. But the policy of import substitution threw up new opportunities, and the group went into automobiles, heavy chemicals, pharmaceuticals, pesticides, fast moving consumer goods, consumer electronics, and consumer durables. Post liberalization, the group moved into high technology areas like information technology, telecommunications, passenger vehicles, and financial services. At the same time, it moved out of fast moving consumer goods like textiles, vegetable oils, soaps and detergents, and toilet and personal products because it did not have the marketing strengths to compete with new entrants.

The problem of controlling group companies really emerged with the abolition of the managing agency system in 1969, when these companies became legally independent. It was tackled in a number of ways:

- The holding company, Tata Sons, did not have substantial shareholding in many of the companies. But there was a web of inter-corporate shareholding. Financial institutions who were large shareholders also wanted the Tata management to continue.

- J.R.D. Tata was the chairman of all group companies and commanded a high degree of loyalty because of his personal stature and charisma.

- He was also the chairman and the chief executives of major operating companies were directors of a shell company called Tata Industries.

- The group companies had a number of common directors who met and exchanged ideas from time to time.

- Professional managers were in short supply. The group recruited bright young people to a central Tata Administrative Service (TAS) and trained and posted them in key middle management positions. TAS officers could go up either one company or across companies and were encouraged to develop a group vision.

- J.R.D. Tata embodied and propagated certain values that he had inherited from Jamsetji Tata. He believed that the group should participate in projects of national importance, give a fair deal to shareholders, employees and customers, and abide by the law. His senior colleagues shared these values.

- As a result, the group acquired an enviable reputation. Group companies wanted to take advantage of this reputation by remaining within the group.

When Ratan Tata began to take over from J.R.D. Tata towards the end of 1980s, he found that the group had certain weaknesses also:

- Thanks to a culture of excessive tolerance and gerontocracy, many of the companies were inefficient and lacked dynamism.

- J. R. D. Tata had encouraged the companies to operate independently. Towards the end of his career, he also started handing over the chairmanship of these companies to the chief executives. As a result, the companies were highly protective of their own turf, unwilling to synergize their activities and even competing with one another.

- Senior people in the group were not very familiar with the 'new economy' and resisted attempts to capitalize on emerging business opportunities in that sector.

To deal with these problems, Ratan Tata made a few changes in the group organization:

- He replaced the old guard over a period of time by fixing a retirement age for executive chairmen and managing directors.

- He put all companies in eight business groups and encouraged people to think in terms of business groups, rather than companies.

- He created a group executive office (GEO), consisting of himself and three executive directors. The GEO would avoid overlaps, exploit synergies and capitalize on new opportunities by vetting business plans of group companies and developing and implementing a group business plan.

- He tried to propagate a culture of excellence by advertising the 'Tata legends' (achievers with a connection with the group) and communicating his vision for the group to employees, directly and through his senior colleagues.

Source: A case study prepared by Ashish Nanda and James E. Austin of Harvard Business School and press reports.

12 Architecture II: Compensation and Performance Evaluation Systems, External Architecture, and Corporate Governance

In the last chapter, we considered one component of internal architecture, namely the organization structure. In this chapter, we deal with the other two components of internal architecture, namely compensation and performance evaluation systems. We also look at a few key issues relating to external architecture and corporate governance.

12.1 DESIGNING THE COMPENSATION SYSTEM

12.1.1 How Much Should We Pay an Employee?

The output of an employee is the amount of value he adds with his physical and mental effort, holding all other inputs constant.[1] The law of diminishing returns suggests that as the employee increases his effort, the total output of the firm increases, but each additional unit of effort results in a progressively lower increase in the output of the firm. We may represent this by assuming the following relationship between E, the number of units of effort put in by the employee, and Q_e, his expected output:

$$Q_e = a.E^\alpha, \tag{12.1}$$

where a and α are constants and $1 > \alpha > 0$. If E increases by 1 per cent, Q_e increases by α per cent, i.e. by less than 1 per cent.[2] The actual output, however, is subject to some random shocks, like variations in market demand or input supplies, which are beyond the employee's control. The employee's actual output may, therefore, be different from the expected output and can be written as:

$$Q = Q_e + \mu, \tag{12.2}$$

where μ is a random variable with a mean value of zero and a variance of σ^2.

---

[1] For a comprehensive treatment of the economics of compensation systems, see Milgrom and Roberts (1992), Chapters 7 to 13.

[2] Note that $(dQ_e/dE)/(Q_e/E) = \alpha$

The compensation that has to be paid to the employee has two parts. He has to be paid a reservation wage without which he will not offer his services in the employment market at all. In addition, he has to be compensated for the actual effort he puts in. By putting in one unit of effort, he incurs a certain amount of disutility that results from his having to do something unpleasant like hauling coal, or not being able to do something more pleasant like watching a film. He will put in this effort only if he is paid a remuneration that gives him enough utility to compensate for the disutility that he suffers as a result of this effort. The law of diminishing marginal utility tells us that as his income increases, the utility that he gets from the last unit of his income falls. He, therefore, has to be paid an increasing amount for putting in one extra unit of effort. We can capture all these points by assuming that the minimum compensation that has to be paid to the employee for putting in E units of effort is:

$$W = W_o + b.E^\beta, \tag{12.3}$$

where W_o is the reservation wage, $b.E^\beta$ the compensation payable to the employee for undertaking E units of effort, b and β are constants with positive values, and $\beta > 1$. If E increases by 1 per cent, $b.E^\beta$ increase by β per cent, i.e. by more than 1 per cent. The firm's expected profit from the employee's effort is:

$$\Pi_e = Q_e - W. \tag{12.4}$$

Figure 12.1 presents all these relationships diagrammatically, by plotting E on the horizontal axis and the corresponding rupee values of Q_e and W on the vertical axis. Π_e is maximized when the vertical distance between the Q_e and W curves is the highest. The profit-maximizing values of E, Q_e, W, and Π_e are denoted as E^*, Q_e^*, W^*, and Π_e^* respectively. It follows from (eqn 12.2) that the corresponding value of actual output is $Q^* = Q_e^* + \mu$. Since the profit accrues to the owner of the firm, the owner's utility is maximized at this point. We know that the employee agrees to work under the authority of the owner, because he is risk-averse. Therefore, the employee's utility is maximized as long as he is paid a fixed W^* for putting in E^* units of effort, regardless of the realized values of μ and Q^*. This leaves the owner with an actual profit of Q^*

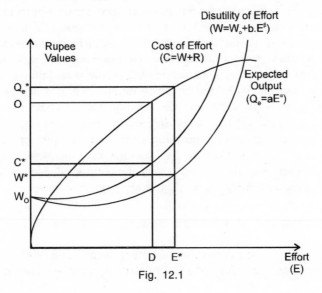

Fig. 12.1

$- W^* = \Pi_e{}^* + \mu$. In other words, under this arrangement, although the owner's expected profit is maximized, there is a risk that the actual profit may deviate from the expected profit. This, however, does not diminish his utility, because he is risk-neutral.

12.1.2 The Principal-Agent Problem

In theory, therefore, both the owner and the employee can maximize their utility by entering into a contract, whereby the employee agrees to supply E^* units of effort and the owner agrees to pay him a fixed compensation of W^*. But in practice, a contract like this tends not to maximize the owner's utility. As we have seen earlier, the owner has to operate by assigning decision rights to his employees. Thus, the owner is the principal and the employee is his agent, or the person through whom he operates. If the agent is paid a fixed compensation, he may renege on his agreement and supply less effort than contracted. The principal could guard against this possibility by observing the effort that is actually put in by his agent. But there is a cost attached to observing effort. Therefore, the principal will observe effort only to the extent the benefits exceed costs and the agent will be inclined to take advantage of this to supply less effort than he had agreed to. This is known as the *principal–agent problem* in economics.

To understand the nature of this problem more fully, consider the following example. A producer of food products employs a salesman. The latter agrees to work E^* hours every month and the former agrees to pay him a fixed salary of W^* rupees every month. The values of a and α are known. Therefore, the food producer expects his salesman to give him an output of $a.(E^*)^\alpha$ every month. He can observe the salesman's effort only by accompanying him on his sales visits. The opportunity cost of this is prohibitive, because in that case the food producer will not be able to do anything else. In effect, therefore, he cannot observe the effort put in by his salesman. On the other hand, the salesman has an incentive to supply as little effort as he can get away with, since any effort he puts in causes him some disutility. But since his salary is fixed, he does not get anything extra for it. He will, therefore, be tempted to take advantage of the food producer's inability to observe his effort, to supply less effort than contracted. Suppose he does so and works for only G hours every month. If he had worked E^* hours, his actual output would have been $a.(E^*)^\alpha + \mu$, μ being the extent to which his actual output would vary from his expected output owing to random shocks beyond his control, like sudden changes in market demand or unexpected moves by competitors. Since he has worked only G hours, his actual output is $a.G^\alpha + \mu = a.(E^*)^\alpha + [\mu - a.(E^*)^\alpha + a.G^\alpha]$. Since, by definition, the value of μ is not known *ex-ante*, the food producer cannot ascertain if the *ex-post* difference between the expected and actual output is due to μ taking on a certain value, or his salesman putting in only G hours of work instead of E^*, as contracted. The salesman can, therefore, supply less effort than contracted every month and still collect the contracted salary. Clearly, this is a suboptimal arrangement from the food producer's point of view.

12.1.3 The Incentive Compensation System

The principal–agent problem arises because the principal cannot observe the agent's effort without incurring a cost and the agent takes advantage of this by supplying less effort than contracted. This problem can be minimized by resorting to a *system of incentive compensation*, in which the realized output of the agent is used as a surrogate for his effort and a part of his compensation is based on his realized output to induce effort. Algebraically, the compensation paid to the agent is:

$$C = F + \lambda.Q, \tag{12.5}$$

where F is a fixed wage, Q the employee's realized output, and λ the proportion of Q that is paid to him as incentive compensation.

To understand why this arrangement induces effort, we go back to Fig. 12.1 and derive from it the rupee values of the employee's *incremental* expected output and disutility, as his effort increases. Figure 12.2 plots the employee's effort on the horizontal axis and the corresponding values of his expected incremental output and disutility on the vertical axis. If the value of λ is fixed at λ_1, then the incremental compensation that the employee can expect to earn by increasing his effort is his expected incremental output multiplied by λ_1 and can be represented by a downward-sloping curve. In that case, the employee maximizes his utility by supplying E_1 units of effort, where his expected incremental earning equals his incremental disutility. If the value of λ is fixed higher, at λ_2 say, then the employee's incremental earnings at each level of effort increases to λ_2 times his incremental expected output, and he maximizes his utility by supplying E_2 units of effort which is higher than E_1. In other words, we can increase E, or the employee's effort, by increasing λ, or the proportion of his output paid to him as incentive compensation. We can now understand why the employee shirks when his compensation is fixed: if the value of λ is zero, the λ multiplied by incremental expected output line is a vertical line that runs through the origin, and the employee maximizes his utility by not working at all.

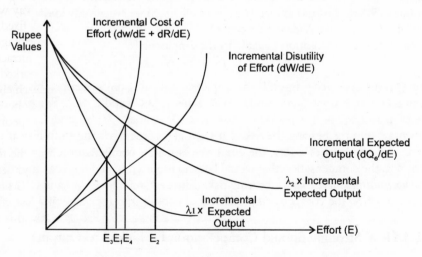

Fig. 12.2

Before we go further, we have to refine our analysis slightly. By combining (eqn 12.1), (eqn 12.2), and (eqn 12.5) it can be seen that:

$$C = F + \lambda.a.E^{\alpha} + \lambda.\mu. \tag{12.6}$$

Ex-ante, the employee knows the *ex-post* values of F and $\lambda.a.E^{\alpha}$, but not of $\lambda.\mu$. This means that under the incentive compensation system, he has to bear a part of the risk. Since the employee is risk-averse, this imposes on him an additional cost. We may denote this cost as R. Equation (12.6) also tells us that as λ increases, the risk that the employee has to bear also increases. We have seen already that an increase in E is induced by an increase in λ. Therefore, the larger the E, the greater is the risk that the employee has to bear and the higher is the value of R. Thus, the incremental cost of the employee's effort is the rupee value of his incremental disutility plus the cost of the incremental risk that he has to bear. This can be represented by an upward-sloping cost-of-effort curve that starts at the origin and lies above the cost-of-disutility curve, with the gap between the two increasing, as E increases. Therefore, when we take into account the cost of risk borne by the employee, his utility-maximizing effort corresponding to λ_1 and λ_2 comes down from E_1 and E_2 to E_3 and E_4, respectively. However, the basic conclusion that an increase in λ leads to an increase in E remains valid.

To find the profit-maximizing value of λ, we have to add to Fig. 12.1 a curve that shows the total cost of effort incurred by the employee at various levels of effort. This curve can be derived from the incremental cost-of-effort curve given in Fig. 12.2, and is shown as C in Fig. 12.1. Now the profit-maximizing effort required of the employee is D units, where the vertical distance between Q_e and C is the highest. The corresponding profit-maximizing expected output and earnings of the employee are O and C^* respectively. C^* is made up of a fixed component, F^*, and a variable component, $\lambda^*.O$, so that:

$$C^* = F^* + \lambda^*.O, \tag{12.7}$$

where $\lambda^* = (C^* - F^*)/O$ and induces D units of effort. We can find out from Fig. 12.2 the value of λ^* that would induce D units of effort. Since we already know the values of C^* and O, we can calculate F^* from λ^*.

The actual compensation payable to the employee is:

$$C = F^* + \lambda^*.Q, \tag{12.8}$$

where Q is his observed output. If the employee puts in D units of effort, his observed output is $O + \mu$. If $\mu > 1$, $Q > O$, and $C > C^*$. If $\mu < 1$, $Q < O$ and $C < C^*$. Since the mean value of μ is zero, over a period of time $\mu = 0$, so that $Q = O$ and $C = C^*$. To compensate him for bearing the risk of his actual income deviating from his expected income, for any level of effort, the employee is paid a compensation $C = W + R$, where W is the compensation that would be paid to him if he did not bear any risk and R a *compensating differential* for bearing risks. Since $\lambda^* = (C^* - F^*)/O$ and C^* includes an element of R, the compensating differential is built into the value of λ^*.

12.1.4 How Strongly Should Compensation be Linked to Output?

It should be noted that the use of the incentive compensation scheme resulted in a fall in the profit-maximizing effort and output from E^* and Q_e^* to D and O respectively. This is because this arrangement leads to *suboptimal sharing of risks*. By passing on a part of the risk to the risk-averse employee, it becomes necessary to pay him a compensatory differential. This imposes an additional cost on the firm, because this cost would be avoided if the owner who is risk-neutral could take all the risks himself.

Thus, the system of incentive compensation is a *second best arrangement*, adopted only because the best arrangement is infeasible. We should, therefore, minimize the cost of risk bearing by tying compensation to output only to the extent necessary. This means that we need to estimate the F^*/C^* ratio with a fair degree of accuracy. As we have seen, this requires us to make reasonable estimates of the responsiveness of the employee's effort to his compensation ($1/\beta$), the responsiveness of output to his effort (α), and the degree of his risk aversion (the value of R at different values of λ). Most firms estimate these values judgmentally. Some use complex mathematical models. These values, and therefore the F^*/C^* ratio, vary from job to job. For example, sales commission typically accounts for a large part of a salesman's income. But an accountant's compensation is rarely based on the quantum of accounting done by him.

12.1.5 Forms of Incentive Compensation

All compensation systems are, in one way or another, variants of the basic incentive compensation system described above. They all try to reward good performance and punish unsatisfactory performance. They differ in the way they measure performance and package rewards. The question of performance evaluation is discussed later in the chapter. We discuss below some of the more important forms that rewards may take.

Incentives can be *explicit*, i.e. linked directly to some quantitative measure of the employee's output, or *implicit*, when no such direct linkage is attempted. The productivity bonus paid to production workers, or the sales commission paid to salesmen, or the profit share paid as bonus to senior managers are examples of explicit incentives. The advantage of this arrangement is that it is easily understood and provides a strong incentive for effort. But it exposes the employee to a high degree of risk for which he has to be compensated handsomely. The other disadvantage is that few jobs are uni-dimensional. By linking an employee's rewards to only one aspect of his job, we may encourage him to neglect other aspects. The production worker may neglect quality. The salesman may neglect profitability. Even the senior manager may be tempted to inflate book profits by resorting to 'creative accounting'.

Another explicit form of incentive compensation is a *one-time award*, like a cash award or a paid holiday or an expensive gift, given to outstanding performers. Since these awards are additional to, and not a part of, the employee's regular compensation, the cost of risk is low, but the incentive effect is also not very strong. Also, these awards are usually based on only one or two dimensions of an employee's job and may encourage him to take an unbalanced view of his job.

Increments and promotions given to employees, on the basis of past performance, are examples of implicit incentive compensation. Conversely, an employee may be given a poor or no increment, sidetracked, demoted, or even dismissed if he performs unsatisfactorily. Since the employee's current income is fixed and his rewards come in the form of a fixed increase in his future income, he is largely protected from the risk of random shocks affecting his performance. Thus, this arrangement provides incentives to employees, without exposing them to business risks. But both the employee and the employer have to bear the risk of moral hazard. An employee may perform well in the hope of being rewarded, but the employer may renege on his promise to reward him if it suits him to do so. On the other hand, the employee may stop performing after he has received his increment and promotion.

Sometimes, incentive compensation is based on *asymmetric sharing of risks*, to encourage effort in risky activities. When an employee works on a project that has an uncertain outcome, he puts his human capital at risk. If the project fails, he may be demoted or dismissed. If his human capital is firm specific, he may not get another job easily. Even if his human capital is not firm specific, it may not be easy for him to get another job, because firms tend to select people on the basis of their performance in other firms. Firms, therefore, find it difficult to persuade people to work on projects that are inherently risky. To circumvent this problem, many firms reward people if they handle a risky project successfully, but do not punish them if they fail. A marketing manager may be rewarded for launching a new product successfully, but not punished if the product fails. An R&D manager may be rewarded if his research leads to the discovery of a new drug, but not punished if it does not. However, this approach may encourage people to promote projects that do not have a high probability of success. To avoid this problem, projects have to be screened very carefully before they are taken up.

12.1.6 Structuring the Compensation Package

The compensation package should be so structured that it maximizes the *employee's utility* at the lowest possible *cost to the employer*. This requires three things. First, the employee should value the benefits provided by the package. Second, the employer should be able to provide these benefits in a cost-effective manner. Third, to the extent possible, the money value of these benefits should be tax-deductible for the employer and non-taxable for the employee.

Typically, *monetary compensation* constitutes the largest component of the package. *Fringe benefits* like company housing and car, medical and educational allowances, etc. have the effect of increasing the employee's monetary compensation. *Concessional loans* enable him to improve his standard of living by acquiring assets like real estate, car, and expensive consumer durables. *Retirement benefits* like provident fund, gratuity, and pension increase his future buying power. *Status symbols* like job titles, lavish offices, the right to travel and live luxuriously on business tours, etc. give him non-monetary utility.

The same benefits may, however, yield different utilities to different people. For example, retirement benefits may be important for an elderly employee, while a young employee may value an allowance for his children's education more. Many firms try to give their employees the best value for their money by offering a *cafetaria approach*. Each employee is allowed to choose a mix of benefits that he considers most valuable, subject to an overall monetary limit. On the other hand, employers tend to offer the benefits that they are best equipped to provide. For example, a construction firm may offer free housing to its employees. An automobile firm may provide free cars. A bank or a financial institution may give low-interest loans.

BOX 12.1. LINKING PAY WITH PERFORMANCE

A survey of 310 Indian companies by Hewitt Associates shows that the percentage increase given to outstanding performers in 2002 is almost five times the percentage increase given to below average performers. What is surprising, however, is that below average performers are given an increase at all. Presumably, this is to take care of inflation and productivity increases because of improvements in technology (see Table A).

TABLE A: SALARY INCREASES GIVEN IN 2002

	per cent of all employees	per cent increase in salary
Outstanding performers	5	18.4
Above average performers	8	14.2
Average performers	79	10.5
Below average performers	8	3.9

The same survey indicates that the practice of paying out a part of the salary as a variable compensation, linked to some objective measure of performance, is also catching on in India. As an employee becomes more senior, the proportion paid out to him as a variable compensation rises (see Table B).

TABLE B: VARIABLE PAY AS PER CENT OF TOTAL SALARY

	2001	2002 (projected)
Top and senior managers	16	19
Managers	13	15
Supervisors	10	12
Clerical and support staff	7	8
Manual workers	5	6

Another survey by PricewaterhouseCoopers shows that two out of three companies in India have adopted the practice of paying out a part of the salary as a variable compensation. Of the companies that have done so, 94 per cent pay out the variable component as cash, 5 per cent as a combination of cash and stock options, and only 1 per cent as stock options only. Companies believe that cash incentives encourage short term performance, while stock options encourage long term performance.

We can get an idea of how salaries are structured at the highest level by looking at the remuneration paid to Vivek Paul, the vice chairman of Wipro. Paul, who is reported to be the highest paid manager in India, was paid Rs 5 crore in 2001–2. Of this, 32 per cent was a fixed salary, 60 per cent commission and incentives, 5 per cent deferred benefits, and 3 per cent other payments. In addition, he was given a stock option of 1.6 lakh shares (ADRs) at an exercise price of $36.40 each (current price is much lower), valid until 2009. If Paul is fired, he will get a severance compensation of Rs 9 crore. This is not surprising. Since only 32 per cent of his salary is fixed, Paul is exposed to considerable business risks.

Sources: The Hewitt Associates survey was reported by *The Indian Express,* Mumbai, 23 June 2002. The PricewaterhouseCoopers survey was reported by *The Economic Times,* Mumbai, 21 May 2001. Vivek Paul's compensation was reported by *The Econmic Times,* Mumbai, 6 June 2002.

12.2 Designing the Performance Evaluation System

12.2.1 Objective Measures of Performance

For some jobs, performance can be measured quantitatively, by comparing the mployee's output with a *performance benchmark*. The performance benchmark is the employee's O in (eqn 12.7), or his expected output if there are no random shocks beyond his control.

One method of establishing performance benchmarks is to conduct *motion and time studies*. These studies analyse existing methods of work, redesign them to make them more efficient and determine how much time an activity should take, using standard methods and under normal circumstances. By concentrating on standard methods and normal work conditions, these studies try to eliminate the effect of random shocks on employees' performance and arrive at an estimate of the expected output directly. However, employees have an incentive to underperform when their work is under study, so that the benchmark is set low.

Some firms try to set performance standards by benchmarking against *best practices*. In this approach, standards are set by adjusting the output levels achieved in the most efficient firm in the industry for differences in technology and other relevant factors. The problem, however, is that these adjustments tend to be arbitrary.

A common method of setting performance standards is to use historical data of *past performance*. In theory, by correcting the standards on the basis of actual performance and making suitable allowances for technical change, we can iron out the effect of random shocks and arrive at an estimate of the expected output. This requires that a good year should lead to an upward revision in the standards and a bad year should lead to a downward revision. In practice, however, most firms tend to raise standards after a good year, but not lower them after a bad year. This induces employees to under-perform in good years, so that they are not faced with unachievable standards in bad years.

Many firms set performance benchmarks by following a system of *management by objectives*. Under this system, the employee's objectives or targets are set jointly by the employer and the employee through a process of consultation. Since the employee has specific knowledge about his own job, he often has a pretty good idea about what his performance benchmark should be. By consulting him, the employer can elicit his private information and estimate his expected output with a fair degree of accuracy, provided the rewards for good performance are attractive enough.

Performance evaluation can be *absolute* or *relative*. In the former case, the employee's performance is measured by his own output. In the latter case, his performance is measured by adjusting his output by the output of other comparable employees. While actual evaluation schemes are quite complex, the basic difference between the two approaches can be explained by using a simple example (see Table 12.1).

Suppose a firm has three employees doing a similar job. Under normal circumstances, the output of the above-average performer is 2 per cent higher than that of the average performer, while the output of the below-average performer is 2 per cent lower. At the profit-maximizing level of effort, the expected monthly output of the average performer is Rs 100,000 and the proportion of output to be paid to him as incentive compensation is 10 per cent. In terms of our symbols, the values of O and λ^* are Rs 100,000 and 10 per cent respectively. The corresponding outputs of the above and below average performers are Rs 102,000 and Rs 98,000 respectively. Now assume that in month 1 business conditions are very favourable and by putting in the profit-maximizing level of effort, the average performer actually produces an output of Rs 105,000. In other words, the effect of random shocks on his output, or the realized value of μ, is + Rs 5000. Assume further that the effect of random shocks, or the realized value of μ, is the same for all the three employees. Therefore, the observed output of the above and below average performers are Rs 107,000 and Rs 103,000 respectively. In month 2, business conditions turn unfavourable. With the same effort, the average performer's output is Rs 95,000 and the realized value of μ is – Rs 5000. Consequently, the outputs of the above and below average performers are Rs 97,000 and Rs 93,000 respectively. Over the two month period, the mean value of μ is zero, and the average performer's mean output is Rs 100,000.

TABLE 12.1 INCENTIVE COMPENSATION PAYABLE UNDER
ABSOLUTE AND RELATIVE PERFORMANCE EVALUATION SCHEMES

	Above Average Employee	Average Employee	Below Average Employee
Expected Output	102,000	100,000 (O)	98,000
Actual Output			
Month 1	107,000	105,000 ($O + \mu$)	103,000
Month 2	97,000	95,000 ($O + \mu$)	93,000
Observed μ (actual – expected output of average employee)			
Month 1		+5000	
Month 2		–5000	
Adjusted Output (Actual output – μ)			
Month 1	102,000	100,000	98,000
Month 2	102,000	100,000	98,000
Incentive Compensation under Absolute PE			
Month 1	10,700	10,500	10,300
Month 2	9700	9500	9300
Incentive Compensation under Relative PE			
Month 1	10,200	10,000	9800
Month 2	10,200	10,000	9800

When the performance of the three employees is measured in absolute terms, their actual outputs are treated as measures of their performance and the incentive compensation paid to them is 10 per cent of these figures. When performance is measured in relative terms, we calculate the observed value of μ by comparing the actual output of the average performer with his expected output (i.e. the performance benchmark), and use it to adjust the actual output of all three employees. The adjusted outputs are treated as measures of their performance and the incentive commission paid to them is 10 per cent of these adjusted figures. In other words, for the purposes of calculating the compensation payable to an employee, his performance is measured in relation to the performance of the average performer.

In the above example, we have assumed that random shocks affect the performance of all employees equally. Therefore, by adjusting the actual outputs of all three by the observed μ of the average employee, we can eliminate the effect of random shocks on their performance completely and stabilize their incomes fully. In reality, random shocks affect the performance of different employees differently and the effect of these shocks on their performance cannot be eliminated completely. Nevertheless, the advantage of relative performance evaluation is that it allows us to reduce the effect of uncontrollable factors on an employee's performance and income. Therefore, he has to be paid a lower compensatory differential than would be necessary if his performance is measured absolutely. The disadvantage is that the employees have an incentive to inflate their performance by depressing, the average performance. They can do so by colluding, ostracizing high performers, or encouraging the recruitment of low performers. This arrangement may also lead to unhealthy competition and loss of cooperation among employees.

12.2.2 Problems with Objective Performance Evaluation

The attraction of objective performance evaluation is that it gives us a precise estimate of the employee's output. But this estimate can be reliable only if we specify all the important tasks that constitute a job, develop performance benchmarks for all the tasks, and weight the benchmarks in terms of their relative contribution to the value generated by the job-holder. If we measure a job-holder's performance along only some dimensions of his job and leave out the others, we are faced with two problems. First, we encourage him to put in *unbalanced effort*, i.e. concentrate only those aspects of his job that are measured and neglect the others. Second, he has an incentive to inflate his performance by *gaming*, or 'cheating', if the effects of cheating are not reflected in his measured performance. To illustrate, even an apparently single-dimensional job like a salesman's has in fact many dimensions to it. He can affect the firm's profits through his volume of sales, the mix of products he sells, the way he relates to his customers, the speed with which he attends to their complaints, how quickly he identifies their new requirements, how closely he follows competitive moves, etc. If we measure his performance only by the volume of sales effected by him, he may maximize his sales by selling unprofitable products and not spending any time on attending to customer complaints or spotting new marketing opportunities. He may also inflate his sales by pushing unwanted stocks into the pipeline, if the resultant increase in the costs of carrying excess inventory and delayed payments are not reflected in his measured performance.

Obviously, there are costs attached to specifying all the tasks that make up a job and developing performance benchmarks for each of them. These costs may be affordable if a job is not too multifaceted, like that of a salesman or a production worker. Even for some multifaceted jobs, it may be possible to measure performance objectively, because summary measures that reflect all aspects of the job are available. A chief executive's performance, for example, can be measured by the short-term profits of his firm and the long-term appreciation in the firm's market value. But in most cases, it becomes prohibitively expensive to develop objective performance standards for all the important aspects of a job, and summary performance measures are not available.

12.2.3 Subjective Performance Evaluation

When objective evaluation of performance becomes infeasible, we have to evaluate performance subjectively. There are two common methods of subjective performance evaluation: the rating scale system and the goal-based system.

In the *rating scale system*, an employee is rated on a number of performance factors, like job knowledge, application, result-orientation, capacity to solve problems, capacity to take decisions, leadership qualities, willingness to cooperate with others, willingness to learn, etc. Typically, the rating is done on a five or seven point scale, ranging from 'far exceeds requirements' to 'does not meet requirements'. Based on these ratings, the employee is given an overall rating, ranging from 'excellent' to 'unsatisfactory'. The evaluator also assesses the employee's strengths and weaknesses and his potential for growth, and gives recommendations for improving his future performance.

In the *goal-based system*, an employee is given a set of goals pertaining to the important aspects of his job and is evaluated by the extent to which he meets these goals. For example, an R&D scientist may be set goals in terms of what new projects he should initiate during the year and what progress he should make with the projects already on hand. At the end of the year, he is judged by the extent to which he meets these goals. Goal-based systems are more objective than rating scale systems, but more subjective than objective evaluation systems.

The main advantage of subjective evaluation systems is that they provide a cost-effective method of assessing an employee's performance along all the important dimensions of his job. But the disadvantage is that the absence of an objective measure of performance may induce dysfunctional behaviour. The employer may define good performance as it suits him and renege on his promise to reward good performance. If the evaluator does not bear the wealth effects of faulty evaluation fully, he may 'shirk'. He may try to become popular with his juniors by overrating their performance or be guided by personal likes and dislikes. The employee may try to influence his evaluators by engaging in unproductive activities like lobbying or politicking. Firms try to guard against these problems in several ways. They may issue extensive guidelines on how an evaluation should be done. The same employee may be assessed by more than one evaluator. The employee may be asked to evaluate himself. Post-evaluation meetings between the employee and his evaluators may be held to reconcile differences in perception. The evaluation of comparable employees by different evaluators may also be compared to remove discrepancies and biases.

12.2.4 Combining Objective and Subjective Evaluation Systems

Clearly, neither the objective nor the subjective system of evaluation is capable of providing a perfectly accurate measure of an employee's performance. For some jobs, the former method may be more suitable than the latter, while for others the latter may be more appropriate. For most jobs, a combination of both methods yields best results. The weights assigned to each method vary, depending on the nature of the job and the kind of business the firm is in. When objective measures dominate, a large part of the compensation is variable and linked to the employee's current output. When subjective measures dominate, most of his income is fixed and incentives take the form of an increase in his future income.

12.2.5 Evaluation on the Basis of Team Performance

When production is the result of team effort and individual team members cannot, by themselves, make a major difference to the team's output, the performance of an individual member is evaluated on the basis of the performance of the team as a whole. This is done for two reasons. First, an individual's output cannot be fully distinguished from the output of his team. Second, team performance is important and individuals have an incentive to improve team performance by coordinating their activities and monitoring one another. For example, the erection and commissioning of a large boiler in a new site requires the joint effort of a team of civil, mechanical, and electrical engineers. The performance of the team can be evaluated objectively by the cost of labour and material used up during the process of erecting and commissioning the boiler, and the time taken to complete the process. The latter is particularly important, because until the boiler is commissioned, it is an asset that costs money but gives no return. How quickly the boiler is erected and commissioned would depend primarily on how well the team performs. No individual member of the team, however hard he works, can speed up the process single-handedly. It, therefore, makes sense to evaluate the engineers on the basis of team performance. If this is done, they have an incentive not only to work hard themselves, but also to cooperate with other members of the team.

The problem with this arrangement is that some members of the team may try to 'free ride'. To avoid this problem, individuals are usually assessed on the basis of both their own performance and the performance of the team. The weights assigned to team and individual performance depend on the extent to which individual performance can affect the performance of the team as a whole. To some extent, the free riders are also monitored and disciplined by other members of the team. If, however, the costs of free riding are so high that they exceed the benefits of team production, then the team members should be assessed purely on the basis of their own performance.

12.2.6 Financial Measures of Team Performance

In the ultimate analysis, the firm is a team and consists of a number of smaller teams. An important component of performance evaluation is, therefore, the evaluation of team performance. Team leaders like the chief executive and heads of divisions and departments are judged primarily by the performance of the teams they lead. As we have just seen, even other team members should be judged by the performance of their teams, if the benefits of team production exceed the costs of free riding.

It is usual to measure team performance objectively, by using summary financial indicators. This is because summary measures for team performance can be developed relatively cheaply and used without running into the pitfalls of unbalanced effort and gaming. Different members of a team may have different priorities, but the team has to balance these priorities and align its own priorities more fully with the firm's priorities. Therefore, teams have less incentive to engage in unbalanced effort and gaming than individuals.

When a team is assigned the task of producing some measurable output, it can be set up as a *cost centre*. A cost centre is given a fixed output budget and a performance benchmark in the form of a cost budget. It has the right to decide what inputs it should use, and how. Its performance is measured by how well it performs against its cost budget, subject to the output budget being met. Cost centres are a common way of organizing manufacturing activities.

Teams responsible for providing services like R&D, HRD, advertizing, market research, accounting, etc. are often established as *expense centres*. The output of these services cannot be measured objectively, making it difficult to measure the cost per unit of output. Typically, the users are not charged for using these services and tend to demand more of these services than they require. The expense centre is given an expense budget and is assessed by the extent to which it meets the demand for its services within the given budget. The expense budget is fixed by looking at past expenditures, or the expenditures of other comparable firms, or as a percentage of the firm's total revenue.

Teams responsible for generating revenue for the firm may be organized as *revenue centres*. Examples are sales, distribution, and service departments. A revenue centre is given fixed manpower and expense budgets and a performance benchmark in the form of a revenue budget. It has the right to decide how its manpower and expense budget should be used. Its performance is measured by how well it performs against its revenue budget, within the framework of the firm's product-mix, pricing, and credit policies.

A *profit centre* consists of one or more cost, revenue, and expense centres. It has the right to decide its mix of products and inputs, output levels, and selling prices. It is given a fixed capital budget and a performance benchmark in the form of a profit budget. Its performance is evaluated by how well it performs against its profit budget.

An *investment centre* is a profit centre, with some decision rights for capital expenditure. The performance of an investment centre is measured by the return on its investment, i.e. the profit generated by the centre divided by the value of the assets invested in it. The return can be compared with external market-based yields to provide a benchmark for the centre's performance. A business division can be a profit centre or an investment centre, depending on its decision rights for capital expenditure.

12.2.7 Transfer Pricing

When a firm consists of more than one profit or investment centres, two problems arise. We have to decide how the transfer of goods and services from one centre to another should be priced and how the cost of corporate overheads should be allocated to them. Many firms deal with these questions by instituting a system of *transfer pricing*. The supplier centre transfers goods and services to the user centre by charging a transfer price. The corporate overheads can also be allocated by the corporate functions charging a transfer price for supplying their services to the operating divisions.

The pitfall of this arrangement is that the firm may undervalue or overvalue the goods and services transferred internally. This may result in the firm making wrong pricing, purchasing, or investment decisions. To avoid this pitfall, transfer prices should be based on the opportunity cost of supplying the goods and services. When there is a well-developed external market for these goods and services, the transfer prices should be the prices that external customers would pay or external suppliers would charge. For example, if an automobile manufacturer makes its own forgings, the transfer prices should be the prices at which they could be sold outside or bought from outside. If an external market does not exist, then the transfer prices should be set by calculating the cost of producing the goods and services on the basis of *shadow prices* of inputs. A shadow price is different from an accounting price, in that the latter is the price the firm actually pays to buy an input, while the former is the income the firm foregoes by not utilizing it in its next best use. Suppose the firm makes its own forgings, because it has superior firm specific knowledge about how a particular type of forging should be made. Then the firm's cost of using this knowledge is not what costs the firm to keep this knowledge in place, but what this knowledge would fetch if it is sold to an external producer of forgings.

12.3 External Architecture

12.3.1 Why External Architecture

When a firm organizes production by establishing an internal architecture, it internalizes the transactions among the partners in production within the firm. This, as we have seen in Chapter 8, enables the firm to produce more efficiently than the market by circumventing the costs of market transactions and promoting teamwork. However, in some situations, the firm can organize production more efficiently by externalizing some of the transactions involved in the production process. This happens for two reasons. First, market transactions offer certain benefits that are lost if the transactions are organized internally. Second, the firm is able to minimize the costs of market transactions by building long-term relationships with other firms. When these two conditions are fulfilled, the firm organizes a part of its production by building an external architecture, i.e. by entering into long term relationships with other firms on the basis of implicit contracts.

12.3.2 Forms of External Architecture

The long-term relationships built by a firm with other firms may be *vertical* or *horizontal*. In a vertical relationship, the firm is a regular customer or supplier of its associates. In a horizontal relationship, both the firm and its associates provide some input to produce an output. An association of two or more equally powerful firms is sometimes referred to as a *strategic alliance*.

Two common forms of vertical relationships are subcontracting and franchising. In a *subcontracting* arrangement, the firm purchases custom-made inputs from another firm on an on-going basis. Automobile manufacturers, for example, subcontract the manufacture of many of their components to small suppliers. In a *franchising* arrangement, the firm supplies its know-how, brand names, and other key inputs to its franchisees who use them to produce the final product and reach it to the consumers. Typically, soft drink firms provide soft drink concentrates and bottling know-how to their bottlers, authorize them to use their brand names, and leave them to bottle and distribute soft drinks in territories assigned to them.

In a horizontal relationship, a firm and its associates usually provide *complementary inputs*. Many multinational companies operate in different countries by joining hands with local firms, on the basis of supplying complementary inputs. The multinational company supplies international expertise in terms of technical know-how, brand names, and other key inputs. The local firm supplies local expertise in terms of knowledge of local laws, markets and business conditions, lobbying power with the local government, and control over supply and distribution channels. A firm may also enter into a horizontal relationship with other firms on the basis of supplying *similar inputs*. This kind of arrangement is quite common when the investments involved are large and risky, as in oil and gas exploration, real estate development, aerospace, and R&D projects.

Production based on horizontal relationships is sometimes undertaken by a *consortium of firms*, and governed by pre-agreed rules and formulae pertaining to the allocation of tasks, costs, and revenues. In many cases, this kind of production is organized by floating a *joint venture*. A joint venture is a separate entity, owned jointly by two or more partners who share the investments, risks, profits, and control of the venture.

12.3.3 Benefits of Externalization

How does a firm benefit by externalizing a part of its production?[3] One answer to this question is provided by the so-called *resource dependence theory*. When two dependent resources, or complementary assets, are capable of generating a rent, underutilized and controlled by two different firms, the firms can maximize their joint profits by using them jointly. These rent-yielding assets may be proprietary assets, like knowledge or reputation, or strategic assets, like a difficult-to-get industrial licence or the exclusive right to exploit some scarce natural resources. If they are complementary and underutilized, then by coming together, each firm can use the asset of the other firm and both firms can benefit from the economies of scale and scope. For example, to produce a motor car, we have to combine automobile engineering with microelectronics and plastic technology. If three different firms have cutting edge technologies in these three areas, all of them will gain by joining hands to produce a state-of-the-art motor car. We may argue that an even more efficient arrangement will be for one of them, say

---

[3]For a useful summary of the benefits of externalization, see Contractor and Lorange (1988).

the engineering firm, to take over the other two. This will not only enable joint use of the three complementary assets, but also avoid the costs of three parties having to transact with one another directly. For strategic assets and simple varieties of proprietary assets, this may indeed be so. But when the development of an asset requires a high degree of specialization and critical competencies that cannot be acquired easily, it is best to leave the development to a firm that has the required focus and competence.

The complementarity between firms may result not only from the assets they control, but also the size of their operations. This is why knowledge and reputation-intensive products, like IT products or internationally known consumer goods, are commonly produced by large and small firms coming together. This arrangement combines *scale with flexibility*. The initial investment in the creation of knowledge or reputation is high in relation to unit costs of production. But once created, the same knowledge or reputation can be used to produce more and more output. Therefore, scale is important: as output increases, the unit cost of production falls sharply. On the other hand, at the point of using these intangible assets to produce a tangible product, flexibility is often more important than scale. Product life cycles tend to be short, necessitating frequent retooling. Demand may be volatile, calling for frequent changes in the product mix. Markets are often segmented, requiring production in small batch quantities. Therefore, a firm has to have flexible productive assets that can be switched from one application to another quickly. A large firm can deal with scale more efficiently. But typically, a small firm is better equipped to meet the demands for flexibility, because it is less constrained by the rigidities in internal systems and the burden of sunk investments. Therefore, many large firms produce knowledge and reputation-intensive products by farming out a part of the production process to small firms. They do not usually take over the small firms, because smallness *per se* is an advantage.

An important motivation for firms coming together is *risk reduction*. Complementarity between two firms may enable both to reduce their business risks in a number of ways. If each uses the other's underutilized assets, their joint investment and the risks resulting therefrom are reduced automatically. The reduction in joint investment may also release resources for the firms to expand their portfolio of products and enable them to diversify their risks more widely. The firms may be able to do the same by pooling their product portfolios. A firm may be able to speed up its entry into and payback from a new market by using the assets of its partner. The reduction in the payback period would reduce the project risks by increasing the net present value of future revenues. As we have noted already, small firms can bear the risks of demand volatility and product obsolescence more efficiently than large firms. Large firms may, therefore, be able to reduce their cost of bearing risks by joining hands with small firms.

Even when firms have similar, rather than complementary assets, they may be able to reduce their risks efficiently by taking up a large and risky project jointly. To understand why this is so, consider a project, say an oil exploration project, which is potentially very profitable, but requires a large investment. Much of the investment is sunk, i.e. project-specific, and the outcome is highly uncertain. If a firm takes up a project like this, it is faced with two scenarios. If the project succeeds, it will make very high profits. But if it fails, the firm will make very heavy losses. If a single firm undertakes the project and the project fails, the firm may go bankrupt. The probability of bankruptcy is high, because the outcome is highly uncertain. On the other hand, if a large enough number of firms undertake the project jointly, none of them will go bankrupt if the project fails. But if the project succeeds, the profits will be high enough to give all of them an adequate return on their investments. Clearly, a project like this will be taken up, only if a large enough number of firms come together and share the risks. This is an efficient arrangement, because without it investment will not flow into the project at all.

Box 12.2. Why do firms cooperate?

Three recent agreements illustrate how parties benefit by entering into alliances in which their assets are vertically related, complementary, or similar.

Rallis India, ICICI, and Hindustan Levers have come together in a 'partnership project', aimed at promoting profitable contract farming in wheat and basmati rice. Under this project, Rallis will provide the farmers with technical knowledge, soil testing facilities, seeds, and pesticides. ICICI will provide farm credit. Hindustan Levers will buy the produce, and brand and market it. The focal point will be the so-called 'kisan kendras'. These kendras will develop tailor-made packages for farmers, taking into account the crop, climatic and geographical conditions, and farming practices, and provide a point where all four parties can meet and transact business. The project has started with wheat in Madhya Pradesh and will be extended to rice in Haryana. Here we have a vertical association, which promises to benefit all the parties. Rallis and ICICI are assured of markets. Farmers are assured of inputs and markets. Hindustan Levers are assured of inputs.

Sterling Holiday Resorts, a time-share company, has entered into a 15-year agreement with Days Inn, USA whereby the former's 11 resorts in India will be managed by the latter. Days Inn, an internationally renowned hotel chain, manages 11 hotels in India already. It will upgrade Sterling's resorts to world standards (at Sterling's expense), take over day-to-day management of the resorts, and train Sterling's personnel. The resorts will be known as Sterling Days Inn resorts. Sterling will concentrate on servicing its existing clients and enlisting new clients. Here we have an association in which each party expects to benefit from the complementary assets of the other. Days Inn will provide a strong brand name, expertise in hotel management, an international reservation system to attract guests from abroad, and synergy with the 11 hotels it manages in India already. Sterling will provide its properties, a client base of 95,000 families who may use other Days Inn properties also, and its expertise in dealing with time-share clients.

The Birla group has been offering cellular telephone services in Gujarat and Maharashtra for some time through a joint venture with AT&T of the USA. The Tata group, which had a licence to offer similar services in Andhra Pradesh, decided to merge its cellular assets into this company in 2000. BPL's cellular business, in which AT&T has some shareholding through a global takeover of Media One, is expected to be merged into the joint venture company in 2002. BPL operates in Tamil Nadu, Kerala, and Maharashtra. All four partners are likely to have roughly similar shareholding in the combined entity, which has been recently christened Idea Cellular. Its brand name, !dea Cellular, is independent of the identity of its sponsors. Here we have an association in which the partners have assets that are similar, but located in different geographical locations. They have come together to widen their market coverage, without increasing their investment or competition.

Source: *The Economic Times,* Mumbai, various issues.

To sum up, externalization enables firms to increase profits by using their assets more efficiently. But sometimes, firms join hands to gain *market dominance*. They may increase their profits by fixing their prices and outputs jointly, or sharing pre-emptive investments to deter new entry, or squeezing the prices and market shares of common competitors to drive them out of the market. In these cases, firms increase profits not by improving their efficiency, but by restricting output and reducing consumer welfare.

12.3.4 How Are Implicit Contracts Enforced?

When production is organized by internalizing transactions, the partners in production are made to cooperate with one another by integrating the ownership of all productive assets and creating an authority relationship among them. But when production is organized by externalizing transactions among the partners, the ownership of productive assets remains dispersed. Some assets may also be owned jointly by all the partners. In this situation, we are back to the problem of transaction costs. Individual partners have an incentive to increase their profits by competing, rather than cooperating, with one another. Instead of maximizing the total pie, they may try to extract a higher share of the pie by 'holding up'. How do we avoid this?

Economic theory provides some useful leads in this direction. Since the partners are bound in a long-term relationship, they have to play *repeated games* with one another. If a partner becomes particularly uncooperative, other partners may punish him by excluding him from future games. Therefore, if he thinks that the one-time gain he can make by holding up is less than the net present value of the future gains he will make by not holding up, he has an incentive to cooperate.

The repeated-games model does indeed provide the basis for many a successful cooperative venture. But it is not foolproof. If a partner takes a short-term view of gains and losses, he can ruin a partnership by behaving opportunistically. Sometimes, the uncooperative partner cannot be excluded from future games for contractual, familial, or other reasons. Then the threat of punishment has to take the form of the threat of reciprocal holding back, or what economists call a *tit-for-tat strategy*. This may indeed persuade the partners to cooperate. But if one of them holds back, it triggers off a series of retaliations, until the costs of externalizing the transactions exceed the benefits of cooperation, and the partnership breaks up.

A more foolproof arrangement is one in which the partners are required to make a *commitment* in the form of transaction-specific investments upfront. If the investments are large enough, they force the partners to cooperate by changing the pay-off structure. Since these investments are sunk, the partners cannot even make a one-time gain by holding back. They have to recover their investments by working with one another over a long enough period of time.

The basic principle underlying all these arrangements is *self-enforcement*. The partners in production abide by the implicit contracts that bind them together, because they think they will gain by doing so. This is the basic difference between internal and external architecture. Implicit contracts underlying the former are enforced by authority, while those underlying the latter are self-enforced.

12.3.5 Sharing Arrangements

Firms come together, because the joint use of their assets creates more value than the total of the values created by these assets separately. How do the firms share the extra value created by the joint use of their assets? This may be seen as the outcome of a bargaining process, where the relative bargaining power of the partners determines their shares of the total pie. In a perfect scenario, the outcome is efficient. Each partner's assets are used until they stop adding further value, so that the size of the pie is maximized. It is then divided among the partners in accordance with their bargaining strengths. The bargaining strength of a partner depends on the capacity of his assets to add value and the extent to which they cannot be substituted or duplicated. Thus a partner's share of the total pie is determined by the contribution that his assets make to the pie. The control that he can exercise over the cooperative venture is also determined by his bargaining power, and therefore his contribution to value. This too is an efficient arrangement. If a partner who contributes more has a greater say in the running of the business, the business is run efficiently.

The above is probably a good description of what happens when two equally powerful firms come together and stick to each other. But the bargaining power of a firm depends not only on its capacity to create value, but also its capacity to dominate its partners, which in turn depends on how easily it can find other partners. Therefore, the value that a firm appropriates from a cooperative venture, and the control that it exercises, also depends on how dominant it is in relation to its partners. This phenomenon is quite evident when a large and a small firm come together, as in a subcontracting or franchising arrangement. Typically, it is much easier for the large firm to find other small firms as partners, than it is for the small firm to find other large firms. This puts the large firm in a position to dominate the small firm and extract a more than fair share of the profits and control. The relationship between the two tends to resemble the relationship between the owners and employees of a firm. Implicit contracts are enforced at least partly by the large firm exercising its authority over the small firm. Quite often, support and incentive systems have to be put in place to get the best out of the small firm. The small firm stays in the relationship not because it gets a fair share of the profits and control, but because it can do no better.

12.3.6 Why Do Alliances Break Up?

Some alliances between firms endure for a long time. But many do not. The reasons for this are not far to seek.[4]

Sometimes, the partners fail to assess the strengths and weaknesses of one another correctly before they enter into a relationship. They cannot therefore live up to the expectations of one another. This leads to disenchantment and eventual dissolution of the alliance.

Sometimes, the partners have the capacity to deliver as expected, but start fighting over the sharing of profits and control after they have come together. This happens

[4]For an interdisciplinary discussion on the creation and termination of joint ventures, see Kogut (1988).

because partners' contributions are difficult to measure and become a bone of contention. This leads to hold-ups, a steady erosion in the joint performance, and eventual breaking up of the alliance.

Different partners have different priorities. Quite often, these differences surface only after they have worked together for some time. The multinational partner of a joint venture may, for example, want the venture to follow tax, dividend, export-import, transfer pricing, and expansion policies that maximize its global profits. The local partner may, on the other hand, want to so design these policies that the local profits are maximized. When such differences become irreconcilable, the partners part company.

BOX 12.3. WHY DO ALLIANCES BREAK UP?

In the mid-1980s, the TVS group joined hands with Suzuki Motor Corporation of Japan to establish TVS Suzuki Limited (TSL), to produce two-wheelers in India. TVS had 32 per cent of the equity and Suzuki had 26 per cent. The rest was held by banks, financial institutions, and the public. This suited both. Because of government restrictions, Suzuki could not come into India except as a minority partner. It was also new to the product and factor markets, distribution and service infrastructure, and the regulatory environment in India. On the other hand, TVS needed Suzuki's technology.

Over time, the equation changed, because the objectives of the two partners did not match. Suzuki wanted to use TSL as a vehicle for using its own products in India, with as little local processing as possible. TVS wanted to acquire the capability to develop and produce two-wheelers in India independently. TSL launched a range of motorbikes like Samurai, Max 100, and Suzuki Fiero, based on Suzuki's technology. Suzuki also wanted TSL to import high-end motorbikes in the 400cc range for the Indian market. But TVS did not agree, because it did not think that there was a large enough market for such products. On the other hand, as TVS saw it, the supply of technology from Suzuki to TSL was inadequate. TSL entered the scooter market with locally developed models like Scooty and Spectra. To take advantage of a booming market for 100cc motorbikes with a 4-stroke engine, it launched, in 2001, an indigenously developed model called Victor, with a 110cc 4-stroke engine.

By 2001, the two partners had reached a situation where they did not need each other any more. Thanks to changes in government policy, Suzuki did not need a local partner to operate in India. It had also picked up enough knowledge about business conditions in India. TVS also did not need a foreign partner any more, because it had acquired the capability to develop and produce two-wheelers on its own. In September 2001, the two partners declared their intention to part. TVS bought up Suzuki's stake in TSL for Rs 9 crore, by paying a premium of Rs 5 per 10-rupee share. Suzuki agreed not to produce or sell two-wheelers in India for the next 30 months. Interestingly, the price at which Suzuki sold its shares was only one-fifth of the prevailing market price of these shares and showed how disinterested Suzuki was in TSL.

Since the Indian market for two-wheelers is large and growing rapidly, there is little doubt that Suzuki will come back to India. Meanwhile, TVS, who now has a 58 per cent stake in TSL will run the company as it considers fit. As the managing director of TSL put it, TVS and Suzuki broke up, because both felt that they needed the freedom to pursue their business interests independently of each other.

Source: *The Economic Times,* Mumbai, various issues.

Perhaps the most important reason why alliances break up is that partners join hands with some specific objectives in mind and have no incentive to continue when these objectives are achieved. A multinational company, for example, may ally with a local partner because it wants to acquire knowledge about local business conditions. Similarly, the local firm may ally with the multinational company because it wants to acquire knowledge about a new technology. When they have learnt enough, they may find it more profitable to strike out on their own.

12.4 CORPORATE GOVERNANCE

12.4.1 What is Corporate Governance?

A firm is a *corporation*, or a group of people who act as one, to produce and share an output. The members of the group are the risk capital provider, the employee, the creditor, the vendor, and the customer. In Business Policy literature, they are called *stakeholders*, because they have a stake in the quality, size, and distribution of the output.

Ideally, each stakeholder should be called upon to contribute to the total output until the value of his marginal contribution equals the cost he incurs to make that contribution, and paid at a rate equal to the value of his marginal contribution. This would ensure that the total output is maximized and each stakeholder is paid in accordance with his contribution to the total output. Typically, however, some, and not all, stakeholders manage the corporation. The *managing stakeholder* can, and often does, *usurp* a higher share of the output than is his due, by denying other stakeholders their rightful shares. This is not only inequitable but, as we shall see later, also inefficient. There are, however, some institutional, market-driven, and regulatory mechanisms that tend to deter the managing stakeholder from appropriating the shares of other stakeholders. The term *corporate governance* refers to the mechanisms by which a corporation is governed, so that it may not overpay some stakeholders by underpaying the others.[5]

12.4.2 Genesis of the Corporate Governance Problem: Closed and Open Corporations

Why does the managing stakeholder usurp? If he usurps, he gets a higher share of the pie. But, for reasons explained below, the size of the pie shrinks. The managing stakeholder has an incentive to usurp, if he gains more from an increase in his share of the pie than he loses from a reduction in the size of the pie.

Why does the pie shrink? If stakeholders can vary their contributions freely, then the stakeholders who are denied their rightful shares respond by reducing their contributions until the cost of their marginal contribution is equal to what they get paid for it. If, for example, the managing stakeholder tries to gain at the expense of the customer by supplying a substandard product, the customer either switches to another

---

[5]For a useful survey of corporate governance issues, see Shleifer and Vishny (1997).

supplier or pays a lower price. If he pays the vendor a lower price than agreed, the vendor switches to another customer or supplies a substandard product. If he does not pay the provider of debt or risk capital the agreed rate of interest or the agreed share of the residual income, the latter switches his capital to another user. If he does not pay the employee the agreed rate of wage, he either switches to another employer or puts in less effort. Consequently, the output of the firm falls.

However, stakeholders cannot always vary their contributions freely, because they make transaction-specific investments that become less productive if they are switched to other uses. The customer who is supplied a substandard product may not be able to switch to another supplier, because he buys a custom-made product and needs time to develop an alternative. The vendor who is paid less than the agreed price may not be able to switch to another customer, because he has invested in customer-specific assets which will become valueless if he switches. The employee who is paid less than the agreed wage may not be able to switch to another employer, because he has developed firm-specific skills that are worth more within the firm than outside. The provider of debt capital may not be able to switch because he is tied up in a long-term contract. Their inability to reduce their contribution exposes them to exploitation by the managing stakeholder. But since they have firm-specific assets, they can try to extract their due by 'holding up'. The customer may withhold purchases. The vendor may withhold supplies. The employee may go slow. As a result, the output of the firm falls.

In what Fama and Jensen[6] call a *closed corporation*, the claim to the residual cash flow is restricted to those who manage it. Examples are proprietary firms, or small partnerships and private limited companies. There are only a few risk capital providers who manage the corporation themselves. They take all the important decisions. To take advantage of specific knowledge, they delegate some decisions to their employees. But they tightly control, by establishing a suitable internal architecture, the decisions taken by these employees. Since the managing stakeholder is the sole beneficiary of the residual cash flow of the firm, he has to bear the cost of any fall in the firm's output fully. Therefore, if he usurps, he is likely to lose more from a fall in the firm's output than he would gain from an increase in his share of the output. For this reason, the managing stakeholder in a closed corporation usually tries to maximize profit, rather than appropriate the shares of other stakeholders. He may sometimes try to pay other stakeholders less than the value of their marginal contribution, but he does so because he underestimates their contribution.

Modern industrial societies, however, are not driven by closed corporations, because they tend to underinvest. Since only a few investors supply the risk capital, the capital available for investment is limited. The rate at which future cash flows are discounted is also high. This happens for two reasons. First, the risks borne by the investors tend to be high, because they cannot be spread over a large number of investors or a wide portfolio of products. Second, the investors want a quick payback, because they cannot encash their future claims by selling them in the capital market freely. An *open corporation* solves these problems by admitting small investors as residual claimants who do not have to participate in the management of the corporation. Examples of an open

[6]See Fama and Jensen (1985).

corporation are public limited companies, large partnerships and private limited companies, and mutual funds. The investors can buy and sell residual claims in an open corporation by buying and selling shares in the total stock of the corporation. The risks they are exposed to are not very high. They can diversify their risks by buying claims in a large number of firms. They can encash their claims to future cash flows by selling their shares at a price that reflects the net present value of future cash flows. The risks are further reduced in a limited liability company: if the firm goes bankrupt, the investors' liability is limited to the face value of their shares. Open corporations are, therefore, better placed to exploit business opportunities. They can mobilize large amounts of money by pooling the savings of a large number of small investors. They do not also have to discount future cash flows at a high rate, because the risks borne by the investors are not very high. Not surprisingly, most large firms are open corporations.

By definition, an open corporation is not managed by all shareholders. Instead, it is managed by a *board of directors* who are elected by the shareholders. The voting power of a shareholder is determined by the number of shares held by him. Typically, a few shareholders have a large number of shares and can take over the management of the corporation by electing themselves as directors. Sometimes, none of the shareholders is large enough to be able to take over the management of the corporation. In that case, the corporation is managed by paid managers under the supervision of an elected board of directors. In either case, there is a *separation of ownership from control*. Some owners have no control over the management of the firm, while the *managing stakeholder*, or the stakeholder who manages the firm, has less than 100 per cent claim on the residual cash flow of the firm. This gives the managing stakeholder an incentive to usurp. If he usurps, the benefit in terms of an increase in his share of the output accrues to him fully. But the cost in terms of a fall in the output is borne by all residual claimants, and not by him alone. The lower his claim on the residual cash flow, the lower is his share of the cost, and the greater is his incentive to usurp. Thus, the problem of corporate governance is associated primarily with open corporations.

12.4.3 Types of Corporate Governance Problems

There are many ways in which the managing stakeholder can gain at the expense of residual claimants who do not manage the firm. He may *steal profits* by giving himself a fat salary and lavish fringe benefits, or by simply spending a part of the residual cash flow for his own benefit. He may sell the firm's output or assets to himself at below market price. This is known as *asset stripping*. He may use his inside knowledge of the firm's operations to sell his shares before their prices start falling in the market or to buy new shares before their prices start rising. By doing so, he passes on his own losses from a fall in the firm's fortune to the shareholders who do not manage the firm, and takes away from them some of the gains from a rise in the firm's fortune. This is called *insider trading*.

When the managing stakeholder is also a residual claimant, he can gain at the expense of the long-term creditor by exposing him to more business risks than is his due. The creditor has a prior claim on the surplus cash that remains after paying for inputs, wages, and salaries. Whatever surplus cash is left after the creditor has been paid his due goes to the residual claimants as profits. If the surplus cash is not large enough, the creditor does not get paid fully. But if it is large enough, he is paid only a fixed amount. In other words, if the firm fares badly, he has to share the losses. But if the firm fares well, he does not share the gains. Typically, the creditor charges an interest rate that factors in the risks he has to bear. But the residual claimant can still gain at his expense, if he takes up new projects that are risky but potentially very profitable, and finances them by raising new debts. This increases the market value of his residual claims, because the probability of his earning high profits increases, without a commensurate increase in the risks that he has to bear. At the same time, the creditor suffers a fall in the market value of the debt held by him, because the probability of his debt not being repaid increases, without any increase in the interest payable to him. A new creditor can offset this by charging a higher rate of interest. But the old creditor ends up by under-recovering his cost of risks and subsidizing the residual claimant.

If the firm is doing badly and is faced with a high probability of bankruptcy, the residual claimant may be able to gain at the expense of the creditor by not investing risk capital to finance a new project, even if the project promises to be profitable. If he invests and the project succeeds, the surplus cash flow increases. But since the creditor has a prior claim on the increased cash flow, the market value of his debt increases, because he now has a better chance of recovering his debt without any fall in the interest payable to him. On the other hand, the market value of residual claims falls, because the residual claimant is now exposed to the risk of the project failing, without a commensurate increase in residual cash flows. This is why firms with a high debt–equity ratio and a high probability of bankruptcy tend to avoid investing in new projects, even if they are profitable.

The managing stakeholder can gain at the expense of non-investor stakeholders like employees, customers, and vendors by going back on implicit contracts, or promises that cannot be enforced legally. For example, the employee may be denied the promised promotions, salary increases, or retirement benefits. He may be forced to invest a part of his earnings in the firm as risk capital, or retrenched when business is down. The customer may be supplied substandard products, or not supplied on time when more profitable sales opportunities arise. The vendor may not be paid on time, or asked to change his production plans frequently, or forced to provide additional services free of charge. We can multiply such examples.

12.4.4 Corporate Governance Mechanisms: The Board of Directors

As we have noted already, an open corporation is governed by a *board of directors* who are elected by all residual claimants. The board has the authority to control all decisions taken by the managers of the corporation and is responsible for safeguarding the interests of all stakeholders. Typically, it consists of executive directors, who are drawn from the paid managers and the residual claimants who manage the corporation, and non-executive directors, who keep an eye on the executive directors. Sometimes, non-executive directors represent specific interest groups. In India, banks and financial institutions who have lent large sums of money to a corporation often nominate their own representatives on the board. In Germany, many corporations have a two-tier board. The upper tier oversees the work of the lower tier which is entrusted with the task of day-to-day management. Half of the members of the upper tier are elected by the shareholders and the other half by the employees. The shareholders, however, have the final say through the casting vote of the chairperson.

Non-executive directors cannot act as an effective check on executive directors, unless they are free from their influence. This, however, is not always the case. Often, executive directors represent the interests of controlling shareholders and have a decisive say in the election of non-executive directors. This problem is mitigated to some extent by the fact that the election of all directors is subject to the approval of statutory authorities. Usually, the election of a non-executive director is not approved unless he has a minimum public standing, and to protect his standing he has to conduct himself in an independent and impartial manner.

12.4.5 Corporate Governance Mechanisms: Market Forces

Several economists have argued that *market forces* act as an effective mechanism for controlling corporate governance problems, because poor corporate governance erodes the profitability of a firm. If the managing stakeholder siphons off a part of the residual cash flow for his own benefit, the reported profit of the firm is reduced automatically. If he tries to gain by under-supplying customers or by underpaying vendors, creditors, or employees, the residual cash flow falls because of a fall in selling prices, or an increase in the cost of inputs or debt capital, or a reduction in the effort put in by employees.

If the managing stakeholder is an employee whose compensation is linked to his performance, and if his performance is measured by the firm's profits, then the fall in the firm's profits leads to a reduction in the compensation payable to him. His failure to earn an adequate profit for the firm also affects his reputation and reduces the value of his human capital in the *managerial labour market*. This, as Fama[7] puts it, leads to an *ex-post settling up*: what he gains at the expense of other stakeholders is offset by what he loses by way of a fall in his compensation and the market value of his human capital.

If the managing stakeholder is a residual claimant with a controlling interest in the firm, he is affected more directly. A part of the gain he makes at the expense of other stakeholders is offset by a reduction in his share of the residual claims. What is more, the fall in the firm's profit induces smaller residual claimants to sell off their shares, so that the stock market value of the residual claims held by him falls. Since his stakes in the firm are large, he cannot exit the firm as painlessly as the smaller residual claimants and has to suffer an erosion in the value of his shares.

Most importantly, if as a result of poor corporate governance, the market value of a firm falls in relation to other firms with comparable assets, the managing stakeholder runs the risk of losing control over his firm. His firm becomes a target for takeover by those who believe that they can use the firm's assets more efficiently and make a capital gain by increasing its residual cash flows. The presence of large minority shareholders tends to facilitate the takeover process, because they tend to join hands with the bidder in the hope that a change in management will improve the efficiency of the firm and

[7]See Fama (1980).

increase the market value of their shares.[8] Thus, the existence of a *market for corporate control*, or a market in which the control over corporations changes hands, tends to deter the managing stakeholder from denying small residual claimants and other stakeholders their rightful shares of the output.

12.4.6 Regulatory Mechanisms

Markets do not always protect non-managing stakeholders, especially small shareholders and creditors, very well. The managing stakeholder, if he is not too greedy, can keep nibbling into the shares of other stakeholders, without the markets detecting it or penalizing him for it. If he becomes too greedy and tries to make a killing, the markets do wake up at some stage. But by the time they do so, he can often make a large one-time profit and exit the company. Even if he is found out in time and faced with a takeover, he is frequently in a position to block the takeover or negotiate a favourable settlement.

Box 12.4. Takeover defences

In the 1980s, North America and the UK witnessed a spate of hostile takeover attempts. In response, the incumbent management devised a host of takeover defences.

- *White knight*: when Mobil Oil attempted a takeover of Marathon Oil, US Steel played the role of a white knight, i.e. a friendly buyer, by making a bid that Marathon's management favoured and finally accepted.

- *Poison pills* are devices aimed at reducing the worth of a company once it has been taken over. One example is a clause requiring that huge dividend payments be made upon takeover. This can raise the cost of acquisition significantly.

- *Scorched earth policies* deliberately reduce the firm's value to the bidder, even if shareholder value is reduced in the process. One way to do this is to sell off *crown jewels*, or the value creating assets of the company, at greatly reduced prices.

- *Golden parachutes* are clauses in the compensation contract that provide for very attractive benefits if a manager leaves after a takeover. Incumbent managers thereby cushion themselves against the risk of losing their current job should a hostile takeover occur.

- *Classified or staggered boards* are boards in which only a fraction of the membership comes up for election every year. It then becomes difficult for an outsider to gain control over the firm quickly.

- *Supermajority rules* require as much as 90 per cent of the votes to effect any change and have the same effect as staggered boards.

- *Greenmail* commonly consists of an offer by the incumbent management to buy out the shares acquired by the raider at an attractive premium.

Source: A. Sen (1998), *Microeconomics: Theory and Applications*, Oxford University Press.

---

[8]See Shleifer and Vishny (1986).

Most countries therefore find it necessary to put in place certain regulatory mechanisms to protect the interests of small shareholders and creditors. In this context, the most important piece of legislation in India is the *Companies Act 1956*. When more than a specified number of persons come together to do business for private gain, they have to register their association as a 'company' under this Act. Thus, the Act governs all corporations, closed or open, if they are of a certain size. But as an instrument of corporate governance, it is of particular importance for open corporations. It covers aspects like the incorporation of a company, issue of shares and debentures, registration of the charges created by the company on its assets, management and administration, and winding up. Among other things, it spells out the rights of the small shareholder to participate in shareholders' meetings, elect the directors, vote in person or by proxy, receive dividends, subscribe to new issues, and seek legal redress against oppression and mismanagement by controlling shareholders. It specifies how companies should keep and consolidate accounts, and requires them to get their accounts audited and disclose critical information about their operations. It also lays down the rules and procedures by which an aggrieved creditor can apply for the winding up of the offending company, having sold its assets to settle his claims.

Another important instrument for corporate governance in India is the Securities and Exchange Board Of India (SEBI). With the gradual dismantling of government controls on capital markets, SEBI was established under the Securities and Exchange Board of India Act 1992, to oversee and regulate the working of capital markets. In 2000, SEBI issued a set of *disclosure and investor protection guidelines* that are binding on firms who wish to access the capital market. These cover eligibility norms for issuing securities, pricing of securities, promoters' contribution and lock-in requirements, pre-issue obligations, contents of offer documents, allotment norms, monitoring reports, redressal of grievances, payment of dividends and interests, and redemption of debts. If a firm violates these guidelines and an investor suffers as a result, the latter can complain to SEBI. SEBI has a duty to investigate the complaint and punish the firm if found guilty. If SEBI does not act, the investor can approach the court to direct SEBI to act.

12.4.7 Corporate Governance Codes

In the ultimate analysis, good corporate governance is possible only if companies follow certain codes of conduct. In view of this, SEBI appointed a committee under the chairmanship of Mr Kumarmangalam Birla in 1999, to recommend codes of behaviour that would raise the standard of corporate governance in India. The committee has adapted to Indian conditions the work done by a similar committee in Britain under the chairmanship of Sir Adrian Cadbury in 1992.

The Birla committee emphasizes the role of the board of directors in ensuring good corporate governance. It recommends that the board should have a few *independent directors* who, apart from receiving director's fees, should 'not have any pecuniary relationship or transactions with the company, its promoters, its management or its subsidiaries, which in the judgement of the board may affect their independence of judgement'. The committee stresses that the *chairman's role* should be separated from the role of the managing director. The former should concentrate on ensuring that the board discharges its duties to all stakeholders, while the latter should concentrate on running the company efficiently. It recommends the formation of *audit committees*, consisting mainly of independent directors, to go into matters that require investigation. It also suggests that a *remuneration committee* consisting of independent directors should fix the remuneration of executive directors.

13

Requirements for
Long-Term Success

Our focus has so far been on how firms make an economic profit in the static context, i.e. at one point of time. But often, firms that have been profitable at some point of time do not remain so over time. We, therefore, now turn to examining what a firm has to do to remain profitable in the dynamic context, i.e. over a long period of time.

13.1 THE BASIC HYPOTHESIS

Business Policy literature tells us that to remain profitable over time, a firm has to keep adapting itself to changes in its business environment. Business environment has many dimensions—economic, political, legal, sociological, scientific, etc. As in other parts of the book, we limit ourselves to only the economic aspects of business environment.

Some changes in economic environment are caused by developments that are *exogenous* to the economic system, like changes in government policy, signing of international agreements, changes in international commodity prices, unexpected technological breakthroughs, etc. Usually, such developments take place abruptly. Firms try to deal with them by *restructuring* themselves, i.e. by making discrete and non-repetitive changes in their business, organization, and capital structures. However, much of the change in economic environment is *endogenous*: it arises because firms compete with one another by *innovating*, or finding better and better methods of using non-proprietary factors of production. A firm cannot, therefore, succeed unless it innovates continuously. What is more, to enjoy the fruits of its innovations, the firm has to grow, make changes in its product portfolio, take an entrepreneurial view of its business and enjoy a certain amount of luck in what it does. In other words, the requirements for the long-term success of a firm are innovation, growth, a changing product portfolio, entrepreneurship, and luck.

13.2 WHY DO SUCCESSFUL FIRMS DECLINE?

13.2.1 The Schumpeterian Process of Creative Destruction

Successful firms have a systematic tendency to decline, because success makes them

BOX 13.1. THE CHANGING FACE OF INDIA INC

The following table compares the ranks of the top 15 companies in terms of market capitalization in October 2001 with their ranks in September 1998. Market capitalization is the market value of shareholders' capital and is the market price of one equity share multiplied by the number of shares.

	Rank in October 2001	Rank in September 1998
Hindustan Lever	1	1
Reliance Industries	2	6
Wipro	3	9
Infosys Technologies	4	17
ONGC	5	2
Reliance Petroleum	6	44
ITC	7	4
Indian Oil Corporation	8	3
State Bank of India	9	7
VSNL	10	10
HDFC	11	26
HCL Technologies	12	-
MTNL	13	5
Cipla	14	41
Dr. Reddy's Laboratories	15	65

Source: *The Economic Times,* Mumbai, ET 500, October 1999 and October 2001 issues.

Six companies are newcomers to the top 15 list in October 2001. This means that six or 40 per cent of the companies that made the list in September 1998 are no longer there. Of the nine that remain, five have fallen through the ranks. Two have managed to hold their ranks. Only two have improved their ranks. In other words, even within a space of 3 years, 11 of the 15 companies who topped the market capitalization chart in 1998 have slipped. In fact, some of them are not doing very well. No doubt, the picture will be starker if these comparisons are made over a longer time span.

prone to becoming a victim of what Joseph Schumpeter[1] calls 'the perennial gale of creative destruction'. Traditional economics has been concerned primarily with how firms maximize profits at one point of time by optimizing resource use and engaging in price competition with one another. This kind of static competition is, in Schumpeter's view, far less important than how firms compete with one another over time by *innovating,* or introducing new and better technologies for using non-proprietary factors of production, so that they may gain a cost or differentiation advantage over their competitors. The capitalist system may thus be viewed as a *process of creative destruction,* a process that keeps upgrading the productive structure of the economy by creating new and superior technologies that displace and destroy old and inferior technologies. At any time, in any market there are firms who, by virtue of having introduced a

[1]See Schumpeter (1942), pp. 73–92.

superior technology in the past, earn a positive profit. But they are soon challenged by other firms with better technologies and face the prospect of being displaced by the latter. The incumbent firm could of course respond by scrapping its existing technology and introducing a new technology that is as good as or better than the challenger's. But all too often the profit maximizing response of the incumbent firm is to stick to its existing technology, so that it gets eliminated eventually.

13.2.2 Incumbency and Technological Inertia

Why should incumbency lead to an unwillingness to innovate, or what economists call *technological inertia*?

Suppose, two firms, one already in the market and making a profit (incumbent) and another not currently in the market but wanting to enter (challenger), have an equal opportunity to introduce a new technology. We may assume that an independent inventor has developed the technology and is willing to sell it to either firm at the same price. The new technology is better than the incumbent's existing technology, in that it can generate a higher profit through lower costs and/or higher prices. The challenger has an incentive to introduce the new technology if

$$I_n < \Pi_n, \tag{13.1}$$

$$(n \doteq \text{new})$$

where I_n is the investment required to buy and commercialize the new technology and Π_n the net present value of the future stream of profit generated by this investment. The incumbent, however, will look at the proposition on an incremental basis. To replace his existing technology by the new technology, his incremental investment is the new investment required *less* the amount he can recover by selling his existing assets. This can be written as $I_n - a.I_0$, where I_0 is the original cost of his existing assets and a the proportion of I_0 that he can recover by selling these assets. His incremental payoff from switching to the new technology is the resultant increase in his profit, *plus* the probable reduction in his existing profit that would take place if he did not upgrade his technology and the challenger entered the market, *less* the sunk cost of his existing assets. This can be written as $(\Pi_n - \Pi_0) + b.\Pi_0 - (1-a)I_0$, where Π_0 is the net present value of the future stream of his current profit and b the probability (in his view) that Π_0 will be lost if he does not switch to the new technology. The incumbent has an incentive to switch if $I_n - a.I_0 < (\Pi_n - \Pi_0) + b.\Pi_0 - (1-a).I_0$, or

$$I_n < \Pi_n - \Pi_0.(1 - b) - I_0.(1 - 2a). \tag{13.2}$$

The right hand side of (eqn 13.2) represents the incumbent's incentive to switch. This is lower than Π_n which, as we know from (eqn 13.1) represents the challenger's incentive to adopt the new technology, if $b<1$ and/or $a<0.5$. In fact, the lower the values of b and a, the lower is the incumbent's incentive to adopt the new technology, compared to the challenger's. A low value of b signifies that, in the incumbent's estimate, non-adoption of the new technology will not lead to a large erosion in his current profit and, therefore, the profit he will make by adopting the new technology will largely be in replacement of the profit that he would have made even otherwise. A low value of a signifies that only a small proportion of the original cost of the incumbent's existing assets is recoverable, or his sunk costs are high. Thus, unlike the challenger, the incumbent has to take into account the *replacement effect* and the *sunk cost effect* of adopting a new technology. These two effects constitute the two most important reasons for the technological inertia of incumbent firms.

13.2.3 Technological Inertia and Erosion of Profits

However, in a world of changing technology, a technologically inactive firm cannot remain profitable indefinitely. To understand why this is so, assume that in period 1, the incumbent firm and the potential entrant are technologically similar. But the former, having moved into the market first, earns a profit by making a commitment in the form of a sunk investment and threatening to fight a price war should the latter try to enter. Table 13.1 summarizes the profit outcomes for the incumbent and the potential entrant under alternative strategic scenarios. Since both have the same technology, both would earn a profit of Π_m, Π_d, and Π_w under conditions of monopoly, duopoly, and a price war respectively. The cost of the commitment made by the incumbent is C which has been so chosen by him that $\Pi_m > \Pi_d > 0 > \Pi_w > \Pi_d - C$, and $\Pi_m - C > 0$. Scenarios 2 and 3 do not represent a Nash equilibrium, because if the potential entrant enters the market, the incumbent finds it less unprofitable to fight than to accommodate, in which event the potential entrant finds it unprofitable to enter. Scenario 1 does, because given the other's strategy, neither has an incentive to change his own strategy.

TABLE 13.1. TECHNOLOGICAL INERTIA AND EROSION OF PROFITS: STRATEGY-PROFIT MATRIX IN PERIOD 1

Strategic Scenarios	*Profit Outcome for*	
	Incumbent	*Potential Entrant*
1. The potential entrant does not enter	$\Pi_m - C$	0
2. The potential entrant enters and the incumbent accommodates	$\Pi_d - C$	Π_d
3. The potential entrant enters and the incumbent fights	Π_W	Π_W

If technology does not change over time, the incumbent can keep making a profit indefinitely by doing two things. First, if his assets depreciate, he has to invest in their renewal, so that the asymmetry between him and the potential entrant does not disappear. Second, if there is a natural growth in the market (because of population growth for example), he has to keep increasing C in line with market growth, so that entry continues to be unprofitable for the potential entrant. But if, as hypothesized by Schumpeter, firms strive constantly to outdo one another by introducing better technologies, the picture changes drastically. Assume that in period 2, the potential entrant challenges the incumbent with a better technology that increases his potential profit by Π_t under all the three scenarios. Assume further that $\Pi_w + \Pi_t > 0$ and the incumbent sticks to his existing technology because he suffers from technological inertia. The strategy–profit matrix in period 2 will then be as shown in Table 13.2.

TABLE 13.2. TECHNOLOGICAL INERTIA AND EROSION OF PROFITS:
STRATEGY–PROFIT MATRIX IN PERIOD 2

Strategic Scenarios	Profit Outcome for	
	Incumbent	Potential Entrant
1. The potential entrant does not enter	$\Pi_m - C$	0
2. The potential entrant enters and the incumbent accommodates	$\Pi_d - C$	$\Pi_d + \Pi_t$
3. The potential entrant enters and the incumbent fights	Π_W	$\Pi_W + \Pi_t$

Now, scenario 3 represents a Nash equilibrium. Regardless of the incumbent's strategy, the potential entrant finds it profitable to enter. When that happens, whether the incumbent accommodates or fights, he makes a loss, but minimizes his loss by fighting. Initially, he may make only an accounting loss but a cash profit, and hang around for a while. But as his assets depreciate and their productive power declines, his cash profit also declines and becomes negative in the end. Since the new entrant has a better technology, the incumbent cannot arrest this decline by making fresh investments in his existing technology and is forced to exit eventually.

13.3 REQUIREMENT 1: INNOVATION

13.3.1 Innovation and Technological Progress

All this really means that technological inertia is profit maximizing only in the short run and reflects strategic myopia. If the market is profitable enough, sooner or later, another firm finds a technology which is so much better than the incumbent's that it nullifies the incumbency advantages. To go back to (eqn 13.2), in the long run $b = 1$, so that $\Pi_o.(1 - b) = 0$. What is more, the correct value of I_o is not its historical cost, but the net present value of the stream of profits that it is likely to generate in future. Thus, if $\Pi_o.(1 - b) = 0$, then $I_o = 0$. In that case, (eqn 13.2) simplifies to $I_n < \Pi_n$, which is the same as (eqn 13.1). In other words, if the incumbent takes a long view of profit maximization, then his incentive to adopt a new technology is exactly the same as that as the challenger.

Thus, the first requirement for a firm to remain profitable over time is that it must maintain its technological superiority over its rivals. In a world of changing technology, this means that the firm must keep *innovating*, or keep introducing new and better technologies for using non-proprietary factors of production. Conceptually, this amounts to *acquiring new proprietary assets*. This can be done by developing new assets in-house (through R&D, building new brands, etc.), or by buying them from outside (e.g. patents, established brands, etc.), or even by replicating the assets of other successful firms (e.g. reverse engineering). Whatever the method, the firm has to make an investment to acquire these new assets.

The firm makes this investment with the expectation that it will lead to a recurring increase in its appropriable surplus and the net present value of this increase will be at

---

Box 13.2. Technological inertia and erosion of profits

For decades, Bajaj Auto Ltd. (BAL) was a virtual monopolist in the Indian market for two-wheelers with its scooters. It maintained its profit at a healthy level primarily by regulating its output. As a result, the waiting period for a Bajaj scooter was several years.

In the 1980s, Hero cycles, the largest producer of bicycles in India, joined hands with Honda Motors of Japan to float a company called Hero Honda to produce two-wheelers in India. Hero has been in the bicycle business for many years and knew the Indian consumer well. The idea was to to combine this knowledge with Honda's technology for making motorbikes. Hero Honda started producing in 1985-6. In that year, it sold 43,000 motorbikes for Rs 49 crore and made a post-tax profit of Rs 1.15 crore.

Traditionally, the motorbike has been seen in India as a two-wheeler used by the flashy youth and designed accordingly. Hero Honda targeted its motorbike at the middle class, office-going adult, whose requirement had so far been met almost entirely by the scooter. It did so by launching its CD 100, a motorbike with a fuel efficient 4-stroke 100cc engine, while other two-wheelers were still using an old fashioned 2-stroke engine. This enabled Hero Honda to combine fuel efficiency with comfort and power and gave it a headstart over its competitors.

BAL did not initially recognize the potential of the new product and was slow to react. Every year, 15–20 per cent of the consumers who wanted to replace their Bajaj scooters switched to Hero Honda's motorbikes. As a result, Hero Honda's share of the two-wheeler market kept rising at the expense of BAL. In 1994, BAL's share had fallen to 53 per cent and Hero Honda's share had risen to 21 per cent and the waiting period for Bajaj scooters had fallen to a few months. BAL started becoming active in the mobike market and introduced its own mobike with a 100cc 4-stroke engine.

By then, however, Hero Honda had become the undisputed leader in the mobike market. Although BAL's motorbike sales grew rapidly, its mobike had to be sold at a low price. At the same time, the sales of its traditional money-spinner, the scooter became static. In 2000-1, BAL sold 12 lakh two-wheelers, 6.5 lakh scooters, and 5.5 lakh motorbikes, while Hero Honda sold 10 lakh motorbikes. But in value terms, BAL's sales at Rs 3121 crore were lower than Hero Honda's sales of Rs 3171 crore. In 1993-4, its sales at Rs 1322 crore were four times Hero Honda's sales of Rs 363 crore. As a result, BAL's profit in 2000-1 was only Rs 98 crore, compared with Rs 541crore in 1998-9.

In recent years, BAL has taken a number of corrective steps. It has invested in new products and processes, introduced new models, stepped up consumer advertising, set itself up as an export platform for Kawasaki motorbikes, and reduced manpower, by laying off temporary workers and offering a voluntary separation scheme to its permanent employees. As a result, its sales and profit in 2001-2 rose to Rs 3695 crore and Rs 262 crore, respectively. But it has lost its dominance in the two-wheeler market in India.

Source: Press reports.

---

least equal to the initial investment. For this to happen, two conditions must be fulfilled. First, the innovations must enable the proprietary assets of the firm to create more value with the same input of non-proprietary factors. Put differently, there must be an increase in the productivity of each weighted input of non-proprietary factors, or in what economists call *total factor productivity*. Second, while some of the increase in factor productivity would accrue to the factors themselves as higher factor prices, some must also accrue to the firm as an increase in its appropriable surplus. This can happen only if the rate at which the firm increases its factor productivity over time, or *the rate of technological progress* achieved by it, is at least equal to the rate of technological progress achieved by the economy as a whole. We develop these points more fully in the next three sections by examining how innovations by firms lead to technological progress in the economy and how firms that achieve a higher rate of technological progress than the economy make a profit.

13.3.2 Technological Progress and Economic Growth: Endogenous Growth Models

It will be useful to start by looking at the basic ideas behind the so-called *endogenous models of innovation and growth*. These models show how economic growth is driven by innovations that are *endogenous* to the economic system, in the sense that they are made by firms in pursuit of profit maximization. The most influential among these is a model developed by Paul Romer.[2] A simplified version of an endogenous growth model is as follows.

Production requires the use of two types of factors of production, those given to us by nature, like human beings and natural resources, and those created by us, like capital goods, knowledge and other intangible assets. To simplify our presentation, we use the term 'labour' to denote all factors given to us by nature. Since these tend to be relatively scarce, we assume that their supply is fixed. We use the term 'capital' to denote all man-made factors. We can increase the supply of capital by saving a part of the output and using the savings to finance the production of new capital. Thus, although the supply of labour is fixed, firms can keep increasing their outputs by expanding their capital stock. But other things being equal, this will lead to diminishing returns to capital. To avoid the prospect of their capital earning less and less, firms use the economy's savings to produce not only new capital goods but also new proprietary assets or technology that enable them to use labour more productively. Thus, the growth in capital stock not only increases the supply of capital, but also the effective supply of labour. Since the actual supply of labour is fixed, the effective supply of labour increases at the same rate as the productivity of labour.

We assume that the economy's time preference for consumption is stable over time. Therefore, the proportion of the output saved by the economy remains constant, regardless of any change in its per capita income. This means that the rate of growth in the economy's capital stock is determined by its labour–capital ratio: the higher the input of labour per unit of capital, the higher is the output, and therefore the quantum of output saved and converted into new capital, per unit of existing capital. At any time, the economy gravitates towards the labour–capital ratio that equates the growth in its capital stock with the growth in its effective supply of labour. If the realized labour–capital ratio is higher, it tends to fall: the capital stock grows faster than the effective labour supply, capital becomes progressively cheaper in relation to labour, and firms substitute labour by capital. Similarly, if the realized labour-capital ratio is lower, it tends to rise. Thus, the economy's savings are so allocated between the production of new capital goods and the creation of new technology that the capital stock and the effective supply of labour grow at the same rate.

[2]See Romer (1990).

It is assumed that there are constant returns to scale: a 1 per cent increase in capital and a 1 per cent increase in effective labour supply lead to a 1 per cent increase in output. This means that the capital–output ratio and the return on capital remain constant over time. Since the actual supply of labour is fixed and the growth in effective supply comes entirely from an increase in productivity, the wage rate keeps increasing at the same rate as the productivity of labour. Most endogenous growth models assume that the rate of technological progress, and therefore the rate of growth in labour productivity, remains constant over time. This leads to what is known as a *steady state growth model*: capital, labour productivity, and output grow at the same constant rate and the capital-output ratio remains constant over time.

Firms will not invest in new proprietary assets unless they can at least recover the costs of doing so. It is, therefore, assumed that the firms compete in a monopolistically competitive market. They are similar in size as well as production and demand characteristics. They are all equally efficient and innovative, and there is free entry into the market. But each firm is differentiated by either the product it produces or the process it employs. It, therefore, has enough market power to charge a price that just covers its full costs, including the interest cost of carrying its capital stock. If it tries to make a profit, however, new firms enter the market with close substitutes of its products or processes and bid prices down until the profit is wiped out.

13.3.3 Implications for the Firm

Table 13.3 shows how the Profit and Loss account of an individual firm evolves over time under these conditions. Labour is counted in terms of numbers. The rest of the accounting is done in terms of number of units of output.

TABLE 13.3. PROFIT AND LOSS ACCOUNT OF THE TYPICAL FIRM

(Labour in numbers; Rest in units of output)

	Period 1		Period 2	
Output		1000	1000 × 1.10 =	1100
Wage Bill	80 Units of Labour @ 10 per unit	800	80 Units of Labour @ 11 per unit	880
Gross Profit		200		200
Interest Charges	Capital stocks of 2500 Units of Output @ 8% per period	200	Capital stocks of 2750 Units of Output @ 8 per cent per period	220
Net Profit		0		0
Accretion to Capital Stock				
Share of Economy's Savings	250 Units of Output			
Accounting Value of Increase in Capital Stock	250 Units of Output			
Growth in Capital Stock		10%		

Suppose there are n number of similar firms in the economy. The output of (i.e. the value added by) each firm is 1000 units in period 1. This output is produced by using 80 units of labour and tangible and intangible capital valued at 2500 units of output. Thus, the productivity of each unit of labour is 12.5 units of output and the capital–output ratio is 2.5. If the firm wants to produce less than 1000 units of output, it can reduce its input of labour. Thus, the wage costs are variable with respect to output. But the capital stock is specific to the firm and represents a sunk cost. Therefore, even if the firm wants to produce less, it cannot reduce its capital stock and the interest charges payable on it. The wage rate is 10 units of output per unit of labour. The rate of interest per period is 8 units of output per 100 units of output borrowed, or 8 per cent. At any time, the economy saves 25 per cent of its output.

In period 1, the firm's variable cost and gross profit are 800 and 200 units of output respectively. The gross profit is just enough to cover the interest charges payable by the firm on its capital stock. Therefore, the firm just breaks even and does not make an economic profit. In period 1, the economy's output is $n \times 1000$ units, and of this, $n \times 250$ units are saved. Since there are n number of firms, each firm borrows 250 units of the output saved by the economy by paying an interest rate of 8 per cent per period and uses it to produce new capital valued at 250 units of output. Thus, in period 1, the accretion to the firm's capital stock is 250 units of output and represents a growth of 10 per cent. This increases the productivity, and therefore the effective supply, of labour by 10 per cent in period 2. With a 10 per cent increase in both the capital stock and the effective supply of labour, the firm's output increases by 10 per cent in period 2, to 1100 units. Since labour productivity increases by 10 per cent, the wage rate increases by 10 per cent, from 10 to 11 units of output. Therefore, the wage bill and the gross profit increase to 880 and 220 units of output respectively. Since the capital stock also increases to 2750 units of output, the interest charges payable on it is 220 units of output which is just covered by the firm's gross profits.

Thus, by improving its technology, the firm has increased its capital stock, effective supply of labour, and output by 10 per cent. It has also held its capital–output ratio constant at 2.5. Since there are n number of such firms in the economy, the economy's capital stock, effective labour supply, and output are n times those of the individual firm. The economy's capital stock, effective labour supply, and output have also increased by 10 per cent and its capital–output ratio is also held constant at 2.5. Both the economy and the individual firm are in steady state growth equilibrium. But the firm's profit continues to be zero: it has had to run hard to stay still.

13.3.4 Profit as the Outcome of Inter-firm Differences in Innovativeness

Let us now see what happens to the Profit and Loss account of an individual firm if all firms are not equally innovative. For this, we make the following assumptions. As before, the economy is in steady state growth equilibrium and has a constant capital–output ratio of 2.5. There are two firms in the economy, firm A and firm B. Both start from an identical position in period 1. But firm A is more innovative than firm B. Since all accounting is in terms of number of units of output, the *accounting value* of the new capital produced by either firm with 1 unit of output saved by the economy is also 1 unit of output. Since the economy's capital-output ratio is 2.5, the average productivity of new capital with an accounting value of 1 unit of output is 0.4 units of output. However, the new capital produced by firm A, with an accounting value of 1 unit of output, produces 10 per cent more than the average, or 0.44 units of output. On the other hand, the new capital produced by firm B, with an accounting value of one unit of output, produces 10 per cent less than the average, or 0.36 units of output. Put differently, the *productive value* of new capital with an accounting value of 1 unit of output is 1 unit of output for the economy as a whole. But it is 1.1 units of output for firm A and 0.9 units of output for firm B.

Table 13.4 shows the impact of this on the Profit and Loss accounts of the two firms in period 2. In period 1, the economy's total output is 2000 units. Of this, 25 per cent or 500 units are saved. Each firm borrows half of these savings or 250 units of output and uses it to produce new capital. The accounting value of the new capital produced by both firms is 250 units of output. But the productive value of the new capital produced by firm A is 275 units of output, which represents an 11 per cent increase in the productive value of its capital stock. Consequently, the productivity of the labour employed by the firm increases by 11 per cent in period 2. With an 11 per cent increase in its effective supply of labour and the productive value of its capital stock, its output in period 2 rises by 11 per cent, to 1110 units. The increase in the productive value of firm B's capital stock, on the other hand, is only 225 units of output or 9 per cent. As a result, firm B's effective labour supply rises by only 9 per cent in period 2 and leads to a 9 per cent increase in its output, to 1090 units. For the economy as a whole, the output in period 2 is 2200 units, representing a growth of 10 per cent. This means that the average labour productivity and the wage rate in the economy rises by 10 per cent, from 10 to 11 units of output, which is applicable to both firms. Therefore, in period 2, the gross profits made by firms A and B are 230 and 210 units of output respectively. The accounting values of the capital stocks of both firms however have increased by 250 units of output, to 2750 units of output. The interest charges payable by both firms is, therefore, 220 units of output. Consequently, firm A makes a net profit of 10 units of output, while firm B makes a net loss of 10 units of output. The economy as a whole breaks even.

This result is hardly surprising. Since the non-proprietary factors of production, namely labour and capital (i.e. the output saved by the economy) are fully employed and competitively priced, their prices equal their *average marginal product* in the economy as a whole and is the same for both A and B. On the other hand, since B is less innovative than A, it achieves a lower, and A a higher, rate of growth in the productive value of its capital stock than the economy as a whole. Consequently, with the revenue growth that they can generate with the same input of non-proprietary factors, B under-recovers, and A over-recovers, its increase in sunk costs. It is important to note, however, that for A to make a profit, B must stay on and make a loss. If B exits the market the moment it starts making a loss, prices of non-proprietary factors will get pushed up to A's productivity levels and A will become a marginal firm. To explain A's profit, therefore, we must also explain why B stays on in the market even after it starts making a loss.

Clearly, the loss made by B is the sunk cost of its capital stock, to the extent it cannot be recovered from its gross profit. By staying on, the firm makes a gross profit of 210 units of output and a net loss of 10 units of output. If the firm withdraws, its

TABLE 13.4. PROFIT AND LOSS ACCOUNT OF FIRMS A AND B

	Firm A		Firm B		Economy (Firms A & B)	
	Period 1	Period 2	Period 1	Period 2	Period 1	Period 2
Output	1000	1000×1.11 = 1110	1000	1000 × 1.09 = 1090	2000	2000 × 1.10 = 2200
Wage Bill	80 units of labour @ 10 per unit 800	80 units of labour @11 per unit 880	80 units of labour @10 per unit 800	80 units of labour @11 per unit 880	160 units of labour @ 10 per unit 1600	160 units of labour @11 per unit 1760
Gross Profit	200	230	200	210	400	440
Interest Charges	2500 units of output @ 8% per period 200	2750 units of output @ 8% per period 220	2500 units of output @8% per period 200	2750 units of output @8% per period 220	5000 units of output @ 8% per period 400	5500 units of out put @ 8% per period 440
Net Profit	0	10	0	−10	0	0
Accretion to Capital Stock						
Share in Economy's Savings	500/2 = 250	250	500/2 = 250	250	2000 × 25% = 500	500
Accounting Value of Increase in Capital Stock	250 × 1 = 250	250	250 × 1 = 250	250	500 × 1 = 500	500
Productive Value of Increase in Capital Stock	250 × 1.1 = 275	275	250 × 0.9 = 225	225	500 × 1 = 500	500
Growth in Productive Value of Capital Stock	11%		9%		10%	

gross profit becomes zero and its net loss rises to 220 units of output. It is, therefore, more sensible for the firm to remain in business and minimize its losses.

When will *B* exit eventually? Within the framework of a two firm economy in which each is committed to employing one half of the economy's labour and savings, *B* will keep expanding its capital stock, regardless of its net loss. Since the average labour productivity in the economy increases by 10 per cent in each period, *B*'s wage bill will keep rising by 10 per cent per period. On the other hand, since it is less innovative than the economy as a whole, its output will increase by only 9 per cent. Consequently, after some time its gross profit will start falling and become zero eventually. When that happens, it will no longer be worthwhile for *B* to stay on in the market.

In a more realistic scenario, *B* will hang around for a while and try to become at least as innovative as the economy as a whole. If it succeeds, it will bounce back. If it fails, it will stop expanding its capital stock and freeze its cash losses when it realizes that by expanding, it adds more to costs than revenue. But even after that, the firm's assets will keep earning less than the cost of carrying them. Its accumulated losses will, therefore, keep rising and the market value of its assets will keep falling. Meanwhile, the profits made by *A* will attract new entrants into the market. At some point of time, *B* may be able to recover some of its sunk costs by selling its assets to another firm who can use them more efficiently.

13.3.5 The Nelson and Winter Model

The basic conclusions may now be summarized as follows. Firms innovate with a view to increasing the productivity of non-proprietary factors and gaining a competitive advantage. As a result of their innovations, the economy experiences steady growth in productivity and output. If a firm increases its productivity at the same rate as the economy, it breaks even. If it increases its productivity faster than the economy, it makes a profit. But if it increases its productivity at a lower rate than the economy, it makes a loss and dies eventually.

These ideas have been put together in an *evolutionary model of growth* by Richard Nelson and Sidney Winter[3] who regard the firm as a behavioural, rather than a profit-maximizing, entity. They argue that the choice set facing a firm is not fully known, and different firms have different beliefs about it. Firms do not, therefore, 'maximize' their profits in any precise sense. They do, however, try to achieve best results by following their *routines*, or decision rules that are peculiar to each firm.

Each firm has two types of routines. It conducts its day-to-day business by following its *operating routines*. But if the results are not considered satisfactory, it looks for ways in which it should change by setting in motion its *search routines*. These would typically consist of *introspection* or a critical analysis of the firm, *imitation* or identification of competitive practices that may be worth emulating, and *innovation* or R&D to uncover new ways of doing things, and lead to proposals for modifications in the existing routines of the firm. These proposals may or may not be accepted. But to the extent they are, they result in a change in the firm's existing routines.

[3]See Nelson and Winter (1982).

Nelson and Winter see the firm as a 'truce' among its various stakeholders, aimed at reconciling their conflicting interests. The firm cannot upset the apple-cart by making drastic changes in its existing routines. A firm's routines in time t_1 are, therefore, a function of three things: its *routines in time* t_0, in that it changes its routines incrementally over time; an *idiosyncratic parameter*, in that each firm has its own way of searching for and adopting new routines; and a *common parameter*, in that there is a commonality in the way all firms respond to general changes in the business environment. Technological progress achieved by the firm is the extent to which it can use non-proprietary factors more productively in time t_1 than in time t_0, by changing its routines. Since each firm has its own distinctive routines in time t_0 and has an idiosyncratic way of searching for new routines, different firms achieve different rates of technological progress. The rate of technological progress in the economy is the weighted average of the rates of progress achieved by all firms in the economy. Firms that just keep pace with the average rate are *marginal firms* who break even and survive. Firms that achieve a higher rate make a profit and grow. Firms that fall below become increasingly unprofitable, decline and die in the end. Thus, the Schumpeterian process of creative destruction is replaced by a more gradual process of *natural selection* whereby the fit survive, the unfit get eliminated, and the productive structure of the economy keeps getting upgraded all the time. While some firms die, new firms enter. At any time we have both profitable and loss-making firms in the economy, but the mix of individual firms keeps changing all the time.

13.4 REQUIREMENT 2: GROWTH

13.4.1 The Link between Innovation and Growth

The second requirement for long term success of a firm follows from the first. By innovating successfully, a firm acquires new proprietary assets that increase the productive potential of the non-proprietary factors it employs. Unless the firm is in the business of selling proprietary assets, it has to grow to exploit this potential. Otherwise, it underrecovers the cost of acquiring these assets.

To understand why this is so, consider what would happen to firm A's profit, if it produced new capital in period 1, but did not use it to expand output. This is shown in Table 13.5. The first column shows the firm's position in period 1, which is exactly the same as in Table 13.4. The second column shows the firm's profit and loss account in period 2, if it uses the new capital produced by it in period 1 to expand its output in period 2. This too is exactly the same as in Table 13.4. The third column shows the firm's profit and loss account in period 2, if it produces new capital in period 1 but does not use it to expand its output in period 2. Since there is no expansion, A's output is the same as in period 1. Since labour productivity increases by 11 per cent, the units of labour required to produce the same output is 11 per cent lower, but the wage rate is 10 per cent higher. Therefore, the gross profit rises to 217 units of output. But the accounting value of the firm's capital stock has now risen to 2750 units of output. Since this represents a sunk cost, the firm has to pay interest charges on its expanded stock of capital, whether it expands its output or not. Therefore, by not expanding it incurs a net loss of 3 units of output.

TABLE 13.5. PROFIT AND LOSS PROJECTIONS FOR FIRM A IN PERIOD 2, WITH AND WITHOUT GROWTH IN OUTPUT

(Labour in numbers, rest in units of output)

	Period 1		Period 2			
			With growth in output		Without growth in output	
Output		1000	$1000 \times 1.11 =$	1110		1000
Wage Bill	80 units of labour @ 10 per unit	800	80 units of labour @ 11 per unit	880	71.2 units of labour @ 11 per unit	783
Gross Profit		200		230		217
Interest Charges	Capital stock of 2500 units of output @ 8% period	200	2750 units of output @ 8% period	220	2750 unit of output @ 8% period	220
Net Proft		0		10		− 3
Accretion of Capital Stock						
Increase in Accounting Value	250 units of output					
Increase in Productive	$250 \times 11. =$ units of output	275				
Growth in Productive Value		1.1%				

We may now restate the link between innovation and growth in more general terms. A firm innovates, because in a world of changing technology it cannot survive otherwise. But innovation involves the acquisition of new proprietary assets by incurring sunk costs. Since these new assets enable the firm to produce more output with the same input of non-proprietary factors, they increase the production potential of the firm. Unless the firm actually utilizes the increased production potential by expanding its output, it under-recovers its sunk costs and may end up by making a loss. Thus, to remain profitable in the long run, not only must a firm innovate, but it must also grow and utilize its ever-expanding production potential.

13.4.2 The Penrose Model of Corporate Growth

The idea that firms have to grow to exploit their underutilized production potential was first propounded by Edith Penrose[4] in a seminal model of corporate growth.

[4] See Penrose (1995), especially Chapters 3 to 5.

Penrose sees the firm as a *bundle of physical and human resources, bound together by an administrative framework*. The administrative framework of the firm consists of its managers who direct and coordinate the activities of the resources at its disposal, optimize their use, and maximize the firm's profits. The boundaries of the firm are not defined by its products, markets, or resources, because it is free to produce any product, operate in any market, or hire any resources. The firm is bounded by the capacity of its managers to direct and coordinate. If it becomes so large that common administrative control becomes infeasible, then it ceases to be one firm.

At any time, the size of a firm is, therefore, limited by the size and quality of its managerial resources. However, the limit so imposed is an ever-expanding one, because with learning, training, and managerial innovations, the capacity of existing managers to manage keeps increasing. The firm has to keep increasing its output to utilize its ever-expanding managerial capacity. Typically, this calls for the hiring of additional physical and human resources. But many of these resources are indivisible (like a human being or a piece of capital equipment) and cannot be increased by the exact amount, or in the exact proportions, required by the growth in its managerial capacity. The firm is, therefore, left with underutilized resources. This provides an inducement for the firm to expand its output faster than the capacity of its existing managers to manage. The firm, therefore, has to expand its managerial resources by recruiting and inducting new managers. The rate at which new managers can be inducted is, however, constrained by the *inherited managerial resources* of the firm. This is because, to become productive, new managers have to acquire firm-specific knowledge by interacting with and learning from the existing managers of the firm. The latter have only a limited amount of time at their disposal and have to allocate it between the running of the firm's business and the training of new managers. Thus, there is an opportunity cost attached to the recruitment and induction of new managers. The firm recruits new managers only if the resulting benefits outweigh the resulting costs. In the ultimate analysis, the rate at which a firm can grow is, therefore, limited by the rate at which it can expand its managerial resources.

In the foreword of the 1995 edition of her book, Penrose restates her basic proposition in more general terms. She says that the growth of a firm is an evolutionary

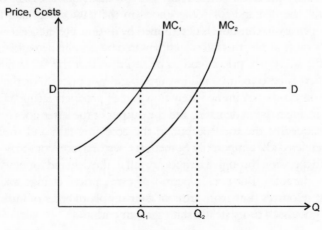

Fig. 13.1

process, based on the cumulative growth in its collective knowledge, and implies that this collective knowledge is embodied in the managers of the firm. We can understand how this process works by looking at Fig. 13.1.

The firm is a small player and can sell in any market it likes at the going price. It, therefore, faces a horizontal demand curve, DD. At any time, its collective knowledge, being embodied in its existing managers, is fixed. Therefore, as the firm expands its output by adding other resources, diminishing returns set in and the marginal cost rises. The marginal cost curve in period 1 is MC_1 and the firm reaches its equilibrium output Q_1, where $DD = MC_1$. In period 2, the firm's managerial resources and the collective knowledge embodied in them increase. Consequently, the marginal cost curve falls to MC_2 and the equilibrium output increases to Q_2. The rate at which Q increases is the rate at which the marginal cost curve shifts to the right.

13.5 REQUIREMENT 3: A CHANGING PRODUCT PORTFOLIO

13.5.1 Does Demand Constrain Growth?: The Supply-side View

In the Penrose model, the lack of demand does not limit the growth of a firm, because the firm is a small player and can sell any amount in any market at the going price. Clearly, this is not always a very realistic assumption. The endogenous growth models rule out the problem of demand by assuming that supply creates its own demand. Only one kind of product is produced. The entire output is distributed as income to wage and interest earners. A fixed proportion of the income is used to buy an equivalent proportion of the output for consumption. The remainder is saved by income earners and used by firms to produce new capital. Thus, whatever output is produced is either consumed or used to produce new capital.

However, as any businessman will tell us, a very common reason why firms cannot grow is lack of demand, rather than their capacity to supply. Why does that happen? Protagonists of endogenous growth models will provide the following explanation. What the economy produces is not really one product, but a basket of goods. For various reasons, the demand for some goods in the basket may fall. But since the economy's propensity to consume is determined by its time preference for consumption that is typically quite stable, this fall is compensated by a rise in demand for some other products. In the short run, prices tend to be *sticky*, so that the fall in demand for the affected products is reflected in a fall in output and not prices. For the same reason, productive resources do not immediately flow out of products facing a fall in demand into products facing a rise in demand, and the output of the latter does not increase for a while. Consequently, the total output in the economy falls and some productive resources are rendered idle temporarily. Sometimes, sectoral recessions may get magnified into a general depression through a temporary fall in the demand for new capital goods and consumer durables. But over a period of time, prices change and find market clearing levels, resources flow from areas of over-supply to areas of under-supply, and the economy goes back to its steady state growth path.

13.5.2 Does Demand Constrain Growth?: The Pasinetti Model

In an interesting model, Luigi Pasinetti[5] shows how these 'temporary' phases of demand constraining growth can result from the process of technological progress itself and last for very long periods of time. This model is worth exploring, because it provides an economic rationale for the commonly observed phenomenon of *product life cycles* and throws up an important action point for firms.

Technological progress increases per capita income by increasing productivity. All empirical evidence shows that as per capita income rises, the consumption of all goods does not rise proportionately. This is because the consumer has a *hierarchy of needs* that determines the order in which she introduces new goods into her consumption basket, as her income rises. Suppose, for example, that there are only three goods in the economy: food, bicycles, and TV. She will first buy food. When her income rises sufficiently, she will also buy a bicycle. When her income increases further, she may be able to afford a TV also. The order in which these three products are introduced into her consumption basket is determined by her hierarchy of needs.

Fig. 13.2 shows the picture that we get by plotting the consumption of various goods against the income of the average consumer in the economy. Essential goods (good 1 in the figure) are consumed first. Their consumption increases as income increases, but at a declining rate because as consumption increases, the marginal utility of consumption falls. However, as income increases and an increasing proportion of it becomes available for buying less essential goods (good 2 and beyond), these are introduced into the consumption basket. The demand curve for these goods is S-shaped. Initially the consumer buys only small quantities of these products on a trial basis. But once she has used and liked them, her consumption of these products rises faster than her income, because the *discretionary income* available after meeting her requirement of essential goods rises faster than her income. Eventually, the marginal utility that the consumer gets by using each product starts to diminish and its

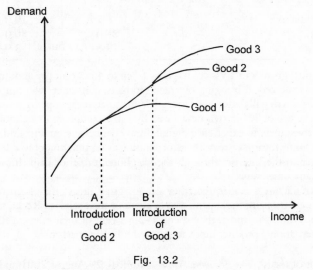

Fig. 13.2

---

[5]See Pasinetti (1981), especially Chapter 4.

consumption tapers off. Thus, as income rises, the consumption of each good is low initially, then rises faster than income, and tapers off eventually. And as the demand for existing goods tapers off, new goods that are considered less essential by the consumer are introduced into her consumption basket.

BOX 13.3. PRODUCT LIFE CYCLE IN THE INDIAN TV INDUSTRY

Consumer durables are subject to short product life cycles, because replacement demand forms a large part of the demand for these products. As a consumer's income rises, she wants to replace her existing product by something better. If the producer cannot give her a better product, she does not buy and the market does not grow. To avoid this, the producer has to keep replacing old products by new products. The television (TV) industry in India is a living example of this phenomenon.

When the TV first came to India 25 years ago, there were only black and white TVs. Over a period of time, black and white TVs were replaced by colour TVs. Now black and white TVs account for less than a third of the TV market. In recent years, the basic colour TV has been losing out to TVs that deliver a booming sound, like Videocon's Bazooka or Onida's KY Thunder or Samsung's Metallica. However, consumers are now becoming more interested in picture quality for which they are willing to pay a premium. As a result, TVs that emphasize the visual effect like sharpness of image, zoom effect, viewing space, stress free viewing, etc. are growing faster than TVs that emphasize the sound effect. At the same time, as the following table shows, larger TVs are replacing smaller TVs and flat screen TVs which now account for only 2 per cent of the market are beginning to take off.

	Segment-wise growth rates (per cent per annum)	
	2001	2002 (expected)
!4 inch	-	1.9
20 inch	2.8	2.5
21 inch	5.1	2.4
25 inch and above	6.7	19.0
Flat screen	38.0	50.0
Total	3.8	3.9

The annual growth in TV sales has now fallen to 4 per cent per annum. Unless the TV producers succeed in bringing out new products, consumers will not replace their old TVs and growth will flatten even more. TV manufacturers hope to boost demand by promoting the use of TV in two new areas. By using compression technology, the TV will enable consumers to experience digital multi-channel surround sound and become the hub of a home theatre system. By incorporating a computer processor, it will connect the consumer to the Internet through the telephone, cable, or dish. It will no doubt evolve in many other ways.

TV manufacturers realize that they cannot grow unless they keep offering new products. Internationally, they spend 4–6 per cent of their sales on R&D, most of it for product innovations. In India, they spend 1–2 per cent of their sales on R&D, mostly to adapt international product innovations to the Indian market.

Sources: 'Out of focus', *The Economic Times,* Mumbai, 29 August 2001 and 'Honing in on the future', *The Times of India,* Mumbai, 17 May 2002.

The implication of this for the growth of the economy is as follows. Technological progress on the supply side increases factor productivity and the per capita income of factor owners. However, as per capita income increases, existing products go through a cycle of introduction, growth, maturity, and decline. Growth in consumption can keep pace with growth in income only if new products are introduced into the consumption basket continuously. In a rich economy, this involves inventing new products, because such an economy is likely to have used all products that have been invented already. If new products are not invented quickly enough and growth in consumption falls consistently short of the growth in factor productivity, demand and supply can be kept in balance only through a growing unemployment of productive resources. If, for example, per capita demand and productivity increase at 2 per cent and 3 per cent per annum respectively, per capita output will grow at 2 per cent per annum and employment will fall at 1 per cent per annum.

Conceptually, it should be possible to develop a steady state growth model in which profit-maximizing firms so allocate their R&D resources that supply-augmenting innovations are matched by demand-augmenting innovations. But such a model can work only if two conditions are fulfilled. Since each firm has its own area of specialization, the R&D efforts of all firms must be well coordinated to ensure that supply and demand augmenting innovations are well matched. Second, there must be a high degree of certainty attached to the innovation process, so that firms can predict the outcome of their R&D efforts and allocate these efforts between supply and demand augmenting projects with a fair degree of precision. Pasinetti solves this problem by designing a model in which vertically integrated sectors operate in a planned economy, charge a *natural price* that yields a *natural rate of profit*, and achieve balanced growth in supply and demand by using this profit to finance new investments. But, as he points out, in a free market economy in which we have to depend on the price mechanism to solve the problems of coordination and uncertainty, full employment of productive resources is by no means automatic. We could have prolonged periods when growth is restricted because no worthwhile new products come up and consumption opportunities are limited.

13.5.3 Implication for the Firm: BCG's Portfolio Planning Model

From the firm's perspective, the import of the Pasinetti model is that to remain profitable, it must not only find new methods to produce its existing products, but also new products to produce. To keep ahead of competition, the firm has to find new methods of producing its existing products. To find new methods of producing its existing products, it has to add to its stock of proprietary assets. To recover the sunk cost of its expanding stock of proprietary assets, it has to make its output grow. And to make its output grow, it has to find new products to produce.

However, to maintain the required rate of growth, it is not enough for the firm to introduce new products that exhibit a high rate of growth. It must also phase out some old products with a low rate of growth. In other words, the firm has to keep changing, rather than expanding, its portfolio of products. Why and how the firm should do this has been spelt out in a *portfolio planning model* by the Boston Consulting Group (BCG), an American firm of management consultants.[6] Take the case of a firm that has a mix of high and low growth products in its portfolio. BCG holds that all products that enjoy a large share of the markets they operate in tend to be profitable. This is because being a large producer of such products, the firm has a *learning*, and therefore a cost, advantage over its competitors. If a product that has a high market share operates in a saturated market, its rate of growth tends to fall short of the rate of profit it generates. If the entire profit generated by such a product is ploughed back into the same product, then its profitability will keep falling. On the other hand, if a product with a high market share operates in a growing market, its rate of growth tends to exceed the rate of profit it generates. If the entire profit generated by such a product is re-invested in the same product, then its profitability will keep rising.[7] BCG calls the first category of products *cash cows* and the second category *stars*. Clearly, cash cows generate more cash than they can use for their own growth, while stars generate less cash than they need. A sensible firm will, therefore, maximize its growth and profits by using the cash surplus generated by its cash cows to fund the cash deficit faced by its stars. This recycling has to be done continuously, because over time today's stars become cash cows and new stars emerge.

What should a firm do if it has only cash cows and no stars in its portfolio? BCG suggests that such a firm should use its cash surplus to buy up another firm that has a high proportion of stars in its portfolio and is, therefore, short of cash. This can be done even if the acquiring firm does not have any special expertise in the businesses of the firm it acquires. By virtue of the large market shares that it enjoys, the acquired firm has the required expertise and this can be passed on to the acquiring firm. Unfortunately, many firms burnt their fingers by going overboard and acquiring a variety of disparate businesses. Consequently, although much of the BCG model is based on ideas that are fundamentally sound, it has lost some of its popularity in recent years.

13.5.4 Limits to Diversification, Growth, and Profits: The Marris Model

We know that proprietary assets are largely *non-rivalrous*: once created, they can be combined with increasing quantities of non-proprietary factors without any diminishing returns setting in. It should, therefore, be possible for a firm to increase its return on capital continuously by adding new products and expanding its output faster than its stock of proprietary assets. This however does not happen very often. Successful firms do manage to increase their earnings per share over time. But they do so by ploughing back profits, expanding their capital base per share, and generating a steady rate of return on an expanding capital base.

Why do firms not increase the utilization of their proprietary assets and the return on capital continuously, by adding new products to their portfolio? We have answered this question in Chapter 10 already, while discussing the case for related diversification. The proprietary assets that yield a quasi-rent for the firm tend to be business-specific.

---

[6]For a standard presentation of the BCG model, see Johnson and Scholes (1999), pp. 170–3.

[7] This point has been explained more fully in section Chapter 9, 9.3.6.

They can yield a quasi-rent in a new business only if they are suited for the new business. The firm can, therefore, grow only to the extent it can match its proprietary assets with new business opportunities or, as Business Policy literature puts it, its internal *strengths and weaknesses* with external *opportunities and threats*. Robin Marris[8] develops a steady state model of corporate growth to show formally how this limits the growth of the firm.

Marris suggests that, for reasons very similar to those outlined by us earlier, a firm can increase the demand for its output by adding new products to its portfolio. The rate of growth in demand facing a firm at any time is, therefore, a function of the number of new products it introduces at that time, or what Marris calls its *rate of diversification*. However, the rate at which the firm diversifies also affects its return on capital. To understand how this works, consider Fig. 13.3.

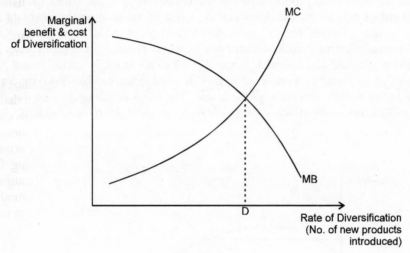

Fig. 13.3

Since the proprietary assets of a firm are generally non-rivalrous, they can be used in a new business without having to be duplicated. If, other things being equal, these assets earn a positive rent in the new business, the firm's average return on capital increases. The *marginal benefit* derived by the firm by adding an extra business to its portfolio is the increase in its average return on capital that results therefrom. However, the proprietary assets are designed specifically for the existing businesses of the firm. As the firm expands its portfolio by moving further and further afield from its existing businesses, the rent earned by its proprietary assets in each additional business falls. This is shown by a downward-sloping marginal benefit curve, *MB*. On the other hand, as the firm expands its business portfolio and becomes bigger, it starts losing some of its existing profits because of information and control losses, agency problems, delays in decision making, etc. (see the chapter on architecture). Thus, the marginal cost of adding an extra business is the loss of profit and the fall in its average rate of return that results therefrom. This loss increases as the firm becomes bigger by adding more and

[8]See Marris (1966), pp. 249–65.

more products to its portfolio. This is shown by a rising marginal cost curve, MC. The optimum rate of diversification, or the optimum number of additions to the product portfolio, at any time is reached at D, beyond which the cost of adding a new product exceeds its benefit.

Marris presents the same information slightly differently by plotting rates of growth on the horizontal axis and the corresponding rates of return on capital, R on the vertical axis (see Fig. 13.4). The gD line shows the R that the firm gets by adding new products to its portfolio and increasing the rate of growth in demand for its output. As gD increases, R increases until the optimum portfolio size is reached and falls thereafter. The gS line shows the rate at which the firm can increase its supply at various levels of R. Marris assumes that given a rate of growth, the capital–output ratio of the firm has a constant value. Therefore, gS is equal to the rate at which the firm can increase the stock of its productive assets. Algebraically, $gS = I/K$, where I is the firm's investment in new assets and K its existing stock of assets at any moment of time. Marris assumes further that all new investments are funded by retaining a fixed proportion of the firm's profit, so that $I = a.\Pi$, where Π is the firm's profit and a is the proportion retained and invested. Since $R = \Pi/K$, $gS = I/K = a.\Pi/K = a.R$. As R increases, gS increases proportionately and this relationship can be shown by drawing a straight line which runs through the origin. The point of intersection of the gS and gD lines determines the steady state growth rate, g^*, and return on capital, R^*, of the firm.

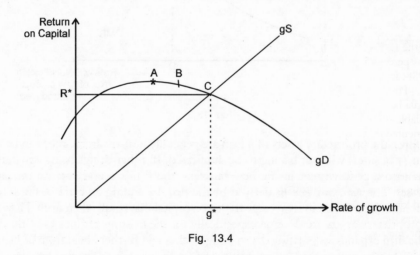

Fig. 13.4

Clearly, a firm can choose its g^* and R^* by choosing its retention ratio a, which determines the slope of the gS line. The value of a chosen by the firm depends on its objectives. A firm that wants to maximize its current profit will so choose its a that the gS line cuts the gD line at A, the point at which R is at its highest. A firm that wants to maximize the market value of its assets will a choose a higher a, so that the gS line intersects the *g*D line at a point to the right of *A*, say *B*, yielding a higher *g** but a lower *R**.[9]

Marris points out that firms that are controlled by their managers tend to be growth maximizers, because the bigger is a firm, the higher are the remuneration, power, and status enjoyed by its managers. Such firms often choose an even higher retention ratio, so that the *g*S line cuts the *g*D line to the right of *B*. However, the growth rate of a firm cannot be increased indefinitely at the expense of its market value. If the market value of a firm falls below a critical level, shareholders want to sell their shares and the firm becomes a candidate for takeover. In Fig. 13.4, *C* represents this point and determines the maximum rate of growth that can be achieved without risking takeover.

The Marris model provides a useful framework for analysing the limits to the growth of a firm, but its steady state methodology is open to question. The *MB* line in Fig. 13.3 is valid only at one point of time. Over time, businesses become more specialized and markets become less imperfect, so that the *MB* line tends to shift downwards. Firms try to prevent the *MB* line from shifting downwards by improving the rent-yielding capacity of their assets and shift the *MC* line downwards by improving their architecture. This means that the *g*D line in Fig. 13.4 keeps shifting over time, so that the point at which it meets the *g*S line and the equilibrium rate of growth that results therefrom also keep changing over time.

The Metal Box story

In the 1960s and 1970s, Metal Box India (MB), the Indian subsidiary of a British MNC, was perceived to be in the same exalted league as Hindustan Levers, ITC, and ICI. In 1988, it became a BIFR case. How did this happen?

Post independence, the production of packaged consumer goods grew rapidly in India because of rising per capita income and import substitution. MB, being the only reliable supplier of tinplate and aluminium cans, caps, closures, and tubes at that time, benefited from this growth and was a highly profitable company throughout the 1950s and 1960s.

High profits attracted a number of new manufacturers into the metal packaging business. The new firms came in with more modern technology and used metal and manpower more efficiently. Initially it did not matter, because thanks to its reputation and long association with customers, MB could get a higher price than its competitors. But as the new firms proved themselves, MB's market shares started falling. At the same time, metal especially tinplate prices rose rapidly. This, coupled with technological advances

---

[9] This is because the market value of a firm's assets at any time is the sum of the discounted value of the future stream of dividends that they are expected to generate. Algebraically, $V = \Sigma[K.R(1-a)(1+g)^t]/[1+r]^{(t+1)} = [K.R(1-a)]/[r-g]$, where V is the market value of the firm's assets and K its capital stock at time t, R the rate of return on capital, $(1-a)$ the proportion of profit paid out as dividend, g the rate at which K grows over time, and r the rate of discount. It can be shown that V is maximized when the gradient of the *g*D line is $(r-R)/(r-g)$. Since typically, $R>r>g$, this gradient is negative and fractional, so that *B* lies to the right of *A*. The reason why V rises even beyond *A* is that the fall in R is more than compensated by a rise in *g* until *B* is reached. Beyond *B*, the rise in *g* can no longer make up for the fall in R, and both V and R fall.

in other types of packaging, led to a steady substitution of metal packages by packages made from paper and plastics. These trends were accentuated by government policy. Because tinplate was largely imported, it was subjected to heavy and ever-rising duties, and its supply was limited by import restrictions. Being Indian, MB's competitors got preferential allocation of whatever tinplate was available. MB responded by increasing its selling prices frequently. This hastened the erosion in its market shares and the shift from metal to paper and plastic packages.

In the meantime, MB had applied for and been given an industrial licence for producing paper and plastic packages. This opened a window of opportunity, which the company did not exploit. In the 1970s, instead of investing heavily in its paper and plastic business to exploit a growing market, its international expertise in packaging, and longstanding relationship with customers, it invested heavily to upgrade its technology for making metal packages. Consequently, it failed to establish its paper and plastics business and remained dependent on its declining metals business.

For the first time, MB made a loss in 1975-6. It reacted by cutting costs through manpower reductions at all levels and use of inferior materials. This, coupled with selective price increases, enabled the company to stay afloat for a few more years. But it was clear by now that to grow and survive, it had to look beyond its metals business. Paper and plastics were no longer a viable option, because a number of other firms had already made the necessary investments and entrenched themselves in this business. Because of government policy, other options available to an MNC like MB were also not very wide. MB came to the conclusion that its strength lay in precision engineering and decided to diversify into ball and roller bearings. It started producing bearings in 1979. As it transpired, MB did not have the required technical and marketing strengths, kept making heavy losses in its bearings business and sold it to the Tata group in 1984. But thanks to the huge losses suffered in bearings already and the poor health of its metals business, MB was terminally sick by now. In 1983, it started making losses and its losses kept mounting every year. In 1986, Metal Box, UK sold off its stake in the company to an Indian group and pulled out of India.

The Metal Box story illustrates the following points made by us in this chapter so far.

- The link between success and technological inertia. Throughout the 1950s and 1960s, MB made no attempt to deter or fight new entrants by upgrading its technology, because it was highly profitable and underestimated the new entrants.

- The link between technological progress and profit. Once the new entrants established themselves, the growth in MB's factor productivity could not keep pace with the industry average. The only way it could maintain its profits was by increasing its selling prices faster than the industry as a whole. This became untenable after some time.

- The link between profit and growth. When MB did finally upgrade its technology in metals in the 1970s, it could not support its new investments by business growth, because the metals business in India had become stagnant by then. Consequently, its return on capital kept falling further.

- The link between growth and diversification. MB did not grow, because it failed to diversify its business portfolio. In the 1960s, its metals business was a 'cash cow' and its paper and plastics business was a potential 'star'. At that time it should have invested the cash surplus generated by the former in the latter, which it did not do.

- The limits to diversification. When MB did try to diversify in the 1980s, it chose bearings, an unrelated line in which the company had no expertise. Consequently, the project failed.

13.6 REQUIREMENT 4: ENTREPRENEURSHIP

13.6.1 Innovation, Uncertainty, and Risk

Firms make some innovations incrementally. Some are the result of R&D undertaken specifically for this purpose: *research* to uncover new ideas about markets, products, processes, and methods of organization, and *development* of these ideas into actionable projects. Both, especially the latter, require the firm to make an investment now with a view to generating a profit later. But, as we have noted while discussing the Nelson and Winter model, innovation involves exploring a choice set which is not fully known. This means that there is an element of *uncertainty* associated with the process of innovation, in the sense that the profit outcome cannot be predicted with 100 per cent accuracy. This leads to a *risk*, or a probability, that the actual profit will deviate from the expected profit. The higher the probability of this happening, the greater is the risk involved.

Why does this risk arise? First, the outcome of individual projects is uncertain. An important empirical study done in the USA shows that about a half of all R&D projects initiated become technically successful, about two-third of the technical successes are commercialized, and about three-fourth of the projects commercialized succeed financially. This means that only one out of four projects initiated succeed. At the time of initiation, there is no way of knowing which one of these four projects will succeed in the end.

Second, even when a project is successful, it is difficult to predict how much of the rent generated by it can be appropriated by the firm, and for how long. This is because, as we have noted already, the output of an R&D project is knowledge which is non-rivalrous: once created, its use by one firm does not physically preclude its use by other firms. To predict appropriability, we have to predict how quickly and how well our competitors will discover our trade secrets or invent 'around' patents, and this is never easy.

Finally, firms often engage in what economists call a *patent race*, or a battle to innovate first. This happens when the winner 'takes all' by getting a patent, or shutting off competition through pre-emptive investments, or moving down the learning curve quickly. In that case, we cannot predict the return from a project unless we can predict whether it can be completed successfully ahead of competitors. This is almost impossible if the patent race is *probabilistic*, i.e. we do not know exactly how long it will take to complete the project. We can use some very reasonable assumptions to show that if there are N number of equally innovative firms in the race, and if they all spend the same amount of money on R&D, then all of them have the same probability of winning, which is $1/N$. If one of them outspends the others, its chances improve. But no amount of spending can guarantee that the firm spending more will actually win.

13.6.2 Risk, Entrepreneurship, and Profit

Since innovation involves risk, a firm cannot innovate successfully unless it has a penchant and facility for taking risks, or what economists call *entrepreneurship*.[10]

The entrepreneur is not the inventor. He notices the profit potential of emerging markets and technologies earlier than others, spots and backs potential winners through the cycle of research, development, and commercialization, and takes the risks involved in making the required investments. He is really an all-purpose arbitrageur. He brings together the inventor and the potential buyer of his inventions by absorbing the risks that separate them and makes a profit by buying cheap and selling dear. The greater the risks, the larger is the gap between buying and selling prices, and the higher is his profit. Thus, the profit he makes is the reward that he gets for taking risks and proving right in an uncertain world.

The implication of this is that the rent earned by a firm by innovating has really two components: the rent that would accrue to a new technology even under conditions of perfect certainty and a middleman's profit that accrues to the entrepreneur for taking the risks involved in introducing it. Schumpeter and his followers believe that the former component tends to be very small, and the entire reward for innovation accrues to the entrepreneur. This, however, is an over-simplification. Many entrepreneurial firms subcontract R&D activities in complex areas like information technology or biotechnology to other firms who have the required expertise, or commercialize new technologies developed by other firms. The price that they pay to the firm that develops a new technology is the rent that accrues to the new technology under conditions of perfect certainty.

If the profits of an entrepreneur are in the nature of a middleman's profit, why do they not dissipate quickly as he succeeds and other middlemen rush in? If the entrepreneur acquires a proprietary right over the new technology, either because he has developed it himself or because he has bought it at a price, his profits are protected by the isolating mechanisms discussed in Chapter 8. Even if he does not own the technology, but has had to make a large investment to commercialize it, he may be able to sustain his profit for a long time by exploiting his first mover advantages. If he is neither the owner nor a large investor, his profit from a particular technology may indeed get eroded fairly soon. However, as several Austrian economists have pointed out, in a changing and uncertain world the market is a process in time, which throws up new opportunities all the time. It drives the economy towards equilibrium through a process of trial and error, in which the plans of all economic agents are reconciled and nobody has an incentive to change his plan. But well before this situation is reached, new developments take place. These may be technological advances, or changes in the socio-economic profile of consumers, or external developments. Economic agents respond to these developments by changing their own plans. Since one agent is not aware of the revised plans of other agents, a new disequilibrium arises and new arbitrage opportunities emerge. An entrepreneurial firm can, therefore, sustain its profits indefinitely by spotting and exploiting one new opportunity after another.

[10]A number of Austrian economists have made important contributions on the link between entrepreneurship and profit. Kirzner (1992) is an influential recent contributor. Lewin (1999) provides a useful survey of how the Austrian thinking has evolved over the years.

DHIRUBHAI AMBANI: THE QUINTESSENTIAL ENTREPRENEUR

Speaking to shareholders at the Annual General Meeting of Reliance Industries Limited (RIL) on 13 June 2000, the–then chairman, the late Dhirubhai Ambani, spelt out his vision for the Reliance group for the next 5–10 years. He wanted the group to become the largest independent power producer and infocom player in India, a significant player in the oil and gas sector, and the leader in petrochemicals.

The group is well on its way to achieving his ambitions. By making massive investments in greenfield projects and acquisitions in the last 20 years, RIL now accounts for two-thirds of India's output of petrochemicals and is ranked between fourth and tenth in the world in all the major products it produces. We have talked about it at some length already.

The group went into oil and gas exploration and has recently struck a natural gas reserve of 7 trillion cubic feet, equivalent to 1.2 million barrels of oil, in the Krishna–Godavari basin of the Bay of Bengal. It plans to produce 40 million cubic metres of gas per day, increasing India's gas availability by a whopping 60 per cent. This will require a total investment of Rs 7000 crore by way of drilling and exploration, laying sub-sea pipelines to bring the crude gas to onshore terminals, creating gas purification facilities at the terminals, and laying pipelines to carry the purified gas to consuming centres.

Reliance Petroleum Limited (RPL) has invested Rs 14,250 crore to set up a 27 million tonne refinery in Jamnagar. In 2000-1, the very first year of its commercial operations, RPL's sales were Rs 30,963 crore, only a little less than the sales of established oil companies like Bharat Petroleum and Hindustan Petroleum. Its net profit at Rs 1464 crores was second only to that of the Indian Oil Corporation. Exports accounted for over 20 per cent of its sales. Its net profit to sales ratio at 5 per cent is already much higher than that of all other oil companies. It plans to add more value by establishing a marketing network, consisting of company-owned and franchised retail outlets and tie-ups with other oil companies.

The group is now concentrating on getting its infocom project off the ground. It plans to invest Rs 25,000 crore in the project. At the heart of this project is a 60,000 kilometre broadband fibre optic cable network, connecting 115 cities in India in 16 states. This network will be used to provide basic telephone services covering local, long distance, and international calls; cellular telephone services; data services like e-commerce, web hosting, virtual private networks, and co-location of large servers of other companies; bandwidth leasing to other Internet service providers; and multi-media broadcasting and trading in financial instruments through the TV, computer, and telephone. To speed up Internet access for its customers, Reliance has tied up with firms in Malaysia, Singapore, and India to lay submarine cables with a capacity of 3 tetrabits per second, connecting India to Malaysia and Singapore. To expand the market for mobile telephony, it proposes to assemble and sell 2 million cell phones at a price of Rs 2500–3000 each. To create a market for Internet through the TV, it plans to produce set-top boxes. The Reliance group expects to start selling its infocom services towards the end of 2002.

The group owes its success to its founder, Dhirubhai Ambani, who embodied the three basic attributes that make up a true entrepreneur.

- He spotted new business opportunities before others. He did so by looking at latent, and not manifest, demand and set his targets accordingly.[1] When he started making polyester, the capacity of his new plant was the same as India's total consumption of polyester at that time. When he went into oil and gas exploration, his was the only private sector firm in India to do so. When he established his petroleum refinery, its capacity was a third of India's total consumption. The fibre optic cable network his group is laying now is three-fourths the size of the network already in place.

- He mobilized latent demand by bridging the gap between potential buyers and potential suppliers of productive resources, thus creating new markets. He did by developing an unparalleled capacity to raise funds at a lower cost than the capital market, absorb and operationalize new technology, complete new projects quickly, and manage government relations.

- He took the risks involved in making very large investments to create new markets. He, however, minimized his risks by doing two things. He integrated vertically, so that in the initial stages he could support the weak links by capturing the value created by the strong links. He also made large investments up-front, so that he could pre-empt the market, deter new entry, and sustain profits.

---

[1]Hamel and Prahalad (1989) call this the 'strategic intent'.
Source: Press reports.

13.7 Requirement 5: Luck

Uncertainty has one other implication. To succeed consistently over time, it is not enough for a firm to be entrepreneurial. It must also be lucky. More often than not, its forays into new markets should work, its new product introductions and advertising campaigns should click, its R&D projects should yield results, and so on. This has prompted several economists to argue that *luck*, more than anything else, accounts for inter-firm differences in profitability over time.[11] They point out that even if there are no entry barriers or isolating mechanisms and all firms have an equal opportunity to make profits, over time some firms will make a higher profit than the others, simply because they are more lucky.

To understand the gist of their argument, consider a particularly simple model. Assume that a new market opportunity has emerged and a number of firms are contemplating entry. The market demand is known and is predicted to grow at a constant rate. The technology is stable and is available to all the firms. The product is homogeneous. All firms are price takers and risk neutral. Entry into the market is completely free. Since all firms are initially identical, all of them have the same *ex-ante* rate of growth, but it is distributed randomly around a mean. Firms know the probability distribution, but the *ex-post* rate of growth of a particular firm can be known only after the firm has entered the market and started producing. Thus, the rate of growth realized by a firm is initially a matter of luck. But once it happens, it persists because, barring random variations, the firm's output in any time period is a fixed proportion of its output in the previous time period. The last two assumptions follow from what is known as *Gibrat's Law of Proportionate Growth*: if we plot the logarithms of the sales of a population of firms by the frequency of their occurrence, we get a normal and symmetrical bell-shaped curve. We assume further that, for reasons explained earlier, the profit made by each firm is a function of its rate of growth.

---

[11]See, for example, Mancke (1974) and Scherer and Ross (1990), pp. 141–6.

Given these assumptions, the *i*th firm's growth and profit functions may be expressed as follows:

$$g_i = g^* + \mu_i, \tag{13.3}$$

where g_i is the *ex-post* rate of growth of the *i*-th firm, g^* is the rate of growth of the market, and μ_i is a normally distributed variable with a mean of zero, and

$$\Pi_i = f(g_i) \tag{13.4}$$

where Π_i is the *ex-post* profit of the *i*th firm. Since entry is free, firms enter the market until the industry as a whole breaks even. In other words, firms with a $g_i = g^*$ make a profit of $\Pi_i = 0$. For 'lucky' firms who have a rate of growth of $g_i > g^*$, $\Pi_i > 0$. 'Unlucky' firms with a $g_i < g^*$ have a $\Pi_i < 0$ and are forced to exit eventually. As they exit, new firms enter.

Most of us will find it difficult to accept that business success is the outcome of chance alone. However, it is probably the result of both deliberate action and luck. Stochastic models of the type described above are, therefore, useful in drawing our attention to the fact that luck is also an important requirement for continuing success.

14 Public Policy I: Regulation and Privatization

Firms interact with many types of agents and institutions—customers, suppliers, the government, other firms, etc. These interactions take place in two sets of interrelated environments. One is the market environment, where markets govern the interactions. In the market environment, firms must compete effectively against rival firms. They must achieve production efficiency, and be responsive to consumer demand. They must adapt to change and innovate new products and technologies.

The performance of a firm also depends on its non-market environment. 'The non-market environment is characterized by the social, political and legal arrangements that structure interactions outside of, and in conjunction with, markets' (Baron, 1993). Issues in the non-market environment include environmental protection, health and safety, regulation and deregulation, corporate governance, business ethics, etc. These are beginning to command increased attention and firms can no longer be oblivious to these issues. In fact, the way in which firms tackle these issues can have a significant bearing on their ability to create and appropriate value.

In the non-market environment, the interaction between the firm and the government is of special interest. The interactions between the government and the private sector can take place in many ways:

- firms owned by the government compete with private sector firms
- sometimes these firms are privatized and come to form a part of the private sector
- firms in the private sector may be subjected to various types of regulations
- the government can try to ensure greater competitiveness in the economy
- the government can do the opposite and pursue an industrial policy that promotes the creation of large, powerful firms, etc.

In this chapter, we take up the issues of regulation and privatization. The next chapter deals with competition policy and law, in general and in the Indian context, where the effects of the earlier industrial policy regime are now sought to be countered through the adoption of a new competition policy.

14.1 REGULATION

Economical and reliable supplies of a variety of basic infrastructural services such as electricity, telecommunications, transportation services, etc. play a critical role in economic development. Till recently, many of these infrastructural services were viewed as natural monopolies and public or private sector monopolies were given the task of supplying them. The conduct parameters of these monopolies—prices, investment programmes, labour policies, rules governing entry of competing suppliers, etc.—are subject to government control. Such governmental regulation may be referred to as 'economic regulation' to distinguish it from other forms of 'social' regulation, for example, environmental, health, and workplace safety regulation.

There are two contradictory views about regulation and its effects. The 'public interest' view holds that market failures of various types provide the rationale for regulation. These include the existence of natural monopolies, external effects and public goods, and imperfect information. Regulation can improve upon unfettered market performance in all these cases. For example, so far as information is concerned, the government can reduce uncertainties by increasing the supply of information (weather reports can benefit farmers) or protect uninformed agents against 'bad' outcomes (forcing drug manufacturers to provide information about possible adverse side-effects).

On the other hand, the 'interest group' theory of regulation holds that organized groups lobby the regulatory agencies and use them to further their own interests. A special case is 'capture' of the regulatory agency by industry interests. The regulators do what the industry wants and, in fact, protect firms from competition. There are several reasons why capture may occur. Experts who work on an industry tend to be sympathetic to the interests of the firms within the industry. Officials in the regulatory agency may hope to get jobs in private firms after their retirement and hence be chary of working against the industry. Regulatory agencies may also get funds from the regulated firms.

In evaluating the net effects of regulation, one must be aware of the various costs associated with regulation. There are not only the direct costs of setting up and maintaining a regulatory agency. There are also the costs of industry complying with regulation. For example, if polluting firms are required to install filtering plants, then this cost should be taken into account. Further, if regulation is inefficient, then the costs of inefficiencies have to be added to the other types of costs.

As noted earlier, we can distinguish between two types of regulation—social and economic. Social regulation relates to concerns like consumer health and safety, environment, workplace safety, etc. Economic regulation refers mainly to price and profit controls. In this section, we focus on the second type of regulation, where some of the conduct variables are sought to be regulated to affect the performance of the firm.

14.1.1 Price Controls

14.1.1.1 Monopoly with increasing marginal costs

First let us consider a private monopoly with increasing marginal costs. In Fig. 14.1, the deadweight loss under monopoly is the area ABC. The objective of regulation might be to get rid of the deadweight loss.

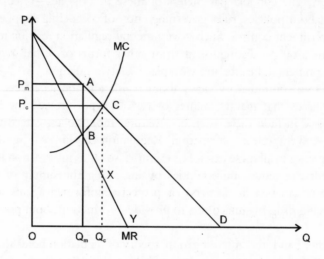

Fig. 14.1

To get rid of the deadweight loss, the regulator imposes a price ceiling of P_c. As a result, the demand curve facing the monopolist becomes P_cCD and the corresponding MR curve is the discontinuous curve P_cCXY. The intersection of the MR and MC curves now take place at C. The monopolist, therefore, produces an amount Q_c (the competitive level of output) and the deadweight loss is eliminated.

Two conditions must be satisfied for this solution to be desirable or feasible: (1) The monopolist must be making a profit at the price P_c, otherwise it will refuse to produce and (2) the cost of running the regulatory agency must be less than the deadweight loss.

Next, let us consider two other possibilities of inefficient regulation. If the regulatory agency does not have full information about costs and demand, it may not be able to choose the right price P_c.

Suppose it sets a price P such that $P_m > P > P_c$. In this case, the consumers benefit, but the deadweight loss is not totally eliminated.

On the other hand, if the price P is set too low, then the monopolist can shut down and the deadweight loss may be greater than under unregulated monopoly. In Fig. 14.2, if the regulator sets a price ceiling of P^*, then the deadweight loss is the area DEC, which is greater than ABC.

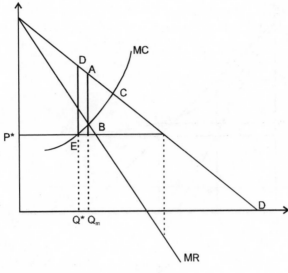

Fig. 14.2

14.1.1.2 Natural Monopoly

A firm is a natural monopoly if it can produce the market quantity Q at a lower cost than two or more firms. Formally, let k firms produce outputs $q_1, q_2, \ldots, q_k$ such that $q_1 + q_2 + q_3 + \ldots + q_k = Q$. If each firm has a cost function $C(.)$, then one firm can produce Q at a lower cost than k firms if $C(Q) < C(q_1) + C(q_2) + \ldots + C(q_k)$. In this case, the least cost (most efficient) way to produce is to have one firm produce all Q units. It is then said to be a natural monopoly. A cost function displaying the above property is said to be subadditive at Q.

   A strictly decreasing average cost curve implies subadditivity, though the opposite does not hold (i.e. the cost function may be subadditive even though the average cost curve is increasing in the relevant range). A firm can be a natural monopoly even with a U-shaped average cost curve.

   To keep things simple, however, let us consider a situation where a firm is a natural monopoly with constant marginal cost and falling average cost. This is represented in Fig. 14.3. It is often argued that utilities providing electricity, gas, or telephone have relatively high fixed costs but constant or falling marginal costs. Marginal cost curve is represented by the horizontal line labelled c.

   In Fig. 14.3, if the natural monopoly is not regulated, it sets a price P_m and produces an amount Q_m. It makes (supernormal) profits because its price is above the average cost.

   If the regulator wants to get rid of the deadweight loss, it must set a price ceiling of p. The demand curve will now become pAD and pA will also be a section of the MR curve. The monopolist's output will be Q^* and there will be no deadweight loss. But, how to induce the monopolist to produce Q^*? It can be seen from the diagram that at $Q^*, p <$ average cost, and so the monopolist will be making a loss and would prefer to shut down operations.

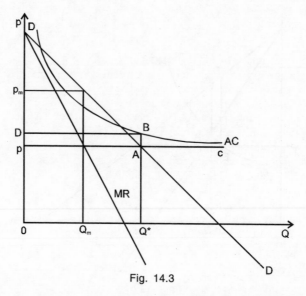

Fig. 14.3

Society can of course keep the monopoly operating by providing it with a subsidy equal to the amount of the loss, so that the monopolist just breaks even. But providing a subsidy to a private monopoly on a continuing basis may not be a politically feasible proposition. Further, the subsidy is often generated by using inefficiently raised tax revenues. Commonly used taxes like income and sales tax drive a wedge between price and marginal cost. Moreover, the subsidy may be at the expense of developmental programmes for governments strapped for cash.

Another problem is that the possibility of transfers from the regulator to the regulated firm gives the former discretionary power and creates an environment for regulatory capture to occur.

An alternative therefore, is, to set a price ceiling P'' based on the equality of price with average cost, as in Fig. 14.4. This allows the monopolist to break even but leaves a deadweight loss.

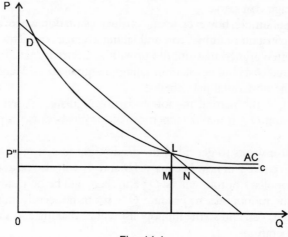

Fig. 14.4

BOX 14.1. ENTRY REGULATION

In many countries, entry is highly regulated and requires a lot of paperwork, time, and money. It might also involve payment of bribes to officials and politicians. On the other hand, it is very easy to start business in some countries. A National Bureau of Economic Research (NBER) paper suggests that the average number of working days needed to complete the administrative procedures in order to set up a new firm is 66 in France and only 7 in the US.

Proponents of high regulation of entry believe that the government should try to prevent 'fly-by-night' operations from taking off, maintaining high quality standards, protecting public health, and reducing pollution. Others believe that regulation of entry only benefits incumbents, politicians, and bureaucrats.

Lopez-de-Silanes and others, in the NBER paper mentioned above, study a data set covering the number of procedures required to set up business in 75 countries, as well as time delays and costs. They try to identify the real beneficiaries of entry regulation. They find that the number of procedures needed to register a company and obtain all required licences varies from 2 in Canada to 20 in Bolivia. The time it takes varies from 2 days in Canada to 6 months in Mozambique. The average delay over all countries is estimated at 2 months, but this underestimates the real time needed to comply with the regulations, since it excludes the time required to gather all information and visit ministries repeatedly. The authors find that entry is highly regulated in developing countries, but some developed countries have stiff regulation as well.

The cost of following the procedures is defined to include licence and other fees, costs of forms, fiscal stamps, and legal and notary charges. Such costs range from 0.4 per cent of per capita Gross Domestic Product (GDP) in New Zealand to 260 per cent in Bolivia. But the real costs are higher, since they should include bribes paid, the opportunity costs of time, and any forgone profits.

The findings of the paper go against the proponents of entry regulation. It is found that stricter regulation does not improve product quality—compliance with international quality standards is lower in countries with more regulation. Nor does it reduce pollution or raise health levels. In fact, filing for a business licence entails very few procedures involving environmental, safety, or health matters.

The stricter regulations give rise to an underground economy where enterpreneurs are helped to escape the burden of regulation. Countries where entry regulation is stiffer are also the countries with more corruption. Entry regulation seems to benefit mainly politicians and bureaucrats who impose it. Surprisingly, stringent regulation does not seem to favour incumbent firms. There is no evidence that its presence raises the return on assets or reduces the intensity of competition.

Source: Simon Djankov, Rafael La Porta, Florencio Lopez-de-Silanes, and Andrei Schleifer, 'The Regulation of Entry', NBER Working Paper, No W7892, September 2000.

14.1.2 Rate of Return Regulation

Instead of controlling prices, the regulatory authorities may seek to ensure a certain rate of return on the capital employed by the regulated monopoly. Suppose that a monopoly uses labour L and capital K to produce electric power. Both L and K are available in unlimited quantities at fixed prices per unit. The firm is restricted only in that it can earn no more than some fixed proportion of the value of its capital. It can pursue maximization of profit subject only to this constraint. It is also assumed that the rate of return permitted to the firm by regulation is less than the return it earns in an unregulated state, but is at least as great as the rate of return on capital.

The firm's rate of return (ROR) on capital is usually defined as the ratio of its profit to the value of its capital stock. Profit will be $PQ - wL - uK$, where w is the wage rate and u is the *user cost* of capital, i.e. the cost of using or renting the capital for one period. On the other hand, the cost of capital is $p_k K$, where p_k is the purchase price per unit of capital stock. Then

$$ROR = \frac{PQ - wL - uK}{p_k K}.$$

Given this definition, an ROR of zero is the normal or competitive rate of return. The unrestricted monopoly would be earning an ROR above zero. The regulatory body might want to restrict the ROR to a *fair rate of return*. However, if the regulated ROR is positive, this provides the firm with an incentive to invest more in capital because the allowed rate of return is more than the competitive rate of return. In other words, the firm, maximizing profit subject to the ROR constraint, will produce its output with an inefficiently high K/L ratio. Thus the rate of return constraint leads the regulated monopoly to inflate its rate base by substituting capital for labour. There will thus be overcapitalization or a *goldplating effect*. More surprising yet, it leads to the choice of factor proportions off the cost curve. Therefore, *profit maximization requires a deviation from cost minimization*. These results are known as the *Averch–Johnson effects* (Averch and Johnson, 1962).

In practice, there is often a lag between the time when the firm's cost conditions change and the new regulated prices come into effect. This is called *regulatory lag*. If the costs have increased, then the firm suffers a loss. If the costs have gone down, the firm makes some gains till the new prices become operative.

Another type of regulation that has been tried out is *price cap regulation* (sometimes viewed as rate-of-return regulation with a very long regulatory lag). Price is set beforehand and does not change even if cost changes. This mechanism provides for the maximum incentive to reduce costs. However, it has been noticed that the reduction in cost is followed quite soon by downward revision in price, reducing the incentive to reduce cost in the first place.

14.1.3 Alternatives to Regulation

Our discussion shows so far that even if we accept the argument that regulation is done in public interest, regulation may not prove to be the panacea for market failure. A couple of alternatives to regulation exist. We now examine these:

• Franchise bidding (Demsetz competition): The idea is that the government would auction off the industry to the highest bidder. If there is competition for the monopoly right, this will allow the government to capture the monopoly rents. The government may require, as a condition of the bidding, that the firm will have to act in a manner that is most favourable to consumers.

However, the idea of franchise bidding faces some problems:

1. In the case of a natural monopoly, a firm would make losses under the price equals marginal cost condition and no firm would bid.

2. The government has to monitor on a long-term basis that the firm is honouring its commitments.

3. Over time the environment changes, so that the initial agreement may not be the best one for the future.

• Government ownership—The other option is for the government to own the natural monopoly in question. The government can then set prices to maximize value. But government ownership has failed to deliver the goods and there has been a movement towards privatization in many countries.

In the latter part of this chapter, we examine the process of privatization in India. But next we turn to another area in which regulation is becoming increasingly important— environmental regulation.

14.1.4 Environmental Regulation

According to Helm and Pearce (1990), 'The fate of natural environments (is) suddenly everyone's concern.' Environmental problems were first viewed as local, or at best national, issues. But in the 1980s, global environmental problems took centrestage. The growing awareness of environmental problems has created new challenges and opportunities for firms. On the one hand, they have to decide how best to respond to environmental regulation; on the other hand, the very existence of regulation created opportunities for some firms to enjoy first-mover advantages by moving early to satisfy regulatory concerns. Therefore, environmental regulation is a key component of the non-market environment facing a firm.

In this section, we examine the economic approaches to environmental regulation. An understanding of the various economic approaches to environmental issues is crucial to the understanding of value creation by firms in today's world, when environmental awareness is rapidly spreading.

14.1.4.1 Economic Approaches

It is important to understand that the economic approach to environment is based on viewing environmental effects as *externalities*. An *externality* is defined as an action by one individual agent that provides benefits or costs affecting another individual agent outside the market mechanism. If I buy a shirt and pay money for it, the seller is benefited. But this is not an externality, because the purchase affects only parties engaged in the transaction process. However, there are other types of actions that affect agents who are not engaged in a related market transaction . If you are smoking in a public place, this might set somebody coughing. You and the non-smoker are not engaging in any transaction via the market, yet your action is affecting the non-smoker.

The externality is *negative* when the action has negative effects on the second agent. For example, if my neighbour plays loud music at night and I lose my sleep, then this is an example of a negative externality. The externality is *positive* if the effect is beneficial, as when one man's flower garden gives enjoyment to another. Again, when a parent inoculates her children against smallpox, this has beneficial effects on other children who come in contact with them.

BOX 14.2. GLOBAL CLIMATE CHANGE AND BUSINESS

Scientists all over the world are becoming increasingly convinced that the earth's surface temperature is rising due to the release of greenhouse gases in the atmosphere.

O'Neill Packard and Reinhardt (2000) note that '. . . business leaders at the most recent World Economic Forum in Davos, Switzerland, voted global climate change as the most pressing issue confronting the world's business community'. Global warming will have an impact on business in three ways—through changing the risks and opportunities associated with shifts in the weather, through potential regulatory changes, and through shifts in public opinion.

Climate changes are of special importance to companies with climate-dependent assets. Thus, agricultural companies may have to invest in regions where the climate has warmed enough to make farming viable and abandon areas where farming has become non-viable. Real estate companies will have to keep abreast of research on flood patterns if they want to ensure that waterfront property investments do not involve them in financial losses. Insurance companies will have to use predictive models that ensure that their prices are accurate.

Regulatory programmes that include additional taxes on fossil fuel consumption and require that cars and appliances use less energy will change asset valuations. Thus cars with low mileage will lose value. When taxes on greenhouse gas emissions are imposed, companies will have to decide whether it is cheaper to pay the tax or invest in reducing emissions.

Some companies like General Motors have supported regulatory measures that make driving more expensive, because they see climate change as an opportunity to gain advantages over technologically less sophisticated rivals. So they are investing in cars that run on a combination of petrol and battery power and in fuel cells.

Finally, companies like Swiss Re and BP Amoco have publicized their investments in knowledge about climate change or their commitment to reducing carbon dioxide emissions. However, others have chosen to remain quiet about their efforts because a too hearty support of regulation may displease their customers in the fossil fuel and electricity sectors.

Source: Kimberly O'Neill Packard and Forest Reinhardt (2000), 'What every executive needs to know about global warming', *Harvard Business Review*, July–August, pp. 129–35.

We can also distinguish between consumption externalities and production externalities. A *consumption externality* occurs when one person is affected directly by another person's production or consumption. An example is when somebody starts smoking and sets another person coughing. A *production externality* occurs when the production possibilities of one firm are affected by the activities of other firms or consumers. Thus, if a large firm in the industry demands more labour and sets off a wage increase, this creates a negative production externality on a smaller firm employing labour.

When an externality exists, efficient allocation of resources may not take place because agents often do not take the externality into consideration. In other words, the maximum value is not created.

We can show this with the help of an example of a negative externality. Suppose that there is a chemical dyes industry that is perfectly competitive. Firms in the industry face a constant *MC* curve and hence the industry supply curve is horizontal. The industry discharges pollutants in a lake which kill off the fish in the lake. Each unit of output, therefore, generates pollution and the harm done by each additional unit of pollution (killing off the fishes in the lake) is represented by the *marginal externality cost (MEC)* curve.

In this industry, the *MC* curve represents the *marginal private cost (MPC)* curve. If unregulated, firms in the industry consider only these costs in deciding on the optimal output, because the effects on fishing do not concern them. The competitive output is obtained at the intersection of the industry supply and demand curves, and this is Q_P.

However, society consists of both the firms in the chemical dyes industry and the fishermen dependent on the lake for their livelihood. The *marginal social cost (MSC)* is, therefore, the sum of *MPC* and *MEC* and is obtained in Fig. 14.5 by vertically adding the two curves. From the society's point of view, both the direct production cost as well as the negative cost of pollution must be taken into account. The *MSC* curve will obviously lie above the *MPC* curve and the resultant output, that is socially optimal, will be Q_C, which is less than Q_P. Thus, if a negative externality is present, the level of production determined in the market by considerations of private cost will be *higher* than the socially optimal level of output. Similarly, it can be shown that if a positive externality is present, the level of production that is determined by considerations of private cost will be lower than the socially optimal level of output.

Note, however, that the socially optimal output in the presence of a negative externality *is not* zero. Achieving a zero pollution level would require shutting down the chemical dyes industry, not an attractive option from the society's point of view.

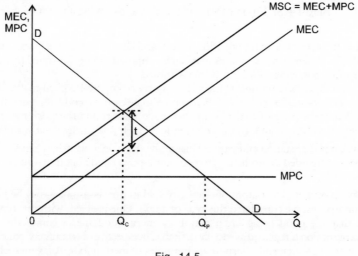

Fig. 14.5

Regulatory approaches to externality are based on the divergence of *MPC* from *MSC* and the need to bring the two into convergence. We discuss the regulatory approaches under the following heads (we continue to consider a negative externality):

1. Standard setting. Such policy instruments are of two types: (a) technology-based standards: these define specific abatement techniques for each source of pollution; and (b) performance standards: these set specific ceilings on emissions from each source, leaving the polluting firm free to determine how best to achieve these.

Punishment for exceeding the standards is administered through the legal system and can range from fines and imprisonments to closure of the offending units.

The problem with this solution is two-fold. The government or the regulatory agency often does not possess enough information about the marginal private and social costs to compute the optimal amount of pollution and secondly, the costs of enforcing limits are ignored. If an industry emits smoke and the firms have to cut down on smoke emission by putting filters on chimneys, then this cost should be taken into account.

2. Pigovian tax: A second solution is to levy a tax on the output so that the price rises to reflect the cost of pollution at the margin. In Fig. 14.5, the rate of tax that should be imposed per unit of output is t. This will ensure that $MSC = MPC$ at the optimal level of output. It should be obvious that in the case of a positive externality, the remedy is an appropriate subsidy rather than a tax. This approach is typically ascribed to Pigou (1920). Crudely, the idea is to impose a tax that will bring the polluter's cost function into line with the true, social cost of production.

This approach assumes that the private costs of the polluting firm and the externality costs are known. Hence the approach is informationally very demanding, since it assumes that all private information is also available to the regulator, there is no strategic revelation of information by affected parties, and no uncertainty about the pollution impacts.

Box 14.3. Different types of taxes on pollution

It may not be practicable to tax pollution directly and hence a number of 'proxy' solutions are used. The different types of taxes that can be imposed can be illustrated by using the example of carbon emissions from power stations.

- Tax on the carbon-producing fuel: The tax may be imposed, e.g. on coal used by the power stations, on the basis of their approximate carbon-producing potential. This will alter the price of coal and (a) encourage substitution towards other types of fuels (gas for coal) and (b) towards non-fossil fuels (like nuclear, water, and winds).

- Tax on power station emissions: This can be done on a plant-by-plant basis. Each plant is regarded as producing two outputs—power and pollution—and emissions are taxed.

- Tax on output: The output of electricity sold to final consumers may be taxed (in our analysis, we considered this type of a tax). One problem with this type of tax is that the good being taxed may be a merit good (i.e. a commodity whose consumption is regarded as socially desirable, irrespective of consumers' preferences). Electricity, water, and transport are examples of merit goods. A tax on such goods may discourage consumption and have important distributional impacts.

Source: D. Helm and D. Pearce (1999), 'Economic Policy towards the Environment', *Oxford Review of Economic Policy*, Vol. 6, No. 1.

3. Missing markets: The problem with externalities is that there is no property right and no market for certain 'goods'. 'There is no explicit market in clean air, in unpolluted bathing beaches, in forest views, and in the carbon-fixing properties of tropical rain-forests' (Helm and Pearce, 1999). Thus, pollution may be considered to be an output of the production process, since both output and pollution are the results of production. However, there is no market for pollution (a 'bad') and no price for it. The firms are the suppliers of pollution. The consumers are the potential 'buyers', and since pollution is a bad, we can anticipate that consumers will buy this good *only if they are paid to buy it*: the price of a 'bad' will be negative.

When one identifies the problem of externalities as the absence of markets, the obvious solution is the creation of appropriate property rights. If a chemical firm pollutes a river, the riverside residents, if given the right to clean water, will demand compensation or sue. Alternatively, if they do not own the right to clean water, they will have the incentive to bribe the chemical firm to reduce pollution. It must then be determined as to which party should be given property rights—the polluter or the victims.

Suppose that parties affected by an externality can negotiate costlessly with each other. Coase pointed out that in this case, an efficient outcome will result, no matter how the initial property rights to the externality-creating variables are assigned. Therefore, under the condition of zero or negligible bargaining costs, it does not matter from the point of view of efficiency who is given the property right.

Coase's idea is quite simple. Suppose that the polluting firm is given the right to pollute. Then the polluted agent will have an incentive to pay the former to restrict pollution. The firm will accept this offer so long as the gain from this outweighs the loss in profit from cutting down production.

Example 14.1 Suppose that firm 1 is a monopoly giving rise to an externality and faces an inverse demand curve $p = 11 - x$. Total cost is $C = 2x$ and $MEC = 2x$.

x	*Profit*= px − 2x	*Marginal Profit*	MEC
1	8		
		6	2
2	14		
		4	4
3	18		
		2	6
4	20		
		0	8
5	20		

The marginal figures are given between two x figures to emphasize their marginal nature. The monopoly will produce 5 units (or 4) to maximize profit. If the victim wants the monopoly to reduce output (and pollution) by one unit, it will be prepared to pay upto 8 (because the cost of pollution will be reduced to this extent), whereas the loss in profit will be 0. Hence, the victim and the polluter should be able to reach agreement over this reduction. This process continues until $x = 3$. For a further one unit reduction in x, the maximum the victim can pay is 4, which is exactly equal to the marginal loss in profit for firm 1. We can expect bargaining to stop here, and the socially optimal amount of x to be produced.

Suppose on the other hand, that the victim is given the right to clean air/water. Then rather than producing nothing, it is in the interest of the polluting firm to offer the victim a sum of money in return for the right to pollute (or to prevent the latter from going to court). By increasing output from 1 to 2, the firm earns an extra profit of 6, while the cost to the victim is 2. The polluter can compensate the victim and still have something left over. For every extra unit of pollution, the firm will weigh the marginal gain in profit it can make and be prepared to offer a maximum amount based on this. The victim will go on accepting so long as this payment adequately compensates her for the extra cost of pollution. The end-result will be the socially optimal level of pollution.

Of course, while the efficiency result is the same in both cases, the distributional implications are quite different. In one instance, the polluted firm has to pay the polluter, in the other the polluted has to pay. The Coase theorem also depends crucially on the absence of any transaction cost, i.e. any cost of bargaining. If bargaining costs are substantial, then the gains from negotiation may be neutralized entirely by such costs, and the socially optimal outcome will not be reached.

The identification of substantial bargaining costs (one type of transaction costs) can alert us to situations where in the absence of government intervention, the market will not be able to reach the desired outcome, even if property rights are established. These costs include, among other things, (a) costs of discovering who is it one must deal with, (b) forming associations of affected agents to conduct bargaining, (c) conducting negotiations, (d) drawing up the contract, (e) undertaking inspection to ensure that the conditions of the contract are being met, and so on.

The bargaining costs increase sharply once we step out of the limits of one-to-one bargaining. In the simple one-to-one cases, the parties are easily identified and they can bargain with each other. It is also going to be easier to calculate the costs of pollution. Pigovian taxes and subsidies can then be used; negotiation and bargaining can take place. For example, neighbours often solve problems of noise pollution through direct complaints.

However, when larger numbers of agents are involved, the problem becomes more difficult to solve. With large numbers of polluters, it becomes difficult to determine how much each is contributing to pollution. With larger numbers of victims, it becomes difficult to measure the damage. There is also the problem of establishing cooperation amongst affected parties, particularly because the incentive to free-ride on others is strong (e.g. I will not spend much effort in fighting polluters since I expect others to do the fighting). Thus, if a number of chemical firms are located along a river and are discharging effluents into the river, it becomes difficult to find out which firm is responsible for what amount of the pollution of the river.

BOX 14.4. CREATING A MARKET FOR EXTERNALITIES

How does one create markets for externalities? One way is to allocate trading permits in pollution. The largest polluters are assigned a quota for their emission of polluting substances. If they exactly meet their quota, no fines or penalties will be levied. On the other hand, if they emit pollution below their quotas, they will be free to sell the difference to others on the open market. Thus, for example, if the firm's quota is 86 tons of nitrogen oxide emission a year, and it actually emits only 80 tons, it will be free to sell the right to emit 6 tons of nitrogen oxide to other firms. Firms can then compare the open market price of emission credit to the cost of reducing emissions and decide what to do. The firms who can reduce emissions more cheaply will sell credits to firms that cannot do so.

A successful example of using tradeable permits to control emissions is the experience of sulphur dioxide emission trading in the USA. In 1990, Title IV of the Amendments to the Clean Air Act introduced in the US the first national programme of environmental regulation based on a system of tradeable permits. The aim was to reduce permanently yearly sulphur dioxide emissions, that contribute to acid rain, to about 50 per cent of their 1980 levels (9 million tonnes). In phase I of the programme, during 1995–9, the largest and dirtiest generating units were targeted and from 2000 onwards, effectively all electricity generating units were targeted. Firms are given 'allowances', each allowance being the right to emit a ton of SO_2, and these are distributed approximately in proportion to the 1985–7 heat input of each unit. Each unit needs to buy allowances if it emits more than the initial allocation, but can sell or bank allowances if it emits less. If a unit is found not in compliance, it must pay $2000 for each ton of emissions not accounted for (which is about 10 times the current price of an allowance).

The market thus created is open and unregulated. Anybody can enter the market and trade. Partners can trade in any manner they choose and new instruments, like swaps of current for future allowances, can be freely created. The volume of market transactions has grown enormously. The environmental objectives have been surpassed—in 1996, for example, emissions were 33 per cent below allowed aggregate levels. The aggregate response hides large differences in individual responses, as is to be expected. Roughly, one quarter of the affected units had emissions exceeding their allowances.

Source: Alessandra Casella (1999), 'Tradeable Deficit Permits', *Economic Policy*, No 29, (October 1999) pp. 323–61.

Another contentious issue relates to valuing the future. Most of the major consequences of the global externalities will affect future generations. However, the future generations are not present to bargain when decisions are being taken in the present—decisions that will affect their lives significantly. Moreover, economic analysis takes account of the future by discounting the future. The value of Rs 100 is higher today than Rs 100 tomorrow, because Rs 100 today can earn returns between now and tomorrow. Discounting means that less weight is placed on the future. But discounting the future shifts the burden of environmental degradation to the future and may be objected to on this ground.

BOX 14.5. ENVIRONMENTAL REGULATION IN INDIA

Several features of environmental regulation in India stand out.

First, it is based on standard-setting and does not employ economic instruments. Many pieces of legislation have been passed to protect the environment. These include, among others, the Water (Prevention and Control of Pollution) Cess Act of 1977, the Forest Conservation Act of 1980, the Air (Prevention and Control of Pollution) Act of 1981, the Environment (Protection) Act of 1986, etc. Under some of these Acts, Pollution Control Boards have been set up. These Boards regulate standards for air and water quality. Industrial units have to supply all pertinent information to these Boards. The Acts also lay down regulatory procedures for ensuring that standards are met by individual units. In case of non-compliance, the Boards can take actions against the offending units, ranging from fines to imprisonment, and cutting off electricity and water connections.

It should be emphasized again that the Government of India has not so far used a pollution tax as a regulatory instrument. There is a water cess on the industrial use of water, but it is very nominal and can, at most, be regarded as a revenue tax.

Secondly, while the necessary laws are quickly passed, enforcement budgets are not forthcoming and government agencies appear to be reluctant to use their power to discipline violators. The institutional mechanism comprising of the Pollution Control Boards, forest bureaucracies, and state agencies is, in many respects, ineffective.

Thirdly, local communities and environmental groups are playing an increasingly important role in fighting environmental pollution. The judiciary has to respond to citizen complaints about environmental degradation and administrative sloth. Because of this, the judiciary has begun to play an active role as '. . . public educator, policy maker, super-administrator and, more generally, *amicus* environment' (Divan and Rosencranz).

Sources: Shyam Divan and Armin Rosencranz (2001), *Environmental Law and Policy in India*, Oxford University Press, New Delhi.
M. N. Murty, A. J. James, and Smita Misra (1999), *Economics of Water Pollution: The Indian Experience*, Oxford University Press.

One of the market-based solutions to environmental solution may be privatization. Privatization involves a transfer of assets from the public to the private sector. It will have an effect only if the private and public sectors behave differently. It has been thought that government objectives in operating firms reflect wider considerations than profit-maximization. For example, the public sector's objectives may be focused on increasing output, rather than profit. This type of objective is likely to lead to levels of output higher than the profit-maximizing level of output. The trend is reinforced by the lower cost of capital to public, compared with private, ownership. If the level of pollution is directly related to the level of output, this will in turn lead to more pollution with public ownership. Some commentators also feel that resources will be used more efficiently in the private sector and hence pollution will be lower. On the other hand, access to the relevant information needed to monitor performance is reduced when industry is turned over to private hands. Therefore, whether privatization will lead to a reduction in environmental pollution is an open question.

In the next section, we examine in a wider context the economic rationale for privatization. We have discussed earlier the need for regulating private monopolies. An important question is whether privatization *per se* leads to any improvements in the performance of firms.

14.2 PRIVATIZATION

What is privatization? Privatization involves a transfer of ownership and control from the public to the private sector, with particular reference to asset sales. Privatization can be accomplished in two ways:

- The government can sell assets it owns to private buyers.
- The government can stop providing a service directly and rely on the private sector to deliver the service.

The public enterprises relevant here are revenue-generating entities originally owned or controlled by the state. An example of a revenue-generating entity is a municipal corporation that gets property taxes.

14.2.1 Reasons for Privatization

Over time, in many countries, the performance of public sector enterprises (PSEs) turned out to be, by and large, unsatisfactory. They incurred losses, or did not make as much profit as they should have, given that they had privileged access to capital, various subsidies, and protection from domestic and foreign competition. Governments have begun to think of privatization of PSEs as a solution to these problems.

We next examine the possible impacts of privatization to determine whether it can transform PSEs.

Fiscal Impact

When a PSE is sold off to the private sector, the government gets the sales proceeds. Further, if the PSE had been making losses and was being subsidized, then these subsidies come to an end, which further helps the government. Thus, the immediate generation of revenues is supplemented by a reduction in recurrent expenditures.

But does the government really gain? In the simplest case, the buyer will be willing to pay only so much as the PSE is expected to bring in the future. The PSE is expected to generate a future stream of returns. The sum of the discounted returns is what a buyer will pay. The government would have got the same revenue had it not sold the PSE. Therefore, it would seem that privatization does not have any real impact on the government's finances.

There are two reasons why privatization might still make a difference. First, a privatized firm might be expected to be more efficient than a PSE. Hence, the sum of discounted returns will be higher than that under government ownership. Secondly, the government, when it privatizes, is getting funds immediately. This added liquidity might be desirable for a number of reasons, for example, because the government might want to spend on education or infrastructure.

It is interesting to note that in theory, for a loss-making PSE, the price might be negative. This is not very far-fetched. Governments have sometimes given so many concessions to the buyer to induce them to buy loss-making concerns, that in effect the price has turned out to be negative.

Efficiency Gains

Proponents of privatization have argued that it can have an important effect on economic efficiency. Two types of efficiency gains are possible: gains in allocative efficiency, and gains in productive efficiency.

- **Allocative efficiency:** Proper allocation of the resources of the economy depends on the prices reflecting correctly relative scarcities of resources. A resource that is more scarce should have a higher price and this would lead to it being used more sparingly. In PSEs, prices sometimes do not reflect scarcities properly. For example, if the government gives a subsidy for an input used by a PSE, the PSE would tend to overuse that resource. Or, if a PSE is a monopoly, then it can set its own price. Thus, kerosene may be sold at a very low price, which would encourage adulteration of diesel with kerosene (i.e. overuse of kerosene).

It is clear that for PSEs operating in competitive markets, prices would better reflect scarcities and, therefore, allocative inefficiency would be less. Then the gains from privatization would also be less. On the other hand, transforming a public sector monopoly into a private sector monopoly would also not lead to increases in allocative efficiency. We can expect large increases in allocative efficiency to be achieved when a public sector monopoly is privatized and the market opened up to other players.

- **Productive efficiency:** Productive efficiency relates to the optimal use of inputs in the production process. It has been argued that PSEs are likely to exhibit greater internal inefficiencies than private firms for various reasons. Public managers are given numerous and inconsistent objectives. Instead of control by shareholders who are interested in profit-maximization, there is bureaucratic control which puts more emphasis on 'playing it safe'. Suppose that productive efficiency requires use of an input that is not available in a competitive market. The manager in a PSE is required to obtain competitive quotations for almost everything, and hence may have no way of using this particular input because there is only one seller.

Distributional Impact

Critics of privatization argue that it is likely to affect adversely weaker sections of the society. First, it might lead to layoffs by the new owners. Or the firm might go bankrupt after privatization and the government will not be there to protect jobs. Secondly, the goods and services made available by the PSE to the poor may become less accessible. For example, a privatized airline may choose not to fly on unprofitable routes.

A counter argument is that the PSEs have not had a very successful record of reaching the poor and the disadvantaged sections. For example, in India, it has been repeatedly shown that the Public Distribution System does not do a good job of reaching essential commodities to the poorest sections; it is more useful to the richer sections.

14.2.2 Techniques of Privatization

• Divestiture: The most well-known technique of privatization is the sale of equity to the general public. This is called divestiture (divestment or disinvestment), and may be complete or partial. That is, the government may sell all its stake in an enterprise or sell only a certain percentage. This can be done through *direct sales* and *equity offerings*.

However, the inadequacy of national stock markets and the lack of domestic capital have sometimes led to a shortage of local buyers, while foreign investors, unable to obtain sound information on the enterprises offered, often lacked sufficient interest. Furthermore, the direct sales approach may be costly and slow, owing to the complexity of preparing each state asset for sale individually, and then ensuring that buyers observed all contract provisions.

• Restitution: Restitution refers to the return of state assets to their former private owners in situations where the government's original acquisition is seen as unjust, such as uncompensated seizure. Restitution, in such cases, it is argued, is essential on moral grounds.

Opponents of restitution counter that the process is necessarily selective, and therefore an unsatisfactory way of achieving justice retroactively. As a practical matter, private claims can often be complicated and drawn out, bogging down privatization unnecessarily. In practice, the transition countries have seldom used restitution, except for Estonia and, to a lesser extent, the Czech Republic.

• Management-Employee Buyouts: Under this approach, shares of an enterprise are sold or given to some combination of managers and other employees. The powerful positions of employees and of managers may give this approach the twin advantages of feasibility and political popularity. It is also rapid and easy to implement. Well-structured management-employee buyouts can sometimes lead to efficient results, since the people who know best about an enterprise, i.e. employees and managers, become the owners.

Nevertheless, experience shows that these buyouts suffer serious disadvantages. Yielding to insider interests often entails large costs in inefficiency and poor management. The new owners may grant excessive wage increases, maintain excessively high employment, and undertake insufficient investment. Insiders may also lack many of the skills necessary to function in a market-oriented economy. Further, the process is seen to be inequitable, handing employees, rather than the population at large, most of the benefits.

• Mass Privatization: In mass, or equal-access, voucher privatization, the government generally gives away, or sells for a nominal fee, vouchers that can be used to purchase shares in enterprises. This technique was rarely used elsewhere in the world before the massive transition in Central and Eastern Europe began, but it has proved popular there, particularly in the Czech Republic.

Voucher privatization helps to overcome the shortage of domestic capital. Voucher schemes can be politically popular because they address the perceived unfairness of other approaches and avoid the charges of a sellout of national assets to foreigners. The difficulties associated with valuing enterprises before privatization are also avoided.

Early proponents argued that the fast pace of voucher privatization would add to the credibility of reform programmes and bolster their chance of success. At times, the speed could prevent employees or other interests from mobilizing opposition to privatization. Furthermore, the widespread participation of a country's citizens fosters a greater understanding of reform and creates a new owner class with a stake in the process.

Mass privatization has its downside, however. The main risk is that a dispersed ownership structure will lack the focus and power to direct effective corporate management. This, in turn, may scare off potential new sources of capital. In practice, these problems have been partly addressed by pooling ownership interests in investment or mutual funds. The funds, however, do not always have adequate management, control, and supervisory powers. In such cases, voucher privatization becomes merely ineffective absentee ownership.

• Contracting out or leasing out of government services can be another technique of privatization. For example, a municipal corporation can contract out the task of garbage collection to a private party.

Associated with privatization usually are the processes of *liberalization* and *deregulation*. Liberalization refers to the introduction/promotion of competition in a traditionally monopolized industry. Deregulation refers to the abolition of statutory barriers to the operation of market forces. For example, the Government of India controls the prices of many commodities through the administered pricing mechanism. If some commodity is taken out of the purview of this mechanism, then this is a dergulatory measure, because the price will now be determined by market forces.

14.2.3 Obstacles to Privatization

Worldwide experience shows that implementation of privatization programmes has lagged well behind the stated intentions. Barring a few countries, privatization has been limited to small PSEs of the manufacturing and the services sectors. Two kinds of obstacles to privatization can be identified: implementation issues and political constraints. We take these up in turn.

Implementation Issues

Technical constraints to privatization are related to both managerial deficiencies and weaknesses within the economy.

First, privatization requires a high level of administrative capacity. In some developing countries, there is a lack of well-established, competent, management consulting groups, accounting firms, and investment bankers. These are needed to provide technical advice and valuation of PSEs. As a result, in some instances, foreign experts have been brought in.

Secondly, a valuation of the PSE has to be carried out before it can be offered for sale, and the valuation exercise has faced severe problems. Valuation is a sensitive subject politically, because governments want to get a high sales price and at the same time the valuation process might raise questions about past public management and investment decisions.There have been inordinate delays in valuation. The problem is aggravated when poor records are maintained by PSEs.

Box 14.6. The BALCO controversy

Bharat Aluminium Company Ltd. (BALCO) was set up in 1965 at Korba in Madhya Pradesh to manufacture aluminium rods and semi-fabricated products. BALCO is today the third largest player in India's aluminium industry. The Korba facility includes bauxite mines, an alumina refinery, a smelter, and a fabrication unit, besides a 270 MW power plant, which meets a substantial part of the unit's power requirements, and a fully built-up township spread over 15,000 acres in which over 4000 families live. In the last quarter of 2000–1, the GOI decided to sell off equity in BALCO. Sterlite Industries won with a bid of Rs 551.5 crore for a 51 per cent stake in the company. But no sooner was the BALCO deal announced than it created a furore within and outside Parliament. The opposition to the deal was on many counts. First, since BALCO is a profitable and cash-rich public sector corporation with an extremely low debt to equity ratio, it was argued that it would have been possible for it to finance its proposed modernization plan (estimated to cost Rs 1000 crore) without recourse to budgetary funds. This would have allowed the corporation to improve its profitability and increase the dividend payable to the exchequer. But BALCO as a PSU has suffered from procedural bottlenecks and lack of managerial autonomy. The company had been unsuccessful in getting clearance from the government for its plans, for example, for setting up 100 per cent captive power generation. As a result, the company had to depend on high cost power from the state electricity board which resulted in avoidable cost increases.

Secondly, it was argued, a direct valuation of BALCO's assets suggested that with an investment of just Rs 550 crore, Sterlite was to get control over assets that according to some were worth around 10 times that value. In fact, officials from the power sector argued that the captive power plant alone would cost more than the sum being paid by Sterlite.

Third, it was alleged that the valuation procedure has been neither transparent, nor undertaken by qualified valuers capable of valuing the plant and machinery of the company and the bauxite mines that it has on lease.

Fourth, the whole procedure was gone through in much haste. Even though the bids had been invited sometime ago, the valuation of the firm, the fixing of the reserve price, and the acceptance of Sterlite's bid was allegedly done within a month's time.

On the other hand, the government argued that the Sterlite offer exceeded that warranted by a reasonable projection of future revenues and indicated that the company was willing to pay a premium for the controlling stake it was being offered in a major player in the aluminium market. Further Sterlite's offer was more than double the competing bid from rival Hindalco.

Source: C.P. Chandrasekhar, 'Lessons from the BALCO fiasco', http://www.indiareacts.com/archivespecialreports/nat2.asp?recno=14&ctg=policy

Thirdly, once the valuation has taken place, administrative capacity is needed to assess buyers' bids, arrange finance and insurance, and deal with a host of complex legal issues. Sometimes, a comprehensive rehabilitation plan for the PSE has to be designed, evaluated, and financed before privatization is possible. Moreover, appropriate regulatory structures may not exist and have to be set up, particularly when privatization leads to the creation of a monopoly.

Fourthly, capital markets in many developing countries are typically weak and poorly regulated. Large investments in equity are quite unusual. PSEs are some of the largest firms in the country and the private sector may not be in a position to fund the purchase of large assets. The private sector may also be suspicious about the government's intentions, given the record of nationalization in the past. On the other hand, the government may not be willing to sell assets to foreign investors.

Political Constraints

Generally, the costs of privatization are borne by a small group of people, e.g. the workers of the enterprise who may lose their jobs or the suppliers who may lose favoured contracts. The benefits, however, are spread out over a large number of people, sometimes a very large section of the population. Public choice theory suggests that in such situations, it will be easier to organize opposition to the privatization programme than support. Experience tells us that in many countries, privatization programmes fail to mobilize popular support, and in fact give rise to strong opposition.

Trade unions, in particular, tend to react strongly against privatization. Trade union power is often concentrated in the public sector and the public sector provides a base for such power. Unions oppose privatization, not only because of the direct effect on employment, but also because of a fear that trade union power will be reduced in the private sector.

14.2.4 Some Critical Issues

Governments considering privatization of PSEs must first decide on a number of critical issues.

Should restructuring occur before or after sale of the unit?
Most PSEs will not fetch a good price if they are sold in their current condition. For historical reasons, many have excess workers, are burdened with obsolete machinery and technology, and often are run bureaucratically. Such unrestructured enterprises will fetch lower prices. One option before the government is to restructure these enterprises before placing them on the market, e.g. by laying off excess workers, by inducting new workers with appropriate skills, by selling off non-strategic parts of the business, computerization of operations, etc. These enterprises will then become attractive to private investors who would be willing to pay high prices for them. On the other hand, proponents of speedy privatization argue that the attempt to restructure these enterprises before sales will inevitably lead to delays and the entire momentum for privatization will be lost. Further, it is doubtful whether the governments are at all adept at restructuring.

How to deal with the problem of laying off workers?
The overstaffing in PSEs means that the restructuring process would generally involve laying off part of the workforce. Usually, forced dismissals are politically infeasible and

only generate more opposition to privatization. Governments therefore try to adopt some kind of voluntary approach. Components of voluntary approaches that have been tried out include monetary compensation (e.g. through voluntary retirement schemes), retraining, and redeployment.

Sometimes the government agrees to accept a lower price for the enterprise in return for an assurance from the new owner that employees will be retained even after privatization. In the East German privatization programme, there is an instance where an enterprise was sold for one Deutschmark, because the bidder promised to retain all the workers.

Retraining can refer to giving workers training in skills that would help them to become productive members of the PSE itself. Or the aim may be to enable them to find alternative jobs in the private sector. Redeployment can be from one government PSE or Department to another, or it can be to the private sector.

The process of laying off workers poses a number of difficulties:

1. The total cost of laying off workers can be quite high and may pose a problem to cash-strapped governments. The problem has been eased to a certain extent because multilateral agencies are now prepared to lend for severance pay packages.

2. It is not easy to estimate the right package. Usually, some rules of thumb are employed to arrive at the compensation package, e.g. paying one year's salary for every year's service. Generally, no attempt is made to find out whether the compensation offered is adequate or not.

   But to properly calculate the present value of the change in earnings resulting from dismissal, one must take account of not only salaries, but also bonuses and other cash benefits. In many industries, salaries in the public sector are higher than in the private sector, except for highly skilled employees. Moreover, it might take a long time for a laid-off worker to find an alternative employment, and earnings might be close to zero in the intervening period. Further, in most developing countries, the public sector provides health coverage as well as old age pension. The greater job security in the public sector also makes employment in this sector more attractive. If all these factors are to be taken into account, then the required compensation becomes sizeable.

   It might also be argued that in developing countries, where job opportunities are so limited, one employee in the public sector might have to support a large number of unemployed members of the family. The loss of this one person's income can affect many more individuals.

3. There is also another subtle problem involved here. Once a severance package has been formulated, only the high-productivity or the superior workers may accept the package and leave, because they are certain of getting jobs elsewhere. The PSE is left with the low-productivity workers. This is called the problem of adverse selection : since the package offered is not tailored to individual needs or characteristics, any employee gets to

consider the same package. But only the high-productivity workers find the package attractive and accept it.

Should the assets be given away or sold?

As we have noted earlier, one way of attempting privatization is to give vouchers to a group of people who can then use these vouchers to get stakes in enterprises of their choice. The free distribution of vouchers, perhaps to all the citizens of the country, is seen to satisfy the goal of equality and to create stakes in the privatization process for everybody. The latter could then help to overcome opposition to the privatization process. However, this method is difficult to implement in large economies. Moreover, dispersed ownership can lead to corporate governance problems. Therefore, many countries have opted for selling off the PSEs rather than giving them away. Those who have money or access to it are usually foreigners or people who have enriched themselves under the old system, and political opposition to the sales to these two groups of people can be quite strong.

One easy way of giving away an enterprise is to give stakes to the 'insiders', i.e. managers and workers of the enterprise. But this is considered to be inherently unfair to the populace at large, since it is their tax payments which helped in the setting up of the enterprise in the first place. Further, since valuation of the PSEs is a tricky business, there have been allegations that insiders often manage to grab hold of PSEs at throwaway prices by deliberately presenting a sick picture of the PSEs to the outside world and undervaluing the assets. This is partcularly important in transition economies with no experience in putting market values on land, buildings, or other assets.

14.2.4 Privatization in India

Privatization in India has followed two routes: disinvestment and granting more autonomy to PSEs.

Disinvestment

The Industrial Policy Statement of 24 July 1991 envisaged, for the first time, disinvestment of part of government equity holdings in selected PSEs. The following objectives were sought to be met through disinvestment of shares: provide market discipline, raise resources, encourage wider public participation, promote greater accountability, and improve the performance of PSEs. It was proposed that the revenue generated from disinvestment would be utilized in the two vital areas of health and education, particularly in the poor backward districts of the country.

On 20 November 1991, the GOI announced that it was offering 'packets' containing shares of 31 PSEs for sale by a competitive bidding process. A reserve price was determined for each packet (i.e. the price below which the packet would not be sold) and each packet was sold to the highest bidder. After about 3–6 months, buyers would be allowed to unbundle the shares and sell them on the stock market.

In 1992–3, buyers were allowed to bid for the shares of individual PSEs through an open auction.

Year	Number of shares sold (crore)	Amount raised (Rs crore)	Target (Rs crore)	Permitted bidders
1991-2	87.21	3038	2500	Insurance companies, mutual funds, banks
1992-3	43.93	1912	2500	All the above and private parties
1993-4	11.37	2292	2500	All the above and foreign institutional investors

Source: R.R. Vaidya (1995).

In the first year, the set of bidders was restricted to insurance companies, mutual funds, and banks. Moreover, shares were sold in bundles. The GOI was not committed to sell all the shares intended to be sold at the reserve price as no underwriters were appointed. Thus there was nobody to take up the unsold shares in the event of undersubscription.

Over time, the set of bidders was enlarged. Moreover, the shares were not sold in bundles. This helped the GOI to get better prices for the shares. Beginning from 1991–2, till 2000, 14 rounds of disinvestments of government share holding have taken place in 39 PSEs and a total amount of about Rs 18,288 crore has been realized.

Underpricing of shares

If one of the primary objectives of disinvestment is to generate revenues for the government, then possible underpricing of shares becomes an important issue. In the Indian context, Vaidya (1995) made an attempt to calculate the extent of underpricing, if any, in the initial rounds. For this purpose, one can look at the difference between the prices at which shares were initially sold by the government and the closing price of the shares on the first day they were traded at a stock exchange (call this 'D'). However, in India, there was a considerable time lapse between the time the shares were sold and the time when they were allowed to be sold on the stock exchanges. During this time period, there would be a general trend of movement of stock prices which should be netted out to find the extent of underpricing. Therefore Vaidya used an adjustment factor based on the *Economic Times* (share price) index to deflate D.

Vaidya's calculations revealed the following:

- In the 1991–2 rounds, the revenue loss due to underpricing of shares was Rs 8916.61 crore. Of this amount, Rs 4383.58 crore could be attributed to the sale of shares of one company only—Neyveli Lignite.
- The extent of underpricing was considerably lower thereafter. For the October 1992 round, it was Rs 319.07 crore, while for the December 1992 round it was Rs 485.73 crore. In the March 1994 round, it was only Rs 90.87 crore.

Why did this underpricing occur? As we have noted, in the earlier rounds, the government was not committed to sell all the shares intended to be sold at the reserve price as no underwriters were appointed. Thus there was nobody to take up the unsold shares in the event of undersubscription. Moreover, the set of bidders was restricted. Over time, the set of bidders was enlarged and there was more competition. Moreover, in the later rounds, the shares were not sold in bundles. This made them more attractive to buyers and helped the government to get better prices for the shares.

The Disinvestment Commission was constituted in 1996, for a limited period of three years, to advise the government on the extent, mode, timing, and pricing of disinvestment. The Commission has submitted 12 Reports in which recommendations have been given in respect of 58 PSEs. The tenure of the Commission was extended up to 30 November 1999. The term of the Commission ended on 30 November 1999 and the Commission as constituted has ceased to exist.

In the Budget Speech 1999–2000, the Finance Minister announced that the strategy towards public sector enterprises will continue to encompass a judicious mix of strengthening strategic units, privatizing non-strategic ones through gradual disinvestment or strategic sale, and devising viable rehabilitation strategies for weak units. It has also been decided that in the generality of cases, the government shareholdings in PSE would be brought down to 26 per cent. In cases of PSEs involving strategic considerations, the government will continue to retain majority holding.

In order to give greater impetus to the disinvestment programme and expedite the disinvestment of government equity, the government has constituted a Cabinet Committee on Disinvestment (CCD). The Committee is headed by the Prime Minister. The government has set up a separate Department of Disinvestment to handle disinvestment of government equity. The government decided, on the recommendations of the Disinvestment Commission, to reduce its shareholding to below 51 per cent through strategic alliance in certain PSEs like Modern Food Industries Limited (MFIL), Bharat Aluminium Company Limited (BALCO), Indian Petrochemicals Corporation Limited (IPCL), and Madras Fertilisers Limited (MFL).

With the exceptions of the Lagan Jute Machinery Company Limited and Modern Food Industries (India) Limited, only minority stakes in different PSEs were sold till 2000. The Government is now emphasizing *strategic sales*. During the last quarter of 2000–1, 51 per cent shares of BALCO have been sold to a strategic investor. The government admits that its policy of selling only minority stakes had created a number of problems:

- It led to lower realizations from the disinvestment process because the management control is not transferred. Moreover, it signalled a lack of commitment to efficient governance of PSEs.

- With the limited holding remaining with the government after minority sales, only small stakes can be offered to the strategic partner, if it is decided to go for a strategic sale subsequently. This depresses the possibility of higher realizations from the strategic partner, especially since the latter has to offer the same price to other shareholders also through an open offer.

- The minority sales also give the impression that the main objective of the government is to obtain funds for reducing its fiscal deficit.

Despite the government's stated objectives, in practice, the revenues generated from the disinvestment process have been utilized to reduce fiscal deficits. Targets have not been met and the entire process has been plagued by huge delays. The process as well as the selection of particular units for sale have generated sharp controversies (the attempt to divest the government's stake in BALCO being the latest example) and the Government of India has not been able to form a national consensus in favour of privatization.

TABLE 14.1 PROCEEDS FROM DISINVESTMENT

Year	Rs in crore
1991–2	3038
1992–3	1913
1993–4*	NIL
1994–5	4843
1995–6	362
1996–7	380
1997–8	902
1998–9	5371
1999–2000	1479
Total	18,288

Source: http://divest.nic.in/performance.htm
* Proceeds received in 1994–5.

Navratnas and Mini-ratnas

In addition to disinvestment, in 1997 the government had identified 11 public sector companies, that have comparative advantages, as *Navratnas* and granted substantially enhanced autonomy to the Boards of Directors of these PSEs to enable them to become global players. These enterprises are IOC, IPCL, ONGC, BPCL, HPCL, NTPC, SAIL, VSNL, BHEL, GAIL, and MTNL. The criteria for selecting the enterprises included factors like size, performance, nature of activity, future prospects, and the potential to develop into world level players.

The Boards of these PSEs have been broad based by appointment of part-time non-official Directors. These enterprises, subject to certain guidelines, would now enjoy freedom to make capital expenditure, enter into joint ventures, effect organizational restructuring, create and wind up posts below Board level, raise capital from the domestic and international markets, establish financial joint ventures subject to equity investments with specified limits, etc.

The government has also granted enhanced financial, managerial, and operational autonomy to other profit-making enterprises, called *mini-ratnas*. These enterprises should have earned profits continuously for the last three years, have positive net worth, not seek budgetary support or guarantees from the government, and have not defaulted in the repayment of loans/interests to the government. These enterprises can incur capital expenditure, enter into joint ventures, set up technological and strategic alliances, formulate schemes of human resources management, etc., subject to certain stipulations and guidelines. This is designed to make them more efficient and competitive. As on 31 December 1999 there were 39 enterprises categorized as mini-ratna.

14.3 A MODEL OF THE INTERACTION BETWEEN PRIVATE AND PUBLIC SECTOR

Finally, we consider a model built by Fershtman that examines the interaction between a private sector and a public sector firm. The model yields some surprising results about the relative performance of these two types of firms.

Consider a duopoly in which the first firm is partly nationalized while the second firm is privately owned. There is no ambiguity about the objective of the second firm—it tries to maximize profit. The partly nationalized firm's objective, on the other hand, is assumed to be a mix of the goals of profit maximization and social welfare maximization.

The inverse demand curve facing the firms is linear and of the form $p = a - (q_1 + q_2)$. Both firms have identical linear cost functions $C_i = cq_i, i = 1, 2$ (so that we are abstracting from any inefficiencies associated with nationalization). Assume that $a > c$. The i-th firm's profit is then

$$\pi_i = \{a - (q_1 + q_2) - c\}q_i, i = 1, 2.$$

The social welfare is obtained by adding the consumer surplus and producer surplus for any output level. It is, therefore, the area under the inverse demand curve less the total cost of production. That is,

$$W(q_1, q_2) = \int_0^{q_1+q_2} (a - z)dz - c(q_1 + q_2) = Q(a - 0.5Q - c), \text{ where } Q = q_1 + q_2.$$

Now, the reaction function of the privately-owned firm is obtained by maximizing its profit, treating q_2 as fixed. The reaction function can then be expressed as

$$q_2 = (a - q_1 - c)/2. \tag{14.1}$$

If the partly nationalized firm were to maximize its profit, then its reaction function would be given by $q_1^{\#} = (a - q_2 - c)/2$. If it were to maximize social welfare, then its reaction function would be $q_1^{\sim} = (a - q_2 - c)$. Let t be the proportion of the government's control of the firm. Fershtman assumes that the conflict between the two interest groups (the government and the private owners) in the first firm is resolved by a compromise. In terms of the compromise, the choice of the output by the partly nationalized firm is a combination of $q_1^{\#}$ and $q_1^{\sim}$:

$$q_1 = tq_1^{\#}(q_2) + (1 - t)q_1^{\sim}(q_2) = (a - q_2 - c)(1 + t)/2. \tag{14.2}$$

From (eqn 14.1) and (eqn 14.2), we can solve for the Cournot–Nash equilibrium. We find that

$$q_1^* = (1 + t)(a - c)/(3 - t) \text{ and } q_2^* = (1 - t)(a - c)/(3 - t),$$

while the equilibrium price is
$$p^* = \{(1 - t)a + 2c\}/(3 - t).$$
The equilibrium profits are $(p^* - c)q_i^*$, and they can be calculated to be
$$\pi_1^* = (a - c)^2(1 - t^2)/(3 - t)^2 \text{ and}$$
$$\pi_2^* = (1 - t)^2(a - c)^2/(3 - t)^2.$$
Several interesting results can now be obtained:

1. The equilibrium total quantity increases, and therefore the equilibrium price declines, as t increases. In other words, stronger the government's control over the partly nationalized firm, the larger is the output produced in the market and smaller the price, and hence the larger the social welfare. It can be easily checked that the output of the partly nationalized firm increases while that of the privately owned firm decreases as t increases.

2. When $0 < t < 0.6$, i.e. when the government owns less than 60 per cent of firm 1, the equilibrium profits of firm 1 are above the regular Cournot equilibrium profits (= 1/3 when both firms maximize profit).

3. In the duopolistic market described above, so long as $0 < t < 1$, the partly nationalized firm has higher profits than the private sector competitor.

Therefore, the partly nationalized firm does unambiguously better than the privately owned firm in terms of the standard capitalist criterion of profit maximization. The result is to be explained by the fact that the objective of the partly nationalized firm—a mixture of profit and social welfare maximization—makes its response in the market strategically more aggressive in that it always chooses to produce more than a purely profit-maximizing firm. As Fershtman explains it, 'the partial nationalization serves as a credible commitment to increase output beyond the profit-maximizing level'.

Of course, these results depend on the assumption that the two firms are equally efficient and have the same cost function. If the partly nationalized firm is less efficient, then nationalization will increase the market share of the inefficient firm and may result in lower social welfare.

15   Public Policy II: Competition Law

As mentioned in the earlier chapter, the performance of a firm also depends critically on its non-market environment. In the non-market environment, of special interest is the interaction between the firm and the government. Even in free market economies, the government plays an important role as a referee to enforce the 'rules of the game'. In this chapter we examine some of these interactions.

15.1 COMPETITION LAW

An important element of the institutional framework in which firms in many countries have to operate is competition policy. There are two main aspects of a competition policy. The first involves putting in place a set of policies that enhance competition in local and national markets. These would include a liberalized trade policy, relaxed foreign investment and ownership requirements, and economic deregulation. The second is legislation designed to prevent anti-competitive business practices and unnecessary government intervention—*competition law*. Competition law (or antitrust law) lays down rules for competitive rivalry which are administered by government agencies created for this purpose.

The fundamental rationale of competition policy lies in the proposition that competition yields benefits that are lost through monopoly and practices that reduce competition. In an earlier chapter, we showed that perfect competition in a market leads to maximum value creation. But this is a rather static result. In a more dynamic setting, competition policy highlights the importance of market competition to drive down costs and prices, induce firms to produce the goods consumers want, and spur innovation and the expansion of new markets from abroad.

What precisely is meant by the terms 'competition' and 'monopoly'? Perfect competition requires fulfilment of a number of conditions simultaneously. Pure monopoly is also an unrealistic concept. Since one cannot hope to meet perfectly competitive and pure monopoly markets in reality, one can try to think of markets that are 'approximately competitive' and 'approximately monopolistic'. But then exactly where does one draw the dividing lines?

An attempt has been made to define 'workable competition'. The idea was first enunciated by economist J. M. Clark in 1940. He argued that the goal of policy should be to make competition 'workable', not necessarily perfect. He proposed criteria for judging whether competition was workable, and this provoked a series of revisions and counter-proposals. The criteria put forward are wide ranging, e.g. the number of firms should be at least large as economies of scale permit, promotional expenses should not be excessive, and advertising should be informative. No consensus has arisen over what might constitute workable competition but all regulatory bodies which administer competition policy in effect employ some version of it.

Moreover, the theory of the second best suggests that when two or more markets are not perfectly competitive, then efforts to correct only one of the distortions may in fact drive the economy further away from Pareto efficiency.[1] Thus, for example, if there is one industry which can never satisfy all the conditions for perfect competition, it is no longer clear that the optimal policy is to move the remaining industries towards perfect competition. Moreover, the conditions under which Pareto efficiency can be achieved under these circumstances are complex and not likely to be implementable.

Thus, the defence of competition policy often requires giving weight to more than Pareto efficiency. For example, competition policy may be defended on the grounds of equity, democracy, and incentives. However, achievement towards Pareto efficiency is generally given more weight in the application of competition policy.

There are two main domains of anitrust law—market structure and business conduct. These two are interlinked, since business conduct can modify market structure and market structure in turn allows certain types of conduct. In the US, the three issues that antitrust laws have sought to address are:

- Monopolies and attempts to monopolize
- Unreasonable restraints of trade
- Potentially anti-competitive actions

Practices that come under antitrust laws can be classified as horizontal or vertical. A horizontal practice involves activities in the same industry. Vertical practices involve firms with supply arrangements or along a channel of distribution. Examples of horizontal practices are: mergers within the same industry, monopolization, predatory pricing, price fixing, bid rigging, allocation of customers and group boycotts. Examples of vertical practices are: allocation of territories, refusals to deal, exclusive dealing arrangements, retail price maintenance, reciprocal arrangements, and tying. Some of these terms are explained below.

15.1.1 Horizontal practices

- Horizontal merger: Two firms in the same industry merge.
- Horizontal price fixing (collusion): Explicit or implicit agreements in an industry to control prices.
- Price discrimination: Charging customers different prices that are not justified by cost differences of serving these customers.
- Predatory pricing: Selling at price below cost to drive out rival firms.
- Bid rigging: Particular form of collusive *price-fixing* behaviour by which firms coordinate their bids on procurement or project contracts. There are

---

[1]Pareto efficiency is attained when it is not possible to make even one agent better off without making somebody worse off.

two common forms of bid rigging. In the first, firms agree to submit common bids, thus eliminating price competition. In the second, firms agree on which firm will be the lowest bidder and rotate in such a way that each firm wins an agreed upon number or value of contracts.

15.1.2 Vertical practices

- Refusal to deal: A manufacturer refuses to sell to a distributor or a retailer.
- Exclusive dealing: A manufacturer grants another firm an exclusive right to distribute a product.
- Exclusive territory: A manufacturer grants an exclusive territory to a seller and no other seller is permitted to sell in that territory.
- Retail price maintenance: A manufacturer sets a minimum price below which a retailer cannot sell.

15.1.3 Per se violations and the Rule of reason

Certain violations of the existing competition law are held to be so serious that they are held to be *per se* (as such) illegal. As the Supreme Court of the USA stated (Northern Pacific Railroad Co. vs. U.S. 1 (1958)): 'there are certain agreements or practices which because of their pernicious effect on competition and lack of any redeeming virtue are conclusively presumed to be unreasonable and therefore illegal without elaborate inquiry as to the precise harm they have caused or the business excuse for their use'. The only defence allowed is that the defendant did not commit the act.

However, other cases are considered by authorities on the basis of a *rule of reason*. Under the rule of reason, a firm's actions have to be shown to be *unreasonable* if they are to be penalized. Thus an attempt is made to evaluate the pro-competitive features of a restrictive business practice against its anti-competitive effects in order to decide whether or not the practice should be prohibited. Some market restrictions which *prima facie* give rise to competition issues may on further examination be found to have valid efficiency-enhancing benefits. For example, a manufacturer may restrict the supply of a product in different geographic markets only to existing retailers so that they earn higher profits and have an incentive to advertise the product and provide better service to customers. This may have the effect of expanding the demand for the manufacturer's product more than the increase in quantity demanded at a lower price.

There are two defences available to a defendant under a rule of reason—either that the act in question was not committed or that it was not unreasonable for the defendant to commit the act. In evaluating whether an act was unreasonable or not, the purpose and the effects of the practice must be considered.

15.2 DIFFERENT APPROACHES

Anitrust or competition law is influenced by the prevailing school of thought about the purposes of antitrust law and the consequences of specific practices. The traditional or structural approach held sway till the 1970s, when it was confronted with the

Chicago school of thought. In recent years, research by economists into strategic interactions has also shaped the thinking on these issues.

15.2.1 The Traditional Approach

The traditional approach is concerned with limiting economic power and providing fairness to market participants. Economic power is a function of the number of firms in the industry, or correspondingly, their market shares. This relationship is captured by the generalized Lerner index:

$$(p - mc)/p = 1/(ne),$$

where p is price, mc is marginal cost, n is the number of firms in the industry, and e is the market price elasticity of demand. In a perfectly competitive industry, $p = mc$. In imperfectly competitive industries, there is a wedge between price and marginal cost, and this wedge is bigger, the smaller is the number of firms and more inelastic the demand. Empirical studies that show a positive correlation between industry concentration and profitability as predicted in the Lerner index support the traditional view.

In the traditional view, therefore, the focus is on rectifying the market structure, through breaking up of monopolies, ordering the divestiture of units, requiring stringent standards for mergers and licensing technologies to all those who want to use them.

The tradititonal approach has some other implications:

1. The larger the number of firms in the market, the better it is. Since a large number of firms are needed to provide vigorous competition, it may be necessary to protect some of them from rivals, particularly from predatory behaviour or from unfair advantages such as not having access to low price inputs.

2. Vertical arrangements should be viewed with suspicion because they necessarily limit opportunities for competitors. Resale price maintenance, exclusive dealerships, etc., foreclose opportunities for competitors.

3. The economic power of the incumbent firms can be checked by the threat of new entry. But the potential for entry is limited by the existence of barriers to entry.

4. Since entry in many industries may be difficult, and economic power is concentrated in a small number of firms, incumbent firms are likely to engage in collusive behaviour. The empirical literature that finds a positive correlation between concentration and profitability could reflect this collusion—for example, collusion can lead to price-fixing. This provides an additional reason why authorities should closely scrutinize concentrated markets.

15.2.2 The Chicago School

The Chicago School views the ultimate purpose of antitrust policy as promoting economic efficiency. In a simple setting, this implies the maximization of the sum of consumers' surplus and producers' surplus. Since economic efficiency depends on the level of prices, the focus is on the prices that consumers pay. A price equal to marginal cost is efficient, regardless of whether it results from a perfectly competitive market or a monopolistic market where the price is kept down by the threat of potential entry. Hence the focus of the Chicago School is on performance rather than the structure of the industry.

In contrast to the traditional approach, which views markets as fragile and prone to failure, the Chicago School feels that markets are resilient. Rather than government intervention, consumers are best protected by competition. The conditions for perfect competition are sufficient, but not necessary, for economic efficiency. Even if there are few firms, competition can be vigorous. Supernormal profits attract entry and the Chicago School is sceptical about the nature and scope of barriers to entry. If entry is relatively easy, then firms cannot exercise market power for long. In fact, the Chicago School feels that the only sustainable barrier to entry is the relative efficiency of incumbent firms. The positive correlation between concentration and profitability can be due to the superior efficiency of the firms that survive the competitive process.

The Chicago School also feels that collusion among firms is unlikely to be sustainable because of the incentive to cheat. Collusion is most likely to be effective when there is government regulation or protection.

One consequence of the emphasis on the strength of competitive forces is that the Chicago School is not generally in favour of applying the *per se* criterion. The performance in a market must be evaluated while judging practices under antitrust laws. This is equally true of vertical practices. Further, it becomes important to define the relevant market. Both present and potential competition must be considered. The relevant market includes not only the product in question but also potential substitutes that can offer competition.

15.2.3 The Strategic Approach

The new economics of industrial organization has given birth to the strategic approach which is different from the other two approaches. The strategic approach emphasizes the repeated interactions between players in the market and the possibility of implicit collusion sustained by these repeated interactions. Even when firms act in a non-cooperative manner, a collusive equilibrium can be sustained through the threat of punishment in future plays. Moreover, interactions over time can allow firms to develop reputations for 'toughness' that dissuade new firms from entering the market. Possibilities for such strategic behaviour are greater when there is incomplete information about various relevant variables.

15.3 Some Issues in Competition Law

15.3.1 Mergers

A merger refers to an *amalgamation* or joining of two or more firms into an existing firm or to form a new firm. A merger is a method by which firms can increase their size and expand into existing or new economic activities and markets.

The UK Fair Trading Act of 1973 gives a very wide definition of a merger situation. According to this Act, as a result of a merger, two or more enterprises cease to be distinct (or, in the case of proposed mergers, arrangements will be in progress or in contemplation which will lead to enterprises ceasing to be distinct). There are two ways in which enterprises can 'cease to be distinct': (a) they are brought under common ownership or control or (b) there is an arrangement or transaction between the persons carrying on the enterprises so that one of them will cease to exist to be carried on in order to prevent competition between them. Control here does not necessarily mean acquisition of outright voting control; situations falling short of outright control where Company A may acquire the ability materially to influence the policy of Company B could be considered by the authorities.

Mergers are classified into three types:

- *Horizontal Merger*: Merger between firms that produce and sell the same products, i.e. between competing firms. Horizontal mergers can be viewed as *horizontal integration* of firms in a market or across markets.

- *Vertical Merger*: Merger between firms operating at different stages of production, e.g. from raw materials to finished products to distribution. An example would be a steel manufacturer merging with an iron ore producer. Vertical mergers usually increase economic efficiency, although they may sometimes have an anti-competitive effect.

- *Conglomerate Merger*: Merger between firms in unrelated business, e.g. between an automobile manufacturer and a food processing firm.

A variety of motives may exist for mergers: to increase economic efficiency, to acquire market power, to diversify, to expand into different geographic markets, to pursue financial and R&D synergies, etc. In evaluating the effects of a merger, the possible anti-competitive effects have to be balanced against the possible gains in efficiency from the merger. Mergers make firms bigger and may enable them to reap economies of scale and scope. There can be better production planning, adjustment to changing technology, and more effective utilization of central staff resources. There are some empirical studies which indicate that even though increases in efficiency or adaptations to changing market conditions can occur through internal growth, mergers and acquisitions may be a speedier and less costly means.

The first step in reviewing a merger is to properly define the relevant market. Next, the government determines whether the proposed merger will greatly increase concentration (and hence, presumably, market power). Concentration is usually measured by the four-firm concentration ratio (where the market shares of the four largest firms are added up) or the Herfindahl–Hirschman Index (HHI, which involves taking the squares of the market shares of the firms in the industry and adding them up). This procedure implicitly assumes that (a) after a merger the firms involved will retain their market shares and (b) the merged firm will have a market share equal to the sum of the pre-merger shares. For example, suppose that initially there are five firms in the market, each with a market share of 20 per cent. Then the pre-merger HHI is $(20)^2 + (20)^2 + (20)^2 + (20)^2 + (20)^2 = 2000$. Two of the firms merge. The post-merger HHI is $(40)^2 + (20)^2 + (20)^2 + (20)^2 = 2800$.

In defining the market, the important thing is to identify competing products and the geographical area in which competition is taking place. It may be obvious that Coke and Pepsi are in the same market but it may not be so obvious that Mirinda is also in the same market. In merger cases, firms try to argue for a broader definition of the market (in which their market share would be smaller). Competing products may either be demand substitutes or supply substitutes. A demand substitute of a product X is a product Y such that buyers will switch to Y if the price of X rises. A supply substitute of X is a product Y which will be produced in greater quantity if X's price goes up. In evaluating the anti-competitive effects of a merger, the potential as well as current substitutes must be identified. Sometimes the degree of substitution depends on the current prices. Fuel cell powered cars may not be susbtitutes for petrol-run cars at current petrol prices, but may become substitutes if the price of petrol increases sufficiently.

The traditional remedy for a merger that has anti-competitive effects is divestiture, complete or partial. Complete divestiture is aimed at completely undoing the merger so that the market is restored to its pre-merger structure. However, sometimes a merger will have anti-competitive effects in some markets but not others. In such cases, divestiture may be confined to the assets serving the markets adversely affected. The authorities can also try to 'prevent and restrain' illegal mergers and acquisitions. This means that the authorities move before the merger is actually completed.

Box 15.1. GE's bid to take over Honeywell

When General Electric (GE) tried to take over Honeywell, the aerospace company, in a $41 billion deal, it ran into opposition from the European Commission. The European Commission, the European Union's (EU's) competition watchdog, estimated in its statement of objections to the deal that the combined company would have more than 90 per cent of the market for large regional jet engines. The Commission also estimated that the merged group would have a 65 per cent market share in marine gas turbines. Much of the statement of objections focused on the potential for GE to bundle its engines with Honeywell's aerospace components and avionics, and offer price discounts. The Commission thought that this could, over the longer term, force rivals out of the market.

In response, the GE said that it was prepared to dispose of some of its business to allay the Commission's fears. GE has already agreed to sell off Honeywell's military helicopter engines division.

Source: *The Financial Times*, various articles from *FT.com*

So far as vertical integration is concerned, a number of arguments have been advanced as to why such integration would have anti-competitive effects. One argument is that vertical integration leads to an increase in the barriers to entry. It makes it difficult to enter a single stage of production and/or distribution, thus requiring integrated entry at both stages. This drives up capital requirements and increases entry barriers. As economists of the Chicago School have pointed out, integrated entry may require more capital, but new firms should be able to raise the required amount of capital from the market. Moreover, it does not follow that vertical integration by one or more firms leads to a situation where integrated entry is the only feasible alternative. Another argument is the foreclosure argument. Suppose X Shoe company takes over a retailer Y who from now on will be required to stock only shoes made by X. Makers of other brands of shoes will now be precluded from Y's segment of the market. However, so long as Y was not the only distributor in the market, the foreclosure argument does not follow. Therefore, horizontal integration in the retail market is required for the vertical integration to have anti-competitive implications, and hence vertical mergers do not seem to provide new cause for concern.

15.3.2 Vertical Arrangements

Vertical arrangements involve restrictions imposed by a manufacturer on the sales and distribution of its products. These restrictions are determined through contractual negotiations between the manufacturer and its distributors. Examples of vertical restrictions are requirements that the dealer sell a minimum number of units (quantity forcing), that dealers charge no lower than a particular price (resale price maintenance), that distributors not locate near to each other (exclusive territories), that distributors not sell competing products (exclusive dealing), etc.

Vertical restrictions may have some anti-competitive effects, but they may also benefit both firms and consumers. First, consider some situations where vertical restrictions can be used to create or support monopolies.

(i) Suppose that there is a group of dealers who can only sell a product A. It is difficult for any new entrants to sell A. Then the dealers can force the manufacturer to grant them exclusive territories, leading to local monopolies and restricted competition.

(ii) A group of manufacturers want to collude and fix prices. Wholesale prices that are charged to dealers are difficult to observe and therefore there is a possibility of cheating on fixed wholesale prices. But if all manufacturers agree to charge the same price at the retail level and use resale price maintenance to do so, then cheating is easier to detect.

(iii) Vertical restrictions can be used to increase the difficulty of entering an industry. This can be done by entering into exclusive dealing arrangements between incumbent manufacturers and dealers, so that new entrants will not be able to find distribution outlets.

On the other hand, it is now clear that vertical restrictions may have beneficial effects.

(i) Under quantity forcing, dealers are forced to sell a minimum amount, even if they have to lower their prices to do so.

(ii) If there is a double monopoly, i.e. there is monopoly both at the manufacturing as well as the distribution stage, then there are two levels of monopoly mark-up. The profit mark-up by the manufacturer raises the wholesale price above the marginal cost, while the profit mark-up by the distributor raises the retail price above the wholesale price. Thus, price paid by the final consumers is high and sales low. If more competition at the distributors' level can be introduced, then this problem can be solved. But if the monopoly at the distribution level cannot be disturbed, then, to counter the fall in volumes, the manufacturer may require the distributor to charge not more than a maximum price. This helps to reduce the gap between the wholesale price and the retail price.

(iii) Typically, several independent distributors distribute a firm's product. Each distributor benefits from the promotional activities of the other distributors without having to pay for them. Therefore, each has an incentive to free ride, i.e. invest less in promotional efforts, hoping that the efforts of the others will fill in the gap. But if every distributor behaves in this manner, then too little promotional activity is undertaken. The problem here is that the distributors do not have property rights over the fruits of their efforts. That is, they cannot exclude other distributors from enjoying the benefits of their efforts. To solve the problem of free-riding, exclusive territories may be granted. Each distributor would then be sure of capturing all the benefits from its promotional endeavours in the territory granted to it. Another solution is to require that each distributor charge a minimum price. It then becomes difficult for distributors to compete on price and gives them an incentive to compete on non-price dimensions, e.g. after-sales service.

It is therefore, clear that vertical arrangements can have both pro-competitive and anti-competitive effects and hence should be considered under the rule of reason rather than as *per se* violations of antitrust law.

The Chicago School distinguishes between interbrand and intrabrand competition in this context. Intrabrand competition refers to competition between dealers of the same brand, as in the case of two Amul cheese dealers competing with each other. These dealers also compete with sellers of Britannia cheese—interbrand competition. If interbrand competition is vigorous, so that a manufacturer does not have horizontal market power, then restrictions on intrabrand competition (Amul imposing resale price maintenance on its dealers) will not have significant anti-competitive effects.

15.3.3 Predatory Pricing

Predatory pricing, as we have already seen in Chapter 5, refers to the possibility of a dominant firm setting its price low to drive out competitors from the market. Obviously, such a low price inflicts losses on the predator. Bearing the losses is rational only if the predator can hope to outlast the victims (possesses greater staying power) and eventually be able to exploit the increased market power by raising prices. An additional argument is that the potential benefits need not be limited to the market where predation takes place. The predatory campaign can be viewed as an investment in reputation for 'toughness' which can benefit the predator in other geographical or product markets.

This theory of predation came under strong attack by a number of writers, including Areeda and Easterbrook, who argued that predation is irrational. First, the cost of predation would be higher for the dominant firm with its larger market share. Against the large and certain costs of predation must be set the discounted, uncertain future revenues. The future revenues are uncertain because the prey might enter into long-term contracts with customers (who would not want to see a competing supplier disappear), find financing to ride out the price-cutting, or shut down and wait for prices to rise.

Even if one particular victim does leave the market, the subsequent price rise will attract new firms and predatory pricing must be undertaken to drive these out. Therefore, the predator will never find a period of sufficient duration in which it can exercise monopoly power and recoup losses. Therefore, it would appear that sharing markets would be the rational option rather than predation.

The debate over the rationality and thus the frequency of predation is reflected in a parallel debate over the best legal rule to control it. Broadly speaking, those who believe that the threat of predation is inherently incredible and thus that attempts to predate will be rare find that the best medicine is no medicine at all, because any prescription could have undesirable effects on *legitimate* competitive pricing. Those who believe that predation is a real possibility are correspondingly more willing to try to curb it, and formulate rules against predatory pricing.

In the literature, the mistaking of predation for competitive pricing is termed a 'false negative' and the mistaking of competitive pricing for predation a 'false positive'. Both types of error pose serious if different problems for competition policy. To impose no rule against predatory pricing may pose risks of greater monopoly power through increased concentration or more disciplined collusion among existing firms. Rules which are overly inclusive can hinder competition either by deterring firms from pricing aggressively or by exposing those who do so to public or private enforcement actions to make them stop. Thus, the risks of false positive or false negative errors should be of concern in evaluating the various rules for analysing predatory pricing that have been suggested in the literature.

Bork, McGee, and Easterbrook[2] argue that predatory pricing is so rare that it should not be a matter of concern for competition policy officials. Most of what appears to be predatory pricing is actually competitive pricing. If predation is rare, practically any rule runs the risk of generating false positive errors, and those errors would multiply with the restrictiveness of the rule. An important point in this argument is that because predation is unlikely to be successful, it is self-deterring and, therefore, government intervention is not needed. Self-deterrence arises because if a firm (foolishly) attempts to predate, it inflicts losses on itself but ultimately gains no market power, as the victim calls its bluff and weathers the predatory campaign. At some point the predation ceases and the predator, having punished itself, refrains from further attempts.

Areeda and Turner (1975) have suggested that a firm's pricing is predatory if its price is less than short run marginal cost. The logic is that no firm will profitably choose to price below marginal cost. But since it is difficult to observe marginal cost, the average variable cost can be used as a proxy for short run marginal cost data. Many economists have responded to the article by Areeda and Turner. Some have suggested the use of average cost, some the use of long-run marginal cost. It is obvious that if such tests were used, then one of the main issues in any antitrust action would be to distinguish a firm's variable costs from its fixed costs.

---

[2]See *References*.

The difficulty of calculation costs led Baumol to suggest a test based on price increases after successful predation. Baumol would require any price cut made in response to entry to continue for a considerable period of time after exit. In effect, Baumol's rule would prohibit the earning of monopoly profits and thus restrict the incentive of the predator to incur losses in the first instance.

15.3.4 International Harmonization of Competition Laws

So far, we have been discussing competition laws that operate at the national level. However, the question of the geographical level at which competition laws should operate is becoming increasingly important. Consider some of the possibilities:

- A firm has a dominant position in the Indian market but claims that the relevant market definition is the whole of South-East Asia.

- A supplier in the Indian national market is the branch of a multinational company (MNC), which has entered into an agreement with other MNCs to share out the world market by assigning different economies to different suppliers.

- The Indian market may be served by a group of American firms that have formed an export cartel.

One can argue that if the relevant market is 'national' in the sense that the good is 'non-tradeable' across national boundaries, then the national competition authority is the natural body to consider issues. If the market is international and the good is widely traded, then a higher (supra-national) authority is required (or full collaboration between the national authorities affected).

There is of course the question as to whether national authorities would be willing to submit to a supra-national authority, because such submission is sometimes viewed as an infringement of national sovereignty. Similarly, cooperation between different national authorities is also hard to achieve. This is particularly because competition policies are sometimes designed to protect domestic markets and to promote domestic producers in export markets. For example, a country may allow domestic producers to agree on predatory responses to attempts by foreign firms to enter the domestic market. Or it might permit vertical restraints that prevent foreign firms from getting access to existing distribution networks.

A further problem is that in practice it may not be easy to distinguish between traded and non-traded goods. An example is a heavy construction material like cement. Because of transport costs, one might expect cement to be non-traded across national boundaries. However, if prices of cement are high in the domestic market, this might make it possible for low-cost suppliers in other countries located at deep-water ports to start supplying cement. The competition authority will need to consider carefully the potential for entry via imports in assessing whether a firm is in a dominant position.

Scherer (1996) has pointed out that international competition policy is an important issue for developing countries. He distinguishes between three types of concerns here:

1. In many developing countries, the export of primary agricultural or mineral commodities is the main source of earnings from foreign trade. To stabilize prices, countries sometimes form cartels for such commodities, e.g. the

leading oil-exporting nations participate in the OPEC cartel. If developing nations believe that cartelization of primary exports will be successful under some circumstances, they will be reluctant to enter into international agreements that prohibit all cartels in international trade.

2. There is a fear that MNCs will agree among themselves on spheres of influence, designating specific customer nations or broad geographic areas as the exclusive market of a single enterprise. Moreover, most industrialized nations exempt export cartels formed by domestic firms from their competition law prohibitions. Cartelization could affect not only the supply of equipment and raw materials to developing nations, but also the supply of licensed technology. In this respect, international competition policy codes that reduce non-tariff barriers to market access in developed countries could increase the export potential of developing country firms in two ways—by curbing buyer cartels and by easing the restrictions resulting from the domestic manufacturers' control over distribution channels.

3. Tough international competition policy codes would hit hard the restrictive practices employed by domestic firms in developing countries. It has been recognized that firms in developing countries may need some sort of infant-industry protection in their formative years to make them internationally competitive later on. As the tariffs are reduced in later years, however, countries like Japan and South Korea have tended to adopt permissive policies towards cartel formation and monopoly positions in home markets. Thus, the developing country government may itself act as 'cartel master' through quota assignments and monitoring, sometimes also through intra-industry coordination. As Scherer (1996) observes, 'Reconciling such trade-policy-induced cartelization with the prevailing norms of international competition policy poses difficult problems'.

15.3.5 Competition Policy in Dynamic Markets

As we have noticed, competition is favoured by competition law because it forces firms to pursue efficiency, product improvement, and vigorous innovation. However, questions have been raised about the usefulness of competition in a dynamic context. Members of the Austrian school (von Mises, Schumpeter, and Demsetz, to name a few), argue that economists in the mainstream tradition misuse the term competition by applying it to a state of affairs rather than a process. In other words, firms are engaged in a continuing dynamic competitive process, '. . . constantly creating new products and processes in order to gain a competitive advantage over their rivals' (Audretsch, Baumol, and Burke, 2001). Firms may temporarily gain monopoly power that allows them to earn monopoly profits. But this can only happen till rivals replicate their innovation or replace it with one that is superior. In industries where entry and exit is easy, firms will continue to enter till an additional firm can expect to earn only normal profit.

The Austrian school would argue that governments should not intervene to reduce the profits of firms, for (a) such profits are temporary prizes for winners in the competitive environment and (b) reducing the profits will reduce the incentive for existing firms and prospective entrants to engage in competitive innovation.

The Austrian approach has drawn attention to the need to reward with monopoly profits the product and process innovators who incur costs and take risks. The standard approach lays emphasis on the short term deadweight losses that follow from such (albeit temporary) monopolies. We must, therefore, conclude that regulation has to tread a thin line between preserving the incentives to engage in dynamic competition and ensuring that these rights are not employed to block entry into further rounds of dynamic competition. For example, entry can be blocked through the promotion of technological lock-in through the creation of network externalities.

BOX 15.2. NETWORK EXTERNALITY

A network externality exists when the value of a good depends on the number of people who use it. Consumers would like to be connected to as large a network as possible (e.g. telephone networks).

The key features of a market with network externality are:

- *Existence of a critical mass*: To be successful, a network must attract a certain number of users.

- *Excess inertia*: It follows that successful networks tend to be large. New entry is difficult and monopoly concerns are present.

- *Tipping*: When successful, product penetration can be very fast. Once consumers expect a standard to 'win', fears about getting stuck with the wrong standard diminish, and there is a self-reinforcing rush to adopt the new standard.

Thus, once a product is established in the market, the demand for similar products will collapse—consumers get 'locked in'. And if they get locked in to a bad product, there is another market failure to compound the first one (i.e. monopoly).

The classic example of the 'bad standard', or of 'path dependence' as this syndrome is called, is the QWERTY keyboard (these are the first 5 letters on the top left hand corner of the keyboard). It is claimed that the layout makes no sense, but by an accident of history it has established itself and there is no getting rid of it.

'But The Fable of the Keys', a paper by Stan Liebowitz and Stephen Margolis, shows that the QWERTY story was wrong, because the standard layout is not in fact demonstrably worse than the alternatives. Lock-in is inefficient (that is, it is a kind of market failure) only if the inferior product survives despite the fact that the benefits of switching would exceed the costs. If the inferior product survives because the costs of switching are high, that is as it should be: in that case it would be inefficient to switch.

Moreover, where lock-in is a factor, on both sides of the transaction, there is an incentive to find ways around the problem:

- On the demand side, groups of consumers can get together and coordinate their choices.

- On the supply side, producers can start by selling their superior new product at a loss: if it really is superior, the market will adopt it and move across.

- Or producers can spend heavily on advertising.

- Or producers can help newcomers to switch by promising compatibility, as when cable-television companies offer to convert old televisions to the new system.

With these and other strategies, it becomes an empirical question whether inefficient lock-in is as common as is often supposed; it is certainly not self-evident.

The Austrian school's view of the welfare-enhancing effects of entrepreneurial activity has been contested by writers who point out that dynamic competition can give rise to excessive product differentiation, excessive advertising, patent hoarding, etc. In such situations, regulation may be needed even though monopoly profits serve to encourage innovation.

15.4 THE INDIAN CONTEXT

In the Indian context, the non-market environment was largely determined by government policy till the mid 1980s. From the mid 1980s, a process of liberalization was set in motion, and other elements of the non-market environment are becoming more important. Yet Indian managers can only build on the industrial and organizational structures that they inherited. It is, therefore, important to understand the nature of industrial policy in the early years.

15.4.1 Industrial Policy Regime on the Eve of Reforms

In the industrial policy regime on the eve of the reforms in 1991, the public sector, financed from public savings, still had the role of prime mover. Certain industries were reserved for public sector. Its scope included

- strategic industries like defence, atomic energy, and aerospace
- industries believed to play a critical role in industrial development like steel and non-ferrous metals.

The second component of the policy regime was import-substitution, and self-reliance in key sectors of the industry was a major objective.

Thirdly, the government arrogated to itself powers to direct private investment into sectors targeted by state planners. Licensing was the main instrument to achieve this, with the stated aims behind licensing being threefold: (i) to prevent concentration of economic power, (ii) development of backward regions, and (iii) exclusive reservation of some areas for SSI (small-scale industry) units.

Import licensing and high tariffs were used to regulate access to imports and foreign technology. There was regulation of technology imports and payments for technology, to prevent 'repetitive import of technology'. Regulatory powers were also vested in the government under the Monopolies and Restrictive Trade Practices Act (MRTP) and Foreign Exchange Regulation Act (FERA). In the original MRTP Act, Section III contained provisions requiring prior approval of the Central Government for establishment of a new undertaking, expansion of existing undertaking, amalgamation, merger, takeover of undertakings, and appointment of directors.

15.4.2 Adverse Consequences of the Pre-reform Industrial Policy

Efficiency

The industrial policy regime had very adverse effects on efficiency in the industrial sector. Among other things, it led to the following:

- Distortions in the incentive structure and promotion of 'rent-seeking' activities. The barriers to entry resulted in some markets coming under the control of one or few firms. The costs of these enterprises due to government policies (high excise duties and other taxes, high costs of materials, and poor quality) could be offset by high prices possible because of the weak competition. Firms, therefore, were given the incentive to try to obtain monopoly status but not attain efficiency in their operations. The import quotas and high tariffs also gifted supernormal profits for the existing firms which tended to become inefficient in the absence of competitive pressures.

- There was large unsatisfied demand in industries with severe entry restrictions— mainly consumer durables. Since consumers had to pay high prices, this also reduced the firms' incentive to export.

- The specification of size and location of the plants resulted in targeted capacity being shared between several medium sized units, which were unable to exploit scale economies.

- The restrictions on technology imports generally did not lead to the development of indigenous technology. On the other hand, it prevented modernization because introduction of advanced technologies and products became more difficult.

Growth

The adverse consequences on growth were equally serious:

- The high rate of protection led to a bias against export industries.

- State monopoly over infrastructure led to critical bottlenecks.

- Controls on the capital market retarded its expansion and deepening, leading to a high dependence on public sector financial institutions, both for debt and equity.

- The financial structure kept long-term interest rates well below short-term rates, resulting in diversion of investment funds into running expenses. Since the Controller of Capital Issues kept issue prices for shares artificially low, companies depended less on equity and more on cheap long-term debt. High debt-equity ratios and subsidized long term credit led to perverse incentives that encouraged siphoning of funds from units.

- Restrictions on repetitive import of technology meant that in several sectors Indian plants were unable to modernize.

15.4.3 Favourable effects of the Pre-reform Industrial Policy

One should not draw the conclusion that the policy regime did not have any merits. In a number of instances, it had favourable effects on the development of Indian industries.

- Due to weak patent protection, Indian drug firms could innovate new processes to manufacture the same molecules and Indian consumers could get drugs at low prices that were unmatched in the world.

- The restrictions on repetitive imports helped standardize the design and size of capital goods in some industries, leading to international competitiveness in the capital goods sector. It also forced the Indian capital good producers to develop considerable reverse engineering capability, along with R&D efforts aimed at modifying designs to suit Indian conditions and available construction materials.

- The restrictions on foreign firms helped Indian joint venture partners to negotiate terms favourable to them.

- The restrictions on the use of foreign brands helped the growth and strengthening of several strong domestic brands, a process not found in many developing countries.

15.4.4 Effects on the structure of Indian industry

How was Indian industry affected by all these factors? We can note a number of features that came to characterize the industry.

- Because of policy induced entry barriers and low level of competition, there was no incentive to develop capabilities for sustainable competitive strategies.

- Corporate growth and diversification strategies were shaped by the licensing policy and the ability of top management to lobby for licenses and procure scarce foreign exchange and bank finance. It was often difficult to expand even in profitable lines of business. On the other hand, entry restrictions meant that setting up units in almost any industry was profitable. Hence, unrelated diversification became a common phenomenon.

- Planners were often keen to encourage entry into targeted industries, and hence, several industries came to be plagued by over-capacity.

- SSI units using domestic inputs often provided severe price competition to large and medium units. Tax concessions and the unorganized nature of the labour market has given the small units cost advantages that are difficult to imitate in the organized segments of the industry.

It must be noted that incumbent foreign and domestic firms often managed to retain their market domination. Many of them began to source from small units and built high entry barriers through large scale advertising, product differentiation, and control over proprietary distribution channels.

It should be noted that the public sector was not always an inefficient monopolist, nor its domination pervasive:

- Many large private Indian and foreign firms were allowed to continue their operations. They undertook expansions during the 1970s, and came to dominate sectors.

- Severe price controls and lags in adjusting PSU product prices despite rapid inflation often crippled the PSUs financially and robbed them of the capacity to invest and modernize. This was compounded by political interference and the use of PSUs to subsidize one or the other pressure group or constituency.

- Some public sector units were well-managed enterprises, with assets, skills, and management that were unmatched in the Indian private sector.

It is in this backdrop that the industrial reforms were set in motion during the early 1990s and to these we now turn. It can be seen that a number of the reforms were liberalization measures, lifting the restrictions that the firms were subjected to in the earlier years. The reform measures can also be viewed as providing components of a competitive policy, since they made it easier for new entry to occur—e.g. complementary trade reforms allowed imports to compete with domestic production.

15.4.5 Industrial Reforms in India

Some of the most important elements of the post 1992 reforms included the following:

1. All licence requirements were abolished except for cars, drugs, coal and petroleum, sugar, defence equipment, white goods, cigarettes, and alcohol.
2. Automatic approval would be given to foreign investment for upto 51 per cent control except in high-tech areas.
3. MNCs were made welcome in most industries.
4. Trading companies were allowed entry.
5. All technology agreements would be on bilateral commercial terms and no restrictions would be imposed on this.
6. Priority for PSU investment would be limited to petroleum, infrastructure, and strategic and defence industries only.
7. Requirements of pre-entry scrutiny were removed by the MRTP (Amendment) Ordinance of 1991. Similarly, restrictions on M&A activity were abolished under the MRTP Act.

15.4.6 Trade Reforms

The industrial reforms were complimented by a host of trade reforms. The salient features of the pre-1991 regime were: import licensing for capital goods and raw materials and intermediates, high tariffs that averaged 80–100 per cent and sometimes were greater than 200 per cent, prohibition of imports of consumer goods and gold, a fixed exchange rate set by the Reserve Bank of India (RBI), requirement of RBI/government prior permission for payment for technology and services, and banning of foreign investment in Indian capital markets. All these measures insulated the domestic sector against competition from imports and prevented foreign investment and technology from entering the Indian economy. The post-1992 trade reforms significantly changed all these:

1. Import licensing was abolished.
2. The average tariff for capital goods came down to below 25 per cent, for intermediates etc. it was 40 per cent. The maximum rate of tariff was reduced to 65 per cent.

3. Consumer goods imports were allowed on the restricted list and against licence to exporters. Gold imports were allowed.

4. Foreign exchange markets now determine exchange rates.

5. Full current account convertibility has taken place; there is now freedom to pay for services.

6. Institutional investors are now allowed to invest in capital markets.

15.5 COMPETITION LAW IN INDIA

In the new liberalized scenario in India, it has become extremely important to ensure that firms do not indulge in anti-competitive practices. The existing Competition Law in India is the Monopolies and Restrictive Trade Practices Act, 1969 (MRTP Act). It has been felt that this Act is not adequate to deal with the challenges thrown up by liberalization and globalization and the contours of a new competition policy have been laid out by the S. V. S. Raghavan Committee. In this section, we examine the main features of the MRTP Act, pointing out its limitations, and then consider the Raghavan Committee's suggestions.

The existing Indian laws promoting competition consist of the following: the MRTP Act, the Consumer Protection Act (CPA) of 1986, the Sick Industries Companies Act, the Indian Companies Act, and the Essential Commodities Act [see Rao (1998)]. There are also other Acts, orders, rules, and procedures, which affect competition, e.g. the Standards, Weights and Measures Act, 1976, the Drugs and Cosmetics (Amendment) Act, 1964, etc. Here we focus on the MRTP Act and the CPA.

15.5.1 The MRTP Act

The present functions of the MRTP Commission may be summarized as follows:

- prevention of concentration of economic power which may be detrimental to public interest;
- control of restrictive trade practices;
- control of unfair trade practices; and
- control of monopolistic trade practices.

So far as prevention of concentration of economic power and control of monopolistic trade practices is concerned, the MRTP Commission's role is of an advisory nature and the power to issue the final order rests with the Central government. The Commission can, however, grant temporary injunctions if it starts some inquiry. So far as the monopolistic and restrictive trade practices are concerned, the MRTP Act is based on the principle of 'abuse' and not 'prohibition'. This is similar to the application of the rule of reason than *per se* illegality. The injury caused by such a practice is to be weighed against the reasonableness of the practice in the context of benefits accruing from it, and the benefits can be pleaded to take advantage of the 'gateways' or exemptions provided under the Act. The practices only become illegal after a 'cease and desist' order is passed: 'cease' means that the practice shall be discontinued and 'desist' means that the practice shall not be repeated.

The concept of an undertaking coming under the purview of the the MRTP Act was originally based on the asset criterion of Rs 1 crore. This asset-based criterion has now been removed, so that the sections under Chapter III now apply to any undertaking. Section 27 of this chapter empowers the government to direct the division of an undertaking, if it is of the opinion that the working of the undertaking is prejudicial to public interest, or has/will lead to monopolistic and restrictive trade practices. Section 27A provides for severance of interconnection between undertakings, if it is found detrimental to the principal undertaking or the growth of the industry or public interest.

Thus, the MRTP Act had the necessary teeth to tackle abuse of dominant or monopolistic positions. However, in practice, these provisions have rarely been employed to penalize or break up undertakings.

Chapter I provides the concept of a dominant undertaking: it is an undertaking that by itself, or along with interconnected undertakings, controls 25 per cent of the share, either with respect to production or supply or distribution. However, the amount exported is not to be included for the purpose of calculation of the share. Monopolistic trade practices are those that keep prices, costs, or profits at unreasonable levels or affect adversely technical development, capital investment, quality, or competition. Prior to 1984, only three references have been made by the Central government to the MRTP Commission for inquiry into monopolistic trade practices. These related to Messrs Coca-Cola Export Corporation, Cadbury Fry, and Colgate Palmolive. The concerned companies went in appeal to the Supreme Court, which granted stay, and the matters are still *sub judice*. In 1987, the Central government made a reference to the Commission in the matter of safety razor blades industry in India, but the Bombay High Court granted a stay and the Commission could not make any headway with its enquiry. In addition, four other cases are pending before the Commission.

The expression 'competition' figures in Section 2(o) of the MRTP Act. This section defines a restrictive trade practice. Section 2(o) of the Act reads as follows:

> 'restrictive trade practice' means a trade practice which has, or may have, the effect of preventing, distorting or restricting competition in any manner and in particular,
>
> (i) which tends to obstruct the flow of capital or resources into the stream of production, or
>
> (ii) which tends to bring about manipulation of prices, or conditions of delivery or to affect the flow of supplies in the market relating to goods or services in such manner as to impose on the consumers unjustified costs or restrictions.

Another section that refers to 'competition' is in fact a gateway or an escape valve from indictment by the MRTP Commission. Section 38(1)(h) of the Act states that if a particular restrictive trade practice 'does not directly or indirectly restrict or discourage competition to any material degree in any relevant trade or industry and is not likely to do so', it can pass through this gateway and escape a cease and desist order by the MRTP Commission.

Under restrictive trade practices, a number of practices are subsumed. These include, among others:

- tie-in sales ('any agreement requiring a purchaser of goods, as a condition of such purchase, to purchase some other good');

- resale price maintenance ('any agreement, to sell goods, on condition that the prices to be charged on re-sale by the purchaser shall be the prices stipulated by the seller unless it is clearly stated that prices lower than those prices may be charged');

- exclusive dealings ('any agreement restricting in any manner the purchaser in the course of his trade from acquiring or otherwise dealing in any goods other than those of the seller or any other person');

- exclusive territories ('any agreement to limit, restrict or withhold the output or supply of any goods or allocate any area or market for the disposal of the goods');

- price fixing/predatory pricing ('any agreement to sell goods at such prices as would have the effect of eliminating competition or a competitor');

- bid rigging ('any agreement as to the bids which any of the parties thereto may offer at an auction for the sale of goods or any agreement whereby any party thereto agrees to abstain from bidding at any auction for the sale of the goods').

Box 15.2. Sample of Cases before the MRTP Commission

Here is a sample of cases where the MRTP Commission found the respondents guilty of indulging in restrictive trade practices:

In reference to JMD Marketing Company, Bangalore (M) and JMD Electric Company Bangalore (E): M and E were partnership firms of the same family, with the wife and the husband being, respectively, the main partners of the companies. M started purchasing Unimex Kitchen Machines from Ambala and these machines were then sold to E. That is, the wife sold the machines to her husband, and at inflated prices, retaining a handsome profit margin. The machines were then sold by E to wholesalers and retailers, again at a handsome margin. The Commission held that the respondents were manipulating prices, thereby imposing unjustified costs on the consumers.

In reference to Borosil Glass Works: The respondent was charged with not supplying amber glass tubing of the size asked for to DAMPL. The Commission held that the primary motive behind the non-supply was to prevent DAMPL from competing with the respondent in the supply of ampoules to Sandoz. Therefore, the respondent's conduct had the effect of preventing and restricting competition.

In reference to United Breweries Ltd. (UB) and Indo Lawenbrau Breweries Ltd. (ILB): The respondents who produced, distributed, and marketed beer, entered into an agreement with ILB. Under the agreement, ILB was to produce beer with the help of technical expertise and know-how provided by UB, and sell the beer to UB. The MRTP Commission found clause 12 of the agreement to constitute a restrictive trade practice. Clause 12 laid down that ILB shall not, without the consent of UB, during the currency of the agreement, manufacture or be involved in any way with the manufacture of beer other than that to be produced under the agreement with UB.

Source: Dugar (1997).

Finally, unfair trade practices are defined under the MRTP Act as trade practices related to the sale, use, or supply of commodities that cause loss or injury to consumers. These practices are of the following types:

(i) Misrepresentation of the quality or attributes.

(ii) Misleading advertising.

(iii) Offering gifts, prizes, etc., either (a) with the intention of not providing them or (b) creating the impression that they are being provided free whereas their charge is fully or partly covered by the amount charged.

(iv) Supplying commodities that do not comply with prescribed standards.

(v) Hoarding or destruction or refusal to sell something, if such action tends to raise the cost of similar goods and services.

15.5.2 Consumer Protection Act and the MRTP Act

The Consumer Protection Act, 1986, has the objective of providing simplified, inexpensive, and speedy remedy for the redressal of the grievances of the consumers in regard to defects in goods purchased by them and/or deficiency in services hired or availed of by them. The CPA has provisions for the establishment of Consumer Councils and for the setting up of quasi-judicial machinery at the district, state, and Central levels, with power to give relief to the consumers and to award compensation for the loss or injury suffered by them. It must, therefore, be viewed as constituting an important component of India's competition policy.

There is substantial overlap in the coverage of the two enactments, namely, the MRTP Act and the CPA. However, there are also several distinctive features of the two enactments which demarcate them from each other. Some important features of difference between the two enactments (as noted by the S. V. S. Raghavan Committee) are the following:

1. Under the MRTP Act, the MRTP Commission is the only Authority to enquire into the allegations of restrictive and unfair trade practices. Under the CPA, there is a three-tier set-up, namely, District Forum, State Commission, and National Commission with each of the three Authorities having its own original pecuniary jurisdiction. An appeal against the order of the MRTP Commission under the MRTP Act or the National Commission under the CPA can be made to the Supreme Court.

2. The provisions of the MRTP Act do not apply to a banking company, State Bank of India, or an insurer in relation to matters for which specific provisions exist in the Reserve Bank of India Act, State Bank of India Act, or Insurance Act, as the case may be. Such an exemption for the banking or insurance companies is not provided in the CPA.

3. Under the MRTP Act, the definition of restrictive trade practice is broad and covers a trade practice which has or may have the effect of preventing, distorting, or restricting competition. Certain trade practices are statutorily declared as restrictive in nature. Under the CPA, a restricted trade practice

relating to a tie-in arrangement indulged in by a trader can only become the subject matter of complaint.

4. A buyer who obtains goods for resale or for a commercial purpose is not regarded as a consumer for the purposes of the CPA and therefore cannot become a complainant under the CPA. There is no such bar for invoking the jurisdiction of the MRTP Commission. (Because of judicial interpretation, the definition of consumer in the CPA has been adopted by the MRTP Commission and this difference no longer subsists.)

5. Under the CPA, the Central or state government cannot make a reference for enquiry whereas under the MRTP Act, there is a specific provision enabling them to do so. A further difference is that the CPA redressal authority cannot *suo motu* initiate any enquiry into restrictive or unfair trade practice, whereas the MRTP Commission can do so.

6. An investigation machinery is available with the MRTP Commission in the form of an office in the nature of the Director General of Investigation and Registration who can be required by the Commission to investigate into a complaint and submit a report to it. There is no such machinery under the CPA.

7. The definition of 'goods' in the CPA is narrower than that in the MRTP Act. For instance, 'goods' in the MRTP Act cover shares and stocks, including the issue of shares before allotment. The CPA does not cover shares and stocks. Similarly, 'service' in the MRTP Act covers a Chit Fund but not in the CPA. Likewise, real estate is covered under 'service' in the MRTP Act whereas only housing construction is covered under 'service' in the CPA.

8. Even though both the enactments provide for a cease and desist order by the tribunal concerned, the power of the MRTP Commission includes issuance of directions for corrective advertisements etc., whereas such a power is not available for the CPA Tribunals.

9. Both the enactments provide for award of compensation. Under the CPA, compensation can be awarded only to consumers whereas under the MRTP Act, compensation can be awarded to consumers, traders, and even state and Central governments.

10. The MRTP Commission has powers of injunction whereas the Tribunals under the CPA do not have such a power.

11. The CPA has a limitation period of 2 years within which a consumer has to lodge a complaint. There is no limitation period under the MRTP Act.

12. Under the CPA, a time frame has been fixed for the National Commission for disposal of a complaint/appeal. There is no such time frame under the MRTP Act.

13. Under the MRTP Act, the Commission has the power to review its order whereas such a facility is not available under the CPA.

14. For violations or contraventions of orders passed by the Tribunal concerned, the punishment is different in the two enactments.

15. Under the CPA, there is a provision for exemplary costs for frivolous or vexatious complaints. There is no such provision in the MRTP Act.

15.5.3 The New Competition Policy

Recently, a New Competition Policy has been submitted to the government by the S. V. S. Raghavan Committee. The proposed New Competition Policy proposes to repeal the Monopolies and Restrictive Trade Practices Act, 1969 (MRTP). It has been felt that in the context of liberalization, deregulation, and privatization, there is a need to design a new competition policy.

Under the New Competition Policy, the Industries (Development and Regulation) Act, 1951, may no longer be necessary except for avoidance of urban-centric location, for environmental protection etc. Moreover, the Industrial Disputes Act, 1947 and the connected statutes will have to be amended to provide for an easy exit to the non-viable, ill-managed, and inefficient units subject to their legal obligations in respect of their liabilities.

It is also envisaged that the Board for Industrial and Financial Reconstruction (BIFR), formulated under the provisions of the Sick Industrial Companies (Special Provisions) Act, 1985, would be abolished.

The MRTP Act, 1969, may be repealed and the MRTP Commission wound up. The provisions relating to unfair trade practices need not figure in the new Competition Act as they are presently covered by the Consumer Protection Act, 1986.

Under the New Competition Policy, all anti-competitive practices would be considered as illegal. Blatant price, quantity, bid, and territory sharing agreements and cartels would be considered illegal. The state monopolies and public enterprises would also be covered by the Competition Policy to prevent monopolistic, restrictive, and unfair trade practices. Government procurement and foreign companies should be subject to the Competition Law. The law would cover all consumers who purchase goods or services, regardless of the purpose for which the purchase is made.

The terms 'dominance' and 'dominant undertaking' would be defined in the Competition Law in terms of 'the position of strength enjoyed by an undertaking which enables it to operate independently of competitive pressure in the relevant market and also to appreciably affect the relevant market, competitors and consumers by its actions'. The definition should also be in terms of 'substantial impact on the market including creating barriers to new entrants'. The *abuse* of dominance rather than dominance *per se* needs to be frowned upon. Predatory pricing should be treated as an abuse, only if it is indulged in by a dominant undertaking.

Exclusionary practices which create a barrier to new entrants or force existing competitors out of the market will attract the competition law.

Pre-notification would be required for mergers beyond a certain limit. The Committee has suggested that the threshold limit may be fixed at the asset value of the merged entity equal to Rs 500 crore or more, or the asset value of the group to which the merged entity belongs being Rs 2000 crore or more, both linked to wholesale price index. The expression 'group' as presently defined in the MRTP Act, 1969, may be adopted for the purpose of merger.

The Raghavan Committee felt that there should be necessary provision and teeth in the new Competition Act to examine and adjudicate upon anti-competition practices that may accompany or follow developments arising out of the implementation of WTO Agreements. In particular, agreements relating to the following should be taken account of by the new law:

- foreign investment
- intellectual property rights
- subsidies
- countervailing duties
- anti-dumping measures
- sanitary and phytosanitary measures
- technical barriers to trade
- Government procurement

In this connection, the statutes governing professions need to be amended to be GATT compatible.

For the implementation of the Indian Competition Act, a Commission would be established which would be named the 'Competition Commission of India' (CCI). It would be a multi-member body comprised of eminent persons from various fields. The CCI will be the sole recipient of all complaints against infringement of the Indian Competition Act from any source whatsoever, be it an ordinary citizen, business firm, or any other entity including the Central and the state governments.There will be no *suo motu* powers for the Director General to initiate any action of investigation. He will only investigate cases referred to him by the Competition Commission.

The Raghavan Committee's recommendations have been criticized on several counts. Members of the Committee have submitted notes of dissent. Dr. Rakesh Mohan has written that '. . . I have had a continuous sinking feeling that I am contributing to something that could possibly stop the growing Indian economy in its tracks.' According to him, 'the root of the problem is that modern competition policy and the kind of law that enforces it has to be discretionary in its essential characteristics. Removal of discretion through enlargement of categories of *per se* illegality would be worse than the cure'. It is always difficult to distinguish competitive actions in the market place from restrictive trade practices. According to Dr Mohan, in India we simply do not have enough experience yet to plunge headlong into such adjudication. Another member, Mr Sudhir Mulji, has stated that promoting competition is a much more important goal than curbing monopolies. Accordingly, 'combative or aggressive rivalry' which leads to innovation and efficiency is the need of the day and the new Competition Act would clamp down on such rivalry. Coming to more specific recommendations, Mr P. M. Narielvala disagreed with the requirement of pre-merger notification. As he put it, 'Our companies are by and large extremely small and the tempo of mergers and amalgamations has not kept pace with the need for large companies to counter the threat of competition from foreign giants abroad. We therefore need, not only to permit and facilitate mergers and amalgamations, we also need to push companies in this direction. A provision for prior notification may have the opposite effect.'

Pushpa Grimaji (*Times of India*) has objected to the recommendation that the provisions relating to unfair trade practices need not feature in the new Act as they are covered by the Consumer Protection Act. The objections are based on the argument that the CPA is likely to be less effective than the new Act. We have already looked at the differences between the CPA and the MRTP Act. Grimaji points out the following:

1. The CPA does not have the provision for a watchdog like the office of the Director General. There is, therefore, no office under the CPA which can investigate unfair trade practices on its own.

2. Unlike the MRTP Act, the consumer courts lack the power to issue interim orders. The power to issue interim injunctions, pending disposal of the case, can be very important in curbing practices like misleading and false advertising.

3. Consumer courts do not have the power to order corrective advertisements.

4. Unlike the MRTP Commission, consumer courts cannot award compensation to victims of unfair trade practices.

If these provisions from the MRTP Act were to be incorporated in the new Act, then taking the unfair trade practices outside the ambit of the Act would leave consumers with less effective means of redressal.

References

Alchian, A. A. and H. Demsetz (1972), 'Production, Information Costs and Economic Organization', *American Economic Review*, Vol. 62, pp. 777–95.

Amihud, Y. and B. Lev (1981), 'Risk Reduction as a Managerial Motive for Conglomerate Mergers', *Bell Journal of Economics*, Vol. 12, pp. 605–17.

Areeda, P. A. (1982), *Antitrust Law: An Analysis of Antitrust Principles and their Applications*, Boston: Little, Brown and Company.

Areeda, Phillip and Donald F. Turner (1975), 'Predatory Pricing and Related Practices under Section 2 of the Sherman Act,' *Harvard Law Review*, Vol. 88, February 697-733.

Audretsch, David B., W. J. Baumol, and A. E. Burke (2001), 'Competition Policy in Dynamic Markets', *International Journal of Industrial Organization*, Vol. 19, No. 5, pp. 613–34.

Averch, H. and L. Johnson (1962), 'Behaviour of the Firm Under Regulatory Constraint', *American Economic Review*, Vol. 52, pp. 53–69.

Axelrod, R. (1984), *The Evolution of Cooperation*, New York: Basic Books.

Bagwell, Kyle and Garey Ramey (1996), 'Capacity, Entry, and Forward Induction', *Rand Journal of Economics*, Vol. 27, No. 4, Winter, pp. 660–80.

Bain, Joe S. (1956), *Barriers to New Competition*, Cambridge, Mass: Harvard University Press.

Barney, Jay (1991), 'Firm Resources and Sustained Competitive Advantage', *Journal of Management*, Vol. 17, pp. 99–120.

Baron, David P. (1993), *Business and its Environment*, New Jersey: Prentice-Hall.

Barros, Pedro P. and Luis Cabral (1994), 'Merger Policy in Open Economies', *European Economic Review*, Vol. 38, pp. 1041–55.

Bartlett, C. and S. Ghoshal (1993), 'Beyond the M-form: Toward a Managerial Theory of the Firm', *Strategic Management Journal*, Vol. 14, pp. 23–46.

Basant, R. (1999), 'Corporate Response to Economic Reforms in India' (mimeo).

Baumol, W. (1958), 'On the Theory of Oligopoly', *Economica*, Vol. 25, pp. 187–98.

——— (1979), 'Quasi-permanence of Price Reductions: A Policy for Prevention of Predatory Pricing', *Yale Law Journal*, Vol. 89, pp. 1–26.

Baumol, W. J., J. C. Panzar, and R. D. Willing (1982), *Contestable Markets and the Theory of Industry Structure*, New York: Harcourt, Brace, Jovanoich.

Bencivenga, V. R., B. D. Smith, and R. M. Starr, (1996), 'Equity Markets, Transaction Costs and Capital Accumulation: An Illustration', *The World Bank Economic Review*, May, Vol. 10, No. 2, pp. 241–65.

Bernheim, B. D. and M. D. Whinston (1990), 'Multimarket Contact and Collusive Behavior', *Rand Journal of Economics*, Vol. 21, pp. 1–26.

Besanko, D. Dranove, and D. and M. Shanley (1996), *The Economics of Strategy*, New York: John Wiley & Sons.

Bhattacharya, Gautam (1984), 'Learning and the Behavior of Potential Entrants', *Rand Journal of Economics*, Vol. 15, No. 2, Summer, pp. 281–9.

Bonnano, G. (1987), 'Location Choice, Product Differentiation and Entry Deterrence', *Review of Economic Studies*, Vol. 54, pp. 37–45.

Bork, Robert H. (1978), *The Antitrust Paradox: A Policy at War with Itself*, New York: The Free Press.

Brandenburger, Adam M. and Barry J. Nalebuff (1995), 'The Right Game: Use Game Theory to Shape Strategy', *Harvard Business Review*, July-August, pp. 57–71.

Brickley, J., C. Smith, and J. Zimmerman (1997), *Managerial Economics and Organisational Architecture*, Chicago: Irwin.

Bulow, Jeremy I., John D. Geanakoplos, and Paul D. Klemperer (1985), 'Multimarket Oligopoly: Strategic Substitutes and Complements', *Journal of Political Economy*, Vol. 93, No. 3, pp. 488–511.

Cabral, Luis M. B. (2000), *Introduction to Industrial Organization*, Cambridge, Mass.: The MIT Press.

Carlton, D.W. and J.M. Perloff (1994), *Modern Industrial Organization*, New York: Warper Collins.

Casella, Alessandra (1999), 'Tradable Deficit Permits', *Economic Policy*, No. 29, October, pp. 323–61.

Caves, R. E. (1996), *Multinational Enterprise and Economic Analysis*, Cambridge: Cambridge University Press.

Caves, R. E. and M. Porter (1977): 'From Entry Barriers to Mobility Barriers', *Quarterly Journal of Economics*, Vol. 91, pp. 241–67.

Chatterjee, Kalyan and Barbara Gray (eds) (1995), *International Joint Ventures: Economic and Organizational Perspectives*, Dordretch: Kluwer Academic Publishers.

Clemons, Eric K. (1997), 'Technology-driven Environmental Shifts and the Sustainable Competitive Disadvantage of Previously Dominant Companies', in George S. Day, David J. Reibstein, and Robert E. Gunther (eds), *Wharton on Dynamic Competitive Strategy*, New York: John Wiley & Sons, Inc.

Coase, R. (1972), 'Durability and Monopoly', *Journal of Law and Economics*, Vol., 15, pp. 143–9.

Contractor, F. and P. Lorange (1988), 'Why Should Firms Cooperate: The Strategy and Economic Basis for Cooperative Ventures', in F. Contractor and P. Lorange (eds), *Cooperative Strategies in International Business*, Lexington: Lexington Books.

Cooke, Terence E. (1986), *Mergers and Acquisitions*, Oxford: Basil Blackwell.

Cyert, R. and J. March (1963), *A Behavioural Theory of the Firm*, New Jersey: Prentice Hall.

D'Aspremont, C. Gabszewicz, J., and J. F. Thisse (1979), 'On Hotelling's Stability in Competition', *Econometrica*, Vol. 47, pp. 1145–50.

Dierickx, I. and K. Cool (1989), 'Asset Stock Accumulation and Sustainability of Competitive Advantage', *Management Science*, Vol. 35, pp. 1504–11.

Divan, Shyam and Armin Rosencranz (2001), *Environmental Law and Policy in India*, New Delhi: Oxford University Press.

Dixit, A. (1979), 'A Model of Oligopoly Suggesting a Theory of Barriers to Entry', *Bell Journal of Economics*, Vol. 10, pp. 20–32.

——— (1981), 'The Role of Investment in Entry Deterrence', *Economic Journal*, pp. 95–106.

Dixit, A. and B. J. Nalebuff (1991), *Thinking Strategically*, New York: W.W. Norton & Co.

Dixit, A. and S., Skeath (1999), *Games of Strategy*. New York: W.W. Norton & Co.

Djankov, S., Rafael La Porta, Florencio Lopez-de-Silanes, and Andrei Schleifer (2000), 'The Regulation of Entry', NBER Working Paper, Vol. W 7892.

Dolan, R. J. and H. Simon (1996), *Power Pricing: How Managing Price Transforms the Bottom Line*, New York: The Free Press.

Dugar, S. M. (1997), *Law of Monopolistic, Restrictive and Unfair Trade Practices*, New Delhi: Wadhwa and Company.

Dunning, J. H. (1988), *Explaining International Production*, London: Unwin Hyman.

Easterbrook, Frank H. (1981), 'Predatory Strategies and Counterstrategies', *University of Chicago Law Review*, Vol. 48, Spring, pp. 263–377.

Fama, E. (1980), 'Agency Problems and the Theory of the Firm', *Journal of Political Economy*, Vol. 88, pp. 288–307.

Fama, E. and M. C. Jensen (1983), 'Separation of Ownership and Control', *Journal of Law and Economics*, Vol. 26, pp. 301–25.

——— (1985), 'Organizational Forms and Investment Decisions', *Journal of Financial Economics*, Vol. 13, pp. 101–19.

Gabszewicz, Jean J. (1999), *Strategic Interaction and Markets*, Oxford: Oxford University Press.

Garda, R. A. and M. V. Marn (1993), 'Price Wars', The McKinsey Quarterly, No. 3, pp. 87–100.

Gelman, J. and S. Salop (1983), 'Judo Economics: Capacity Limitation and Coupon Competition', *Bell Journal of Economics*, Vol. 14, pp. 315–25.

Gilbert, Richard J. and David M. Newbery (1992), 'Alternative Entry Paths: The Build or Buy Decision', *Journal of Economics and Management Strategy*, Vol. 1, No. 1, Spring, pp. 129–50.

Grossman, H. J. and O. D. Hart (1980): 'Takeover Bids, the Free Rider Problem and the Theory of the Corporations', *Bell Journal of Economics*, Vol. 11, pp. 42–64.

Hall, Bronwyn H. (1988), 'The Effect of Takeover Activity on Corporate Research and Development', in Alan J. Auerbach (ed.), *Corporate Takeovers: Causes and Consequence*, Chicago: The University of Chicago Press. Also Comment by Ariel Pakes on Hall in the same volume.

Hamel, G. and C. K. Prahalad (1989), 'Strategic Intent', *Harvard Business Review*, May–June, pp. 63–76.

Helm, D. and D. Pearce (1999), 'Economic Policy towards the Environment', *Oxford Review of Economic Policy*, Vol. 6, No. 1.

Johnson, G. and K. Scholes (1999), *Exploring Corporate Strategy*, Singapore: Pearson Education.

Judd, K. (1985), 'Credible Spatial Pre-emption', *Rand Journal of Economics*, Vol. 16, pp. 153–66.

Kakabadse, A. and N. Kakabadse (2002), 'Trends in Outsourcing: Contrasting USA and Europe', *European Management Journal*, Vol. 20, pp. 189–98.

Kaplan, S. and Mohanbir Sawhney (2000), 'B2B E-commerce Hubs: Towards a Taxonomy of Business Models', *Harvard Business Review*, May–June, pp. 97–103.

Kay, John (1993), *Foundations of Corporate Success: How Business Strategies Add Value*, Oxford: Oxford University Press.

Khanna, T. and K. Palepu (1997), 'Why Focussed Strategies may be Wrong for Emerging Markets', *Harvard Business Review*, July–August, pp. 41–51.

Kirzner, I. M. (1992), *The Meaning of Market Process: Essays in the Development of Modern Austrian Economics*, London: Routledge.

Klein, B., G. Crawford, and A. Alchian (1978), 'Vertical Integration, Appropriable Rents and the Competitive Contracting Process', *Journal of Law and Economics*, Vol. 21, pp. 297–326.

Klein, B. and K. B. Leffler (1981), 'The Role of Market Forces in Assuring Contract Performance', *Journal of Political Economy*, Vol. 89, pp. 615–41.

Knickerbocker, F. T. (1973), *Oligopolistic Reaction and Multinational Enterprise*, Boston: Harvard University Press.

Kodama, F. (1992), 'Technology Fusion and the New R&D', *Harvard Business Review*, July–August, pp. 70–8.

Kogut, B. (1988), 'A Study of the Life Cycle of Joint Ventures', in F. Contractor and P. Lorange, *Cooperative Strategies in International Business*, Lexington: Lexington Books.

—— (ed.) (1993), *Country Competitiveness: Technology and Organising of Work*, Oxford: Oxford University Press.

Krugman, P. and M. Obstfeld (1991), *International Economics: Theory and Policy*, Reading: Addison Wesley.

Leibenstein, H. (1966), 'Allocative Efficiency v. X-efficiency', *American Economic Review*, Vol. 56, pp. 392–415.

Liebowitz, S. J. and Stephen E. Margolis (1990), 'The Fable of Keys', *Journal of Law and Economics*, April, No. 1, pp. 1–26.

Levy, D. (1984), 'Testing Stigler's Interpretation of "The Division of Labour is Limited by the Size of the Market" ', *Journal of Industrial Economics*, Vol. 32, pp. 377–89.

Lewin, P. (1999), *Capital in Disequilibrium*, London: Routledge.

Lippman, S. A. and R. P. Rumelt (1982), 'Uncertain Imitability: An Analysis of Interfirm Differences in Efficiency under Competition', *Bell Journal of Economics*, Vol. 13, pp. 418–38.

Malueg, David A. and Marius Schwartz (1991), 'Pre-emptive Investment, Toehold Entry, and the Mimicking Principle', *Rand Journal of Economics*, Vol. 22, No. 1, Spring, pp. 1–11.

Mancke, R. B. (1974), 'Causes of Inter-firm Profitability Differences: A New Interpretation of the Evidence', *The Quarterly Journal of Economics*, Vol. 88, pp. 181–93.

Marris, R. (1963), 'A Model of the Managerial Enterprise', *The Quarterly Journal of Economics*, Vol. 77, pp. 185–209.

—— (1966), *The Economic Theory of Managerial Capitalism*, Glencoe, IL: The Free Press.

Martin, S. (2002), *Advanced Industrial Economics*, Cambridge, Mass: Blackwell.

McGee, John S. (1958), 'Predatory Price Cutting: The Standard Oil (N.J.) Case,' *Journal of Law and Economics*, Vol. 1, October, pp. 137–69.

—— (1980), 'Predatory Pricing Revisited', *Journal of Law and Economics*, Vol. 23, pp. 289–330.

McMillan, J. (1994), 'Selling Spectrum Rights', *Journal of Economic Perspectives*, Vol. 8, No. 3, pp 145–62.

Milgrom, P. and J. Roberts (1992), *Economics, Organization and Management*, New Jersey: Prentice Hall.

Morck, Randall, Andrei Shleifer, and Robert W. Vishny (1988), 'Characteristics of Targets of Hostile and Friendly Takeovers', in Alan J. Auerbach (ed.), *Corporate Takeovers: Causes and Consequence*, Chicago: The University of Chicago Press.

Mueller, D. C. (1972), 'A Life Cycle Theory of the Firm', *Journal of Industrial Economics*, Vol. 20, pp. 199–219.

Murty, M. N., A. J. James, and Smita Misra (1999), *Economics of Water Pollution: The Indian Experience*, New Delhi: Oxford University Press.

Neary, J. P. (1978), 'Short-run Capital Specificity and the Pure Theory of International Trade', *Economic Journal*, Vol. 88, pp. 488–510.

Nelson, R. R. and S. G. Winter (1982), *An Evolutionary Theory of Economic Change*, Cambridge, Mass: Harvard University Press.

Nonaka, I. (1991), 'The Knowledge-creating Company', *Harvard Business Review*, November–December pp. 96–104.

Packard, Kimberly O'Neill and Forest Reinhardt (2000), 'What Every Executive Needs to Know about Global Warming', *Harvard Business Review*, July–August, pp. 129–35.

Pakes, A. (1988) in A.J. Auerbach (ed.), *Corprate Takeovers: Causes and Consequences*, Chicago: The University of Chicago Press.

Pasinetti, L. (1981), *Structural Change and Economic Growth: A Theoretical Essay on the Dynamics of the Wealth of Nations*, Cambridge: Cambridge University Press.

Penrose, Edith (1995), *The Theory of the Growth of the Firm*, Oxford: Oxford University Press.

Peteraf, Margaret A. (1993), 'The Cornerstones of Competitive Advantage: A Resource-based View', *Strategic Management Journal*, Vol. 14, pp. 179–91.

Pigou, A. C. (1920), *The Economics of Welfare,* London: Macmillan

Porter, M. E. (1985), *Competitive Advantage: Creating and Sustaining Superior Performance*, Glencoe, IL: The Free Press.

———— (ed.) (1986), *Competition in Global Industries*, Boston: Harvard Business School Press.

Prahalad, C. K. and Y. L. Doz (1987), *The Multinational Mission: Balancing Local Demands and Global Vision*, Glencoe, IL: The Free Press.

Prahalad, C. K. and G. Hamel (1990), 'The Core Competence of the Corporation', *Harvard Business Review*, May–June, pp. 79–91.

Prescott, E. and M. Vischer (1980), 'Organization Capital', *Journal of Political Economy*, Vol. 88, pp. 446–61.

Puri, Ashwani (1998), 'Intangibles in Action', *The Economic Times,* Mumbai, 28 December.

Reed, R. and R. J. DeFillippi (1990), 'Causal Ambiguity, Barriers to Imitation and Sustainable Competitive Advantage', *Academy of Management Review*, Vol. 15, pp. 88–102.

Romer, P. M. (1990), 'Endogenous Technological Change', *Journal of Political Economy*, Vol. 98, No. 5, Part 2, pp. S71–S102.

Roquebert, J. A., R. L. Phillips, and P. A. Westfall (1996), 'Markets vs. Management: What "Drives" Profitability?', *Strategic Management Journal*, Vol. 17, pp. 653–64.

Rumelt, R. P. (1984), 'Toward a Strategic Theory of the Firm', in R. Lamb (ed.), *Competitive Strategic Management*, New Jersey: Prentice Hall.

———— (1991), 'How Much does Industry Matter?', *Strategic Management Journal*, Vol. 12, pp. 167–85.

Saloner, G. (1987), 'Predation, Merger and Incomplete Information', *Rand Journal of Economics,* Vol. 18, pp. 165–86.

Salop, S. (1986), 'Practices that Credibly Facilitate Oligopoly Consideration' in J. Stiglitz and F. Mathewson (eds) *New Developments in the Analysis of Market Structure*, Cambridge, Mass: MIT Press.

Scherer, F. M. (1996), 'International Trade and Competition Policy', Discussion Paper No. 96-18, *Zew Industrial Economics and International Management Series*, Mannheim, Germany.

Scherer, F. M. and D. Ross (1990), *Industrial Market Structure and Economic Performance*, Boston: Houghton Mifflin.

Schmalensee, R. (1978), 'Entry Deterrence in the Ready-to-eat Breakfast Cereal Industry', *Bell Journal of Economics*, pp. 305–27.

Schumpeter, J. A. (1942), *Capitalism, Socialism and Democracy* , New York: Harper and Row.

Scott, J. T. (1993), *Purposive Diversification and Economic Performance*, Cambridge: Cambridge University Press.

Sen, A. (1997), 'Entry Strategies: A Survey', *Economic and Political Weekly*, 29 November–5 December 1997, Vol. 32, No. 48, M-99 to M-106.

—— (1999), *Microeconomics : Theory and Applications*, New Delhi : Oxford University Press.

Shapiro, Carl (1989), 'Theories of Oligopoly Behavior', in Richard Schmalensee and Robert D. Willig (eds), *Handbook of Industrial Organization*, Vol. I, North-Holland, Amsterdam.

Shapiro, C. and Hal Varian, (1999), *Information Rules,* Boston : Harvard Business School Press.

Shleifer, A. and R. Vishny (1986), 'Large Shareholders and Corporate Control', *Journal of Political Economy*, Vol. 94, pp. 461–88.

—— (1997), 'A Survey of Corporate Governance', *Journal of Finance*, Vol. 52, pp 737–83.

Sinn, Mans-Werner and Alfons J. Weichenrieder (1997), 'Foreign Direct Investment, Political Resentment and the Privatization Process in Eastern Europe', *Economic Policy*, Vol. 24, April, pp. 179–210.

Stewart, G. Bennet (1990), *The Quest for Value: The EVA^{TM} Management Guide,* New York: HarperBusiness.

—— (1993), 'EVA^{TM}: Fact and Fantasy', *Journal of Applied Corporate Finance*, pp. 6–19.

Stigler, G. J. (1951), 'The Division of Labour is Limited by the Size of the Market', *Journal of Political Economy*, 59, pp. 185–93.

Teece, D. J. (1982), 'Towards an Economic Theory of the Multi-product Firm', *Journal of Economic Behaviour and Organisation*, Vol. 3, pp. 39–63.

—— (1998), 'Capturing Value from Knowledge Assets', *California Management Review*, Vol. 40, pp. 55–79.

Telser, L. G. (1966), 'Cut-throat Competition and the Long Purse', *Journal of Law and Economics*, Vol 9, pp. 259–77.

Vaidya, R. R. (1995), 'Disinvestment of Public Enterprise Shares', in Kirit S. Parikh (ed.), *Mid-Year Review of The Economy 1994-95*, New Delhi: Konark Publishers Pvt. Ltd.

Wegberg, Marc van and Arjen van Witteloostuijn (1991), 'Multi-market Competition: Entry Strategies and Entry Deterrence When the Entrant has a Home Market', in Jacques Thepot and Raymond Alain Thietart (eds), *Microeconomic Contributions to Strategic Management*, North Holland, Amsterdam.

Williamson, O. E. (1967), 'Hierarchical Control and Optimum Firm Size', *Journal of Political Economy*, Vol. 75, pp. 123–38.

—— (1975), *Markets and Hierarchies*, New York: The Free Press.

—— (1981), 'The Modern Corporation: Origins, Evolution, Attributes', *Journal of Economic Literature*, Vol. 19, pp. 1537–68.

Index